Transformation and Crisis in Central and Eastern Europe

T0384138

The global financial crisis has provided an important opportunity to revisit debates about post-socialist transition and the relative success of different reform paths. Post-communist Central and Eastern Europe (CEECs) in particular show resilience in the wake of the international crisis with a diverse range of economic transformations.

Transformation and Crisis in Central and Eastern Europe offers an in-depth analysis of a diverse range of countries, including Poland, Hungary, the Czech Republic, Slovakia, Russia and Ukraine. This volume assesses each country's institutional transformations, geopolitical policies, and local adaptations that have led them down divergent post-communist paths. Chapters take the reader systematically through the evolution of former communist national economic systems, before ending with lessons and conclusions for the future. Subsequent chapters demonstrate that economic performance crucially depends on achieving a sustainable balance between sound institutional design and policies on one hand, and local characteristics on the other.

This new volume offers a fascinating and timely study which will be of interest to all scholars and policy makers with an interest in European Economics, Russian and East European Studies, Transition Economies, Political Economy and the post-2008 world more generally.

Bruno Dallago is Professor of Economics at the University of Trento and Director of the Research Unit on Local Development and Global Governance, Italy.

Steven Rosefielde is Professor of Economics at the University of North Carolina, USA.

Routledge Studies in the European Economy

Transformation and Crisis in Central and Eastern Europe

Challenges and prospects

Bruno Dallago and Steven Rosefielde

Routledge
Taylor & Francis Group

LONDON AND NEW YORK

First published 2016
by Routledge

2 Park Square, Milton Park, Abingdon, Oxfordshire OX14 4RN
52 Vanderbilt Avenue, New York, NY 10017

Routledge is an imprint of the Taylor & Francis Group, an informa business

First issued in paperback 2020

British Library Cataloguing in Publication Data
A catalogue record for this book is available from the British Library

Library of Congress Cataloging in Publication Data
Names: Rosefielde, Steven, author. | Dallago, Bruno, 1950- author.
Title: Transformation and crisis in Central and Eastern Europe : challenges
    and prospects / Steven Rosefielde and Bruno Dallago.
Description: Abingdon, Oxon ; New York, NY : Routledge, 2016.
Identifiers: LCCN 2015049341| ISBN 9781138801141 (hardback) |
    ISBN 9781315754819 (ebook)
Subjects: LCSH: Post-communism—Europe, Central. | Post-communism—
    Europe, Eastern. | Global Financial Crisis, 2008-2009. | Europe,
    Central—Economic policy—1989- | Europe, Eastern—Economic
    policy—1989-
Classification: LCC HC244 .R593 2016 | DDC 330.943—dc23
LC record available at http://lccn.loc.gov/2015049341

ISBN: 978-1-138-80114-1 (hbk)
ISBN: 978-0-367-66838-9 (pbk)

Typeset in Times New Roman
by Swales & Willis Ltd, Exeter, Devon, UK

Contents

Tables

Figures

Preface

This book investigates the economic evolution of two former communist national economic systems: Russia and Ukraine (previously the RSFSR and UkSFSR), and the Central European states (Hungary, Poland, the Czech Republic and Slovakia), remnants of the Austro-Hungarian Empire. Although these once filial communist systems displayed many common characteristics during the Soviet era, institutions, cultures, national aspirations and the geopolitical situation led them along divergent post-communist paths. Institutions, cultures, national aspirations and the geopolitical situation differed enough to lead these countries along divergent post-communist paths.

Authoritarianism was a central feature of tsarist and Soviet rule. It has resurfaced in the post-Soviet era in a comparatively liberal guise. The Central European states (the Visegrád Four), spurred by more tolerant traditions, have hitched their stars to the European Union. Russia and Ukraine have modernized their command economic control mechanisms. Their economic systems have been transformed, but neither country has transitioned to democratic free enterprise, socialist democracy, German social market, or American liberal economy. Central Europe by contrast has broadly embraced the western paradigm. Hungary, Poland, the Czech Republic and Slovakia have not just changed, they have evolved mostly in the direction of social market economies. The divergence between the two formerly filial communist economic systems reflects the re-emergence of historical, cultural and geopolitical influences veiled during the Cold War by Soviet power, as well as the full emancipation of national aspirations and new opportunities.

The challenges and prospects confronting Russia and Ukraine on one hand, and Central Europe on the other, consequently are strikingly different despite their geographical proximity. This volume documents the evolutionary process that has led the former Soviet republics and the Visegrád Four to part ways in the post-communist era, analyzes the effect of the international crisis and assesses their comparative performance from an inclusive economic benchmark.

The authors discussed at length the idea for this book, its approach and content in various meetings and joint work in Chapel Hill, Trento, Budapest and Tokyo.

The Introduction and the Conclusion are of joint authorship and serve to give a broad unified frame to the book. Steven Rosefielde is the author of the chapters on the Soviet Union, Russia and Ukraine (Part I: Chapters 1 through 6), while Bruno Dallago wrote the chapters on the Central European countries (Part II: Chapters 7 through 12).

Bruno Dallago and Steven Rosefielde
Trento, October 2015

Introduction

The slow motion collapse of Soviet power triggered by Mikhail Gorbachev's radical economic and political reforms opened the way to the destruction of the Soviet system and central planning in Russia, Ukraine, and Central Europe.[1] Radical reform had precedents, especially in Central Europe, but perestroika alone destroyed communism.

The post-communist systems of the Visegrád Four, Russia and Ukraine that evolved after 1989 and 1991 are a blend of continuity and change. All have modernized and westernized in various degrees. They have decriminalized private property where it was forbidden and liberalized it where it was restricted. Both have promoted market entrepreneurship and competition and opened foreign trade with the West. They have embraced multiparty balloting in their own fashion. Their institutions and economic structures today more closely resemble those of the European Union and the United States than they did a quarter century ago, but their national idiosyncrasies remain evident. Agricultural and industrial production and employment have contracted, while their service sectors have expanded. Balanced trade and the fiscal and monetary conservatism characteristic of Soviet-type regimes are now largely forgotten in Russia and Ukraine, while Central European countries have pursued remarkable fiscal and monetary moderation. In short, as Andrei Shleifer and Daniel Triesman conceive things, former Soviet republics and satellites have become normal middle-income countries.[2]

Command planning in Russia, Ukraine and Central Europe has been discarded, a process begun in Hungary and Poland decades before the Soviet Union's collapse, but this doesn't mean that the new market economies of Russia, Ukraine, Poland, Hungary, the Czech Republic and Slovakia all and equally practice free enterprise and are full-fledged democracies. In Russia and Ukraine, the old communist orders have changed, but haven't yet fully assimilated western values. In Central Europe, the four countries have made rapid progress. They have become well-functioning market economies and authentic pluralist democracies, enabling them to accede to the EU in 2004, but their transformation left some old problems and opened new ones.

The assessment of transformative merit, as Abram Bergson explained more than three quarters of a century ago, depends both on positive and normative criteria;[3] that is, the degree to which specific systems realize their technical potential, and the merit of their ends. The best from each individual's perspective requires the efficient attainment of the ideal. The worst from the same standpoint results from willful actions that wreak national havoc.

This volume applies Bergson's method. It examines Russia's, Ukraine's, Poland's, Hungary's, the Czech Republic's and Slovakia's complex institutions and goals and the effectiveness of their policies. Some of these transformations were failures, while others were successes to various degrees.

Causation is also examined with blame and praise appropriately assigned. Sometimes responsibility lies with domestic actors, other times external influences including those of the World Bank Group and the International Monetary Fund are determinative. In the case of Central European countries, the role of the EU is particularly important.

Moreover, national welfare isn't always policymakers' ultimate objective. Supranationality is an essential aspect of the Visegrád Four's experience. When it is taken into account together with the other positive and normative criteria, the comparative transformational performance of Russia, Ukraine, Poland, Hungary, the Czech Republic and Slovakia is cast in sharp relief. Poland is the main post-communist success story in both the macro- and micro-economic domain. Its accomplishments are primarily due to its judicious mix of shock therapy and gradualism. Slovakia is another relative success, despite a rocky start. The Czech Republic started strong, but has subsequently sputtered. Hungary's performance was disappointing until recently, largely due to domestic political constraints. Russia under Putin scores well in terms of its own objectives, but not from the West's perspective. Ukraine is an abject failure, partly because it defied the World Bank Group's shock therapeutic advice. However, it probably would have floundered anyway due to destructive intra-national oligarchic clan rivalries.

The future of Russia, Ukraine, Poland, Hungary, the Czech Republic and Slovakia cannot be prudently extrapolated from the experience of the past quarter century. According to Francis Fukuyama, the post-Soviet era was supposed to be the "end of history," but he now acknowledges his misplaced optimism.[4] Other approaches show that there isn't one unique best institutional system and that the most effective outcome depends upon the quality of the new institutional system as much as it depends upon the local circumstances.[5]

The EU's domestic economic troubles and problematic eastern enlargement project, Russia's authoritarian consolidation and its annexation of Crimea together with America's "decay" and China's economic slowdown have altered the prognosis.[6] The world finds itself today entangled in a new Cold War that under favorable circumstances could soften into Cold Peace. The Kremlin is committed to expanding its sphere of influence in Russia's neighborhood, a *sine qua non* that cannot be reconciled with transition. It is determined to dominate Ukraine, a policy that will severely impede any effort Kyiv may make to follow in the Visegrád Four's footsteps. Moscow is no longer in a position to bulldoze Central Europe, but the new Cold War will roil the waters, complicating the full recovery and development of the Polish, Hungarian, Czech and Slovak economies and the evolution of their economic systems. American and EU secular economic stagnation, over-indebtedness, the danger of another major global financial crisis and the mounting European refugee problem if they persist could also compel Central European leaders to rethink their options and further sour Russia on the West.[7]

Nothing prevents the winds from changing direction. The ongoing economic and political crises could move countries in different directions. The fate of Russia, Ukraine and Central Europe could be governed in the long run by universalizing or local economic forces. The former is important, because they make international interaction easier and more effective and economic calculation possible for economic actors. Similarly, local circumstances define what is feasible and what is economically appropriate in a particular reality.[8] However, the danger of making either one absolute is always present and thus the dangers of universalism and particularism abound.

One system might triumph over its competitors, or a multitude of systems might coexist. This treatise supports the pluralist outlook on theoretical grounds, but there is no need for dogmatism.[9] *Transformation and Crisis* provides useful insight into what was and is. Readers can appraise the debate about the end of history themselves.

Methodology

This volume utilizes an inclusive methodology that identifies how the micro and macro economies of Russia, Ukraine, Poland, Hungary, the Czech Republic and Slovakia are organized and function for the purpose of creating and distributing value added.[10] The approach documents the forces driving systems and shaping their potentials. It avoids attributing behavior to signal causes like rationality, institutions, culture, groups, or individuals because causality varies by case and context. The inclusive approach doesn't preclude the possibility of unitary global causality, but presumes that it is implausible because individual behavior often is governed by a-rational factors, culture and local institutions. Optimal and satisficing neoclassical theory is sometimes used to judge the shortcomings of real behavior. Care, however, is taken not to conflate what "ought to be" with what actually happens in Russia, Ukraine and the Visegrád Four.

The techniques appropriate for analyzing Russia's, Ukraine's, Poland's, Hungary's, the Czech Republic's and Slovakia's transformational experience 1985–2015 are:

1 identification of key events;
2 chronology of key events (timeline);
3 identification of key narrative documents;
4 identification of key institutions, laws, regulations and cultural forces governing behavior;
5 assembling, cleaning and adjusting pertinent statistics;
6 modeling rational behavior;
7 formulating statistically testable sub-hypotheses;

8   assembling results and complementary evidence;
9   identifying sets of alternative plausible explanations;
10   probing alternative futures.

Most economists focus their attention on points 5–8, ignoring "neo-realist" influences including power-seeking, anti-competitiveness, willfulness and unscrupulousness. For example, post-war studies of Soviet economic performance were dominated by Abram Bergson's adjusted factor cost method (point 5),[11] index number relativity theory, and the duality theorem which established the formal mathematical correspondence between perfect planning and perfect competition (point 6) 1947–70.[12] Thereafter, theory-normed econometrics became fashionable, shifting attention from planning theory to testable sub-hypotheses (point 7).[13] There was an evaluative phase associated with each of these methods (point 8), but for the most part individual specialists tended to claim that adjusted factor costing, index number relativity, planning theory, and econometrics were sufficient to identify causation. The dissolution of the Soviet Union has disproven the adequacy of these methodologies. Nearly all respected specialists (including the CIA) predicted that Soviet economic performance would be good enough to assure its survival well into the twenty-first century.

Historians, political scientists and international relations specialists prefer methodologies 1–4 supplemented with rational actor theory (point 6).[14] They build cases by citing events and documents; describing institutions, laws and regulations, and critically evaluating them from a rationalist perspective. The approach is sensible, but fallible because it is affected by the criteria used to select events and documents. Moreover, events, documents, institutions, laws and regulations are subject to multiple interpretations, and may conceal informal realities. "Facts" seldom speak for themselves, with the result that science often degenerates into persuasion.[15]

Economists run afoul of the same problem, but core neoclassical theory and econometrics give their analyses more, but still insufficient, solidity. As a consequence, the social sciences can never provide predictions that are as reliable as those made in the natural sciences.[16]

Inclusive economic theory cannot overcome this debility. However, it can clarify what is and isn't knowable by combining all ten methods, and provides a superior foundation for assessing Russia's, Ukraine's, Poland's, Hungary's, the Czech Republic's and Slovakia's transformational experience and future prospects.

Notes

1 The terms Central Europe or Visegrád Four (V4) are used throughout to identify Poland, Hungary, the Czech Republic and Slovakia (formerly Czechoslovakia). Central-Eastern Europe or Central-Eastern European countries (CEECs) are used to identify the group of countries between the former Soviet Union and Germany. This group includes Central Europe, Bulgaria, Romania and, after transformation, the Baltic countries. Post-Soviet countries other than the Baltic countries are included in Eastern Europe.

2 Andrei Schleifer and Daniel Treisman, *Without a Map: Political Tactics and Economic Reform in Russia*, Cambridge, MA: MIT Press, 2001; Andrei Schliefer and Daniel Treisman (2004), "Russia: A Normal Country," *Foreign Affairs*, Vol. 83, March/April, pp. 20–38.
3 Abram Bergson, "A Reformulation of Certain Aspects of Welfare Economics," *Quarterly Journal of Economics*, Vol. 52, No. 1, 1938, pp. 310–34.
4 Francis Fukuyama, *The End of History and the Last Man Standing*, New York: Free Press, 1992; Francis Fukuyama (2014), "America in Decay: The Sources of Political Dysfunction," *Foreign Affairs*, Vol. 93, September/October; and Francis Fukuyama, *Political Order and Political Decay: From the Industrial Revolution to the Globalization of Democracy*, New York: Farrar, Straus and Giroux, 2014.
5 See on this the literature on the varieties of capitalism, for example Hall and Soskice (2001). Similarly, Rodrik (2007) maintains that, while the general rules that overlook globalization can be a boon for countries that are striving for development, success requires that policies are tailored to local economic and political realities.
6 Steven Rosefielde and Quinn Mills, *Realpolitik in an Age of Ignorance: Exiting the Global Morass*, Oxford: Oxford University Press, forthcoming.
7 Rosefielde and Quinn Mills, *Global Economic Turmoil and the Public Good*, Singapore: World Scientific Publishers, 2015.
8 Local circumstances in this book identify the typical features of a country which distinguish it from other countries.
9 Experience shows that there are different types of well-functioning market economies. The main issue of transformation was to define whether transformation countries should adopt a standard blueprint of systemic change or whether they should adapt their new institutions to their own local features and circumstances. Economists give different answers to this critical question (Kingston and Caballero 2009). To simplify a rather tangled issue, two opposite positions exist. One is the mainstream position of economics: there is only one type of well-working market economy. According to the other position, each country is different and its institutions reflect also local circumstances. A substantial amount of recent literature tries to disentangle what is of general meaning in any well-working market economy and what is of more particular, local meaning. Many scholars in the institutional economics stream share this position, and in particular those in law and economics and the new comparative economics (Dallago 2004, Djankov et al. 2003, La Porta et al. 1998, Roland 2004, Shleifer 2002). These strands of research reach three important conclusions. First, there are important differences between institutional systems. Second, different institutional systems have different degrees of effectiveness on economic performance. Third, the effect of a particular institutional system depends critically upon the context in which it operates. In particular and when a new institutional system evolves in a country, the affinity and the familiarity with the new system generates more effective results than is obtained in a country that received an alien system without having a similar inclination and predisposition. An alien system is also less effective because it increases the adaptation and transaction costs imposed upon a particular country and its economic actors. An interesting example comes from the latter stream of research and in particular from the study of the transplantation of institutions. This literature shows that legal systems are important determinants of economic performance and that there are important differences in the effect of different legal systems (Glaeser and Shleifer 2002). However, this literature also shows that transplanting institutions is usually not a good business for countries, that suffer as a consequence higher costs and lower institutional effectiveness (Berkowitz et al. 2003a, 2003b).
10 Steven Rosefielde and Ralph W. Pfouts, *Inclusive Economic Theory*, Singapore: World Scientific Publishers, 2014.
11 Abram Bergson, "Soviet National Income and Product in 1937," parts I and II, *Quarterly Journal of Economics*, Vol. 64, Nos. 2, 3, May–August) 1950, pp. 208–41,

408–41; and Bergson, "Reliability and Usability of Soviet Statistics: A Summary Appraisal," *American Statistician*, Vol. 7, No. 3, (June–July) 1953, pp. 13–16.

12 Abram Bergson, *The Economics of Soviet Planning*, New Haven, CT: Yale University Press, 1964.

13 Steven Rosefielde, *Efficiency and the Economic Recovery Potential of Russia*, Aldershot: Ashgate, 1998; and Rosefielde, "Tea Leaves and Productivity: Bergsonian Norms for Gauging the Soviet Future," *Comparative Economic Studies*, Vol. 47, No. 2, June, 2005, pp. 259–73.

14 Martin Hollis and Edward J. Nell, *Rational Economic Man*, Cambridge: Cambridge University Press, 1975; Susanne Lohmann, "Rational Choice and Political Science," in Steven Durdaul and Lawrence Blume (eds.), *The New Palgrave Dictionary of Economics*, London: Palgrave Macmillan, 2008, second edn; and Peter Hedström and Charlotta Stern, "Rational Choice and Sociology," *The New Palgrave Dictionary of Economics*, ibid.

15 John Maynard Keynes, *Essays in Persuasion*, New York: W.W. Norton, 1962.

16 Romano Harre and P.F. Secord, *The Explanation of Social Behaviour*, Oxford: Basil Blackwell, 1972.

Part I

Post-communism transformation in Russia and Ukraine

1 Transformation

Russia, Ukraine and the former socialist countries of Eastern, Central and Southern Europe today are all market economies, unlike the 1980s when many of them were centrally planned command regimes. They have been transformed, but many have not fully transitioned to democratic free enterprise or European social democracy.[1]

The nature of these transformations can be discerned and grasped by carefully considering the Soviet command model which serves as a benchmark for distinguishing the new transformed economies from their predecessors. The requirements for going beyond transformation to transition will be discussed later.

Command economy[2]

All the eastern economies were authoritarian command regimes governed as one-party states before 1990, with the exception of the former Yugoslavia. This meant that they were undemocratic, and that employment, capital allocation, intermediate input technologies, production, wholesale and retail distribution were predominantly determined by authoritarian government directives of various types (edicts, plans, administration, regulations, controls, mandates and laws) rather than competitive markets. Communist authorities (sovereigns) decided what should be produced, how things should be manufactured and distributed, whether or not consumers and suppliers agreed; these authorities justified themselves by claiming to be guardians of the people's assets and protectors of the proletariat's welfare. Vladimir Lenin criminalized private property (nationalization of the means of production, markets and entrepreneurship) in November 1917 and ran the economy as a state directive conglomerate. Lenin in his capacities of Bolshevik Party leader, Chairman of the Council of People's Commissars, and Council of Labor and Defense issued legally binding orders down a chain of command, running from the Supreme Economic Council (VSNKha) at the top, and descending to workers at the bottom. Obedience in his scheme replaced discretion and voluntary competitive negotiations. Those who complied were rewarded; those who resisted were coerced.

The command principle wasn't a novel one. It was the backbone of military and bureaucratic organizations from the dawn of civilization and is widely

employed in varying degrees by governments and business organizations every-where. It worked well enough, together with coercion, to survive the evolutionary test, despite conspicuous inefficiencies and rigidities. The Bolsheviks were unde-terred by its shortcomings, contending that defects would be eliminated in the fullness of time.

Lenin and his successors accordingly chose to improve command by marrying it to scientific central planning. They claimed that central planners could acquire and utilize all the information available in markets to assure superior outcomes, even though markets themselves were proscribed.

Planners, as the Bolsheviks imagined it, would choose the best technologies and allocation of resources to produce the optimal assortment of outputs with superior characteristics, and distribute them efficiently on the basis of need. Planners would do their job correctly, and virtuous commanders would assure faithful plan implementation down the chain of command.

Figure 1.1 illustrates the command concept for the post-NEP Soviet industrial supply regime (1929–90).[3] The supreme commanders (Stalin and his successors) reigned from on high, acquiring essential information in the form of draft plans from the Central Planning authority.

The State Planning Agency (Gosplan) is positioned at the top of the information acquisition and processing column on the right. Leaders reviewed draft plans and demanded revisions until they were satisfied, and then ordered subordinates down the central supply column to implement plan-informed directives. The results were presumed to be superior, if everyone complied. If they didn't, then some entity in the civilian administrative control apparatus located in the left-hand column, or the "justice" system on the far left was assigned to intervene. Serious offenders in the Soviet era were shot, or sent to the state concentration camp network (the Gulag) for re-education.[4] Perhaps, Eastern governments could have been more compassion-ate, but insubordination was a grave threat. Economic misbehavior in competitive market economies is automatically disciplined by the "invisible hand," but not in command regimes that amputate competitive adjustment mechanisms.[5]

This was the core communist command model. It was enhanced over time with better planning methodologies, statistics and computational technologies and by tightening discipline. Better techniques and discipline campaigns were perpetual post-Stalin refrains on what Gertrude Schroeder dubbed the "treadmill of economic reform."[6]

The model was also amenable to motivational reforms supplementing the com-mand principle, but sophisticated incentive schemes yielded meager results. Stalin understood the potential usefulness of carrots and sticks. He adopted progressive piece-work bonuses for workers and rewarded managers for over-fulfilling plan targets both in the civilian sector and the Gulag.[7] Underperformers had their pay docked.

These reforms shifted part of the disciplinary burden from administrative supervisors to workers and managers. The system became partly self-regulating (markets remained proscribed), instead of wholly directive. The reform movement gained momentum shortly after Stalin's death with the decision to link rewards

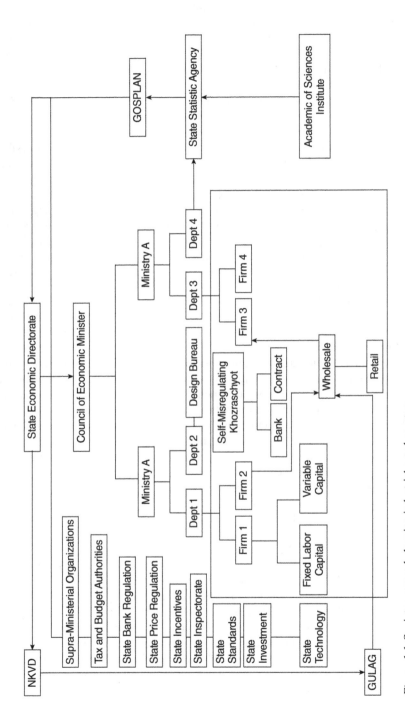

Figure 1.1 Soviet command planning industrial supply system

to profit maximizing, a subtle but important change that induced managers to be cost wise and price conscious.[8] During Stalin's reign, managers were incentivized to pay only secondary attention to costs and prices. Plan fulfillment measured in physical units was king. The post-Stalin managerial bonus-incentive revolution tacitly acknowledged that command planning couldn't function satisfactorily without back-up mechanisms.

Managerial bonus incentives improved efficiency in two ways. First, they deterred the overproduction of low-value/high-cost outputs, with resources transferred to manufacturing high-value goods in short supply.

Second, bonus maximizing assisted Red directors in coping with infeasible plan assignments. If they couldn't fully comply, profit-linked bonus incentives impelled them to sub-optimize.[9]

This wasn't tantamount to a *true* second best because Red directors' hands were tied, compared to their western counterparts.[10] They could not manage cash. All sales receipts and payments were cleared by the State bank on a bookkeeping basis. Red directors were prohibited from entrepreneurial activities, and had little voice in modernizing enterprise technologies. Likewise, they could not competitively negotiate wages or prices with other state firms except for special order items. Wages and prices were set by the State Price Board and often remained fixed for decades. This meant that when Red directors bonus-maximized profits, they were doing so with fiat wages and prices rather than competitive equilibrium values. False prices generated false profits, degrading the efficiency benefit of Soviet profit incentives.

In a nutshell, Soviet authoritarian economic reform was straitjacketed by the leadership's unwillingness to increase consumer and managerial autonomy enough to seriously challenge the command principle. Constructive reforms within these imposed limits were welcome; those that crossed the threshold were opposed.

The reform variant of administrative command planning was probably better than the core model, and certainly less despotic. The improvements were positive, but not enough to counteract the forces pressing for transformation. Communist leaders insisted to the bitter end that administrative command planning was superlative,[11] but by the late 1980s few insiders believed it.

Their disillusionment was justified. Judged from the competitive market benchmark, the system delivered a squalid existence for the vast majority. The reasons always should have been obvious. Planners had no knowledge of consumer preferences or needs. Consumers were prohibited from discussing their tastes with product designers, and planners weren't mind readers. Product characteristics accordingly were whatever bureaucratic designers desired. Consumers were forced to take whatever they could get in an economy of shortage,[12] while the demands of the military industrial complex were prioritized.

Planning itself, despite the hype portraying it as an optimal automatic system of planning and management (ASUP),[13] was in fact merely a crude process of hodge-podge adjustments from achieved levels of production for a small set of "composite" goods.[14] The Soviet product directory listed approximately 27 million products,[15] but central planners only computed approximately 125 plan aggregates.[16]

This meant that the detail of Soviet industrial supply was mostly a matter of serendipity, except for the ad hoc intervention of ministers, Communist Party troubleshooters, the KGB and military officials, and the inscrutable effects of "false profit" guided bonus incentives. Discipline campaigns could force the nation to exert itself, but this didn't translate into a decent living standard or superior quality of life.

These insights can be crisply restated in neoclassical terms. The command model was powerless to maximize consumer utility either on an optimal or satisficing (second-best) basis. Competitive market economies offer second-best outcomes; command systems are mostly second-worst.[17]

Nonetheless, the command model did have a few compensating virtues. Wages and prices were as stable as the supreme commander wanted them to be.[18] There was little overt inflation. Wages and prices were fixed by the state and it was a crime to exchange goods on other terms. The system was designed to insure full or overfull employment. This was accomplished by creating perpetual excess aggregate effective demand (managers were bonus incentivized to overproduce), providing guaranteed state purchase of everything enterprises produced (except defective goods) and criminalizing freeloading (anti-parasite laws). Also, the government had little interest in borrowing from private citizens (negligible national debt) or in abetting speculative bubbles (among Red directors) because, unlike market regimes, it could always commandeer whatever it wanted. These pluses should be weighed in any balance sheet comparing command and transformed planning systems, with appropriate caveats.

The macroeconomic stability of the Soviet system is sometimes conflated with command communism's idealist ends. This puts the cart before the horse. The East's supreme commanders didn't sacrifice microeconomic efficiency to secure the blessings of macroeconomic stability. They provided workers with job security, price stability and public provision of housing, health care, education, transport and other essential services to enlist their support for communist power, development and military might. The provision of barebones public services and basic security were essential for sustaining the regime's legitimacy. Once these conditions were satisfied, the supreme commander's primary goals were insider privilege and state superpower with scant concern for efficiency. Command from this perspective wasn't about optimizing anything. It was the time-honored and effective authoritarian strategy of building cadre loyalty and hence insider power by pretending to comprehensively command, while permitting key personnel to get the job done by all means fair and foul. The system in its entirety was an inferior anti-democratic satisficing venture with slender rationality beyond the primary mission of bolstering Communist Party power at home and abroad.

The precise nature of the supreme commander's satisficing varied from country to country. In the Soviet Union, the goal was the traditional imperial insider privilege and superpower in a communist guise. It entailed the criminalization of private property, business and entrepreneurship, egalitarianism for the masses, Spartan public services, modernization, and an austere public face for the purpose of

vouchsafing the "revolution," building Soviet power and spreading Marxist–Leninist blessings across the globe.

These objectives behind the façade of planning and incentives relied on rent-granting. The supreme commander (tsar) fixed agendas and then ordered his vassals (rent-seekers) to fulfill assignments any way they could, with no questions asked. The supreme commander in this arrangement allowed his servitors to enrich themselves (rent-grants) in return for crudely fulfilling missions and loyal support.

The command principle was a fig leaf. The Soviet Union at its core was a Muscovite servitor state,[19] largely divorced from the twin neoclassical concepts of rational utilitarian optimization and bounded rational satisficing. Rent-granting controlled the way the system actually behaved, given the structural goals set forth in the central plan. Insiders ran the economy in crude authoritarian fashion for their own benefit in the name of the proletariat.

The model worked in the sense that it secured the power of the Bolshevik Party for 73 years, but it ultimately failed because the results as insiders perceived them weren't good enough. An insurgent faction of the Communist Party led by Boris Yeltsin seized the reins of power and sought to rule in its own interest by combining rent-granting and markets with remnants of command in the military industrial complex,[20] under a liberalizing veneer. This was accomplished by striking out the central column in Figure 1.1, replacing it with markets managed by edicts, mandates, administration, regulations, non-planning controls and by revising the nation's ideocracy.[21] The retention of state authority with softer directive methods and the persistence of rent-granting explain why the scuttling of civilian command planning in favor of markets has in most eastern cases resulted in transformation rather than transition to the neoclassical paradigm. Russia's transformed economic mechanism preserves its historical Muscovite rent-granting, and state-managed and superpower-seeking priorities. Other eastern nations display similar characteristics, preserving rent-granting and using "soft" state-management techniques to pursue their social agendas.

Notes

1 The concepts of democratic free enterprise and social democracy can be rigorously formulated in neoclassical and political economic terms. We shall do so in the next chapter to provide clear benchmarks for gauging the special characteristics of Europe's former socialist economies.
2 Steven Rosefielde, *Russian Economy from Lenin to Putin*, New York: Wiley, 2007.
3 NEP.
4 Steven Rosefielde, *Red Holocaust*, London: Routledge, 2010.
5 Steven Rosefielde and Ralph W. Pfouts, *Inclusive Economic Theory*, Singapore: World Scientific Publishers, 2014.
6 Gertrude Schroeder, "The Soviet Economy on a Treadmill of Reforms," in *Soviet Economy in a Time of Change*, Washington, DC: Joint Economic Committee of Congress, 1979, pp. 312–66.
7 Abram Bergson, *The Structure of Soviet Wages*, Cambridge, MA: Harvard University Press, 1944.
8 Evsei Liberman, *Economic Methods and the Effectiveness of Production*, New York: Doubleday, 1973.

9 Steven Rosefielde, *Russian Economy from Lenin to Putin*, New York: Wiley, 2007.
10 Steven Rosefielde, "Economic Theory of the Second Worst," *Higher School of Economics Journal* (HSE), (Moscow), 2015, pp. 30–44.
11 Materials from the Plenum of the Communist Party Central Committee, January 27–9, 1987, Politizdat, 1987, pp. 6–7, quoted in *Narodnoye Khoziastvo SSSR za 70 Let, Iubileinyi Statisticheskii Ezhegodnik*, Finansy I Statistika, 1987, p. 12.
12 Igor Birman, *Ekonomika Nedostach* (Economy of Shortage), New York: Chaldize Publishers, 1983.
13 Martin Cave, *Computers and Economic Planning: The Soviet Experience*, Cambridge: Cambridge University Press, 1980.
14 Igor Birman, "From the Achieved Level," *Soviet Studies*, Vol. 30, No. 2, 1978, pp. 153–72.
15 Steven Rosefielde, *Russian Economy from Lenin to Putin*, London: Routledge, 2007.
16 Steven Rosefielde, *Russian Economy from Lenin to Putin*, London: Routledge, 2007.
17 Steven Rosefielde and Ralph W. Pfouts, *Inclusive Economic Theory*, Singapore: World Scientific Publishers, 2014; Steven Rosefielde, "Economic Theory of the Second Worst," *Higher School of Economics Journal* (HSE), (Moscow), 2015.
18 There was rampant inflation during World War II, but consumer price increases were negligible 1960–87.
19 Muscovite culture is traceable to Ivan III Vasilevich, known as Ivan the Great, Grand Prince of Muscovy (1440–1505). The Muscovite idea is that the ruler, whether he is called grand duke, tsar, *vozhd* (leader), general secretary, or president, is an autocrat who, de facto or de jure, owns all of the country's productive assets and governs for himself in the name of the nation. He is the law and rules by edict absolutely or behind a facade of parliamentary constitutionalism. Everyone else is a *rab* (slave of the ruler). Individuals of other stations may have private lives and may seek to maximize their happiness, but they are always subject to commands, edicts, and rules imposed from above by their supreme lord, without protection of the rule of law. They have no inviolable human, property, economic, political, or social rights. Whatever has been given can be rescinded, regardless of custom or precedent. Social welfare in this cultural framework is synonymous with the autocrat's welfare, given whatever allotment he chooses to share with his people.
20 Steven Rosefielde and Stefan Hedlund, *Russia Since 1980*, Cambridge: Cambridge University Press, 2010.
21 Systems governed by ideas and ideals, including neoclassical idealism and realism. The term was coined by Martin Malia. See Martin Malia, *The Soviet Tragedy: A History of Socialism in Russia, 1917–1991*, New York: Free Press, 1994.

2 Benchmarks

The transformed economic systems of the East can be judged from several perspectives. They all rely heavily on markets, but markets aren't alike. Some are ideal, others imperfect in varying degrees. One benchmark deserves special attention because it comprehensively illuminates the special features of the transformed Russian and East European economies. It is the inclusive economic standard that takes explicit account of markets' ideal and bounded rational potentials, as well as insider power.

The ideal aspect of market potential is derived from Enlightenment philosophy. Enlightenment philosophers like Baruch Spinoza and Jean Jacques Rousseau in the seventeenth and eighteenth centuries claimed that individuals were rational and moral enough to freely determine what was best for them without state guidance. People didn't need to be governed by public authorities. Reason and morality made them autonomous. Contrary to command communist doctrine, people are entitled to be free, own private property, enjoy religious liberty and democratically govern themselves in any fashion they believe advances their well-being.

Enlightenment philosophers, in other words, contended that people could and should be permitted to pursue and maximize their utility within the framework of a fair play social contract that protected minority and majority civic and property rights. If each individual competitively maximizes their utility in employment, production, distribution and consumption, Enlightenment philosophers asserted that this would also maximize the utility of the collective and be socially just in the sense that each individual receives the full value of what they earn. No one in this scheme is entitled to receive a portion of other people's earnings, even if some earn more than others. Those who outperform fully benefit. Those who underperform suffer the consequences, except insofar as the wealthy choose to assist the poor.

This model accepts everyone's right to advocate charity, and the majority right to tax some for the benefit of others within narrow limits that protect minority property rights. The result can be described as the Pareto ideal because if achieved it is impossible for individuals to voluntarily enhance their utility by altering their employment, production, distribution, or redistribution of goods and services. A deviation from equilibrium necessarily prevents at least one participant from improving utility without diminishing the utility of others.[1]

The Pareto ideal, however, only serves as a lucid benchmark for gauging when transformations are transitions to Enlightenment regimes with respect to a single criterion: the democratic consumer utility standard. It is a consumer sovereign efficiency test that can be used to measure the distance Russia and the European East have traversed from authoritarian command toward democratic free enterprise or social democracy.

The benchmark is useful, but incomplete because real economies aren't neoclassically ideal. Individual rationality does not govern outcomes with textbook precision, because the twenty neoclassical axioms required for complete optimization are invalid. The excessively strong axioms are:

1 Consumers don't possess well-defined continuous preferences.
2 Consumer preferences are not interpersonally independent.
3 Consumers do not comprehensively select rationally.
4 Consumers do not exhaustively utility search (optimizing rather than satisficing).
5 Consumers do not autonomously choose (individuals and households).
6 Consumers do not universally act ethically (competitively) within the framework of a Lockean social contract.
7 Well-being is not solely determined by successive rational marginal choices.
8 Consumer preferences are not entirely formed rationally.
9 Production and cost functions are not continuous, twice differentiable and monotonic.
10 Suppliers do not have complete knowledge of demand and intermediate input acquisition possibilities.
11 Suppliers do not possess well-defined continuous preferences that enable them to optimize with discrete production and cost functions, as well as restricted information on intermediate-input supplies and demand.
12 Supplier (manager) preferences are not interpersonally independent.
13 Managers do not comprehensively rationally select.
14 Managers do not exhaustively search profit and cost minimization possibilities (optimizing rather than satisficing).
15 Managers do not autonomously choose (CEOs and collective corporate decision makers).
16 Managers do not always act ethically (competitively) within the framework of a Lockean social contract.
17 Managers' preferences are not comprehensively formed rationally.
18 Humans can either directly intuit ideal founding institutions, or can learn how to do so by trial and error.
19 Rational competition doesn't always provide market participants with the clear signals needed to support generally competitive full employment outcomes.
20 Popularly elected governments aren't the people's faithful agent. Government programs cannot maximize individual Paretian welfare.

The axiomatic shortcomings of ideal neoclassical theory were recognized by Paul Samuelson in the late 1940s and addressed by Herbert Simon in the 1950s.

The upshot of Simon's work and subsequent elaborations by others is that human rationality is bounded by various informational, computational, cognitive and evaluative limitations that preclude a complete marginalist utility-maximizing equilibrium. The proof of the existence of a general equilibrium using fixed point methods like those devised by Kakutani is sometimes cited as a counter-example, but the assumptions invoked are unrealistic.[2]

There are innumerable bounded rational satisficing solutions, instead of a unique competitively best utility-maximizing outcome. The most that can be claimed is that Pareto utility outcomes are individually best in the fuzzy sense imposed both by the bounded nature of information and human rationality.

The boundedness of rationality varies from system to system. The ability of consumers and producers to effectively satisfice depends on property rights, legal, tax, regulatory, political, social and civil regimes. Nations with superior institutions will outperform the norm even if private markets everywhere are competitive.

The inclusive economic standard also takes explicit account of insider power that often over-rides consumer sovereignty. Sometimes individuals and officials exert authority for good, but more often for evil. The balance varies across Russia's and East Europe's transformed economies and strongly affects their comparative merit.

Analysts are aware that institutions and power affect systems performance, but treat them as if they were extraneous policy matters outside the economic core. This gives the misleading impression that the productivity of markets, and consumer utility potential are independent of institutions and political regimes, when in fact the comparative merit of market regimes is co-determined by competitiveness and the quality of economic, legal, political, social and civic institutions and policies. The conflation of "economics" with neoclassical analysis sustains this false dichotomy; the inclusive economic standard remedies the error and provides a superior benchmark for judging the comparative merit of Russia's and Eastern Europe's transformed economic systems.

Notes

1 See Steven Rosefielde, *Asian Economic Systems*, Singapore: World Scientific Publishers, 2013, Chapter 1 for a geometric demonstration of these claims.
2 Shizuo Kakutani, "A Generalization of Brouwer's Fixed Point Theorem," *Duke Mathematical Journal*, Vol. 8, No. 3, 1941, pp. 457–9.

Part II
The former Soviet Union

(misleadingly labeled "shock therapy"),[2] proved catastrophic for most Red directors and the general population, with the exception of a handful of insiders who through diverse methods spontaneously privatized lucrative assets to themselves and/or were awarded lavish state contracts. Marshall Goldman aptly described the process as "piratization."[3] While the gross domestic product declined between 37 and 50 percent in the period 1990–98, causing 3.4 million excess deaths,[4] a small coterie of "oligarchs" in Yeltsin's private circle became billionaires.[5]

Russian intellectuals quickly condemned Yeltsin's "transition" policy (*perekhod*). They considered it rash and catastrophic (*katastroika*), but the regime and its external supporters – for example, the IMF and the World Bank – applauded what they claimed to be a fundamentally successful transition to American-style democratic free enterprise.[6] They lauded Yeltsin's boldness and resolve. Anders Åslund celebrated Russia's capitalist coming of age as early as 1995,[7] and soon thereafter heralded the triumph of Russian democracy before reversing his outlook later in the new millennium.[8] Somehow, without ever acknowledging error or fault, the West is grudgingly accepting the bitter truth that Russia's transition was a mirage in the wake of Crimea's annexation in 2014.[9] The regime has been profoundly transformed, but has not embraced democratic free enterprise or social democracy. It has morphed into something very different, despite marketization and liberalization.

As many had foreseen, the Kremlin has gone back to the future, relying on its Muscovite culture to re-create an authoritarian,[10] martial, rent-granting police state. Like Xi Jinping's contemporary market communist China, Russia has sharply curtailed the role of command in its industrial supply system (see Figure 1.1), circumscribing it mostly to the military-industrial activities, with responsibility for all other industrial supplies, finance and product distribution shifted to the market. But the Kremlin has not surrendered its authority over the supply of private and public goods. The *vozhd* (leader) is firmly in control.

This has been accomplished by adroit rent-granting, both an institution and government policy shaping the Russia's market core. In the tradition of Ivan the Great, all the assets of the realm, including the right to bestow privilege belong exclusively to the tsar, who is the freehold property owner – not the people, the party, or the state. Half a millennium ago, the sovereign's divine right of unrestricted freehold ownership was explicit. Now it is implied, overtly surfacing only when the *vozhd*'s authority is mocked or challenged.[11]

The issue is moot in the state sector. Putin reigns as lord of the military-industrial complex,[12] Rosatom,[13] and huge natural resource companies like Gasprom. He grants usage rights to his favorites (rent-granting) in return for personal tribute, state revenue, service and loyal support. Favorites of all varieties, including oligarchs, aren't obligated to profit maximize or satisfice within the parameters of "bounded rationality." They are permitted wide latitude in serving themselves and Putin outside of the competitive market framework.[14] The *vozhd* prefers neither to micromanage nor command. He sets broad assignments like weapons modernization, and expects the task to be expediently fulfilled by his appointees and subrent-grantees operating under the same rules.[15] The tasks assigned are fuzzy, not legally binding plans as they were previously under the communist command system.

3   Russia

The Soviet Union was the world's flagship command economy when Mikhail Gorbachev was appointed the seventh General Secretary of the Communist Party in 1985. The country was a military superpower and industrial powerhouse with vast natural resource reserves and a well-educated labor force. Its 290 million citizens enjoyed free public education, health care and highly subsidized housing, utilities and transportation. Official statistics reported that no one was unemployed from September 1929 until 1989, and that economic growth surpassed the western norm, except during World War II. Moreover, echoing Lenin, leaders contended that Soviet democracy was a million times more democratic than bourgeois parliamentary democracy. The Soviet Constitution was said to be the world's most progressive founding document and the party claimed that the quality of people's lives was lofty. There seemed to be no grounds for advocating transformation or transition.[1] Nonetheless, six years later, the Supreme Soviet voluntarily dissolved the USSR. Apparently, the face in the statistical mirror bore no resemblance to command communist reality.

Yes everyone worked, but few produced anything of value. The Japanese, for example, refused to purchase raw timber from Russian suppliers because Soviet processing in their view subtracted value instead of adding it. Yes, people sometimes voted, but the system was fundamentally authoritarian. Yes, Soviet constitutions were progressive, but only on paper. Yes, living standards in 1985 were higher than in 1917, but the quality of life was worse for anyone who valued personal freedom. Some citizens were satisfied to accept stability in lieu of opportunity, but many thwarted men and women in high party positions were desperate to escape.

Transformation for them was about self-empowerment. They weren't utopians. They set their sights on destroying command communism to improve their own lot. The process of destruction unfolded with astonishing rapidity. Immediately after the Soviet Union dissolved itself on December 25, 1991, Russia's President Boris Yeltsin canceled all state orders and rescinded the Soviet policy of guaranteed state purchase. Former Red directors, now transformed willy-nilly into enterprise managers, were left to fend for themselves. They had to either figure out how to produce goods people wanted, and self-finance their operations, or go out of business. Needless to say, this callous strategy of state abandonment

Favorites and their vassals in the rent-granting hierarchy are dependent allies of their liege. They own nothing in a freehold sense, appearances to the contrary notwithstanding. The usufruct granted them can be withdrawn any time without notice or explanation, and their freehold claims arising from derivative activities can be set aside at will. This point was first driven home to everyone both inside and outside the state sector when, in 2003, Vladimir Putin seized Mikhail Khordorkovsky's Yukos oil company to punish him for insubordination and sent him to prison for a decade.[16] The confiscation of an asset worth more than US$15 billion at the time, and Khordorkovsky's incarceration, sent a message to Russia's other rent-grantees that could not be and wasn't ignored.[17] The *vozhd*'s servitors instantaneously appreciated that no one in Russia is fully protected by the rule of law. Putin, like all Russian Communist Party general secretaries and tsars, reigns with an iron fist. He controls the secret police and doesn't hesitate to use it as an instrument of personal power.

The commanding heights of the private sector are organized on the same principle. Most of the natural resource sector, banking, finance, insurance, media and foreign trade activities are run as private rent-granted monopolies. Insiders receive privileged contracts, are protected against would-be domestic and foreign competitors and are permitted to live like princes, often immune to market discipline as long as they refrain from biting the hand that feeds them, pay their dues to the *vozhd*, carry out collateral political and diplomatic obligations and defend the realm. Competitive efficiency, profit maximizing and "bounded rational satisficing" here, as in the state-run military-industrial sector are afterthoughts.

The lower depths lying beneath the commanding heights operate on mixed principles. Insiders are permitted to outsource to smaller concerns on a rent-granting basis, but also often find it beneficial to tolerate independent competitors operating on narrow margins. Small- and medium-sized private freehold and leasehold companies competitively profit-seek and profit-maximize to the best of their abilities within the system's institutional constraints. They allow a multitude to survive on little, while providing intermediate and final goods to the powerful, including the secret police (FSB) and the mafia at least competitive cost.[18] Small- and medium-sized proprietors prosper by their wit, energy and initiative to the extent the system permits, filling a void that straitjacketed the command model.

The modification makes the post-Soviet transformed Russian economic system better. Its competitive aspect is compatible with the transition ideal; however, the scope and prospects of competitiveness are limited because there is no reliable rule of law. Successful firms are routinely seized by predators, including the FSB and the mafia, as soon as their promise becomes visible. The new Russia system of Putin's design thus is restrictive. It has the potential to transition, just like its tsarist predecessor, but is stifled by institutionalized privilege.

A deeper appreciation of the nature and potential of Russia's transformed economic mechanism can be gleaned by interpreting the fundamentals elaborated above from the perspective of the inclusive economic theory outlined in Chapter 2. There is no place in Putin's system for complete neoclassical optimization. The dominant force in the Russian economy today is rent-granting, not profit maximizing or bounded rational competitive satisficing.

Rent-granting's fatal defect is motivational. Bounded rational satisficing, as Herbert Simon conceives it, is an informational and computational aberration.[19] Businesspeople want to profit maximize, but they cannot figure out how to do it with confidence, and therefore hedge their bets by combining profit-seeking with other objectives. Their motivation is utility-seeking within the competitive paradigm. They are cost conscious, invest wisely and innovate regardless of whether bounded rationality induces them to maximize market share, or sales subject to a minimum rate of return on capital. The motivation of Russian rent-seekers by contrast is only obliquely connected to these competitive stratagems. Russian rent-seekers concentrate their energies on simulating compliance with the *vozhd*'s wishes, diverting revenue streams toward themselves, suppressing competition, defrauding others and inveigling subsidies. Efficiently managing the state's assets or the usufruct granted to them is a tangential concern because property rights are insecure, and the Pareto mindset conflicts with insiders' willfulness, grandiose ambitions and predatory schemes.

Rent-seekers' swashbuckling approach to satisficing gratifies big egos and pays immense dividends to fortunate high rollers, but harms outsiders. Rent-granting depresses efficiency and productivity, corrupts economic relations, increases catastrophic risks, and embeds extreme disparities of income and wealth.

The same principles apply to the Kremlin's public policies. Russian *vozhds* have always paid lip service to the people's well-being, but are largely uninterested in mobilizing national resources to promote general empowerment, affluence, egalitarianism, entitlement and social justice. Moreover, they oppose any form of globalization that threatens Muscovite authoritarianism and limits empire building when opportunity knocks. These principles are reflected in the Kremlin's preference for grand projects, large land armies, superpower status, spheres of influence and strategic opportunism, as well as in its opposition to true democracy, free enterprise, human rights, constitutionalism, the rule of law and international constraints on its sovereign independence. The ideal neoclassical standard implicitly assumes that the people's preferences determine the provision of public goods. Market Muscovy assures that popular desires are subordinated to Putin's will, even though he claims to be serving the people.

The ideocracy his regime has created to rationalize Muscovite rule ("enlightened conservatism" and sovereign democracy) is bereft of neoclassical rationality.[20] There is no democratic or consumer sovereignty.[21] The state doesn't try to maximize individual welfare as the people themselves perceive it. The Kremlin doesn't apply neoclassical optimization concepts in implementing its authoritarian agenda.

Vozhds don't economize resources to construct virtuous and harmonious societies. They simply rely on repression, rent-granting and public attitude management. Moreover, there are no automatic economic or political adjustment mechanisms fostering a transition to democratic free enterprise of social democracy any time soon. Authoritarian politics is fully in command, and committed to marginalizing economic optimization and second-best satsificing for the foreseeable future. Command communism is gone. Russia has been transformed, but it looks nothing like the post-transition utopia western statesmen promised.

Notes

1 "Almost seventy years ago our Leninist party raised over the nation the victorious banner of the socialist revolution, the struggle for socialism, freedom and equality, for social justice and societal progress against oppression and exploitation, poverty and national subjugation. For the first time in human history, the interests and needs of the workers were placed at the center of the state's agenda. There have been many successes during socialist construction of the Soviet Union in the political, economic, social and spiritual realms. Under party guidance, the Soviet people have built social-ism, defeated fascism in the Great Patriotic War, established and strengthened the national economy, and transformed their homeland into a great power. Our achieve-ments have been immense and indisputable, and the Soviet people are justifiably proud of their successes. They are the true guarantee of the realization of the current plan, and our future dreams": *Materials for the Plenum of the Communist Party Central Committee*, January 27–29, 1987, Politizadat, 1987, pp. 6–7, quoted in *Narodnoe Khoziastvo SSSR za 70 Let, Iubileinyi Statisticheskii Ezhegodnik*, Fianansy i Statistika, 1987, p. 12.
2 Jeffrey Sachs, "Russia's Tumultuous Decade," *The Washington Monthly*, March 2000: http://www.washingtonmonthly.com/books/2000/0003.sachs.html.
3 Marshall Goldman, *The Piratization of Russia: Russian Reform Goes Awry*, London: Routledge, 2003. Cf. Yuko Adachi, *Building Big Business in Russia: The Impact of Informal Corporate Governance Practices*, London: Routledge, 2010; and Yuko Adachi, "Subsoil Law Reform in Russia under the Putin Administration," *Europe-Asia Studies*, Vol. 61, No. 8, October 2009, pp. 1393–414.
4 Steven Rosefielde and Stefan Hedlund, *Russia Since 1980: Wrestling with Westernization*, Cambridge: Cambridge University Press, 2008; and Steven Rosefielde, "Premature Deaths: Russia's Radical Transition," *Europe-Asia Studies*, Vol. 53, No. 8, December 2001, pp. 1159–76.
5 Richard Sakwa, *Putin and the Oligarchs: The Khodorkovsky-Yukos Affair*, Washington, DC: I.B. Tauris, 2014.
6 Konstantin George, "How IMF Shock Therapy Was Imposed on Russia," *EIR*, Vol. 25, No. 32, August 14, 1998, pp. 56–62.
7 Anders Åslund, *How Russia Became a Market Economy*, Washington, DC: Brookings Institute, 1995.
8 Anders Åslund, *How Capitalism Was Built: The Transformation of Central and Eastern Europe, Russia, the Caucasus, and Central Asia*, Cambridge: Cambridge University Press, 2007, and Anders Åslund, group email, December 12, 2011.
9 Steven Rosefielde, *The Kremlin Strikes Back: Russia and the West after Crimea's Annexation*, London: Cambridge University Press, 2016.
10 Steven Rosefielde, "Russia's Productive Potential: Limitations of Muscovite Authoritarianism," *Comparative Economic Studies*, No. 10, July 2003, pp. 83–4; Steven Rosefielde, "Illusion of Transition: Russia's Muscovite Future," *Eastern Economic Journal*, Vol. 31, No. 2, Spring 2005, pp. 283–96; and Steven Rosefielde, "Soviet Economy: An Ideocratic Reassessment," *Ekonomicheskaya Nauka Sovremennoy Rossii*, No. 3, November 2013. Russia has been a rent-granting "public service" busi-ness since the rise of Muscovy under Ivan III Vasilevich, known as Ivan the Great (1440–1505), the Grand Prince of Moscow, the "gatherer of Russian lands," and Grand Prince of all the Rus. Ivan the Terrible (1530–84), Russia's first tsar crowned with the Monomakh Cap in 1547, and all his successors rent-granted, taxed, decreed, price- and wage-fixed, administered, supervised, managed, regulated and contracted to enrich themselves, while posing as the selfless protectors of the Russian people. Statecraft in these respects is similar in both the East and the West, but frameworks, strategies and tactics differ. Russia's tsars and autocratic chief commissars ruled by divine right (or ineluctable dialectic), whereas legitimacy, authority and ownership in today's West

derive constitutionally from the people. Tsars and Communist Party leaders were both the "law," and the ultimate arbiters of "holy" writ. They deferred to no one, acting as masters over everything and everyone they surveyed.

The Russian approach to state governance is an especially vicious form of patrimonialism (patriarchal rule) called the "Muscovite model," associated with Ivan the Grozny (the Terrible, or Awe-inspiring). Its principal features are absolutism, predation, oppression and rent-granting, with secondary characteristics such as slavery, serfdom and perfunctory forms of popular participation.

Absolute Muscovite tsars ruled by authoritarian outsourcing rather than as "philosopher kings" (rulers of Kallipolis), market regulators, or totalitarian commanders. Supporters (including the *oprichniki*) were granted the privilege of managing portions of the tsars' domains (*pomestie*, service-landholding) in return for state service, fixed payments and peasant taxes. Appointees were ennobled, deputized and empowered to govern their custodial realms with little or no direct state oversight, but served at the tsar's sufferance without tenure or constitutional rights (unlike feudalism). Muscovite nobles were required to serve in the military and/or state administration, and for the most part subdelegated estate management to overseers and foremen who satisfied (made do), rather than profit maximized. The control strategy was indulgent, inefficient, underproductive and egregiously exploited the peasantry (serfs and slaves), but suited the tsars' need for loyalty, internal security, state service, economic management and tax collection. The process sometimes was colorful.

Catherine the Great gave her paramours estates, complete with tens of thousands of serfs (slaves). Gregory Potemkin of "Potemkin village" fame was gifted with 16,000 and Peter Zavadovsky 4,000 souls. Institutional details evolved over the centuries, but the core ideas of absolutism, revocable *pomestie*, the servitor state and squeezing ordinary people to provide a lavish life for the few persisted.

This style of rule is often described as "rent-granting" ("*kormlenie*," "feeding"). The term is a short hand phrase that expresses both the Muscovite governance strategy, and the inequity of the compensation package. Rent-granting is a servile subcontracting scheme where each sub-entity is compelled to self-sufficiently fend for itself by exploiting subordinate links down the chain of command. The chiefs of each subordinate entity contribute little added value beyond lashing those directly under their control. Compulsion (and Stalinist terror) mobilize labor and resources, and produce appropriable surpluses, but factors don't receive the values of their marginal products as they are supposed to in competitive theory, and society is degraded. Appropriable income (income available to be commandeered) can be interpreted as rent (unearned income) extorted from the weak and transferred to the powerful. Muscovite "rent-granting" accordingly is little more than a primitive device for feeding loyal supporters on "unearned incomes" coerced from servile peasants (serf and slaves) in return for the tsar's share of the booty, and government service. It is akin to the western practice of granting royal charters to businesses like the British East India Company during the age of absolutism, but is cruder and less efficient.

Muscovite autocratic rent-granting is the antithesis of true democracy. It is autocratic; the people don't count. The autocrat rules by edicts (including granting rents). There are no elections, unauthorized autonomous institutions, or activities. The system is "of the autocrat," "by the autocrat" (with spoils sharing), and "for the autocrat" (who lavishly showers supporters with favors). There is no binding constitution or rule of law, only autocratic rule. There are no entitlements. The market is the tsar's handmaiden, not the consumer's.

Culture, custom and all informal modes of social interaction are subordinate to the emperor's will. The autocrat alone owns and has the right to control everything and everyone in the realm without limitation; whereas contemporary monarchs, state appointees, and elected representatives in the West are the people's agents, entitled in principle to nothing more than fair compensation for their labor services. Public services are whatever the tsar wants them to be, and their business aspects are tolerated only insofar as they are compatible with the imperial agenda. By contrast, in well-functioning true democracies, state regulation and programs efficiently satisfy popular demand (consumer sovereignty). Muscovite autocratic legitimacy is self-proclaimed, justified by divine appointment and naked power, instead of being the constitutional expression of the people's will.

11 "Yevtushenkov Is a Warning to Russian Business," *Moscow Times*, October 6, 2014: http://www.themoscowtimes.com/opinion/article/yevtushenkov-is-a-warning-to-russian-business/508500.html—"The early September arrest of Vladimir Yevtushenkov, the majority owner of the industrial conglomerate Sistema and one of Russia's richest men, has inevitably invited comparisons with the arrest of Mikhail Khodorkovsky in 2003 . . . it is logical for Putin to fear dissent among the business elite and the formation of interest groups that could unite to challenge his course in Ukraine. By showing that a loyal figure such as Yevtushenkov is not invulnerable, Russia's business leaders have been put on notice that the slightest sign of protest could lead straight to a prison cell."

12 Steven Rosefielde, "Economics of the Military-Industrial Complex," in Michael Alexeev and Shlomo Weber (eds.), *The Oxford Handbook of Russian Economy*, Oxford: Oxford University Press, 2012.

13 Rosatom State Atomic Energy Corporation (Rosatom) controls nuclear power holding Atomenergoprom, nuclear weapons companies, research institutes and nuclear and radiation safety agencies. It also represents Russia in the world in the field of peaceful use of nuclear energy and protection of the non-proliferation regime.

14 Oligarchs are powerful cronies of the *vozhd* acting as private Muscovite-style big businessmen.

15 Stephen Blank, "Voodoo Economics: Notes on the Political Economy of Russian Defense," paper prepared the 44th ASEEES (Association for Slavic, East European and Eurasian Studies) Conference, New Orleans, November 15, 2012; Stephen Blank, "Lt. Kizhe Rides Again: Magical Realism and Russian National Security Perspectives," paper presented at the Annual Strategy Conference of the US Army War College, April 9–11, 2013; and Steven Rosefielde, "Russian Economic Reform 2012: "Déjà Vu All Over Again," in Stephen Blank, ed., *Politics and Economics in Putin's Russia*, Strategic Studies Institute and US Army War College, Carlisle Barracks, December 2013.

16 Richard Sakwa, *Quality of Freedom: Putin, Khodorkovsky and the Yukos Affair*, Oxford: Oxford University Press, 2009; and Richard Sakwa, *Putin and the Oligarchs: The Khodorkovsky-Yukos Affair*, London: I.B. Tauris, 2014.

17 Steven Rosefielde, "Illusion of Transition: Russia's Muscovite Future," *Eastern Economic Journal*, Vol. 31, No. 2, Spring 2005, pp. 283–96.

18 "Mafia Capitalism or Red Legacy in Russia?" (Commentary): www.cato.org, March 4, 2000.

19 Herbert Simon, "A Behavioral Model of Rational Choice," in Simon, *Models of Man: Social and Rational: Mathematical Essays on Rational Human Behavior in a Social Setting*. New York: Wiley, 1957; Herbert Simon, "A Mechanism for Social Selection and Successful Altruism," *Science*, Vol. 250, No. 4988, 1990, pp. 1665–8; and Herbert Simon, "Bounded Rationality and Organizational Learning," *Organization Science*, Vol. 2, No, 1, 1991, pp. 125–34.

20 For a discussion of "enlightened conservatism" (*prosveshchyonnyi conservatism*) see Tatiana Stanovaya, "In Search of Lost Ideology," *Institute of Modern Russia*, April 25, 2014: http://www.imrussia.org/en/society/725-in-search-of-lost-ideology—"Alexander Shirinyants is known for writing extensively in his doctoral dissertation about the 'possibility of forming a new ideology in Russia without adopting any Western models.' He also emphasized the concept of 'social conservatism, combining the patriotism and loyalty of cultural conservatism with the social idea of the right to a decent life, solidarity, and justice.' The audience will be offered the doctrines of such ideologists of

conservatism as Nikolai Berdyaev, Ivan Ilyin, Lev Tikhomirov, Nikolai Danilevski, Metropolitan Philaret (Drozdov), and Konstantin Pobedonostsev." On "sovereign democracy" (*suveryennaya demokratiya*), see Vladislav Surkov, Transcript of a speech by the Deputy Head of the Administration of the President of Russia, aide to the president of the Russian Federation, Vladislav Surkov for the center of partisan study and preparation of the staff of "United Russian," February 7, 2006. According to Vladislav Surkov, sovereign democracy is a society's political life where the political powers, their authorities and decisions are decided and controlled by a diverse Russian nation for the purpose of reaching material welfare, freedom and fairness by all citizens, social groups and nationalities, by the people that formed it.

21 Surkov's "sovereign democracy" isn't democratic at all because the leader governing society's political life decides what the people want, rather than the people doing it themselves through the ballot box.

4 The Kremlin strikes back

From malevolent to benevolent despotism

Russia's Muscovite rulers have been wrestling with the challenges posed by the Enlightenment and western modernization from the late seventeenth century under the reign of Peter the Great to the present.[1] Tsars, commissars and presidents all sought to craft reforms that would preserve the Kremlin's imperial authoritarian powers and rent-granting, while tolerating productivity-enhancing liberalization that furthered its purposes. Markets developed in the eighteenth century, serf-slavery was abolished in 1861, and aspects of western civil society emerged thereafter. The central tendency, zigzags aside, has been toward "benevolent despotism," that is, the creation of a liberal imperial martial police state with a humanistic face.[2] Scholars and politicians often deny Russian authoritarianism's staying power, periodically predicting the impending triumph of liberty, fraternity and democracy, but the Kremlin constantly disappoints them.[3]

The drift toward benevolent despotism in the Soviet period began immediately after Stalin died. Nikita Khrushchev, First Secretary of the Communist Party (March 1953–October 1964), repudiated Stalin's crimes against humanity in his secret speech to the 20th Party Congress on February 25, 1956.[4] This led to the launching of a campaign soon thereafter known as the "Thaw" (*Khrushchevkaia ottepel'*) which permitted candid critiques of Soviet reality,[5] paving the way for the release of more than 6 million prisoners from the Gulag,[6] and the adoption of a non-confrontational foreign policy known as "peaceful coexistence" (*mirnoe sosushchestvovanie*) that renounced armed conflict as a means of eradicating capitalism.

Liberalizing momentum ebbed after Khrushchev was displaced by Leonid Brezhnev, but then resumed again in sundry economic reforms and political "détente" (relaxation of tensions) with the West,[7] rising to a fresh crescendo with Gorbachev's 1987 programs of *perestroika* (radical economic reform), *glasnost* (candor), *demokratizatsia* (democracy) and *novoe myslenie* (new thinking),[8] and Boris Yeltsin's call for *perekhod* (transition). Shortly before the Soviet Union dissolved itself, citizens had obtained considerable freedom of speech, publishing and religion, as well as freedom to demonstrate, travel and engage in entrepreneurship and enterprise management, and the negotiated exchange of products and prices. Collectives were formally permitted to acquire leaseholds (*arenda*),[9] and some

individuals were informally empowered to privatize state property. Moreover, the KGB was instructed to take an indulgent approach toward dissidence, and weapons production may have peaked in 1989.[10]

Thus on the eve of the USSR's self-liquidation, the Kremlin had transformed itself from a malevolent Stalinist communist tyranny into a benevolent despotism that many observers believed was on a fast track to European-style social democracy. Gorbachev himself described *perestroika* as Russia returning to its "common European home."[11]

Authoritarian abandonment

The high hopes in many quarters that Russia would expeditiously transition from benevolent despotism to social democracy or democratic free enterprise were based on a shallow grasp of the complexities of transition fostered by idealist neoclassical theory, and disregard for various hidden political agendas and the personality quirks of Kremlin leaders. Gorbachev was erratic and superficial. He may have foolishly believed that his catastrophic programs would somehow improve the communist command system, but he failed to take the necessary steps to insure the creation of well-functioning markets. Alternatively, he may have presumed that destroying administrative command planning would in and of itself spur a swift and painless transition to the western model.[12] Whichever explanation is closest to the truth, the rationale was unrealistic. Empty talk of transition to a market economy in 500 days was a dereliction of duty,[13] not a viable strategy for eradicating Muscovite authoritarianism. Some contemporary parliamentary leaders accordingly are demanding that Gorbachev be investigated to determine whether he should be indicted for treason![14]

There is no doubt that Gorbachev was goaded by advisors bent on radically revising, or destroying, Soviet power, but he should have soberly reconsidered their advice in 1990 when it became clear that the economy was hurtling toward catastrophe.[15] Instead, he twiddled his thumbs, letting events take their own disastrous course. Gorbachev in his role as destroyer of the Soviet Union fully deserves credit or blame, depending on one's viewpoint. He terminated the Bolshevik experiment, but failed to achieve any constructive purpose.[16]

The dissolution of the Soviet Union on December 25, 1991 didn't settle the fate of communism, the political order in each new independent state of the former Soviet Union, or the relationships among members of the Commonwealth of Independent States. Each fledgling nation was free to determine its own future. Some, like Latvia, Estonia and Lithuania, forged democratic market regimes and eventually joined the European Union. The rest, including Russia, adopted democratic façades similar to communist people's democracies,[17] where the *vozhd* (president) was the supreme authority assisted by mock elected legislatures, and puppet judiciaries. Their actions would prove to be the arbiter of transformation. They would each determine their preferred economic and political system, and had the power to reconstitute the Soviet Union or forge new alliances with China and the West, subject to Kremlin pressure and intrigue.

Boris Yeltsin, Russia's first president, chose a quixotic path determined more by his personal enmities against the Communist Party, the military and secret police than commitment to democratic free enterprise, or empire. Like Gorbachev, he was a destroyer, drawn to grandiose schemes like shock therapy with no serious concern for outcomes other than the preservation of his personal authority.[18] This callousness was most clearly manifested in his cancellation of state procurement contracts, dismantlement of industrial ministerial administration, scuttling of the tax system, approval of insider privatization schemes, rampant inflation policy, deferred wage payments to state employees and endorsement of "foraging."[19] The people in effect were forced to fend for themselves in a lawless environment without preparation or assistance. There was no talk of Keynesian deficit spending or stimulatory public programming.[20] Yeltsin's notion of government was making billionaires out of his drinking buddies by allowing them to privatize media and natural resource-processing companies,[21] supplemented with lucrative state contracts. Destroying the old economic order and reviving market Muscovite rent-granting were the sum and substance of his prosperity strategy, despite claims of "competitive market building" and democratization.[22]

Yeltsin's animosity toward the military and secret police compounded the problem. He was bent on punishing the communist establishment for opposing his road to power. Gorbachev had rusticated him for insubordination in 1987,[23] and senior military and secret police officers were suspected of having planned to arrest him before Gorbachev's abduction on August 19, 1991.[24] Yeltsin stopped short of outlawing the Communist Party, and openly declaring war on the military and secret police, but curbed them. He rigged elections to prevent the democratic restoration of communist power,[25] cut weapons production by 90 percent,[26] reduced military manpower by 50 percent and kept the FSB (*Federal'naia sluzhba bezopasnosti Rossiiskoi Federatsii*) on a short leash, while simultaneously maintaining cordial relations with sympathetic senior power service officials satisfied with their rent-grants. Everything was up for grabs, including the sale of nuclear power plants to China and Iran.[27]

Yeltsin's approach to democracy was similar. He rose to power championing fair electoral democracy, but called in the military to suppress Parliament when legislators rejected his autocratic constitution.[28] His electoral victory in 1996 was assured by vote rigging and in 2000 he appointed Vladimir Putin as his successor.[29] Although, Yeltsin is still lauded in the West as the father of Russian democracy,[30] his promises remain unfulfilled.

Russia was a sorry spectacle at the outset of the new millennium. The economy had modestly rebounded from its 1996 low in response to the massive devaluation of 1998 caused by the flimflam sale of dollar-denominated foreign debt,[31] but any sustainable recovery to the Soviet-era standard of living seemed hopelessly out of reach, due in part to the obsolescence and depreciation of Russia's capital stock driven in part by massive capital flight.[32] Yeltsin like Nero had chosen to fiddle while the Russian Federation burned, and he seemed content to allow the nation to languish.

But then along came Vladimir Putin, a leader committed to rebuilding Russia's greatness. Putin was a man of a very different stripe than his immediate predecessors. He was a disciplined KGB operative and head of the FSB,[33] rather than an inner Communist Party politician like Gorbachev or Yeltsin. He understood the importance of hierarchical discipline within a Muscovite rent-granting framework (the "power vertical"),[34] and the desirability of restoring Russia's clout in the international arena. Unlike Stalin after 1928, and Hitler after 1933, Putin didn't rush to rearm or restore Russia's empire. Although, it must have seemed to him that Gorbachev and Yeltsin had stabbed Russia in the back,[35] destroying the Soviet empire and forcing the Kremlin to grovel before the West for more than a decade, he patiently reassembled the power vertical. He began by abolishing the election of regional governors and appointing them instead. He revitalized the country's bureaucracy, the military and secret police, and adopted an assertive foreign policy aimed at shoring up Russia's spheres of influence everywhere, including the former Soviet Union, even though the West was cutting its conventional and nuclear capabilities in Europe.[36] While the West pressed its twin policies of reset and partnership, Putin seized the day by restoring the credibility of Russia's armed might in Europe,[37] allowing the "Kremlin to strike back," first by thwarting Obama's regime change campaign against Syria in September 2013,[38] and then by annexing the Crimea in March 2014. Putin, who now openly laments the destruction of the Soviet Union,[39] hasn't been able to fully settle scores for the West's role in goading Gorbachev and Yeltsin to destroy Russia's empire, but by doggedly pursuing this end, he has made a good start.[40]

A verdict on the nature of Russia's post-Soviet transformation during the preceding quarter century doesn't depend on whether Putin fulfills his ambitions. The fundamental lesson taught by the Soviet transformation experience is the enduring stamina of Russian liberal authoritarianism. The contemporary system which is a version of the Soviet scheme that combines command direction of the renationalized military-industrial complex (without guaranteed state purchase) with oligarchic rent-granting and ancillary competitive markets is hardly perfect,[41] but it is good enough from Moscow's perspective to give the West a run for its money, a fact American and EU politicians refuse to continence.[42]

Russian liberal authoritarianism today is superior to Stalin's despotism and the post-Stalin thaw. Soviet reality was bleak. It was aptly called an "economy of shortage."[43] Retail stores were understocked and only offered a Spartan selection of goods. Everything was inconvenient. Apartments were austere and often cockroach infested (especially flats constructed by Khrushchev). Appliances were obsolete. Communal areas were poorly maintained. A small minority owned automobiles. There were few leisure outlets. Foreign vacations outside the Soviet bloc were tightly restricted. These depravations were lightened for the privileged who had access to special stores, musical performance and recreational facilities, and state provision of affordable basic medical services (including on-demand abortions in lieu of contraceptives), mass transportation (good in urban centers, otherwise poor), mass vocational education, and primitive burial facilities. In a nutshell, Soviet citizens had few degrees of freedom. The toiling masses couldn't

imagine brighter material futures, and satisfied by substituting chauvinism, communist idealism, personal relationships, vodka and carousing for material affluence, and civil and political liberties.

The Yeltsin years were worse. Per capita income plummeted, unemployment skyrocketed and the social safety net was shredded. There were some compensations: civil liberties improved and shortages reduced for new rent-grantees; restaurants and entertainment facilities mushroomed for the privileged, and cars (many stolen in Europe) began clogging Moscow's inadequate roadways.[44]

These improvements dramatically accelerated after Putin seized the reins of power, aided by high natural resource prices in the wake of 9/11.[45] Wage arrears were paid and pensions improved. The Internet and cellphones became commonplace.[46] Automobile ownership burgeoned and new highway networks were built in major urban centers. Russia's GDP rebounded rapidly enough that national income may have recovered to the 1989 level by 2007, despite the drag of a falling population, a sharp decline in scientists and engineers, and adverse public health conditions.[47]

People acquired broad effective rights of religion, the press, and civic and political participation as long as they didn't threaten the *vozhd* or were fortunate enough to escape random victimization. Life became indisputably better for a large segment of Russia's cosmopolitans, although the neglected hinterland bore a closer resemblance to ramshackle Soviet realities than Moscow's city lights.

These gains gave Russia the superficial luster of what Andrei Shleifer and Daniel Treisman call a "normal middle income developing country,"[48] rough around the edges, but nonetheless on the express track to progressive democratic free enterprise. Their characterization was well received in the Kremlin and Foggy Bottom precisely because it glossed the distinction between Muscovite liberal authoritarianism and democratic free enterprise, making it seem as if Russia deserved to be a full-fledged member of the G-8 club.[49]

Russia's annexation of the Crimea has prodded western leaders and academics to reassess their positions, but it will be difficult to resist reverting to a policy of "reset" and partnership after a discrete interlude. Western governments cannot easily reconfigure domestic priorities to accommodate Russia's resurgent liberal authoritarianism and Putin is likely to maneuver them into embracing a "new normal." Everything it seems is thinkable in the West except the possibility that the Kremlin adamantly rejects the West's agenda.

This wishful thinking appears to assure that Russia and the West will be at loggerheads for the foreseeable future, while both sides continue to tout their common ideals. The Kremlin today is weaker in many ways than it was in Soviet times. Its arsenal, military manpower, population and territory are smaller, and the regime no longer enjoys its former ideological luster.

Nonetheless, Russia's Muscovite system has passed the test of *katastroika*, and modernized in its own peculiar fashion. The Kremlin's grip on power today may well be more robust than it has been since the early years of Tsar Nicholas II's reign and may continue strengthening well into the future despite significant authoritarian vulnerabilities and lingering popular resentment over the oligarchs' theft

of the "people's assets." Russia has transformed while preserving its Muscovite characteristics. Its economic system is inferior, just as it always has been for the last half millennium from the perspective of ideal democratic free enterprise, but is good enough to sustain the Kremlin's strategic opportunism in international affairs. Putin's Russia is consolidating its hegemony over the Commonwealth of Independent States. The Kremlin appears willing and able to strike back.[50]

Notes

1 Alexander Gerschenkron, *Economic Backwardness in Historical Perspective*, Cambridge, MA: Harvard University Press, 1962.
2 Benevolent despotism, or enlightened despotism was a form of government in the eighteenth century in which absolute monarchs pursued legal, social and educational reforms inspired by the Enlightenment. Among the most prominent enlightened despots were Frederick II (the Great), Peter I (the Great), Catherine II (the Great), Maria Theresa, Joseph II and Leopold II. They typically instituted administrative reform, religious toleration and economic development but did not propose reforms that would undermine their sovereignty or disrupt the social order: http://global.britannica.com/EBchecked/topic/931000/enlightened-despotism.
3 Francis Fukuyama, *The End of History and the Last Man*, New York: Free Press, 1992; and Jack Matlock, *Reagan and Gorbachev: How the Cold War Ended*, New York: Random House, 2004.
4 "On the Cult of Personality and Its Consequences," (*"O kult'te lichnosti I ego posledstviyakh"*), *Congressional Record: Proceedings and Debates* of *the 84th Congress, 2nd Session* (May 22, 1956–June 11, 1956), C11, Part 7 (June 4, 1956), pp. 9389–403: http://www.fordham.edu/halsall/mod/1956khrushchev-secret1.html.
5 Benjamin Nathans, "Uncertainty and Anxiety: On Khrushchev's Thaw: Why Did Different Segments of the Soviet Population Experience Khrushchev's Reforms in Radically Different Ways?" *The Nation*, September 26, 2011: http://www.thenation.com/article/163187/uncertainty-and-anxiety-khrushchevs-thaw.
6 Steven Rosefielde, *Red Holocaust*, London: Routledge, 2010. Those who prefer lower Gulag numbers usually put the number of prisoners released by Khrushchev at 3 million. The Gulag population in 1960 reliably estimated with "national technical means" is 4 million.
7 Presidents Nixon and Ford used the term "détente"; the Russians preferred *razpiadka*.
8 Mikhail Gorbachev, *Perestroika: New Thinking for Our Country and the World*, New York: HarperCollins, 1987.
9 Pekka Sutela, *Economic Thought and Economic Reform in the Soviet Union*, Cambridge: Cambridge University Press, 1991.
10 Steven Rosefielde, *Russia in the 21st Century: Prodigal Superpower*, Cambridge: Cambridge University Press, 2005.
11 Gorbachev first used the phrase to 1984. Brezhnev employed it in 1981. See Robert Legvold, ed., *Russian Foreign Policy in the Twenty-First Century and the Shadow of the Past*, New York: Columbia University Press, 2007, p. 395.
12 Mikhail Gorbachev, *Memoirs*, New York: Doubleday, 1996; Archie Brown, *The Gorbachev Factor*, Oxford: Oxford University Press, 1996; and Jack Matlock, Jr., "Gorbachev: Lingering Mysteries," *New York Review of Books*, December 19, 1996.
13 Stanislav Shatalin, *Transition to the Market: 500 Days*, Moscow: Arkhangelskoe, 1990. Shatalin declared that he didn't really care whether transition took 500 hundred days or 500 years as long as it eventually led to the eradication of communism. Public speech, Duke University, November 1991. Cf. Ed Hewett, "The New Soviet Plan," *Foreign Affairs*, Vol. 69, No. 5, 1990, pp. 146–66.

14 Gabriela Baczynska "Group of Deputies Wants Gorbachev Investigated over Soviet Break-up," *Reuters*, April 10, 2014: http://news.yahoo.com/group-deputies-wants-gorbachev-investigated-over-soviet-break-124523136.html. This isn't the first time indictment has been considered. The issue was also raised in 2012. "Critics Demand High Treason Trial for Gorbachev," *RT*, January 19, 2012: http://rt.com/politics/gorbachev-high-treason-trial-175/—"A small group of lawmakers have asked Russia's top prosecutor to investigate whether the last Soviet leader, Mikhail Gorbachev, should face treason charges over his role in the 1991 collapse of the Soviet Union. The seven-page request for an investigation says Gorbachev and other senior Soviet officials violated the law and the will of the people by letting the republics that made up the Soviet Union declare independence and break away. 'As a result of these criminal actions, the Union of Soviet Socialist Republics, a global superpower, was destroyed and ceased existing as a geopolitical reality,' says the letter."

15 Steven Rosefielde, *Russian Economy from Lenin to Putin*, New York: Wiley, 2007.

16 The dissolution of the Soviet Union was not tantamount to eradicating communism, but Gorbachev claimed in 2000 that this was his intention. See "My Ambition Was To Liquidate Communism": http://www.revolutionarydemocracy.org/rdv6n1/gorbach.htm.

17 One party "proletarian" states with controlled elections.

18 Celestine Bohlen, "Yeltsin Deputy Calls Reforms 'Economic Genocide'," *The New York Times*, February 9, 1992. The chief domestic architect of Yeltsin's shock therapy was Yegor Gaidar who served sequentially as Minister of Economics, Minister of Finance and Prime Minister under the Yeltsin government.

19 Traffic police in Moscow for example stopped cars at random and demanded that drivers pay their "salary." Military forces in the Caucasus operated on the same principle.

20 American advisers deliberately avoided recommending Keynesian "pump priming" because they wanted the Kremlin out of the economic management business. Even though many prominent economists today advocate generous deficit spending to reinvigorate the US's economy, they adopted a double standard toward Russia by urging austerity. See Paul Krugman, *The Return of Depression Economics and the Crisis of 2008*, New York: W.W. Norton Company, 2009; and Lawrence Summers, "Washington Must Not Settle for Secular Stagnation," *Financial Times*, December 5, 2013: http://www.ft.com/cms/s/2/ba0f1386-7169-11e3-8f92-00144feabdc0.html#ixzz2pi6xfiEe.

21 The most influential oligarchs from the Yeltsin era were Boris Berezovsky, Alexander Smolensky, Mikhail Khodorkovsky, Alex Konanykhin, Mikhail Fridman, Anatoly Chubais, Vladimir Gusinsky, Vitaly Malkin and Vladimir Potanin. Putin purged all of them except Potanin, Malkin and Fridman.

22 The World Bank, IMF and G-7 provided and promoted Yeltsin's cover agenda of constructing democratic free enterprise. Some may have been motivated by devotion to the "Washington Consensus," but breaking the back of communism was the hidden goal: John Williamson, "Development and the 'Washington Consensus'," in *World Development*, Vol. 21, 1993, pp. 1239–336.

23 Yeltsin, first party secretary of Moscow, seized the spotlight at the Communist Party's festivities celebrating the seventieth anniversary of the Bolshevik Revolution in November 1987 by announcing his desire to reign from the Politburo, a defiant gesture that called attention to him as a prospective independent political force. Gorbachev retaliated by publicly humiliating his former protégé and then sending him into internal exile where he was barred from meeting with foreigners. See Steven Rosefielde and Stefan Hedlund, *Russia Since 1980*, Cambridge: Cambridge University Press, 2009.

24 Yuri Stroganov, "Oleg Shenin: It's a Pity Yeltsin Wasn't Arrested," *Johnson's Russia List*, Vol. 8333, Article 9, August 19, 2004. Oleg Shenin was one of the masterminds of the GKChP's (State Emergency Committee) plot against Gorbachev. He now claims that "one of the Committee's key errors was that it did not dissociate itself from Gorbachev. The goals declared by Gorbachev at the dawn of perestroika sounded correct . . . But words were at variance with his deeds and it became clear that if the

situation persisted, the Soviet Union would collapse." Also Shenin contends that the coup failed because the GKChP didn't use its military forces. And he goes on to assert that Yeltsin should have been arrested: "We should have detained him in Kazakhstan, where he had been the day before. We should have isolated Popov, Luzhkov, Gdlyan, Ivanov and others. I don't understand why it was not done. This was stupid."

25 Steven Rosefielde and Stefan Hedlund, *Russia Since 1980*, Cambridge: Cambridge University Press, 2009.
26 Steven Rosefielde, *Russia in the 21st Century: Prodigal Superpower*, Cambridge: Cambridge University Press, 2005.
27 Brando Fite, *U.S. and Iranian Strategic Competition: The Impact of China and Russia*, Washington, DC: CSIS, March 2012.
28 Ongoing confrontations with the Supreme Soviet climaxed in the October 1993 Russian constitutional crisis. Yeltsin illegally ordered the dissolution of the Parliament, which then attempted to remove him from office. The military eventually sided with Yeltsin and besieged and shelled the Russian White House, resulting in the deaths of 187 people. Yeltsin then scrapped the existing constitution, temporarily banned political opposition and deepened his economic experimentation. He introduced a new constitution with stronger presidential power and it was approved by referendum on December 12, 1993 with 58.5 percent of voters in favor.
29 Steven Rosefielde and Stefan Hedlund, *Russia Since 1980*, Cambridge: Cambridge University Press, 2009.
30 Leon Aron, *Yeltsin: A Revolutionary Life*, New York: St. Martin's Press, 2000.
31 Steven Rosefielde, "Review of Andrey Vavilov, *The Russian Public Debt and Financial Meltdowns*, New York: Palgrave Macmillan, 2010," *Slavic Review*, 2011.
32 Oligarchs went on a capital asset buying spree abroad because of the ever-present threat that the rents granted to them would be rescinded, and their assets confiscated.
33 Putin served for 16 years as a KGB officer rising to the rank of lieutenant colonel. He was stationed in East Germany where he ran industrial intelligence operations in West Germany. He was appointed director of the FSB in July 1998.
34 The power vertical is a term introduced by Putin to describe his recentralization of Russian state power. Andrew Monaghan, "The Vertikal: Power and Authority in Russia," *International Affairs*, Vol. 88, No. 1, January 2012.
35 Putin believes that the West deliberately egged on Gorbachev and Yeltsin, and that the US and the EU are still trying to destroy the Kremlin with "color revolutions" and other related initiatives. He also blames the West for exploiting Russia's weakness to destroy the former Yugoslavia in 1999. See Colonel General Leonid Ivashov, "NATO Versus Yugoslavia: 15 Years On," *Valdai*, March 24, 2014: http://valdaiclub.com/europe/67608.html.
36 Steven Rosefielde, *Russia in the 21st Century: Prodigal Superpower*, Cambridge: Cambridge University Press, 2005.
37 Steven Rosefielde and Quinn Mills, *Democracy and Its Elected Enemies*, Cambridge: Cambridge University Press, 2013.
38 Steven Rosefielde, "Cold Peace: 'Reset' and Coexistence," *The Northeast Asian Review*, Vol. 1, No. 3, March 2014, pp. 39–50.
39 Leon Aron, "Beware the Rise of Putin the Terrible," *AEI*, March 27, 2014: http://www.aei.org/article/foreign-and-defense-policy/regional/middle-east-and-north-africa/beware-the-rise-of-putin-the-terrible/?utm_source=today&utm_medium=paramount&utm_campaign=032814—"Putin heralded the birth of this new politics in an extraordinarily frank and disturbing nationally televised speech on March 18 to the Russian political elite. In it, he lamented the breakup of the Soviet Union, saying that 'after the dissolution of bipolarity on the planet, we no longer have stability.' Since then, he said, the West, and the United States in particular, have preferred not to be 'guided by international law in their practical policies but by the rule of the gun' and have been seeking to 'drive Russia into the corner.'"

40 Angus Roxburgh, "Russia's Revenge: Why the West Will Never Understand the Kremlin," *New Statesman*, March 27, 2014: www.newstatesman.com—"The events in Ukraine are Putin's payback for what he considers to be a quarter-century of humiliation since the collapse of the Soviet Union."

41 The new command mechanism can be easily visualized in Figure 1.1 by defining Ministry A as the military-industrial complex and state natural resource-processing directorate, with Ministry B and Gosplan deleted. Gosplan in this scheme is replaced by the MOD's and VPK's internal planning arrangements.

42 Scott Wilson, "Obama Dismisses Russia as 'Regional Power' Acting out of Weakness," *Washington Post*, March 25, 2014: http://www.washingtonpost.com/world/national-security/obama-dismisses-russia-as-regional-power-acting-out-of-weakness/2014/03/25/1e5a678e-b439-11e3-b899-20667de76985_story.html, and Philip Bump, "Obama: No, Romney Was Wrong. Russia Is Weak, Not Strong," *Yahoo!News*, March 25, 2014: http://news.yahoo.com/obama-no-romney-wrong-russia-weak-not-strong-155823223.html.

43 Igor Birman, *Ekonomika Nedostach* (The Economy of Shortages). Benson Vermont: Chalidze Publishing, 1983.

44 Western rental car agencies for years refused to permit cars leased in Europe to be driven to Eastern Europe and Russia.

45 The price of oil was around US$12.50 per barrel in the early 2000s. After 9/11, 2011 petroleum prices rose tenfold before settling above US$100 per barrel. The price change was a bonanza for Russia's treasury, and sharply increased the ruble's purchasing power.

46 The cellphone was a godsend for Russia. Telephone wires and cables were in wretched conditions during the 1980s and many forecast that the USSR wouldn't be able to participate effectively in the computer revolution because its electronic transmission system was hopeless defective. The emergence of satellite-based communications obviated the peril.

47 Steven Rosefielde and Stefan Hedlund, *Russia Since 1980*, Cambridge: Cambridge University Press, 2009.

48 Andrei Shleifer and Daniel Treisman, "A Normal Country," *Foreign Affairs*, Vol. 83, No. 2 (2004), pp. 20–39; Andrei Shleifer, *A Normal Country: Russia after Communism*, Cambridge, MA: Harvard University Press, 2005; and Steven Rosefielde, "An Abnormal Country," *The European Journal of Comparative Economics*, Vol. 2, No. 1 (2005), pp. 3–16.

49 Julia Ioffe, "Booting Russia from the G8 Ends 16 Years of Pretending Moscow Should Sit at the Big-Kids Table," *New Republic*, March 24, 2014: http:newrepublic.com/article/117140/g7-boots-russia-g8-relief.

50 Putin has been assiduously cultivating Russian patriotism and recently re-instituted a Joseph Stalin-era fitness program called "Ready for Labor and Defense." See Mike Krumboltz, "Putin Wants Russians to Get in Shape. Can Steven Seagal help?" *Yahoo News*, March 27, 2014.

5   Economic prospects

Russian economic reform, together with Moscow's prospects for catching up with and overtaking the West, is a perennial theme, "a tale of two cities,"[1] where some see future glory if the Kremlin embraces democratic free enterprise, and others anticipate a "treadmill of Muscovite reform."[2] No one therefore should be astonished that discussions of Russian economic reform are "déjà vu all over again."[3] This doesn't mean that the two views are equally meritorious. There is only one correct view and it is the "treadmill of Muscovite reform," with limited learning possibilities because Putin is adamantly opposed to democracy and competitive free enterprise. The importance of the double vision lies elsewhere in the Kremlin's conviction that balloting and rent-granting are sufficient to garner most of the efficiency benefits of democratic free enterprise,[4] and the West's willingness to laud or descry Russia's economic system as political expedience dictates. Institutions like the World Bank Group are always ready to portray Russia as a large developing nation with superior growth prospects when the Kremlin is viewed as a prospective partner,[5] or to condemn it as permanently backward when Moscow challenges the West's authority.

Convergence and divergence

Official Soviet and Russian characterizations of economic performance and potential usually were optimistic, and used by some western observers to paint rosy assessments of past accomplishments and future prospects. During the 1980s, official Soviet data (Goskomstat) indicated that the USSR's GDP was growing more rapidly than the US's, even though Mikhail Gorbachev himself acknowledged that the Soviet economy had been stagnant since 1978![6] During the early 2000s, Russia set its sights on catching up with Portugal in twenty years, assuming a 4 percent annual rate of GDP growth.[7]

These assessments were echoed in 2000–08 by the World Bank Group (including the International Bank for Reconstruction and Development, International Finance Corporation and the Multilateral Investment Guarantee Agency), which classified Russia as a normal developing middle-income country.[8] Thereafter, the World Bank Group (WBG) judged that Russia had weathered the global financial crisis of 2008 admirably,[9] and foresaw Russia once again catching up to Portugal at a rapid clip,[10] a claim said to be confirmed by the Kremlin's success at reducing poverty and fostering a burgeoning middle class,[11] until Russia annexed the Crimea. The protracted effects of the 2008 global financial crisis compelled the WBG to revise its GDP growth forecast for Russia downward in 2013 from 8 to 3.6 percent per annum[12] (the actual 2012–13 figure was 2.4 percent per annum), before adopting an even more sober view in the wake of Russia's Crimean annexation that includes a potential decline of 1.8 percent in 2014.[13]

Russia's economy now is said to be at risk of massive capital flight as a consequence of economic sanctions imposed by the West after March 2014, and therefore vulnerable to secular stagnation.[14]

The likelihood of a prolonged malaise is said to be increased by anticipated budgetary constraints (non-oil fiscal deficit connected with expected declines in petro revenues) and long-standing structural issues, including the need to significantly improve the investment climate,[15] and close large infrastructure gaps, diversify exports and taxes. Russia's economic base must be broadened, its governance improved and institutions strengthened.[16] The WBG contends that Russia's investment climate is poor, its infrastructure is laggard, its exports are excessively concentrated in natural resources,[17] its tax and economic bases are too narrow, and its governance and institutions are weak.[18]

Until March 2014 these deficiencies weren't considered fatal because the WBG claimed that Russia's leaders recognized the shortcomings and were vigorously responding by devising four broad economic reform initiatives to achieve "Growth and Diversification, Skills and Social Services, Russia's Global and Regional Role, Governance and Transparency." Now the WBG is confident that Russia's leadership cannot meet the challenge.

Systems, structure and capital flight

The WBG's forecasts until March 2014 assumed that Russia's "normal middle income" market system was, or soon could be made sound ("reasonably" neoclassically efficient). The Kremlin's prospects accordingly were said to depend mostly on prudent macroeconomic policy, structural issues and capital inflows (outflows), and if Russia rescinds its annexation of the Crimea, it should once again be able to overtake Portugal (and other lower-tier EU countries).

The path to prosperity as the WBG sees it, therefore is clear. The Kremlin needs to abandon its misguided ways and undertake four broad economic reform initiatives: "Growth and Diversification, Skills and Social Services, Russia's Global and Regional Role, Governance and Transparency."

Growth and diversification

Russia's economy, the WBG asserts, is dominated by natural resource extraction undertaken by a few large corporations, a concentration reflected in its output, export structures and fiscal dependence.[19] Accepting the WBG's technical advice, the Kremlin has launched economic reforms to encourage "non-strategic" small- and medium-sized enterprises,[20] to increase the size and modernize Russia's high-tech (for example, Skolkovo's "innovation city")[21] and financial sectors,[22] disregarding the political conditionality. This diversification not only will improve the structural balance, but also is intended to spur growth through the curtailment of state-owned enterprises and the rapid modernization of underdeveloped activities,[23] including innovation ("innovative Russia-2020").[24] These goals will be facilitated further by regional diversification ("Strategic Projects"),[25] improved public management,[26] enhanced business competition (achieved through better government regulation),[27] better financial management,[28] and infrastructural investment.[29]

Skills and social services

Skills and social services is the second major category on the Putin regime's economic reform agenda.[30] The World Bank contends that Russia has made immense strides in the areas of universal primary education, equality for women, eradication of extreme poverty and malnutrition, lowering child and maternal mortality, and reaching very high levels of higher education enrollment. Putin's reforms will build on these accomplishments. Russia will strengthen its social safety net,[31] improve demographics and public health,[32] adjust education to provide a better mix of labor skills,[33] ameliorate inequality and social exclusion,[34] and soften interregional disparities.[35]

Russia's global and regional role

Russia's global and regional role is the third major component of Moscow's economic reform agenda.[36] This includes initiatives facilitating economic integration in the Commonwealth of Independent States (CIS),[37] and ecological and environmental defense, especially in the Arctic. Globally, Russia claims to be intensifying its international partnerships,[38] even amidst its current confrontation with the West.

Governance and transparency

Finally, Russia's governance and transparency is the fourth major element of Moscow's economic reform agenda,[39] especially in the area of self-government,[40] fighting corruption,[41] and judicial efficiency.[42]

This survey revealed that Russian economic reform from the World Bank's perspective until March 2014 was mostly about routine public policy and state regulation appropriate for any MIC (middle-income country) or BRIC (Brazil, Russia, India, China), not market economic transformation. There was no core transition strategy, just a programmatic vision and promise that Russia's government will do everything better. The World Bank's report, which paralleled the OECD's counterpart 2006 study provided a valuable inventory of these initiatives,[43] and made the case for the proposition that Russia should be on the fast track to becoming a normal country like the United States, if the Kremlin reversed its prodigal ways. If this condition had been met, the WBG pre-March 2014 forecast should have applied, with Russia's GDP growing at 3.5 percent per annum 2012–15,[44] far higher than the negative growth which actually transpired. Others holding similar views press this or that aspect of Russia's reform agenda reflecting diverse parochial interests, but nonetheless adopt the position that the Putin administration can move forward with a progressive state regulatory and pro-competitive market agenda if the Kremlin recommits itself anew to westernization.

Reality check

The WBG's inventory of Russian governmental economic reform programs and policies although accurate as far as it goes, provides a misleading impression of the character and intent of the Kremlin's post-communist regime. Russia's government is anti-democratic, contrary to the WBG's contention,[45] and its economy is organized for the benefit of privileged insiders, not the Russian people. The Federation is no longer communist, but this should not be construed as a radical break from Russia's tradition. Its autocratic Muscovite rent-granting system has been continuously in force since the reign of Ivan III (The Great), Grand Prince of Moscow and Grand Prince of all Rus in the fifteenth century.

Vladimir Putin's government today, like Boris Yeltsin's earlier one, is a market Muscovite autocracy organized for the benefit of privileged insiders, not the Russian people. The "people's assets" from the Soviet period were granted by Boris Yeltsin to his favorites through various subterfuges,[46] creating the social foundations for the new post-Soviet Muscovy. The regime's predominant features are one-man rule and rent-granting, not democracy and market competition. This makes the regime intrinsically inefficient compared with the popular and consumer sovereign (neoclassical democratic competitive) model ascribed to Russia by the World Bank, and radically alters the potential for real economic reform. The policies and reforms if undertaken by the Kremlin as enumerated by the World Bank are merely efforts to enhance the efficiency of the Muscovite paradigm, not to move beyond it to democratic free enterprise. As a consequence, these endeavors can streamline and modernize a retrograde economic governance mechanism (including the public sector), but cannot westernize it. They cannot make public programs responsive to the electorate, or prevent the supply of goods in the private sector being primarily responsive to the demands of Putin and his "servitors" (oligarchs).

This judgment is confirmed by Russia's wretched economic performance from 1989–2012. Although the way the World Bank casts the statistics Russia's GDP doubled in 2005–08 (18.9 percent per annum),[47] in reality using OECD data the Federation's per capita GDP was virtually flat for more than two decades (there was a hyper-depression during the interval).[48] This assessment is easily confirmed by comparing the CIA's estimate of Russian per capita income in 1989 of $23,546 (adjusted to a 2011 dollar price base) which should be more or less the same today because there was little or no real growth in 1989–2011, with the World Bank's contemporary figure of $10,500.[49] Obviously, the World Bank's picture of post-communist Russian economic progress 2000–08 is amiss. If the CIA was right in 1989, Russian living standards have declined substantially since 1989 using the World Bank's contemporary estimate. Most of the discrepancy between the $23,546 and $10,500 figures is attributable to the CIA's exaggerated 1991 purchasing power parity estimates, but the point remains. Russia has not converged toward the developed West's living standard under Yeltsin and Putin from the 1989 benchmark; it has diverged, falling further behind, and the disparity may worsen unless the West succumbs to secular stagnation as Larry Summers and Paul Krugman contend.[50]

Muscovy and the Washington Consensus

Muscovite rent-granting is a governance strategy used by Kremlin autocrats to create a cadre of loyal supporters by privileging the few to exploit the many. Muscovite rulers are primarily concerned with defending their realm and acquiring sufficient revenues to support the courts and the power services (secret police and armed forces). They don't care if their servitors (contemporary oligarchs and other insiders), those subordinated to them and peripheral players are inefficient as long as revenues are adequate, even though everyone is urged to do better. They don't care if servitors are overpaid, and everyone else is under-remunerated (Russia has a Gini coefficient of 42).[51] Servitors for their part are more concerned with obtaining additional rents from the autocrat than competitively maximizing profits. Like their liege, they prefer to enrich themselves through insider channels than competitively cost minimize and revenue maximize (profit maximization) in accordance with the neoclassical paradigm. Rulers and servitors often appreciate that democracy and free enterprise are better for the many, but place their own well-being above the people's desires. This makes Muscovy intrinsically anti-democratic and anti-competitive, disclaimers to the contrary notwithstanding. History has demonstrated that autocratic rent-granting can be combined with state ownership, markets, central planning and economic regulation without ceding sovereignty to the people or consumers, and this is the way that Putin has chosen to play the game. The approach is the antithesis of the Washington Consensus.[52] The programs, regulations and reforms of the Russia government are primarily for the autocrat not the *demos*, and improved competitiveness insofar as it is permitted serves the same purpose.

The treadmill of Muscovite reform

The policies and reforms undertaken by the Kremlin in partnership with the World Bank Group could have positive results. Technology transfer and modernization in the public and private sectors, together with an expanded role for competitive markets, could improve productivity. The tsarist, Soviet and post-Soviet experience however reveal that benefits aren't automatic. The liberalization of Nicholas II's economy, including high-tech foreign direct investment, had mixed results, mostly negative as the Bolshevik Revolution attests. The Soviet Union tried most of the World Bank Group's economic reform recommendations including technology transfer and leasehold marketization. The result was stagnation and collapse. Boris Yeltsin adopted the G-7 transition strategy and immediately precipitated a decade long hyper-depression. The WBG now expects secular stagnation or worse, a lackluster performance given the country's relative economic backwardness.

What precisely is there about Muscovite rent-granting that makes it productively inferior, unjust and impervious to energizing reform? The answer is simple. The Muscovite paradigm encourages rent-grantees to concentrate their attention on acquiring unearned incomes rather than creating value-add, and protects the privileged from competitive forces that might mitigate the harm. Rent-granting is intrinsically underproductive, immoral and corrupt from an Enlightenment neoclassical perspective because it allows the privileged to receive income and wealth without earning them. The fortunes of Russia's oligarchs are tied to currying favor with the Kremlin more than efficiently managing companies and adding value. Insiders receive state contracts without any obligation to perform creating the semblance, but not the substance of value-added (rent-fabrication).[53] The Muscovite system in this way at times offers an illusion of progress that masks its inefficiency and under-productivity. Corruption (privilege granting) in the Kremlin's scheme of things isn't merely moral failure; it is the system's lifeblood.

None of this precludes Russia's privileged from trying to enrich themselves doubly by acquiring rents and maximizing profits; however the regime's culture of corruption inhibits constructive impulses. The rent-seeking mentality keeps servitors' attention riveted on state handouts, with profit maximizing little more than an afterthought.

Adam Smith famously claimed that the potential losses caused by corruption, including conspiracies in restraint of trade were less severe than might be anticipated due to the positive effects of moral self-restraint,[54] and free competition (the "invisible hand").[55] It is easily supposed that the defects of rent-granting are self-correcting too, however, this doesn't follow because the Muscovite ethic is predatory and the Kremlin is committed to creating privilege by suppressing competition. Putin has no objection to ordinary people competing among themselves and supplying services to the privileged at least cost, but any business that is lucrative is "taken over" by the privileged and absorbed into the protected sphere. The same tactics are used in the Kremlin's dealings with foreign companies at home and abroad. Russia's Muscovite economy consequently is woefully inefficient. Labor is miseducated, misallocated and under-incentivized. Privileged companies don't profit maximize. They under-invest and misinvest, a problem exacerbated by the financial sector's misallocation of loanable funds. Foreign direct investors like petroleum giant BP operate in treacherous waters and are routinely bilked.[56] Government regulation and programs are rent-granting activities, not handmaidens to market competition. The people's will is irrelevant and consumers merely have limited market choice, not consumer sovereignty (that is, their demand doesn't govern competitive supply).

The problem of course can be solved by the Kremlin voluntarily repudiating Muscovy, or being forced to do so by a popular awakening as many today seem to anticipate, but not otherwise. Better plans and regulations of the sort recommended by World Bank Group cannot compensate for the inefficiencies imposed by rent-granting, and of course as the Soviet experience proved they are inferior substitutes for competitive markets.[57] Expanding the scope and competitiveness of ancillary markets should be beneficial, but this is precisely what Muscovy opposes to the extent that it leashes privilege. This is why Gertrude Schroeder's dictum continues to hold undiminished. Russia after its post-Soviet transformation is on a treadmill of futile reform (not transition).[58] Both the Kremlin's and the World Bank Group's nostrums are "déjà vu all over again."[59]

Structural militarization

Stephen Blank has recently embellished on this theme by insisting that while Muscovite rent-granting assures a flow of income into the ruler's coffers, the autocrat's primary motive isn't pecuniary. It is the preservation of power.[60]

He contends that Russian governance from the time of Ivan the Great always has been about securing power through internal and external colonization,[61] and links this to the revitalization of what Vitaly Shylkov has dubbed "structural militarization,"[62] despite former Defense Minister Anatoly Serdyukov's attempt to break the thrall of the *genshtab* (Russia's General Staff).[63]

Russia's economy consequently cannot be normal in the WBG's sense because the Muscovite model doesn't work for the people, sacrificing economic efficiency for the higher good of autocracy and placing military priorities at the center of the regime's agenda insofar as they bolster its rule. Where the WBG envisions Moscow embracing the Obama administration's globalizing mission by liberalizing, democratizing and integrating Russia's economy into the emerging free enterprise order (including its 2012 accession to the World Trade Organization), Blank counter-argues that the Muscovite model requires the regime to be illiberal, autocratic, adversarial and martial.[64]

Blank then goes on to document these claims with evidence from Russia's State Armaments Program plans and other corroborative sources,[65] which in their totality demonstrate that the incompleteness of the WBG's neoclassical economic conceptual framework distorts Russian reality just as it did during the Soviet era. Russia's future someday may be fully governed by the principles of democratic free enterprise, contemporary trans-systemic microeconomic and macroeconomic theory, but these tools will only be of ancillary value as long as Muscovy prevails with or without markets.

Notes

1 Charles Dickens, *A Tale of Two Cities*, Book I, Chapter 1, 1859: "It was the best of times, it was the worst of times, it was the age of wisdom, it was the age of foolishness, it was the epoch of belief, it was the epoch of incredulity, it was the season of Light, it was the season of Darkness, it was the spring of hope, it was the winter of despair, we

had everything before us, we had nothing before us, we were all going direct to Heaven, we were all going direct the other way—in short, the period was so far like the present period, that some of its noisiest authorities insisted on its being received, for good or for evil, in the superlative degree of comparison only."

2 Gertrude Schroeder, "The Soviet Economy on a Treadmill of 'Reforms'," in *Soviet Economy in a Time of Change*, Joint Economic Committee of Congress, Washington, DC, October 10, 1979, pp. 312–66.
3 "It's déjà vu all over again": American baseball player and coach Yogi Berra explained that this quote originated when he witnessed Mickey Mantle and Roger Maris repeatedly hit back-to-back home runs in the Yankees' seasons in the early 1960s.
4 Western assessments of Russia's prospects depend on the political climate. From the late 1980 until 2008s, when the G-7 was peddling shock therapy and the "Washington Consensus," forecasts for Russian economic growth and development were consistently rosy, especially after signs of a turnaround appeared in 1999. However, after the financial crisis of 2008 when the Russian GDP plunged and Russo–American relations soured, the outlook reversed, driven by hope that tepid economic prospects would keep the Kremlin's imperial ambitions in check: "The current World Bank outlook confirms the political linkage: Russia's economy is navigating an economic downturn with real GDP growth slowing to an estimated 1.3 percent in 2013 from 3.4 percent of 2012. The lack of more comprehensive structural reforms has led to the erosion in businesses' and consumers' confidence, which became the decisive factor for the downward revision of the World Bank's November growth projections for Russia, says the World Bank's Russian Economic Report No. 31 launched today in Moscow. In the past, the lack of comprehensive structural reforms was masked by a growth model based on large investment projects, continued increases in public wages, and transfers—all fueled by sizeable oil revenues. Recent events around the Crimea crisis have compounded the lingering confidence problem into a confidence crisis and more clearly exposed the economic weakness of this growth model": "Russian Economic Report 31: Confidence Crisis Exposes Economic Weakness," *World Bank*, March 26, 2014: http://www.worldbank.org/en/news/press-release/2014/03/26/russian-economic-report-31.
5 The acronym was coined by Jim O'Neill in a 2001 paper entitled "Building Better Global Economic BRICs": http://www.content.gs.com/japan/ideas/brics/building-better-pdf.pdf; Goldman-Sachs, "Dreaming With BRICS: The Path to 2050," New York, October 2003 <http://www2.goldmansachs.com/insight/research/reports/report6.html>. BRICs originally covered Brazil, Russia, India and China, but more recently has been revised to BRICS by the addition of South Africa.
6 Abel Aganbegyan, *Inside Perestroika: The Future of the Soviet Economy*, New York: Harper and Row, 1989.
7 Fyodor Lukyanov, "Putin's Russia: The Quest for a New Place," *Social Research: An International Quarterly*, Vol. 765, No. 1, Spring 2009, pp. 117–50: http://muse.jhu.edu/journals/social_research/summary/v076/76.1.lukyanov.html.
8 World Bank, *Country Partnership Strategy (CPS) for the Russian Federation*, Report No. 65115-RU, November 2011: "Russia is a middle income country (MIC) that strives to move to a high income status. In the period since 2005, the per capita GDP of Russia doubled to approximately US$10,500 in 2010, and the country moved to an upper MIC status. The current country context was formed in the course of a decade of turbulent adjustment following the transition from a centrally planned to a market economy and another decade of rapid economic growth driven largely by natural resources, interrupted by the 2008–2009 global financial and economic crisis. As a result of a strong fiscal and monetary counter-cyclical package, the country emerged from the global recession with lower-than expected unemployment and poverty and has returned to moderate growth rates. To escape the 'middle income trap,' Russia's government pursues economic policy and institutional development that aim to modernize, diversify, and increase the competitiveness of the economy and improve the

well-being of its citizens." Another version of the same document is entitled: Russian Federation—Country Partnership Strategy for the Period 2012–2016 (English).

9 World Bank, *Country Partnership Strategy (CPS) for the Russian Federation*, Report No. 65115-RU, November 2011: "Russia has weathered the global crisis well despite the massive oil and capital account shocks. This was mainly because of the large pre-crisis fiscal reserves and fiscal surpluses that allowed the Government to mount a large countercyclical stimulus package in support of the financial system, enterprises, and households. Despite a large drop in real GDP in 2009 (−7.8 percent), an acute liquidity crisis, and a sharp increase in unemployment, the crisis was managed without systemic bank failures, and economic and labor market conditions began to improve during 2009 in line with the rise in oil prices and the recovery in domestic demand and credit. Large increases in public sector wages and pensions cushioned the impact on the middle class and the poor, making the social impact less severe than it would otherwise have been. With the cyclical demand recovery in the global and Russian economies as well as energy commodities, Russia's real GDP grew 4 percent, and unemployment fell 2 percentage points from its peak during the crisis to 7.2 percent at the end of 2010."

10 World Bank, *Country Partnership Strategy (CPS) for the Russian Federation*, Report No. 65115-RU, November 2011: "Following a cyclical recovery of oil prices, economic activity and employment during 2010, Russia's current macroeconomic situation remains favorable. After a 4 percent growth in 2010, the Russian economy continues to expand in an environment of declining unemployment (6.5 percent in July 2011) and inflation, rising domestic consumption, and still high oil prices. All sectors of the economy are growing and domestic consumption—while less buoyant than anticipated—increasingly acts as an engine of demand growth (Figure 1). With a good harvest and favorable food price outlook, annual inflation is expected to end at around 7.5 percent in 2011, somewhat higher than the Government's target of 6–7 percent, but lower than at any time in recent years. The federal budget is likely to be in near-balance in 2011. A large current account surplus of almost US$70 billion significantly exceeds the deficit in the capital account, which will allow the Central Bank to accumulate additional reserves."

11 World Bank, *Country Partnership Strategy (CPS) for the Russian Federation*, Report No. 65115-RU, November 2011: "The special focus section of the new Russian Economic Report looks at poverty reduction and middle-class formation in the country. The Bank's research indicates that poverty reduction and middle-class growth in Russia were explained by high growth in average incomes and consumption during the period of 2000–2010. The poverty rate fell down from 35 percent in 2001 to 10 percent in 2010. At the same time, the size of the middle class grew from 30 percent to 60 percent of the total population. However, weaker growth prospects and stabilizing consumption at a lower rate dim the economic mobility outlook. Economic factors, such as the wage growth and access to good, productive jobs, rather than the demographic factors drove the middle-class growth in Russia. However, in the current environment of a much slower economic growth and constrained fiscal resources, job creation will be an important condition for the future economic mobility, as well as for strengthening the role of labor income as the main driver of the middle-income growth."

12 World Bank, *Russia Economic Report, Confidence Crisis Exposes Economic Weaknesses*, Report 31, March 2014: http://www.worldbank.org/en/news/press-release/2014/03/26/russian-economic-report-31—"Yet the risks to the global economy are growing and so are risks to Russia's growth. Reflecting the slowdown in major developed economies, and rising risks associated with the European debt crisis during the summer of 2011, the WBG's outlook for Russia's real GDP growth was revised to 4 percent in 2011 (down from 4.4 percent earlier in the year), and to 3.8 percent in 2012. This is predicated on the lower oil price outlook for Russia (Figure 2) and the global economy growing at

more moderate rates, especially high income countries." The full report is available at http://www.worldbank.org/content/dam/Worldbank/document/eca/RER-31-eng.pdf.

13 World Bank, *Russia Economic Report, Confidence Crisis Exposes Economic Weaknesses*, Report 31, March 2014.

14 Andrey Ostroukh, "Russia's Capital Outflows at Whopping $63 Billion in 2013," January 17, 2014: http://blogs.wsj.com/emergingeurope/2014/01/17/russias-capital-outflows-at-whopping-63-billion-in-2013/—"Analysts say it was because state oil firm OAO Rosneft's acquisition of TNK-BP for some $60 billion boosted the number, although it's not clear what part of the complex deal was counted as outflows," and Lidia Kelly, "UPDATE 1-World Bank Sees Russian Capital Flight, Hit To GDP if Crimea Crisis Deepens," *Reuters*, March 26, 2014: http://www.reuters.com/article/2014/03/26/russia-economy-worldbank-idUSL5N0MN25X20140326—"The Russian economy may contract markedly this year and the country could see record capital outflow of $150 billion if the crisis over Moscow's annexation of Ukraine's Crimea deepens, the World Bank warned on Wednesday."

15 OECD, "Economic Policy Reforms 2012: Going for Growth," 2012: "The narrowing in March 2011 of the list of activities of strategic importance performed by non-state-owned banks removed the need for prior government approval for foreign acquisitions in this sector. Tariffs for selected agricultural products were reduced in response to the food price shock resulting from the drought in the summer 2011."

16 World Bank, *Country Partnership Strategy (CPS) for the Russian Federation*, Report No. 65115-RU, November 2011: "Beyond this favorable short-term picture lie heightened vulnerabilities of the Russian budget and long-standing structural issues. First, there is the large non-oil fiscal deficit of about 11 percent of GDP, compared with the sustainable 4.5 percent level. Second, with much smaller fiscal reserves than before 2008, Russia's budget is now more vulnerable to a new, sustained drop in oil prices. Third, Russia faces major structural problems in the medium term, including the need to significantly improve the investment climate, close large infrastructure gaps, diversify its export, tax, and broader economic base, improve governance, and strengthen institutions."

17 Marshall Goldman, *Petrostate: Putin, Power, and the New Russia*, London: Oxford University Press, 2010.

18 World Bank, *Country Partnership Strategy (CPS) for the Russian Federation*, Report No. 65115-RU, November 2011: "Finally, on the structural reform front, the Russian economy is facing multiple, long-term challenges. These include, first and foremost, improving the investment climate, addressing the large infrastructure gaps, diversifying Russia's tax, export and broader economic base, and strengthening governance and institutions. In each of these areas, Russia scores comparatively low on many measures of performance, especially for a very large middle-income country aspiring to achieve high-income status within the next decade. These challenges underpin the government's broader modernization agenda and the ongoing broad consultative discussions about the country's revised Strategy 2020. The extent to which these long-term challenges are met will determine the longer-term dynamics of the Russian economy, its catch-up with developed countries, and its ability to improve the living standards of its citizens."

19 World Bank, *Country Partnership Strategy (CPS) for the Russian Federation*, Report No. 65115-RU, November 2011: "The dominant concern for Russia's economic model remains the dependency on fossil fuel production and exports and the associated challenge of using hydrocarbon revenues effectively and efficiently. Russia is a global energy powerhouse. It is the world's largest exporter of natural gas and the second largest oil exporter. Energy resources combined with stronger social and economic policies have resulted in rapid social and economic progress during 2002–2008 and allowed it to weather the global crisis well. At the same time, however, as in many other major hydrocarbon producers, these resources are also the source of many of its development

challenges. Relative to its structural endowments and trade potential, Russia appears to be under-exporting. Only approximately 9 percent of total exports in 2009 were accounted for by high-tech exports, mainly from the defense industry. There has been some shift to services over the years but the economic structure is dominated by large corporations with concentration in natural resources and low value-added industries, while contributions from the SME sector are limited. The financial sector remains underdeveloped in terms of its capacity to mobilize and intermediate savings and is vulnerable to fluctuations in commodity prices and capital flows. Capital markets are inadequately developed and gaps exist in the oversight of the banking system."

20 Russia has a lengthy list of "strategic" enterprises, both military and key suppliers to the military that prohibit foreign participation. Military-industrial enterprises are all nationalized. "Strategic" enterprises essentially are state controlled. The number of strategic enterprises has not been reduced, or is there any officially stated intention to do so. See OECD, "Economic Policy Reforms 2012: Going for Growth," 2012.

21 OECD, "Economic Policy Reforms 2012: Going for Growth," 2012.

22 OECD, "Economic Policy Reforms 2012: Going for Growth," 2012: "An April 2011 legislative act requires that all draft legislation be subject to regulatory impact analysis in order to identify the provisions that create unjustified obstacles to investment."

23 World Bank, *Country Partnership Strategy (CPS) for the Russian Federation*, Report No. 65115-RU, November 2011: "Russian businesses are often inefficient and tend to operate at low levels of technology and knowledge. Russia's product base has narrowed considerably over the past decade. In manufacturing, value-added per worker is similar to that of workers in China and India, but when labor costs are accounted for, overall productivity is lower. State-owned enterprises are present in more sectors of the economy than in any OECD country bar Poland. These enterprises also account for around 17 percent of total employment. Competition and the institutional and policy framework provide insufficient pressure or incentives to stimulate innovation. A difficult environment for the financial system leads to deficiencies in new company formation. External know-how transfers are limited with gross FDI inflows from 2005–2010 averaging a low 1.5 percent of GDP, with only 21 percent of these funds going to non-energy manufacturing."

24 OECD, "Economic Policy Reforms 2012: Going for Growth," 2012: "The Government's new innovation strategy 'innovative Russia-2020' emphasizes the importance of private sector innovation activity. The creation of the Kolkovo 'innovation city' may facilitate innovation, but its special legal and tax regimes go against the principles of universally applied rules and incentives."

25 World Bank, *Country Partnership Strategy (CPS) for the Russian Federation*, Report No. 65115-RU, November 2011: "Russia, as the largest country in the world by land area, faces significant challenges in development of its regions as average numbers for the country mask huge regional variations. Large and dynamic cities with high growth rates such as Moscow and St. Petersburg are highly congested and create substantial problems for urban transport management, while outside these cities poverty levels and unemployment can reach significantly high levels. According to Rosstat, the average level of unemployment from November 2010 to January 2011 varied from only 1.4 percent in Moscow to 47.5 percent in the Republic of Ingushetia. Headcount poverty rates (2008) ranged from 38 percent in Kalmykia (in the south) to 7.4 percent in oil-rich Khanty-Mansiysk. Providing access to infrastructure of comparable quality is a principal development objective of the Federation, yet is also a significant challenge given its huge size. Three strategic projects, including a Pacific oil pipeline, a drilling rig and an auto plant have been launched in the Far East." See "Strategic Projects to Boost Russia's Far Eastern Economy," www.chinaview.cn, January 5, 2010.

26 World Bank, *Country Partnership Strategy (CPS) for the Russian Federation*, Report No. 65115-RU, November 2011: "Russia has a strong interest in continuing to improve efficiency and effectiveness of public financial management. Among other measures, the

Government already introduced a three-year budget framework, implemented legal and institutional mechanisms for monitoring sub-national public finance and Treasury principles of budget execution, created budget authority at the municipal level, and adopted legislation on insolvency of budgets of the regions. In late 2010 and 2011, Russia experienced large oil windfalls. Rising public expenditure commitments—including on the military, public sector wages, and pensions—are threatening to undermine fiscal and overall macroeconomic stability. The Government needs to substantially improve its long-term fiscal position by rationalizing public expenditures, managing the effects on public finances of an aging population, creating fiscal space for productive infrastructure spending, returning to an explicit fiscal rule, and broadening the tax base."

27 World Bank, *Country Partnership Strategy (CPS) for the Russian Federation*, Report No. 65115-RU, November 2011: "The Government has renewed and stepped up efforts to improve the business environment. Over the past few years these efforts have included the reduction of the burden of regulatory compliance on business, particularly in dealing with licensing and inspections at the subnational level, systematic monitoring of business environment indicators at the level of the regions, strengthening the enforcement of competition regulations, automating key administrative processes concerning business (e-filing of taxes), and stemming the proliferation of new regulations through the introduction of regulatory impact assessments. Despite the promising recent initiatives aiming at improving the business climate, perception indicators of the business environment remain poor. Russia ranks 120th among 183 economies in the 2012 Doing Business report. Government efforts now focus on streamlining key regulatory processes (e.g., issuance of licenses and permits) and monitoring administrative corruption affecting business at the level of the regions, where most regulatory processes occur. See further details in Annex 3."

28 World Bank, *Country Partnership Strategy (CPS) for the Russian Federation*, Report No. 65115-RU, November 2011: "The Russian Government is prepared to address existing weaknesses in the financial system. Prudential and non-prudential supervision requires strengthening through an improved regulatory framework in line with the G20 objectives. In particular, the Central Bank of Russia needs supervisory powers for several areas to mitigate banking sector risks. Also, financial system assets are concentrated in the banking sector where loan quality may be overestimated and the level of provisions is still lower than it should be. The breadth and depth of the equity, bond and investment fund markets remain well below capacity. Russia's capital markets also face deficiencies in market infrastructure (clearing and settlement) and a small institutional and retail investor base. The issues in the banking system and capital markets mean that there are problems in access to finance. The lack of access to finance is an obstacle for micro, small and medium firms, but is a particularly significant obstacle for medium and large firms. Structural obstacles to an enhanced access to finance remain to be addressed."

29 World Bank, *Country Partnership Strategy (CPS) for the Russian Federation*, Report No. 65115-RU, November 2011: "The Government regards infrastructure as a key development constraint with estimates for necessary investments at about US$1 trillion until 2020. According to a joint Bank/IFC study, Russia's potential energy savings are roughly equal to the annual primary energy consumption of France. Russia's transport infrastructure is generally poor and has been declining because of underinvestment in maintenance and rehabilitation. Major weaknesses are evident in the quantity, quality and institutions of several large infrastructure sectors. Upgrading Russia's infrastructure would require not only significant investments but also a strengthening of the country's institutional framework. Russia's environmental management suffers from poor governance and sometimes obsolete management practices. Environmental quality and control are poor for a majority of Russians living in the country's population centers. This has detrimental effects not only for those peoples' well-being but also a significant negative impact on Russia's economy."

30 World Bank, *Country Partnership Strategy (CPS) for the Russian Federation*, Report No. 65115-RU, November 2011: "The Russian Federation has made significant achievements in social and human capital development. The most notable achievements are in the areas of universal primary education, equality for women, eradication of extreme poverty and malnutrition, lowering child and maternal mortality, and reaching very high levels of higher education enrollment. With these achievements, the Russian Government is increasingly focusing its strategies on moving Russia closer to the level of achievements of other G8/OECD countries. In light of these ambitious goals, despite the impressive achievements to date, Russia is facing new challenges that will be critical to address if the government goals under the updated Strategy 2020 are to be achieved."

31 World Bank, *Country Partnership Strategy (CPS) for the Russian Federation*, Report No. 65115-RU, November 2011: "While general poverty levels have fallen sharply since the early 2000s, vulnerability to poverty remains a concern. Poverty rates are declining but remain significant with more than 18.5 million Russians living in poverty in 2010. Chronic poverty is now at about 7 percent, but the relatively high vulnerability to poverty affects about a quarter of the population (some 37 million people). (3) Efficiency in social spending, better targeting of social programs, as well as new transfers will be of critical importance in the future, especially with Russia's efforts to reduce the fiscal deficit and its exposure to changes in oil prices. Social protection is the largest budget item (55 percent) within the social expenditures. (4) Up to one quarter of social support beneficiaries are not poor. Furthermore, some of the social programs are suffering from low quality and weak integration with active policies that will bring people into jobs and out of poverty or social care. As Russia continues to develop, social transfers and programs will take up an increasing share of the national budget as in other OECD countries. Thus, enhancing its efficiency will be paramount as will be improving the quality of care and social programs."

32 OECD, "Economic Policy Reforms 2012: Going for Growth," 2012: "Since January 2011, citizens have got the right to choose a primary care doctor and an insurance company within the mandatory health insurance system." World Bank, *Country Partnership Strategy (CPS) for the Russian Federation*, Report No. 65115-RU, November 2011: "Demographic and health trends are characterized by low fertility, high adult mortality and morbidity rates, and inefficient health spending, in addition to a rising pressure on pensions. The demographic profile of the Russian Federation shows a shrinking and aging population. Average male life expectancy in Russia is only 62.8 years (13.8 years less than the EU average), as opposed to 74.7 for women (7.9 years less than the EU average). The excess mortality is overwhelmingly attributable to cardiovascular diseases, cancer, alcohol poisoning, as well as injuries due to traffic accidents. According to Rosstat estimates, the working age population size will decrease by 10.4 million between 2011 and 2025, which is a major challenge for the Russian economy. Labor force shortages are expected to be compensated through labor immigration. Progress has been made in the fight against AIDS/HIV and TB. Still, Russia is among the 10 countries with the highest multi-drug resistant TB burden in the world. Furthermore, the Russian health system suffers from poor quality and inefficient spending with limited resources flowing to preventive care and an excessive amount of resources going to the hospital sector. Despite these challenges, Russia's total health expenditures is only 5.4 percent of GDP compared to an OECD average of 8.8 percent. Health indicators generally remain low in an international perspective and when compared to countries with similar levels of development. Given the relative low retirement age and the aging population, the fiscal burden arising from pensions will continue to grow."

33 World Bank, *Country Partnership Strategy (CPS) for the Russian Federation*, Report No. 65115-RU, November 2011: "Skill mismatches in the labor market are turning into an increasingly important development constraint. Professional education and the renewal of skills for labor market entrants as well as existing workers are critical for adopting new

technologies, diversifying the economy, and improving productivity levels. The latest EBRD-World Bank Business Environment and Enterprise Performance Survey (BEEPS) ranks skills as the number one concern for businesses in Russia. This is further exemplified by the fact that excess labor market capacity appears to have been exhausted. Combined with the changes to the demographics of the Russian population, this indicates a serious and tightening bottleneck in the economy with regard to the provision of skilled workers, the quality of higher education and the renewal of skills within the existing labor force. Labor force shortages resulting from demographic trends make the Russian economy dependent on immigrant labor. The Russian Government is undertaking steps to attract more highly skilled immigrants to the country and is currently developing a scheme of organized recruitment of migrant workers. During 1999–2007, Russian GDP grew by an average of 7 percent annually with labor productivity growing an average of 6 percent per year accounting for 2/3 of the expansion in per capita GDP. Both female and male employment rates are below the EU average. The Russian Government is aware of the challenges which are to be addressed in the updated Strategy 2020. See further details in Annex 4."

34 World Bank, *Country Partnership Strategy (CPS) for the Russian Federation*, Report No. 65115-RU, November 2011: "The country's strong economic recovery and downward poverty trends belie significant challenges of inequality and social exclusion. Since Russia began its transition from a planned economy to a market economy some 20 years ago, economic growth has been steady and GDP per capita has increased threefold. Inequality as measured by the Gini coefficient rose significantly, however, from 28.9 to 42.2 between 1992 and 2009. Social stresses have been similarly magnified. Given that federal spending on social services in 2007–2008 already accounted for about 17 percent of GDP, or half of total federal spending, and was further increased by around 1.3 percent of GDP in 2009 and 2.2 percent of GDP in 2010, effectively addressing the issues of inequality and social exclusion will require an alternative preventative approach that can tackle the root causes of these issues."

35 World Bank, *Country Partnership Strategy (CPS) for the Russian Federation*, Report No. 65115-RU, November 2011: "The sharp disparities in development and living standards among Russia's regions require a differentiated policy approach. Russia's achievements conceal huge variations among regions in the level of social spending and poverty rates. For example, 82 percent of preschool education is financed through local government budgets, and therefore poorer regions will be more disadvantaged in their capacity to finance preschool education than richer regions. Substantial differences among Russia's regions are also apparent in per student spending and in the quality of education at the primary and secondary education level. 7. Finally, vulnerable children including those with mental or physical disabilities and those who are infected with HIV suffer from educational exclusion. Addressing these variations among the regions across the human development spectrum will be critical for maintaining the path of achievements and calls for a more differentiated approach to policies and interventions."

36 World Bank, *Country Partnership Strategy (CPS) for the Russian Federation*, Report No. 65115-RU, November 2011: "Russia's national choices have critical impact on regional and global challenges. Russia is one of ECA's regional engines of growth, both as the major destination of exports and migrant labor from the CIS countries. The Russian Government wants to support economic integration within the CIS, including the creation of a common migration space and common labor market, but also has to grapple with social integration and adaptation of labor immigrants. The Russian territory contains about 22 percent of the world's undisturbed ecosystems. These have global value and significance for biodiversity protection, carbon storage and sequestration, and other critically important environmental functions. Strengthening forestry governance and management is particularly critical. The country's forests are at risk from forest fire, pest and disease outbreaks, and low rates

of reforestation. Further strengthening of the national system for weather forecasting, hydro-meteorological services and climate monitoring remains a high priority for the Government as the impact of climate change is expected to increase the frequency of extreme and hazardous weather events. Due to the large-scale economic development and climate warming in recent decades, Russia's remote Arctic areas have become more accessible, resulting in a significant increase in human activities. This has led to more pressures on the pristine but fragile environment in the Arctic zone."

37 World Bank, *Country Partnership Strategy (CPS) for the Russian Federation*, Report No. 65115-RU, November 2011: "At the ECA regional level, Russia has become a prominent emerging donor. Over the last CPS period, it has implemented an ambitious development assistance program with significant contributions. With the approval of 75 percent of the population according to a 2010 WBG-managed opinion survey by the Levada Center, Russia will focus its assistance on LICs and lower-income MICs in ECA where it has many social and economic ties, and will also become active in other LICs. As a member of the Eurasian Economic Community, it initiated the establishment of a regional multilateral mechanism (EurAsEC Anti-Crisis Fund) administered by EDB to help deal with crisis-related challenges in affected EurAsEC countries. Russian lead agencies have developed an understanding of the complexity of development aid communications and a sense of urgency for more active work in ensuring adequate information in support of Russian development aid. The Russian Government now plans to create a stronger institutional framework for development aid. It wants to set up a new bilateral development aid agency and enhance capacity within existing public agencies through better staffing, increased staff training, and development of expert potential."

38 World Bank, *Country Partnership Strategy (CPS) for the Russian Federation*, Report No. 65115-RU, November 2011: "At the global level, Russia has made important steps toward deeper integration into the international community. Russia is already a member of the G8, G20, and APEC. It is also making significant progress toward becoming a member of the OECD and the WTO. To reach its full potential as a prominent member of these global institutions, the Russian Government would like to employ the whole array of available policy instruments. Yet, with regard to the area of global public goods, where Russia is showing special interest in decisive issues like financial stability and food security, the Department for International Financial Relations in the Ministry of Finance is understaffed and the Government needs to strengthen the institutional structures and technical expertise necessary to provide effective leadership."

39 World Bank, *Country Partnership Strategy (CPS) for the Russian Federation*, Report No. 65115-RU, November 2011: "In recent years, the Government of Russia has completed or initiated a number of major reforms in the public sector. These efforts were intended to ensure sound management of public resources, create a more favorable business environment, and enhance public service delivery. Still, many challenges remain. Annex 5 analyzes recent developments and their impact, the main challenges, and the Government's current strategies for improving public sector governance."

40 World Bank, *Country Partnership Strategy (CPS) for the Russian Federation*, Report No. 65115-RU, November 2011: "Improving effectiveness and efficiency of public administration has been a high priority for the Russian Government in the last decade. The Government has undertaken a major effort to clarify and delineate functions between levels of executive government and establish local self government. The Government also launched a broad set of public sector reforms in areas such as civil service, budget process, and public administration. Some of these reforms, however, were only partially implemented and are not fully visible to the average citizen. The reforms are yet to translate into tangible and noticeable improvements in the quality and effectiveness of public administration in the eyes of the citizens and businesses. Government functions and civil service staff kept growing between 2004 and 2010. Government regulation is seen as excessive and often ineffective. Public services are

heavily embedded in traditional administrative arrangements, which often encourage corruption and are burdensome for citizens and businesses."

41 World Bank, *Country Partnership Strategy (CPS) for the Russian Federation*, Report No. 65115-RU, November 2011: "Corruption has been recognized as one of the major obstacles for investments and growth. In response, the Government has embarked on a comprehensive anti-corruption program. Anti-corruption efforts have received new impetus in recent years under the leadership of President Medvedev. A Federal Anti-corruption Law and National Anticorruption Plan have been adopted and civil servants are required to declare their assets. Surveys of corruption perceptions show that Russia continues to lag relative to the ECA region and in global terms. The Government has made reform of the state contracting systems a key priority. Reported unofficial payments to obtain public procurement contracts were relatively high (BEEPS 2008), with 30 percent of firms reporting having made such payments, amounting to an average 11.5 percent of the value of the contract. Some improvements have been made, including introducing e-procurement through a single government portal, and according to Rosstat, competition in public procurement tenders has increased (average number of bidders in electronic auctions increased from 7 in 2007 to 26 in 2009)."

42 World Bank, *Country Partnership Strategy (CPS) for the Russian Federation*, Report No. 65115-RU, November 2011: "The judiciary is viewed as weak despite some improvements in recent years. Some high-profile court cases have caused international concern about the full independence of the criminal justice system. However, according to surveys by the Levada Center, citizens' confidence in the courts rose from 45 percent in 2006 to 64 percent in 2010. According to the latest Business Environment and Enterprise Performance Survey (BEEPS), the share of firms using the legal system increased from 27 percent in 2005 to 43 percent in 2008, while only 3 percent of the companies surveyed reported corrupt practices. Two areas stand out for continued state attention in the judicial system: (i) continuing the trend towards greater transparency and efficiency in the functioning of courts (through investments in information technology and disseminating information to citizens on judicial decisions and the functioning of courts), and (ii) strengthening the enforcement of judicial and administrative procedures through the bailiff system, ensuring efficiency, transparency and integrity."

43 OECD, *Economics Surveys: Russian Federation 2006*, Paris: OECD, 2006.

44 World Bank, *Country Partnership Strategy (CPS) for the Russian Federation*, Report No. 65115-RU, November 2011, p. 52.

45 World Bank, *Country Partnership Strategy (CPS) for the Russian Federation*, Report No. 65115-RU, November 2011: Another version of the same document is entitled: *Russian Federation: Country Partnership Strategy for the period 2012–2016* (in English), p. 2: "According to the 1993 Constitution, Russia is a democratic federal law-governed state with a republican form of government, comprising 83 federal subjects." The next parliamentary elections will be held on December 4, 2011, to be followed by presidential elections on March 4, 2012. President Dmitry Medvedev came to power in March 2008 and appointed Prime Minister Vladimir Putin. This ruling tandem has operated well since then. According to recent polls, the approval ratings for both the president and prime minister remain high, albeit lower than in 2010. The ruling party, United Russia, dominates the State Duma by holding 315 seats. The 2011 parliamentary elections will be the sixth in the history of modern-day Russia. Vladimir Putin announced that he will run for president. According to latest public opinion polls, the political situation is not likely to change significantly after the elections, with the four leading parties retaining their dominance in the Duma." Cf. Michael McFaul and Kathryn Stoner-Weiss, "Mission to Moscow: Why Authoritarian Stability Is a Myth," *Foreign Affairs*, January/February 2008. McFaul worked for the US National Security Council as Special Assistant to the President and Senior Director of Russian and Eurasian Affairs. McFaul is one of the architect's

of the "reset." See Leon Aron, "A Tormenting in Moscow," *Foreign Policy*, April 12, 2012. He was the Obama administration's ambassador to Russia, and champions the view that Putin's authoritarianism soon would give way to democracy, a belief shared by Anders Åslund.

46 Steven Rosefielde and Stefan Hedlund, *Russia Since 1980: Wrestling With Westernization*, Cambridge: Cambridge University Press, 2008.

47 "In the period since 2005, the per capita GDP of Russia doubled to approximately $10,500 in 2010." The year 2008 is used as the endpoint in the text because Russian per capita GDP was lower in 2010 than 2008. World Bank, *Country Partnership Strategy (CPS) for the Russian Federation*, Report No. 65115-RU, November 2011, p. 47.

48 Angus Maddison, http://www.ggdc.net/maddison/Historical_Statistics/horizontal-file_03-2009xls (last updated: March 2009). West Europe includes Austria, Belgium, Denmark, Finland, France, Germany, Italy, Netherlands, Norway, Sweden, Switzerland and the United Kingdom. GDP for West Europe and Russia is calculated in 1990 international Geary-Khamis dollars.

49 Steven Rosefielde, *Efficiency and the Economic Recovery Potential of Russia,* Ashgate, 1998, Table S1, p. xxii. CIA, *Handbook of International Economic Statistics*, CPAS92-10005, September 1992. Russian per capita income valued in 1991 dollars was 15,631. The inverse of GDP deflator 1991–2011 is 1.5. Russian 1989 GDP in 2011 US$ prices is $23,546: http://www.economagic.com/em-cgi/data.exe/fedstl/gdpdef+1.

50 Paul Krugman, *The Return of Depression Economics and the Crisis of 2008*, New York: W.W. Norton Company, 2009; Lawrence Summers, "Washington Must Not Settle for Secular Stagnation," *Financial Times*, December 5, 2013: http://www.ft.com/cms/s/2/ba0f1386-7169-11e3-8f92-00144feabdc0.html#ixzz2pi6xfiEe; James Pethokoukis, "The Slump That Never Ends: Does the US Face 'Secular Stagnation'?" *AEI*, November 19, 2013; Henry Blodget, "Has the US Entered a 'Permanent Slump'?" *Daily Ticker*, November 18, 2013: http://finance.yahoo.com/blogs/daily-ticker/u-economy-entered-permanent-slump-165120719.html—"Summers speculates that the natural interest rate 'consistent with full employment' fell 'to negative 2% or negative 3% sometime in the middle of the last decade.' But conventional monetary policy can't push rates that low. The dreaded Zero Lower Bound. Thus Summers concludes, 'We may well need, in the years ahead, to think about how we manage an economy in which the zero nominal interest rate is a chronic and systemic inhibitor of economic activity, holding our economies back, below their potential'"; Alan Greenspan, "Never Saw It Coming," *Foreign Affairs*, November/December 2013: http://www.foreignaffairs.com/articles/140161/alan-greenspan/never-saw-it-coming, and Jenny Cosgrave, "Summers: US faces a 'Downton Abbey' Economy," *CNBC*, February 17, 2014: http://www.cnbc.com/id/101421153.

51 *Russia-CIA World Factbook*, 2012.

52 John Williamson, "Democracy and the 'Washington Consensus'," *World Development*, Vol. 21, No. 8, 1993, pp. 1329–36.

53 This was an aspect of the notorious phenomenon of hidden inflation during the Soviet era.

54 Adam Smith, *The Theory of Moral Sentiments*, 1759. His attitude reflected the values later called the Protestant ethic, and an Enlightenment reverence for the righteousness of pure reason. Muscovite autocrats would have scoffed.

55 Adam Smith, *Wealth of Nations*, 1776.

56 British Petroleum is being forced by the Kremlin to sell its lucrative stake in TNK-BP. See Stephen Blank, "Is Russia Riding to BP's Rescue?" *Huffington Post*, October 25, 2010; Julia Werdigier, "BP to Seek Sale of Russian Venture TNK-BP," *New York Times*, June 1, 2012. Cf. the case of Avianova LLC, where majority foreign shareholders were peremptorily thrown out by the government on June 24, 2011.

57 Steven Rosefielde, "The Impossibility of Russian Economic Reform: Waiting for Godot," US Army War College, Carlisle Barracks, 2012.

58 Gertrude Schroeder, "The Soviet Economy on a Treadmill of 'Reforms'," in *Soviet Economy in a Time of Change*, Joint Economic Committee of Congress, Washington, DC, October 10, 1979, pp. 312–66.

59 Cf. Clifford Gaddy and Barry Ickes, *Bear Traps on Russia's Road to Modernization*, London: Routledge, 2013.

60 Stephen Blank, "Voodoo Economics: Notes on the Political Economy of Russian Defense," paper prepared for the 44th ASEEES (Association for Slavic, East European and Eurasian Studies) Conference, New Orleans, November 15, 2012.

61 Douglass C. North, John Joseph Wallis and Barry R. Weingast, *Violence and Social Orders: A Conceptual Framework for Interpreting Recorded Human History*; Cambridge: Cambridge University Press, 2009; Vitaly V. Shlykov, "Back into the Future, or Cold War Lessons for Russia," *Russia in Global Affairs*, No. 2, April–June, 2006: http://eng.globalaffairs.ru/number/n_6571; Daron Acemoglu and James A. Robinson, *Why Nations Fail: The Origins of Power, Prosperity, and Poverty*, New York: Crown Business Books, 2012; Alexander Etkind, *Internal Colonization: Russia's Imperial Experience*, London: Polity Press, 2011; Richard Hellie, "The Structure of Russian Imperial History," *History and Theory*, No. 44 (2005), pp. 88–112; and Peter Baker and Susan Glasser, *Kremlin Rising: Vladimir Putin's Russia and the End of Revolution*, New York: Scribner's, 2005, p. 417.

62 Vitaly V. Shlykov, "Back into the Future, Or Cold War Lessons for Russia," *Russia in Global Affairs*, No. 2, April–June, 2006: http://eng.globalaffairs.ru/number/n_6571.

63 Serdyukov was replaced as defense minister November 6, 2012. Vladimir Isachenkov, "Kremlin Chief Says He Knew About Corruption Probe," *Yahoo!News*, November 12, 2012. Deputy Prime Minister and Chief of the Presidential Administration, Sergei Ivanov is widely seen as the driving force behind Serdyukov's ouster. Most experts believe that Serdyukov was sacked because of an intensifying behind-the-scenes battle for the distribution of 20 trillion rubles (US$635 billion) that the Kremlin plans to spend on buying new weapons through 2020. Serdyukov was refusing to sign new weapons contracts, demanding higher quality and cheaper prices from the military industry, a stance that angered industry leaders with strong Kremlin connections. The Serdyukov camp has struck back by raising allegations of embezzlement of 6.5 billion rubles (over US$200 million) earmarked for Russia's GLONASS satellite navigation system under Ivanov's watch. Cf. Alexandr Golts, "Why Russia Smuggles U.S. Electronics," *St. Petersburg Times*, October 10, 2012, p. 12: "60 to 70 percent of all electronics used in Russia's defense equipment are purchased abroad. The much-discussed 20 trillion ruble ($644 billion) rearmament program through 2020 is supposed to finally introduce serial production in the country's military production chain. But sooner or later, it will become evident that the new "advanced weapons" Russia is supposed to produce will be missing the electronics needed to make them work. Still, does anyone really believe that serial production will ever be implemented? Isn't the real goal to embezzle as much money as possible by promising to flood the army with modern equipment?"

64 In other words, rent-seeking and rent-granting presuppose rule by force and the ready resort to excessive reliance on force, a reliance compounded by the fact that Russia has always tended to over-militarization of its economy and state because its institutions did not allow it to compete with foreign neighbors and interlocutors for influence on an equal basis. Therefore in today's Russia the rent-granting state with a rent-seeking elite is not just a major attribute of the system, rather it is an essential precondition of its survival. As many have noted, corruption is the system not an excrescence upon it or an undesirable but inevitable cost of doing business.

65 Blank, "Voodoo Economics: Notes on the Political Economy of Russian Defense": Putin now says that by 2020 the armed forces will get over 1,500 new aircraft and helicopters and about 200 new air defense systems. Furthermore he too has demanded 70 percent modernization (although it is nowhere specified what the criteria of such modernization is) by 2020. Furthermore he called for producing by this

date over 400 ICBMs, 8 strategic missile submarines and SLBMs, 20 multipurpose submarines, 50 combat surface ships. Over 600 modern aircraft, including fifth generation fighters, over 600 modern helicopters, 28S-400 Surface to air anti-aircraft missiles, 38 Vityaz air defense systems, 10 Islander-M systems, over 2,300 modern tanks, some 2,000 self-propelled artillery systems and guns, over 17,000 motor vehicles, and 100 military satellites. Blank, citing Julian Cooper also contends that Russian defense spending has recovered significantly since the early 1990s to about 50 percent of the Soviet level on a territorially adjusted basis. See Julian Cooper, *Reviewing Russian Strategic Planning: The Emergence of Strategy 2020*, NDC Research Review, NATO Defense College, 2012, www.ndc.nato.int. Elsewhere, Cooper provides data that puts weapons procurement at more than 60 percent of the Soviet era level. See Steven Rosefielde, "Economics of the Military-Industrial Complex," in Michael Alexeev and Shlomo Weber, *The Oxford Handbook of Russian Economy*, Oxford: Oxford University Press, 2012, and "Postcrisis Russia: Counting on Miracles in Uncertain Times," in Carolina Vendil Pallin and Bertil Nygren, eds., *Russian Defense Prospects*, New York: Macmillan, 2011.

6 Ukraine

The Union of Soviet Socialist Republics (*Soyuz Sovetskikh Sotsialisticheskikh Respublik*) or USSR was a federation of 15 nominally independent member republics,[1] even though Ukraine, Belarus and Kazakhstan held UN seats from 1945 onwards.[2] Most republics had been administrative units of the Russian empire (*Rossiiskaya Imperiya*).[3] The Russian empire and Soviet Union were unitary states, not federations of independent republics.[4] The Ukraine was one of the Soviet Union's founding republics (*Ukrainskaya SSR*) together with the RSFSR, the Transcaucasian SFSR, and the Belorussian SSR in December 1922.[5] Its Soviet version was larger than imperial Russian Ukraine. Both included a sub-division called "Novorossiya" (New Russia) that contemporary separatists want re-annexed to Russia.[6]

Ukraine's roots can be traced back to "Kievan Rus" in AD 882,[7] a loose federation of East Slavic tribes residing in Europe from the late ninth to the mid-thirteenth century, under the Rurik dynasty.[8] The modern peoples of Belarus, Ukraine and Russia all claim Kievan Rus as their cultural inheritance.[9] Following its fragmentation in the thirteenth century, Ukraine was contested, ruled and partitioned by a variety of powers. A Cossack republic emerged and prospered during the seventeenth and eighteenth centuries (the Zaporizhian Host),[10] but Ukraine remained otherwise divided until its consolidation into a Soviet republic in the twentieth century, becoming a true independent state only in 1991.

"Ukrainian" is an ambiguous ethnonym (ethnic name) and toponym (geographic marker) because it means different things to different segments of the population currently resident in the post-Soviet Ukrainian political space.[11] Contemporary Ukraine contains numerous, predominantly western Slavic, ethnicities including Russian and Polish, and sub-ethnicities including Hutsuls, Volhynians, Boykos, Lemkos, Polishchuks, Bodnars, Kuban Cossacks, Belorussians, Romanians and Tartars.[12] The term "Ukrainian" only became generally accepted after 1917 and was affected by the Molotov-Ribbentrop "non-aggression" treaty's secret partitioning of Poland, which resulted in the permanent transfer of Northern Bukovina, Southern Bessarabia and Hertza into the Ukrainian SSR.[13] This annexation increased the latent regional tug of war between Poland (and in the background Lithuania and Germany) and Russia, a problem compounded at the 1945 Yalta Conference by Franklyn Roosevelt's acceptance of the Curzon Line, which ceded significant additional portions of Poland abutting

Ukraine to the Soviet Union.[14] Broadly speaking, populations formerly under Polish, Lithuanian and German control lean westward while significant portions of pre-Soviet annexation residents lean toward the Kremlin. Ukraine's secession initiative from the Soviet Union which began in March 1990 was spearheaded by west Ukrainians.[15]

Economic transformation

The Ukrainian and Soviet economic systems before 1990 were one and the same thing. The means of production in the Ukrainian SSR belonged to the Soviet people. Markets and entrepreneurship were criminalized.[16] Ukrainian officials and citizens were legally obliged to abide by plan directives, and economic activity was administered, supervised and incentivized by Soviet ministries, the Communist Party of the USSR, the Ministry of Defense (MOD) and the KGB. Like all Soviet firms, Ukrainian enterprises enjoyed guaranteed purchase. The state agreed to buy as much as "Red directors" could produce if goods weren't defective. Guaranteed purchase combined with managerial bonuses tied to output or profit maximizing constituted a formal back-up mechanism supporting the command system whenever enterprise micro-plans (*tekhpromfinplans*) were unfeasible.[17] Moreover, Mikhail Gorbachev's *perestroika* reforms and unauthorized "spontaneous privatizations" in the late 1980s applied across the Soviet space. Consequently, there were no institutional factors pressing Ukraine to embark on its own unique post-Soviet transformation path, but parochial political forces did impose some distinctive characteristics.

Ukraine's transformation drama began on February 7, 1990, when the Communist Party of the Soviet Union relinquished its monopoly on political participation creating the possibility for open nationalist political opposition within Republican parliaments.[18] This mostly meant that nationalist factions could be openly formed throughout the Communist Party hierarchy.

On July 16, 1990, four months after Lithuania unilaterally declared its independence from the Soviet Union,[19] Ukraine's Parliament emboldened by Gorbachev's policy of *glasnost* (openness) approved a Declaration of Independence in advance of Mikhail Gorbachev's March 17, 1991 Soviet-wide referendum on the preservation of the Soviet Federation. This didn't constitute formal secession, and the results of the March referendum temporarily spiked Ukraine's secessionist ambitions. However, 76.4 percent of Union-wide voters rejected secession, opting instead for the preservation of a reformed unitary Soviet state based on Gorbachev's principles of *perestroika*, *glasnost* and *demokratizatsia*.[20] Nonetheless, the July 16, 1990 Declaration of Independence was founded on the principles of self-determination, democracy, and political and economic autonomy, and the priority of Ukrainian over Soviet law was a milestone in the Ukrainian secession process.[21]

During the ensuing six months after the referendum, prospects for immediate Ukrainian independence dimmed, but the failure of the August 19, 1991 *coup d'état* against Mikhail Gorbachev (then president of the USSR and general secretary of the Communist Party) by the State Committee on the Emergency Situation

(*Gosudarstvenniy Komitet po Chrezvichaynomu Polozheniyu*) undermined the credibility of Soviet power. The Ukrainian Parliament seized the opportunity five days later on August 24, 1991 by adopting the Act of Independence declaring Ukraine an independent democratic state.[22] Formal secession had begun. Belarus immediately followed suit.

Ukraine's gambit emulating Lithuania's prior success was spearheaded by Leonid Kravchuk (the chairman of the secessionist Parliament and former second secretary of the Ukrainian Communist Party Central Committee in charge of ideology), who soon "traveled to the United States, Canada and France for discussions on the head-of-state level about Ukraine's impending independence. On both the domestic and international fronts, therefore, Ukraine prepared the groundwork to support the widely anticipated vote for independence."[23] This carefully orchestrated second-round referendum undertaken to ratify Parliament's declaration of independence together with the first Ukrainian secessionist presidential election took place on December 1, 1991. That day, more than 90 percent of the electorate expressed their support for the Act of Independence, and elected Kravchuk to serve as the country's first president. The leaders of Belarus, Russia and Ukraine formally dissolved the Soviet Union in Brest on December 8, and formed the Commonwealth of Independent States (CIS) (*Sodruzhestvo Nezavisimykh Gosudarstv*, SNG) on December 21 in Alma Ata, Kazakhstan). Gorbachev ratified the decision four days later completing the legal disestablishment of the Soviet Union. The former Yugoslavia was torn asunder in a similar manner. Apparently, opportunists seeking personal advancement believed that the nationalist card provided the surest route to power when communist parties in Eurasia began crumbling.[24]

Yeltsin's, Kravchuk's (Ukraine) and Stanislav Shushkevich's (chairman of the Supreme Soviet of Belarus) ploys to destroy Soviet power succeeded, but the adventure had no constructive purpose other than to create an independent basis for enhancing their personal authority. Although all three marched under the banner of secession, *perekhod* (transition) and democracy, they had no commitment to responsibly establishing democratic free enterprise from the ashes of the Soviet command economy, and had only vague ideas about future mutual relations other than the creation of the SNG.[25]

This opportunistic approach left Ukraine vulnerable on many crucial scores. Its peoples were ethnically and culturally divided broadly into western and eastern camps, with opposing attitudes toward personal liberty and collectivism. Ukraine's economy and armed forces had been fully integrated in the Soviet command system and a transition plan should have been devised to preserve effectiveness in the new, independent post-Soviet environment. Ukraine's industries, for example, were dependent on inter-industrial supplies from, and sales to, the rest of the former Soviet Union, but this seems to have escaped Kravchuk's (and the World Bank Group's) attention.[26] Likewise, and now a matter of some controversy, Kravchuk misgauged the threat of Russia's re-annexing Ukraine (Novorossiya),[27] and consequently the need for retaining Kyiv's nuclear deterrent.[28] This miscalculation made it a relatively easy for Russia, the US, Britain, France and China to coax Kravchuk and his successor Leonid Kuchma into transferring Ukraine's nuclear weapons to the Kremlin in exchange for now apparently worthless security guarantees provided by the Budapest Memorandum on Security Assurances of 1994.[29] The result was that Russian and Ukrainian defense policies moved in opposite directions. Russia retained its nuclear superpower status and Ukraine was denuclearized.[30]

Russia's and Ukraine's economic transformation goals seemed more compatible. Boris Yeltsin and Leonid Kravchuk both claimed to reject communist authoritarianism in favor of democracy. Both endorsed harmonious multiculturalism, applauded the "rule of law" and condemned the "rule of men." Both abandoned directive central planning, guaranteed state purchase, price fixing and monopoly state ownership of land;[31] as well as state control of the means of production, banking and finance. Both decriminalized markets for labor, capital, land, finance, goods and services, and entrepreneurship, and paid lip service to macroeconomic stabilization. Both liberalized the foreign trade sector by permitting competitive importing and exporting, decontrolling the foreign exchange rate ("dirty floats") and encouraging direct foreign investment.

These goals and actions shifted Russian and Ukrainian proprietary and decision-making responsibility from obedient state officials to independent actors, who were supposed to competitively utility and profit-seek without "guaranteed purchase" in accordance with the principles of democratic free enterprise, but culture, politics and institutions caused things to turn out differently in practice. Russia and Ukraine rejected true democracy,[32] competitive markets and popular government in favor of their own versions of rent-granting Muscovy.[33] Russia and Ukraine both plowed the "enlightened conservative" authoritarian course charted by Tsar Nicholas II, but Ukraine was more conflicted. East Ukraine was comfortable with Putin's style of rule; west Ukraine looked toward the European Union.

Ukraine, like Russia, faced two critical problems. On the demand side, Kravchuk had to create new mechanisms to make consumer demand effective in lieu of plan and edict. Once command planning, guaranteed state purchase and enterprise turnover taxes were scuttled,[34] Ukraine's government had no directive or incentive tools for making enterprise managers responsive to consumer (purchaser) demand, and could not partially remedy the problem with Keynesian public spending (including weapons procurement) because it lacked sufficient tax revenues and borrowing possibilities. On the supply side, enterprise managers were disoriented. They were granted the right to profit maximize, but were forced to operate without secure ownership of their firms and a credible rule of law for contract enforcement. Moreover, when demand for Soviet-era products evaporated with the command system, managers lacked the requisite skills to design and market desirable products.

Kravchuk's solution to these challenges was allowing problems to solve themselves. He acted as if he believed that competitive markets would spring forth fully formed like Athena from Zeus's head,[35] more or less in line with the World Bank Group's advocacy of "shock therapy" (more accurately, shock *without* therapy).[36] Western economists promised that while shock therapy would temporarily inflict acute pain, it would be quickly compensated by skyrocketing production up the "J" curve,[37] but their predictions went unfulfilled. Although Ukraine suffered, it failed to achieve prosperity.

Kravchuk could not compel enterprises to produce because the state had repudiated command, and could not have done so effectively in any case because Ukraine had abolished central planning. He didn't launch a crash deficit public spending program of the sort Paul Krugman now advocates for the US because there was no market for Ukrainian public debt,[38] and he could not have paid for large-scale public projects in cash without recklessly printing money, because the tax collection system had collapsed.[39] Enterprise managers didn't fill the void because they didn't know how, and had no incentive to bear the risks.

Kravchuk's disregard for current production and mass unemployment (invisible in public statistics)[40] didn't mean that he and other insiders were idle. They preoccupied themselves with rent-seeking, other forms of public plunder, and asset-grabbing in that order. The Yeltsin administration set out to transfer the means of production from the people (state ownership of the means of production) to well-connected insiders (oligarchs). Privatization proceeded briskly. Kravchuk and his presidential successor Leonid Kuchma by contrast were operating in a more fractious environment as they were forced to deal with ethnic rivalries. They moved more cautiously, transferring control rather than ownership of state enterprises to insiders. Privatization didn't begin in earnest until 1995 and only picked up steam in 2000. Results were uneven, both in terms of the volume of successful privatizations and the scope of enterprise restructuring. Cumulative privatization receipts as a share of GDP only amounted to 3 percent of GDP through 2000, compared to the 9 percent post-Soviet average:

> As measured by EBRD's indices of structural reform, Ukraine's progress likewise has been slow, with the indices rising from 1.0 to 3.3 for small-scale privatization and from 1.0 to 2.7 for large-scale privatization (on a scale of 1 to 4.3), respectively, over the 1991–2000 period.[41]

Rival regional clans of Ukraine's insiders contented themselves for much of the 1990s with controlling state-owned enterprises' corporate governance.[42] They dispensed with maximizing the present discounted value of the state's assets, concentrating instead on using revenue streams from state enterprises for their private purposes. The economy suffered because rent-seeking, collusion, monopoly power and fraud took precedence over competitive efficiency. Many insiders became billionaires. The system fostered the illusion of value adding more than the reality, because rents granted and received were unrelated to services rendered and marginal utility.[43]

Ukraine didn't have to transform itself in this way, and it didn't have to suffer the ravages of *katastroika* as the Chinese and Slovenian transformation experiences clearly demonstrate,[44] but it stumbled into hyper-depression by refusing to responsibly orchestrate the transformation process. Some analysts blame political infighting which pitted conservatives against reformers for this outcome; others fault a Ukrainian model that tried to navigate the transformation by controlling price formation and using a variety of economic levers.[45] These factors no doubt played a role, but were peripheral. The real reasons for Ukraine's woes were twofold. First, its leadership, under pressure from rival regional oligarchic clans, refused to directly address the challenge of building efficient bridge mechanisms empowering consumer demand (consumer sovereignty) after Ukraine scuttled command planning, guaranteed state purchase and enterprise turnover taxes. The government needed to empower small-business and consumer sovereignty, but preoccupied itself with the agendas of powerful insiders.

Second, and relatedly, Kravchuk and his successors failed to provide would-be competitive enterprise managers with secure ownership, contract protection, essential business skills and financial credit. Ukraine's leaders and World Bank Group advisors chanted the microeconomic and macroeconomic mantras of the Washington Consensus,[46] but avoided taking the practical steps needed to transform abstractions into realities.[47]

As a consequence, Ukraine was a depressing spectacle at the outset of the new millennium, despite rudimentary privatization efforts, patchwork reforms and gradual oligarchic modernization begun after 1995. Its population plummeted,[48] and per capita income fell unrelentingly throughout the 1990s, bottoming at 60 percent below the 1990 level in 1999 (Russian per capita GDP declined by 40 percent).[49] The prosperous transition confidently anticipated by shock therapy advocates was nowhere to be seen.

The new millennium

Then suddenly, and without warning, everything changed—driven by external forces. Russia's economy, stimulated by spiraling petroleum prices after 9/11, mounted an impressive recovery (due to reactivation of idle machinery and equipment, not growth beyond the prior 1989 achieved level). Global economic growth surged (especially in emerging countries) in 2000–08. International trade flourished and speculative foreign direct investment (FDI) increased across the planet, pulling Ukrainian economic activity along with it. Foreign direct investment may have been especially important for Ukraine. According to the OECD, every 1 percent increase in FDI generated a 0.4 percent rise in Ukrainian GDP during this period, and FDI beginning in 2000 was vibrant.[50] Starting from a low base of $3.3 billion,[51] cumulative FDI (from the EU, 43 percent; from Russia, 28 percent) increased tenfold, to $36.5 billion.[52]

This explanation, supported by Pekka Sutela,[53] is disputed by other scholars, who assign credit primarily to domestic factors. Anders Åslund, for example, claims that Viktor Yushchenko's "100 days" of economic reform in January–March 2000 (a fragment of what was intended to be a 1,000-day reform) was not only responsible for Ukraine's ephemeral growth spurt in 2000–08, but allowed it to achieve a complete market transition and become a full-fledged democracy.[54] This judgment, Åslund asserts, is supported by the depth and comprehensiveness of Yushchenko's program, which covered government administration, state finances, energy trade, agricultural land privatization, large privatizations and the deregulation of small firms:

> Yushchenko already had a reform program called 1,000 Days of Reform in Ukraine. It had been prepared in cooperation with the German Advisory Group on Economic Reforms with the Ukrainian Government (1999). This program summed up a consensus achieved in the market economic reform debate in Ukraine, calling for a retreat of the state from economic intervention through subsidies and tax privileges as well as administrative reforms and anticorruption measures . . . Soon, Kuchma wanted to get back into the act. On February 28, 2000, he made a national address to parliament with a new long-term economic and social strategy for 2000–2004, which he labeled Ukraine Toward the XXIst Century. His policy prescriptions coincided with the Yushchenko program. He focused on regulatory reform for entrepreneurship, advocating that intrusive regulations be replaced with general laws and that administrative barriers to business development be eliminated. In mid-March, Kuchma followed up by presenting about 80 draft laws to parliament that were urgently needed to accelerate reforms. These drafts included many key laws that Ukraine was still missing, notably a tax code, a land code, a housing code, and a new criminal code. The first four months of 2000 saw the greatest reform drive that Ukraine had seen since the fall of 1994. It was broader and more comprehensive, and it would put the market economy right. The main measures can be summarized as central government reform, fiscal reform, energy reform, land reform, large privatizations, and anticorruption measures. Yushchenko and his allies knew that the oligarchs would not tolerate them for long, so they struck while the iron was hot.[55]

The reforms Åslund lauds were technical or policy matters appropriate for improving the performance of any economic system that side stepped the parochial problems bedeviling the building of competitive self-regulating markets, wise government oversight and regulation in post-Soviet transition regimes. Government decision-making structures and processes were rationalized.[56] The budget deficit was reduced by lowering expenditures (including subsidies) more than increasing revenues, and the economy was remonetized after a disastrous bout of barter.[57] Transparency was emphasized in the domestic energy market and tax collections were improved.[58] Agriculture was formally decollectivized and over the ensuing eight years Ukraine became a country of large estates controlled both by private agribusiness and old collective farm managers operating in new structures.[59] Large industrial firms, especially those in the energy and utilities sectors, were sold to private companies both at home and abroad (mostly Russian firms). This process had already been ongoing in 1998–2000, but became fairer after 2000.[60] The substitution of token registration fees and taxes for more complicated arrangements encouraged small businesses to exit the informal sector and participate in the formal economy: "As a consequence, the number of single entrepreneurs swiftly skyrocketed to an estimated 2.7 million by 1999, and 250,000 enterprises had 1 to 10 employees."[61] Small- and medium-sized enterprises were also cultivated by reducing excessive regulations. The number of state agencies was cut and streamlined. Licensing was reduced and simplified.

It is difficult to see how any of these generic regulatory, tax and policy measures mostly initiated before the 100-day reform program began could have changed anything fundamental in the underlying rent-granting demand/supply equation,[62] especially when Yushchenko was ousted in April 2000, and Yulia Tymoshenko (minister of energy, 30 December 1999–19 January 2001)[63] arrested in February 2001, accused of three crimes committed during her time as a gas trader in 1996–97. Åslund attributes the miracle to the fact that Yushchenko's reforms were "legislated." Good laws, he insists, allowed Yushchenko's bland reforms to clip the oligarchs' wings and eradicate Ukraine's rent-granting society,[64] but this invisible victory if it occurred,[65] was ephemeral and cannot plausibly justify attributing Ukraine's post-2000 growth spurt to fundamental domestic economic and democratic political reforms.

Perhaps, there is another domestic explanation. A series of demonstrations from November 2004 through January 2005 and known as the "Orange Revolution" (*Pomarancheva revolyutsiya*) toppled Viktor Yanukovych's government via a court-mandated run-off election, and raised hopes for democracy and fundamental economic reform.[66] Viktor Yushchenko, who as prime minister had overseen the 100 days reform in early 2000, was elected president with 52 percent of the ballot.

His victory and the empowerment of Parliament have been portrayed as a blow for Ukrainian democracy,[67] representing the people's triumph over insider vote rigging. As such they can be praised as a milestone in a march from an oligarchic variant of "sovereign democracy" toward a liberal governance system more responsive to the people's will, but they failed to advance the cause of post-Soviet Ukrainian economic transition because the people were split over how to redesign the core economic system. Democracy for westernizing liberals was synonymous with laissez-faire. It implied individual economic empowerment (eradication of oligarchic rent-granting) and Ukraine's eventual absorption into the European Union. Democracy for easternizing social democrats, socialists and communists was synonymous with state paternalism, Surkov's "sovereign democracy" and Putin's "enlightened conservatism."[68] It implied collectivist empowerment and the rejection of the EU as Ukraine's common home.

The Orange Revolution's democratic victory consequently proved to be a fatal obstacle to progressive post-Soviet Ukrainian economic systems building. It paralyzed neoliberal economic reform without advancing the cause of a well-functioning alternative, as parliamentarians and oligarchs battled over socioeconomic inclusion and exclusion.[69] The global financial crisis of 2008 exacerbated matters further by pitting rival westernizers and easternizers (neoliberals versus collectivists) against each other in a struggle over a shrinking pie.

Yushchenko did adopt liberal legislation to accelerate privatization, but to no one's surprise the process came to benefit oligarchs. Most big enterprises were sold via closed discount cash sales:

Today, without an effective legal system, all property remains insecure. Violent corporate raiding is widespread; oligarchs use mafia muscle to take over each other's firms and scare away most foreign investors. The black economy accounts for 40 to 50 percent of official GDP. Ukraine has received support from international financial institutions, but these funds have been small relative to Ukraine's GDP. The country's failure to enact reforms has repeatedly marred its relationship with the International Monetary Fund.[70]

The economic distress inadvertently caused by the Orange Revolution and the global financial crisis eventually pushed the electorate away from laissez-faire and toward social protectionism, culminating in a tidal political shift against Yushchenko who received only 5 percent of the residential electoral vote in 2010. Yanukovych regained political control on a unity platform that promised an end to the rancor, but he could not fulfill his promise. Instead, he curtailed freedom of assembly, increased executive control over the judiciary and used the security and tax services to harass activists, paving the way toward Euromaiden (political and civic confrontation in Yevromaidan Square) in autumn 2013, Russia's annexation of the Crimea on March 21, 2014, and continued domestic and foreign strife. At the end of the day, Russia and the Ukraine have been polarized into two distinct systems. Russia is a relatively stable multi-ethnic unitary state with a "sovereign democratic," "enlightened conservative" ideocracy that harkens back to Tsar Nicholas II's Russian empire. It is a nuclear superpower sustained by an authoritarian rent-granting economic system. Ukraine is a failed non-nuclear state with a divided polis and weak president ruled on an insider basis by rival regional oligarchic clans—a recipe for dismemberment and annexation.

The World Bank Group and other international organizations don't dispute this assessment,[71] but consider recent setbacks as just another air pocket of turbulence on the flight path to democracy and free enterprise with compassionate social characteristics. They contend against weighty evidence that Ukraine is a "normal" middle-income developing country, rough around the edges, that can reach the promised land by adhering to bland generic remedies.[72] They preach fiscal responsibility, monetary discipline and balanced international payments to achieve and sustain macroeconomic equilibrium. They counsel eliminating subsidies and tariffs to improve microeconomic efficiency and stress the need for improved corporate governance and competitiveness.[73] They recommend good state governance, modernization, enhanced innovation, better public health and social justice initiatives. There is nothing wrong with this advice. Better factor allocation, technology and diffusion, management, production, retail distribution and transfers will always improve economic performance regardless of the economic system, but the counsel misreads Ukraine's systemic plight.

Kyiv has failed to construct a satisfactory economic mechanism to replace the Soviet-era command economy. It has transformed the informal Muscovite rent-granting arrangements based on guaranteed state purchase, managerial bonus incentives and spurious innovation (hidden inflation) that underlay Soviet administrative command planning into a condominium of regional oligarchic clans that expend their energies struggling to expand their turf behind the faux politics of liberalization rather than promoting competitive efficiency. Ukraine's system has been recast in this sense, but the country has failed to transition to democratic free enterprise.[74] Lawmakers have created a constitution and laws, but economic actors don't abide by them. They have established property rights, but they are restrictive and biased in favor of privilege rather than competitive efficiency. The government praises profit-seeking, but promotes productivity depressing rival clan rent-granting. There is balloting, but no well-functioning democracy. In short, Ukraine's clan variant of Ivan Grozny's Muscovy has triumphed over liberal idealism and placed the nation's survival in jeopardy. According to the Heritage Foundation's Index of Economic Freedom, Ukraine ranks one-hundred and sixty-second in economic freedom, just ahead of Myanmar and behind Bolivia! It is the most illiberal economy in the European region.[75]

Primary responsibility for this bleak outcome lies with Ukraine's politicians. They could have soberly assessed the perils of transformation and among other alternatives, emulated Beijing, Slovakia, or even Putin's power vertical.[76] Outsiders, however, also share the blame.[77] The US, the EU, Poland, Lithuania and the Baltic states, under the cover of their institutions (including the G-7 and the World Bank Group) have striven for diverse reasons to prepare Ukraine for financial, economic and military absorption into the West (OECD, EU, NATO).[78] Their primary hidden agenda initially was to complete the mop-up phase of post-communist destruction after Gorbachev, Yeltsin, Kravchuk and Shushkevich dissolved the USSR and repressed their national communist parties.[79] Thereafter, they concentrated on coaching Ukraine about the virtues of financial integration and trade integration with the West, the requirements for EU accession, and benefits of NATO membership.[80]

Russia, nursing its wounds after losing the Cold War,[81] initially tried to salvage whatever relationships it could with its former tsarist vassal based on ethnic ties and residual economic interests. This passivity however was short lived. Putin's restoration of Russia's power vertical and great power in response to what he deemed Gorbachev's and Yeltsin's stab in the USSR's back soon revived the Kremlin's dreams for re-establishing a sphere of influence, economic advantage and re-annexation.[82] Moscow meddled in Ukraine's internal affairs formally and informally through state and oligarchic channels to assert its imperial authority and to repulse western poaching.

Ukraine, as too often had been the case, became a battleground between the western cultural zone and resurgent Muscovy to Kyiv's detriment. Although Putin still pays lip service to the World Bank Group's economic mantras, he has crossed the Rubicon and will not be constrained by the idea of the West.[83] This means that, if the *vozhd* prevails, Ukraine cannot accede to the EU, cannot enjoy the consolation prize status of a dual East–West protectorate, or transition to democratic free enterprise, and will be fortunate to survive intact.[84] The Kremlin is striking back![85]

Current economic prospects

Ukraine's economic performance since the global financial crisis has been bleak and deteriorated further after Russia's annexation of Crimea. The data are suspect, conflicting and must be taken with a bucket of salt;[86] nonetheless, the consensus estimates are illuminating. According to Focus Economics,[87] a for-profit international consulting firm, Ukraine's population declined 6 percent 2010–15. Its GDP plummeted 15 percent in 2009;[88] another 5 percent 2010–14,[89] before falling 17.2 percent in the first quarter of 2015,[90] and was expected to plunge 9.5 percent for the entire year.[91] Consumption dropped 9.6 percent and investment 23.1 percent in 2014, while unemployment burgeoned to 9.3 percent and inflation soared to 12.1 percent. The Ukrainian hyrvnia at the end of June 2015 was 62 percent below its 2010 value.[92] Public debt skyrocketed 75 percent after 2010 from 40.1 to 70.1 percent of GDP in 2014, and is forecast to increase to 135 percent in 2015,[93] threatening a "Greek tragedy."[94] Ukrainian and IMF sources tell a broadly similar story.[95]

These disastrous results occurred despite substantial on-again/off-again financial assistance both from the EU and Russia,[96] and purported progress in liberalizing its economic system.[97] While more assistance is on its way, it may well be offset by a looming debt crisis that threatens to seriously exacerbate matters. As part of the Minsk II process, the IMF agreed to provide a new financial rescue package worth $17.5 billion in February 2015, bringing the international community's total bailout commitment to $40 billion.[98] This constitutes the country's fourth bailout in ten years, and comes on the heels of the April 2014 rescue program that failed to stabilize Ukraine's finances as it battled pro-Russian separatists in the east.[99]

Four months after the deal was initialed, however, it was already in tatters because it was unrealistic from the outset. The IMF rescue which imposes austerity as a quid pro quo for liquidity without providing long-term investment support was predicated on the implausible assumption that the "primary" budget deficit (which excludes interest repayments) would disappear entirely by 2016, "setting debt on a firm downward path."[100]

This is wishful thinking. The IMF expects Ukraine to achieve a Greek level of adjustment that took four years, in just one, by cutting the massive deficit of Naftogaz. It assumes that Ukraine will double domestic gas prices to eliminate the losses on gas imports, but the trimming is still nowhere in sight. IMF predictions for economic growth are similarly optimistic.

The prognosis therefore is grim. The IMF is bleeding its patient to make it well, with a high probability that the cure will be worse than the disease. It is providing liquidity, but doing little to eradicate the roving banditry that makes Ukraine's economy inferior to China's and Russia's.[101] Although this may be better than doing nothing, President Petro Poroshenko's four-year reform program and the IMF's assistance do not appear to pose a serious deterrent to Putin's great power restoration campaign.

Notes

1 The Soviet Union created the Moldavian SSR from parts of the Ukrainian SSR and Bessarabia and North Bukovina, both spoils of the infamous Molotov-Ribbentrop "non-aggression" treaty, August 23, 1939. The Baltic states (Estonia, Latvia and Lithuania) were annexed and transformed into Soviet Socialist Republics in 1940.

2 Stalin negotiated two additional UN seats for the Soviet Union: Ukraine and Belarus. Britain received a seat for colonial India, and the US one for the Philippines.

3 In addition to almost the entire territory of modern Russia, prior to 1917 the Russian Empire included most of Ukraine (Dnieper Ukraine), Belarus, Moldova (Bessarabia), Finland (Grand Principality of Finland), Armenia, Azerbaijan, Georgia (including Mengrelia), the Central Asian states of Kazakhstan, Kyrgyzstan, Tajikistan, Turkmenistan and Uzbekistan (Russian Turkestan), most of Lithuania, Estonia and Latvia (Baltic provinces), as well as a significant portion of Poland (Kingdom of Poland) and Ardahan, Artvin, Iğdır, Kars and northeastern part of Erzurum from Turkey (then part of the Ottoman Empire).

4 According to the 1st article of the Organic Law, the Russian Empire was one indivisible state. In addition, the 26th article stated that "With the Imperial Russian throne are indivisible the Kingdom of Poland and Grand Principality of Finland."

5 Richard Sakwa, *Soviet Politics in Perspective*, London: Routledge, 1998, second edn.; Richard Pipes, *The Formation of the Soviet Union, Communism and Nationalism, 1917–1923*, Cambridge MA: Harvard University Press, 1997.

6 Novorossiya (New Russia) included Odessa, Donetsk, Dnepropetrovsk and Nikolayev: Nick Robins-Early, "Here's Why Putin Calling Eastern Ukraine 'Novorossiya' Is Important," *The Huffington Post*, April 18, 2014. http://www.huffingtonpost.com/2014/04/18/putin-novorossiya-ukraine_n_5173559.html#es_share_ended.

7 Kievan Rus begins with the rule (882–912) of Prince Oleg, who extended his control from Novgorod south along the Dnieper River valley in order to protect trade from Khazar incursions from the east and moved his capital to the more strategic Kiev. Sviatoslav I (died 972) achieved the first major expansion of Kievan Rus's territorial control, fighting a war of conquest against the Khazar Empire. Vladimir the Great (980–1015) introduced Christianity with his own baptism and, by decree, that of all the inhabitants of Kiev and beyond. Kievan Rus reached its greatest extent under Yaroslav I (1019–54); his sons assembled and issued its first written legal code, the Rus Justice, shortly after his death. The state declined beginning in the late eleventh century and during the twelfth century, disintegrating into various rival regional powers. It was further weakened by economic factors such as the collapse of Rus commercial ties to Byzantium due to the decline of Constantinople and the accompanying diminution of trade routes through its territory. The state finally fell to the Mongol invasion of the 1240s.

8 The Rurik dynasty was founded by the Varangian (Viking) prince Rurik, who established himself in Novgorod around the year 862 AD. The Rurikids were the ruling dynasty of Kievan Rus (after 862), the successor principalities of Galicia-Volhynia (after 1199), Chernigov, Vladimir-Suzdal and the Grand Duchy of Moscow, and the founders of the Tsardom of Russia.

9 The word "Rus" in this context means the people of Rus, which were East Slavic tribes living in Ruthenia. At its greatest extent in the mid-eleventh century, it stretched from the Baltic Sea in the north to the Black Sea in the south and from the headwaters of the Vistula in the west to the Taman Peninsula in the east.

10 Cossacks were mostly made up of Ukrainian serfs who preferred the dangerous freedom of the Wild Steppes, rather than life under the rule of Polish aristocrats. However, many serfs from Poland and Muscovy and even Tatars from Crimea could become part of the Cossack host. There were certain tests they had to pass, including accepting Orthodoxy as their religion, crossing themselves and reciting the Creed and other prayers.

11 Andrew Wilson, *The Ukrainians: Unexpected Nation*, New Haven, CT: Yale University Press, 2000.

12 "Crimean Tatars not granted status of indigenous population of Ukraine": *Novosti*, April 11, 2014: http://voiceofrussia.com/news/2014_04_11/Crimean-Tatars-not-granted-status-of-indigenous-population-of-Ukraine-3799/.

13 *Modern History Sourcebook: The Molotov-Ribbentrop Pact, 1939*: http://www. fordham.edu/halsall/mod/1939pact.html—"The three heads of Government consider that the eastern frontier of Poland should follow the Curzon Line with digressions from it in some regions of five to eight kilometers in favor of Poland. They recognize that Poland must receive substantial accessions in territory in the north and west. They feel that the opinion of the new Polish Provisional Government of National Unity should be sought in due course of the extent of these accessions and that the final delimitation of the western frontier of Poland should thereafter await the peace conference."

14 *Modern History Sourcebook: The Yalta Conference, February 1945.* The Curzon Line gave the Soviet Union the cities of Lwov, Stanislavawov, Brzesc, Baranowicze and Wizno, while Poland received Gdansk, Szczecin and Woclaw. The Curzon Line was put forward by the Supreme War Council after World War I as the demarcation line between the Second Polish Republic and Bolshevik Russia, and was supposed to serve as the basis for a future border.

15 United States Congress, *The December 1, 1991 Referendum/Presidential Election in Ukraine* (A Report Prepared by the Staff of the Commission on Security and Cooperation in Europe), 1992, p. 2: http://www.google.com/url?sa=t&rct=j&q=&esrc= s&source=web&cd=13&ved=0CG8QFjAM&url=http%3A%2F%2Fcsce. gov%2Findex.cfm%3FFuseAction%3DFiles.Download%26FileStore_ id%3D297&ei=jxlRU6LYMMmnsQS-sIHgBw&usg=AFQjCNHx62W05zpwiYDW̄ mrDK9DDDBLiYzQ&bvm=bv.65058239,d.cWcOn.

16 These general principles were eroded after *perestroika* began in 1987.

17 Steven Rosefielde, *Russian Economy from Lenin to Putin*, New York: Wiley, 2007.

18 "Soviet Communist Party gives up monopoly on political power—History.com This Day in History—2/7/1990": http://www.history.com/this-day-in-history/soviet-communist-party-gives-up-monopoly-on-political-power.

19 Bill Keller, "Upheaval in the East: The Baltic Bind; Lithuania Seems to Dare Gorbachev to Act and He Seems Only to Harden Its Resolve," *New York Times*, March 24, 1990: http://www.nytimes.com/1990/03/24/world/upheaval-east-baltic-bind-lithuania-seems-dare-gorbachev-act-he-seems-only.html.

20 "1991: March Referendum," SovietHistory.org: The Baltics, Armenia, Georgia, Checheno-Ingushetia (an autonomous republic within Russia that had a strong desire for independence, and Moldova boycotted the referendum. In each of the other nine republics, a majority of the voters supported the retention of the renewed Soviet Union.

21 United States Congress, *The December 1, 1991 Referendum/Presidential Election in Ukraine.*

22 Olexiy Haran, "Disintegration of the Soviet Union and the US Position on the Independence of Ukraine," Belfer Center, Discussion Paper 95-09, 1995.

23 United States Congress, *The December 1, 1991 Referendum/Presidential Election in Ukraine*, p. 2. The Commission on Security and Cooperation in Europe (CSCE), also known as the Helsinki Commission, is a US government agency created in 1976 to monitor and encourage compliance with the agreements of the OSCE. The Commission consists of nine members from the US House of Representatives, nine members from the US Senate, and one member each from the Departments of State, Defense and Commerce. The positions of chair and co-chair are shared by the House and Senate and rotate every two years, when a new Congress convenes. A professional staff assists the commissioners in their work.

24 Yoji Koyama, *EU's Eastward Enlargement: Central and Eastern Europe's Strategies for Development*, Singapore: World Scientific Publishers, 2015.

25 Ukraine however never ratified the agreement and is merely a "participating state." On March 14, 2014, a bill was introduced to Ukraine's Parliament to withdraw from the CIS following the annexation of Crimea by Russia: "Bill introduced to withdraw

Ukraine from CIS," *Kyiv Post*, March 15, 2014: http://www.kyivpost.com/content/politics/bill-introduced-to-withdraw-ukraine-from-cis-339433.html.

26 The G-7 and World Bank Group opted initially for "shock therapy": http://www.larouchepub.com/eiw/public/1998/eirv25n32-19980814/eirv25n32-19980814_056-how_imf_shock_therapy_was_impose.pdf. Shock therapy meant abolishing administrative command planning without regard for macroeconomic stabilization. Later, the G-7 and World Bank Group reversed polarities stressing macro management while cheerleading for competition. General Mikhail Kalashnikov wrote that "We did not lose from the Americans. It was our party bosses who stabbed us in the back with a dagger. The vermin of the nomenclatura and the young communists killed us." See Marcel Van Herpen, *Putinism: The Slow Rise of a Radical Right Regime in Russia*, New York: Rowman & Littlefield Publishers, 2014, p. 58.

27 Many Russians nurture the idea that the Soviet Union was destroyed by a stab-in-the-back, and are using the notion to justify the annexation of Novorossiya. The analogy is to the German nationalist claim that Germany's defeat in World War I was caused by republicans' betrayal of the Kaiser, an idea exploited by Hitler. The post-Soviet variant blames Gorbachev, Yeltsin, Kravchuk, Shushkevich (the *zapadniki*) and western agents for the Soviet Union's destruction. Current efforts to try Gorbachev for high treason are part of this process.

28 United States Congress, *The December 1, 1991 Referendum/Presidential Election in Ukraine*, p. 9. Kravchuk's secessionist party had endorsed denuclearization before Ukrainian independence, but this needn't have been any more binding than his commitment to privatization and democracy.

29 Ukraine had the world's third largest nuclear arsenal, larger than Britain's, France's and China's combined. On June 1, 1996, Ukraine became a non-nuclear nation when it sent the last of its 1,900 strategic nuclear warheads to Russia for dismantling. In return for giving up its nuclear weapons, Ukraine, the United States, Russia and the United Kingdom signed the 1994 Budapest Memorandum on Security Assurances, pledging to respect Ukraine territorial integrity, a pledge that was broken by Russia's 2014 invasion of Crimea. Belarus and Kazakhstan also transferred their nuclear weapons to Russia. Belarus had 81 single warhead missiles stationed on its territory after the Soviet Union collapsed in 1991. They were all transferred to Russia by 1996. In May 1992, Belarus acceded to the Nuclear Non-Proliferation Treaty. Kazakhstan inherited 1,400 nuclear weapons from the Soviet Union, and transferred them all to Russia by 1995. Kazakhstan has since acceded to the Nuclear Non-Proliferation Treaty. Strobe Talbott was a key player in the US's effort to make the Ukraine a non-nuclear state. See Sarah Mend, "The View From Above: An Insider's Take on Clinton's Russia Policy," *Foreign Affairs*, July/August 2002. Rose Gottemoeller, former US assistant secretary of state and new START negotiator insists the US wisely counseled Ukraine to denuclearize, and has honored its Budapest Memorandum. See "US rejects criticism of historic Ukraine nuclear deal," *AFP*, December 5, 2014: http://news.yahoo.com/us-rejects-criticism-historic-ukraine-nuclear-deal-213809874.html—"Rose Gottemoeller, head of arms control and international security for the US government, said her country 'has gone every step towards continuing to defend and develop a means of bolstering Ukraine.' Gottemoeller, who was a negotiator at the Budapest talks 20 years ago, sidestepped questions from reporters on whether Ukraine would have been spared a Russian invasion if it still had nuclear weapons."

30 Olexiy Haran, "Disintegration of the Soviet Union and the US Position on the Independence of Ukraine," Belfer Center, Discussion Paper 95-09, 1995.

31 Anatoliy Bondar and Boo Lilje, *Land Privatization in Ukraine*, Fig. XXII International Congress; Washington, DC, April 19–26, 2002: https://www.fig.net/pub/fig_2002/Ts7-6/TS7_6_bondar_lilje.pdf.

32 Steven Rosefielde and Quinn Mills, *Democracy and Its Elected Enemies*, Cambridge: Cambridge University Press, 2013.

33 Russia has been a rent-granting "public service" business since the rise of Muscovy under Ivan III Vasilevich, known as Ivan the Great (1440–1505), the Grand Prince of Moscow, the "gatherer of Russian lands," and Grand Prince of all the Rus. Ivan the Terrible (1530–84), Russia's first tsar crowned with the Monomakh Cap in 1547, and all his successors rent-granted, taxed, decreed, price and wage fixed, administrated, supervised, managed, regulated, and contracted to enrich themselves, while posing as selfless protectors of the Russian people. See Alexander Gerschenkron, "Russia: Patterns and Problems of Economic Development, 1861–1958," in Alexander Gerschenkron (ed.), *Economic Backwardness in Historical Perspective*, Cambridge MA: Harvard University Press, 1962, pp. 119–51; and Steven Rosefielde and Stefan Hedlund, *Russia Since 1980*, Cambridge: Cambridge University Press, 2009.

34 The lion's share of Soviet tax revenues were generated by "turnover" taxes levied on enterprise production at the wholesale level. When production plummeted due to the abolition of planning and guaranteed purchase, turnover over tax revenue nosedived.

35 Athena was the goddess of wisdom, courage, inspiration, civilization, law and justice, just warfare, mathematics, strength, strategy, the arts, crafts and skill.

36 Peter Murrell, "What Is Shock Therapy? What Did It Do in Poland and Russia," *Post-Soviet Affairs*, Vol. 9, No. 2, 1993, pp. 111–40: http://econ-server.umd.edu/~murrell/articles/What%20is%20Shock%20Therapy.pdf.

37 Josef Brada and Arthur King, "Is there a J-curve for the Economic Transition from Socialism to Capitalism," *Economics of Planning*, Vol. 25, No. 1, 1992, pp. 37–53.

38 Paul Krugman, *The Return of Depression Economics and the Crisis of 2008*, New York: W.W. Norton Company, 2009; and Lawrence Summers, "Washington Must Not Settle for Secular Stagnation," *Financial Times*, December 5, 2013: http://www.ft.com/cms/s/2/ba0f1386-7169-11e3-8f92-00144feabdc0.html#ixzz2pi6xfiEe.

39 Post-Soviet Ukraine initially relied on Russia's ruble for its currency and soon found itself mired in the hyperinflation caused by Yeltsin's excessive money printing.

40 The government reported "registered unemployment" which was negligible when the real figure exceeded 20 percent. See Steven Rosefielde, "The Civilian Labor Force and Unemployment in the Russian Federation," *Europe-Asia Studies*, Vol. 52, No. 8, December 2000, pp. 1433–47.

41 Katrin Elborgh-Woytek and Mark Lewis, "Privatization in Ukraine: Challenges of Assessment and Coverage in Fund Conditionality," IMF Policy Discussion Paper, PDP/02/7, May 2002, pp. 2–3: http://www.imf.org/external/pubs/ft/pdp/2002/pdp07.pdf.

42 Paul Hare, Mohammed Ishaq and Saul Estrin, "The Legacies of Central Planning and the Transition to a Market Economy: Ukrainian Contradictions," *CERT*, October 1996, pp. 1–26: http://www.sml.hw.ac.uk/downloads/cert/wpa/1996/dp9618.pdf.

43 Clifford Gaddy and Barry Ickes, *Bear Traps on Russia's Road to Modernization*, London: Routledge, 2013.

44 Steven Rosefielde, "The Illusion of Westernization in Russia and China," *Comparative Economic Studies*, Vol. 49, 2007, pp. 495–513; and Yoji Koyama, *EU's Eastward Enlargement: Central and Eastern Europe's Strategies for Development*, Singapore: World Scientific Publishers, 2015.

45 Paul Hare, Mohammed Ishaq and Saul Estrin, "The Legacies of Central Planning and the Transition to a Market Economy: Ukrainian Contradictions," *CERT*, October 1996, p. 10.

46 Ronald Mckinnon, *The Order of Economic Liberalization: Financial Control in the Transition to a Market Economy*, Baltimore, MD: Johns Hopkins University Press, 1992.

47 Anders Åslund, *How Ukraine Became a Market Economy and Democracy*, Washington, DC: Peterson Institute for International Economics, 2009.

48 Oleksandr Kramar, "We Were 52 Million: Where Did 6 Million Ukrainians Go?" *The Ukrainian Week*, March 14, 2012: http://ukrainianweek.com/Society/43071—"Based

on official statistics, the Ukrainian population has shrunk by 6.2mn people from 51.8 to 45.6mn since 1990." The decline is evenly concentrated in the 1990s and new millennium. The decline was 12 percent compared with 1.3 percent for Russia. Excess deaths in Russia were more severe than suggested, masked by in-migration from other parts of the former USSR. See Steven Rosefielde, "Premature Deaths: Russia's Radical Transition," *Europe-Asia Studies*, Vol. 53, No. 8, December 2001, pp. 1159–76.

49 Angus Maddison, *The World Economy: Historical Statistics*, Paris: OECD, 2003, Table D-3c, p. 341. Cf. The World Bank, "GDP per capita growth (annual %)": http://data.worldbank.org/indicator/NY.GDP.PCAP.KD.ZG.

50 *FDI in Ukraine: New Approach*, OECD, 2009: oecd.org/globalrelations/psd/43361570.pdf.

51 Ibid.

52 Most of the Russian contribution came indirectly from Cyprus.

53 Pekka Sutela, "The Underachiever: Ukraine's Economy Since 1991," *Carnegie Endowment for International Peace*, March 9, 2012: http://carnegieendowment.org/2012/03/09/underachiever-ukraine-s-economy-since-1991/a1nf#.

54 Anders Åslund, *How Ukraine Become a Market Economy and Democracy*, Washington, DC: Peterson Institute for International Economics, 2009, p. 128: piie.com/publications/chapters_preview/4273/05iie4273.pdf. Leonid Kuchma appointed Viktor Yushchenko prime minister December 22, 1999, a post held until April 2000 when he was ousted. Åslund claims that in a mere hundred days Yushchenko instituted deep reforms, including the government itself, state finances, energy trade, agricultural land privatization, large privatizations and deregulation of small firms that transformed Kuchma's system into a productive economy.

55 Ibid.

56 Ibid., pp. 133–5: "Ukraine introduced regular weekly cabinet meetings. Four government commissions were set up within the cabinet, each headed by one of the four deputy prime ministers. Any government decision had to be prepared by one of these commissions, and the respective deputy prime minister was held personally responsible."

57 Anders Åslund, *How Ukraine Become a Market Economy and Democracy*, Washington, DC: Peterson Institute for International Economics, 2009, pp. 135–7: piie.com/publications/chapters_preview/4273/05iie4273.pdf. Barter has emerged as a rational response to hyper-inflation throughout the post-Soviet economic space and was eventually eliminated everywhere by responsible money emission.

58 Ibid., pp. 135–7: "Yushchenko invited the dissident oligarch Yuliya Tymoshenko to battle her previous competitors as deputy prime minister for energy . . . Tymoshenko knew all the tricks of the gas trade and did her utmost to clean it up."

59 Ibid., pp. 139–40: "Initially, most land was leased back to the old managers of the state and collective farms for minimal payment, but much of the land went to private plots, private farms, and increasingly to large commercial holdings." By 2008 several agrofirms had accumulated a few hundred thousand hectares of land, and they occupied about half of the agricultural land. Ukraine had become a country of large estates. The remaining quarter or so of agricultural land was still controlled by the old state and collective farm managers." "Land Grabs in the Black Earth: Ukrainian Oligarchs and International Investors," October 30, 2013: http://www.boell.de/en/2013/10/30/land-grabs-black-earth-ukrainian-oligarchs-and-international-investors—"Only with the adoption of the presidential decree in December 1999 was the land officially given to the approximately 7 million rural habitants and the leasing of land started. In 2001, the Land Code came into force, which officially guaranteed land titles. Yet, at the same time, a moratorium on the sale and purchase of farmland was introduced. This has been extended several times and is now in place until 1 January 2016."

60 Anders Åslund, *How Ukraine Become a Market Economy and Democracy*, pp. 140–1: "By 2000 the EBRD (2000) assessed that the private sector generated 60 percent of Ukraine's GDP."

61 Ibid., p. 142.
62 Gertrude Schroeder, "Soviet Economic 'Reform' Decrees: More Steps on the Treadmill," In *The Soviet Economy in the 1980s: Problems and Prospects*, Vol. 1, Washington, DC: Joint Economic Committee of the Congress of the United States, 1982, pp. 79–84.
63 Tymoshenko was prime minister of Ukraine twice: 24 January 2005–8 September 2005, and 18 December 2007–4 March 2010.
64 Anders Åslund, *How Ukraine Become a Market Economy and Democracy*, pp. 149–50.
65 Andrew Wilson, *Political and Economic Lessons From Democratic Transitions*, New York: Council on Foreign Relations Press, 2013: "In December 1999, an impending balance of payments crisis forced Kuchma to appoint a reformist prime minister, Viktor Yushchenko. Yushchenko's reforms boosted growth, but this enriched the oligarchs and made them harder to dislodge."
66 Yanukovich was governor of Donetsk May 14, 1997–November 21, 2002, prime minister of the Ukraine twice—November 21, 2002–January 5, 2005 and December 28, 2004–January 5, 2005—and president of Ukraine February 25, 2010—February 22, 2014. Tymoshenko was prime minister under his Presidential regime.
67 As part of the Orange Revolution, the Ukrainian Constitution was changed to shift powers from the presidency to the Parliament. This was the Speaker Verkhovna Rada Oleksandr Moroz's price for his decisive role in winning Yushchenko the presidency. The communists also supported these measures.
68 For a discussion of "enlightened conservatism" (*prosveshchyonnyi conservatism*), see Tatiana Stanovaya, "In Search of Lost Ideology," *Institute of Modern Russia*, April 25, 2014: http://www.imrussia.org/en/society/725-in-search-of-lost-ideology— "Alexander Shirinyants is known for writing extensively in his doctoral dissertation about the 'possibility of forming a new ideology in Russia without adopting any Western models.' He also emphasized the concept of 'social conservatism, combining the patriotism and loyalty of cultural conservatism with the social idea of the right to a decent life, solidarity, and justice.' The audience will be offered the doctrines of such ideologists of conservatism as Nikolai Berdyaev, Ivan Ilyin, Lev Tikhomirov, Nikolai Danilevski, Metropolitan Philaret (Drozdov), and Konstantin Pobedonostsev." On "sovereign democracy" (*suveryennaya demokratiya*), see Vladislav Surkov, "Transcript of a speech by the Deputy Head of the Administration of the President of Russia, aide to the president of the Russian Federation, Vladislav Surkov for the centre of partisan study and preparation of the staff of 'United Russian'," February 7, 2006. According to Vladislav Surkov, sovereign democracy is a society's political life where the political powers, their authorities and decisions are decided and controlled by a diverse Russian nation for the purpose of reaching material welfare, freedom and fairness by all citizens, social groups and nationalities, by the people that formed it. Surkov's "sovereign democracy" isn't democratic at all, because the leader decides what the people want, rather than the people doing it themselves through the ballot box.
69 Andrew Wilson, *Political and Economic Lessons From Democratic Transitions*: "Yanukovych's Party of Regions won the parliamentary election in 2006, creating a coalition government with the Socialists and the Communists under his leadership. As a result, President Viktor Yushchenko had to deal with a powerful Prime Minister Viktor Yanukovych who had control of many important portfolios. His premiership ended in late 2007 after Yushchenko had succeeded in his months-long attempt to dissolve parliament. After the election, Yanukovych's party again was the largest, but Tymoshenko's finished far ahead of Yushchenko's for second place. The Orange parties won a very narrow majority, permitting a new government under Tymoshenko, but Yushchenko's political decline continued to his poor showing in the 2010 presidential election."
70 Ibid.

71 European Bank for Reconstruction and Development, *Country Assessments: Ukraine*, 2013: http://tr.ebrd.com/tr13/en/country-assessments/3/ukraine; *World Bank Group— Ukraine Partnership: Country Program Snapshot*, April 2014: worldbank.org/content/dam/Worldbank/document/Ukraine-Snapshot.pdf.

72 Andrei Shleifer and Daniel Treisman. "A Normal Country," *Foreign Affairs*, Vol. 83, No. 2, 2004, pp. 20–39; Andrei Shleifer, *A Normal Country: Russia after Communism*, Cambridge, MA: Harvard University Press, 2005.

73 World Bank, *Ukraine System of Financial Oversight and Governance of State-Owned Enterprises*, Report No. 59950-UA, February 22, 2011: http://www wds.worldbank.org/external/default/WDSContentServer/WDSP/IB/2012/05/21/000425970_20120521113855/Rendered/PDF/599500ESW0P1120mance0budgeting0MTEF.pdf; *World Bank Group—Ukraine Partnership: Country Program Snapshot*, April 2014.

74 Shock therapy had the same effect in the Balkans. See Yoji Koyama, *EU's Eastward Enlargement: Central and Eastern Europe's Strategies for Development*, Singapore: World Scientific Publishers, 2015.

75 Heritage Foundation 2015 Index of Economic Freedom: http://www.heritage.org/index/country/ukraine.

76 Steven Rosefielde, "The Illusion of Westernization in Russia and China," *Comparative Economic Studies*, Vol. 49, 2007, pp. 495–13; and Steven Rosefielde, *Asian Economic Systems*, Singapore: World Scientific Publishers, 2013. An extensive literature on the decisive role of the state in economic development also weighed against shock therapy. See Yoji Koyama, *EU's Eastward Enlargement: Central and Eastern Europe's Strategies for Development*, Singapore: World Scientific Publishers, 2015; and Alice Amsden, Jacek Kochanowicz and Lance Taylor, *The Market Meets Its Match: Restructuring the Economies of Eastern Europe*, Cambridge MA: Harvard University Press, 1994.

77 United States Congress, *The December 1, 1991 Referendum/Presidential Election in Ukraine* (A Report Prepared by the Staff of the Commission on Security and Cooperation in Europe), 1992, p. 2. http://www.google.com/url?sa=t&rct=j&q=&esrc=s&source=web&cd=13&ved=0CG8QFjAM&url=http%3A%2F%2Fcsce.gov%2Findex.cfm%3FFuseAction%3DFiles.Download%26FileStore_id%3D297&ei=jxlRU6LYMMmnsQS-sIHgBw&usg=AFQjCNHx62W05zpwiYDWmrDK9DDDBLiYzQ&bvm=bv.65058239,d.cWcOn.

78 Jonathan Marcus, "Ukraine Crisis: Transcript of Leaked Nuland-Pyatt Call," *BBC*, February 7, 2014. www.bbc.com/news/world-europe-26079957: "An apparently bugged phone conversation in which a senior US diplomat disparages the EU over the Ukraine crisis has been posted online. The alleged conversation between Assistant Secretary of State Victoria Nuland and the US Ambassador to Ukraine, Geoffrey Pyatt, appeared on YouTube on Thursday. It is not clearly when the alleged conversation took place. Voice thought to be Pyatt's: 'I think we're in play. The Klitschko [Vitaly Klitschko, one of three main opposition leaders] piece is obviously the complicated electron here. Especially the announcement of him as deputy prime minister and you've seen some of my notes on the troubles in the marriage right now so we're trying to get a read really fast on where he is on this stuff. But I think your argument to him, which you'll need to make, I think that's the next phone call you want to set up, is exactly the one you made to Yats [Arseniy Yatseniuk, another opposition leader]. And I'm glad you sort of put him on the spot on where he fits in this scenario. And I'm very glad that he said what he said in response.' [Jonathan Marcus writes:] The US says that it is working with all sides in the crisis to reach a peaceful solution, noting that 'ultimately it is up to the Ukrainian people to decide their future. However this transcript suggests that the US has very clear ideas about what the outcome should be and is striving to achieve these goals. Russian spokesmen have insisted that the US is meddling in Ukraine's affairs—no more than Moscow, the cynic might say—but Washington clearly has its own game-plan. The clear purpose in leaking this conversation is to

embarrass Washington and for audiences susceptible to Moscow's message to portray the US as interfering in Ukraine's domestic affairs. Nuland: 'Good. I don't think Klitsch should go into the government. I don't think it's necessary, I don't think it's a good idea. Anti-government protesters in Kiev, anti-government protesters have been camped out in Kiev since November.' Pyatt: 'Yeah. I guess . . . in terms of him not going into the government, just let him stay out and do his political homework and stuff. I'm just thinking in terms of sort of the process moving ahead we want to keep the moderate democrats together. The problem is going to be Tyahnybok [Oleh Tyahnybok, the other opposition leader] and his guys and I'm sure that's part of what [President Viktor] Yanukovych is calculating on all this.' Nuland: [Breaks in] 'I think Yats is the guy who's got the economic experience, the governing experience. He's the . . . what he needs is Klitsch and Tyahnybok on the outside. He needs to be talking to them four times a week, you know. I just think Klitsch going in . . . he's going to be at that level working for Yatseniuk, it's just not going to work.' Pyatt: 'Yeah, no, I think that's right. OK. Good. Do you want us to set up a call with him as the next step?' Nuland: 'My understanding from that call—but you tell me—was that the big three were going into their own meeting and that Yats was going to offer in that context a . . . three-plus-one conversation or three-plus-two with you. Is that not how you understood it?' Pyatt: 'No. I think . . . I mean that's what he proposed but I think, just knowing the dynamic that's been with them where Klitschko has been the top dog, he's going to take a while to show up for whatever meeting they've got and he's probably talking to his guys at this point, so I think you reaching out directly to him helps with the personality management among the three and it gives you also a chance to move fast on all this stuff and put us behind it before they all sit down and he explains why he doesn't like it.' Nuland: 'OK, good. I'm happy. Why don't you reach out to him and see if he wants to talk before or after.' Pyatt: 'OK, will do. Thanks. Nuland: OK . . . one more wrinkle for you Geoff. [A click can be heard] I can't remember if I told you this, or if I only told Washington this, that when I talked to Jeff Feltman [United Nations Under-Secretary-General for Political Affairs] this morning, he had a new name for the UN guy Robert Serry did I write you that this morning?' [Jonathan Marcus writes:] An intriguing insight into the foreign policy process with work going on at a number of levels: Various officials attempting to marshal the Ukrainian opposition; efforts to get the UN to play an active role in bolstering a deal; and (as you can see below) the big guns waiting in the wings—US Vice President Joe Biden clearly being lined up to give private words of encouragement at the appropriate moment. Pyatt: 'Yeah I saw that.' Nuland: 'OK. He's now gotten both Serry and [UN Secretary General] Ban Ki-moon to agree that Serry could come in Monday or Tuesday. So that would be great, I think, to help glue this thing and to have the UN help glue it and, you know, Fuck the EU.' [Jonathan Marcus writes:] Not for the first time in an international crisis, the US expresses frustration at the EU's efforts. Washington and Brussels have not been completely in step during the Ukraine crisis. The EU is divided and to some extent hesitant about picking a fight with Moscow. It certainly cannot win a short-term battle for Ukraine's affections with Moscow—it just does not have the cash inducements available. The EU has sought to play a longer game; banking on its attraction over time. But the US clearly is determined to take a much more activist role. Pyatt: 'No, exactly. And I think we've got to do something to make it stick together because you can be pretty sure that if it does start to gain altitude, that the Russians will be working behind the scenes to try to torpedo it. And again the fact that this is out there right now, I'm still trying to figure out in my mind why Yanukovych (garbled) that. In the meantime there's a Party of Regions faction meeting going on right now and I'm sure there's a lively argument going on in that group at this point. But anyway we could land jelly side up on this one if we move fast. So let me work on Klitschko and if you can just keep . . . we want to try to get somebody with an international personality to come out here and help to midwife this thing. The other issue is some kind of outreach to

Yanukovych but we probably regroup on that tomorrow as we see how things start to fall into place.' Nuland: 'So on that piece Geoff, when I wrote the note [US vice president's national security adviser Jake] Sullivan's come back to me VFR [direct to me], saying you need [US Vice President Joe] Biden and I said probably tomorrow for an atta-boy and to get the deets [details] to stick. So Biden's willing.' Pyatt: 'OK. Great. Thanks.' [Jonathan Marcus writes:]: Overall this is a damaging episode between Washington and Moscow. Nobody really emerges with any credit. The US is clearly much more involved in trying to broker a deal in Ukraine than it publicly lets on. There is some embarrassment too for the Americans given the ease with which their communications were hacked. But is the interception and leaking of communications really the way Russia wants to conduct its foreign policy? Goodness—after Wikileaks, Edward Snowden and the like could the Russian government be joining the radical apostles of open government? I doubt it. Though given some of the comments from Vladimir Putin's advisor on Ukraine Sergei Glazyev—for example his interview with the *Kommersant-Ukraine* newspaper the other day—you don't need your own listening station to be clear about Russia's intentions. Russia he said 'must interfere in Ukraine' and the authorities there should use force against the demonstrators. Ukrainian opposition leaders Vitaly Klitschko (L) and Arseny Yatsenyuk (R) meet with US Assistant Secretary of State for European and Eurasian Affairs Victoria Nuland (2nd L) in Kiev February 6, 2014. Ms Nuland and Mr Pyatt (center) met Ukrainian opposition leaders Vitaly Klitschko (L) and Arseny Yatsenyuk (R) on Thursday US Assistant Secretary of State Victoria Nuland meets President Viktor Yanukovych in Kiev. Photo: February 6, 2014. She also met President Yanukovych."

79 This judgment is based on extensive discussions by Rosefielde at the time with insiders in the American military, intelligence, public policy and White House communities.

80 This explains why the West never encouraged Ukraine to follow Paul Krugman's and Larry Summers's advice about shunning "austerity." Big deficit spenders are considered unfit candidates for EU membership. They are only urged to misbehave like Spain after they have joined the club.

81 Robert Gates, *Duty: Memoirs of a Secretary at War*, New York: Alfred A. Knopf, 2014.

82 Hitler's supporters contended that Germany hadn't lost World War I militarily; it had been stabbed in the back by social democratic politicians. Putin today echoes this attitude toward Gorbachev's and Yeltsin's destruction of communism: Gabriela Baczynska, "Group of Deputies Wants Gorbachev Investigated over Soviet Break-Up," *Reuters*, April 10, 2014: http://news.yahoo.com/group-deputies-wants-gorbachev-investigated-over-soviet-break-124523136.html. This isn't the first time indictment has been considered. The issue was also raised in 2012: "Critics demand high treason trial for Gorbachev," *RT*, January 19, 2012; http://rt.com/politics/gorbachev-high-treason-trial-175/.

83 Samuel Huntington, "The West: Unique, Not Universal." *Foreign* Affairs, Vol. 75, No. 6, 1996, pp. 28–46.

84 Patrick Smith, "How Obama's White House Lost Ukraine in a Few Stupid Steps," *The Fiscal Times*, April 21, 2014: http://finance.yahoo.com/news/obama-whitehouse-lost-ukraine-093000155.html—"For a while it was possible to pretend, just barely, that supporting the coup against Viktor Yanukovych, the elected president hounded into exile in February, would prove a sound judgment. Obama always came across as a welterweight in the ring with Vladimir Putin, simply not up to the Russian leader's command of all available moves. But one could imagine Secretary of State Kerry clearing an exit corridor with Russian Foreign Minister Sergei Lavrov . . . It is all by the boards now. Regardless of how you may construe these past six months in Ukraine, we have just watched a failed effort to wrest the nation straight out of Russia's sphere of influence and insert it into the West's. It is now easy to conclude

that the second-term Obama White House has not one foreign policy success to its credit and none in prospect."

85 Steven Rosefielde, *The Empire Strikes Back: Russia and the West after Putin's Ukrainian Gambit*, Cambridge: Cambridge University Press, 2015.

86 https://www.cia.gov/library/publications/the-world-factbook/geos/up.html.

87 Focus Economics is a private service company that provides economic analysis and compiles over 1,600 macroeconomic forecasts for over 105 countries. It is supported by an extensive global network of analysts and its research is derived from projections by international banks, national financial institutions, consultancies and other economic think tanks.

88 https://www.cia.gov/library/publications/the-world-factbook/geos/up.html.

89 Focus Economics, *Ukraine Economic Outlook*, June 9, 2015: http://www.focus-economics.com/countries/ukraine.

90 Focus Economics, *Ukraine: Consumption*, June 19, 2015: http://www.focus-economics.com/country-indicator/ukraine/consumption—"According to official data released by State Statistics Service Ukraine, GDP contracted 17.2% in Q1 over the same period of the previous year, which was less than the previously released estimate of a 17.6% decrease. In addition, the contraction still represented a notable deterioration from Q4's 14.8% decrease and represents the worst result since Q2 2009. Ukraine has entered a downward economic spiral as a result of the military conflict and political instability in the east of the country. The large contraction was driven by a worsening of the external sector combined with shrinking domestic demand. Private consumption fell 20.7% annually in Q1, which was a larger contraction than Q4's 13.6% decline. Fixed investment plummeted 25.1%, which followed Q4's 26.2% decrease. In contrast, government consumption recorded the only expansion, growing 5.0% in Q1, which was up from the 3.5% increase in Q4. On the external front, exports tumbled 26.2% in the first quarter (Q4: −31.0% yoy) and imports plummeted 20.1% (Q4: −29.0% yoy). As a result, the net contribution of the external sector to GDP growth swung from plus 4.9 percentage points in Q4 to minus 0.6 percentage points in Q1. Focus Economics participants see the economy contracting 7.4% in 2015, which is down 1.1 percentage points from last month's forecast. For 2016, panelists expect that the economy will rebound to grow 1.8%."

91 Jeremy Tordjman, "IMF Approves Loan to Ukraine Despite Debt Concerns," *AFP*, July 31, 2015.

92 http://finance.yahoo.com/currency-investing: A dollar bought 8 hryvnia in 2010 and 21 in 2015.

93 Jeremy Tordjman, "IMF Approves Loan to Ukraine Despite Debt Concerns," *AFP*, July 31, 2015.

94 Focus Economics, *Ukraine Economic Outlook*, June 9, 2015: http://www.focus-economics.com/countries/ukraine Ukraine's economy, and "The New Greece in the East," *Economist*, March 12, 2015. http://www.economist.com/blogs/freeexchange/2015/03/ukraine-s-economy.

95 "Ukraine GDP Growth Rate 2010–2015," *Trading Economics*, June 28, 2015: http://www.tradingeconomics.com/ukraine/gdp-growth, and "Ukraine," IMF Country Report 15/59, March 2015: https://www.imf.org/external/pubs/ft/scr/2015/cr1569.pdf.

96 https://www.cia.gov/library/publications/the-world-factbook/geos/up.html, updated June 28, 2015. The CIA reports that "In April 2010, Ukraine negotiated a price discount on Russian gas imports in exchange for extending Russia's lease on its naval base in Crimea. Movement toward an Association Agreement with the European Union, which would commit Ukraine to economic and financial reforms in exchange for preferential access to EU markets, was curtailed by the November 2013 decision of President Yanukovych against signing this treaty. In response, on 17 December 2013 President Yanukovych and President Putin concluded a financial assistance package containing $15 billion in loans and lower gas prices. However, the end of

the Yanukovych government in February 2014 caused Russia to halt further funding. With the formation of an interim government in late February 2014, the international community began efforts to stabilize the Ukrainian economy, including a 27 March 2014 IMF assistance package of $14–18 billion. Russia's seizure of the Crimean Peninsula has created uncertainty as to the annual rate of growth of the Ukrainian economy in 2014."

97 Jeremy Tordjman, "IMF Approves Loan to Ukraine Despite Debt Concerns," *AFP*, July 31, 2015: "David Lipton, the IMF's first deputy managing director, said that the Ukrainian authorities had made a 'strong start' in implementing their economic program. 'The momentum needs to be sustained, as significant structural and institutional reforms are still needed to address economic imbalances that held Ukraine back in the past,' Lipton said in a separate statement."

98 "IMF: Ukraine to Get $40 Billion Bailout," *DW*, February 12, 2015: http://www. dw.com/en/imf-ukraine-to-get-40-billion-bailout/a-18250993.

99 Ibid. The bailout is said to include an in-depth restructuring of Naftogaz, Ukraine's state-owned natural gas firm, and to be a realistic program that can represent a turning point for Ukraine.

100 "The New Greece in the East," *Economist*, March 12, 2015: http://www.economist. com/blogs/freeexchange/2015/03/ukraine-s-economy.

101 Mancur Olson, "Dictatorship, Democracy, and Development," *American Political Science Review*, Vol. 87, No. 3, September, 1993, pp. 567–76: "Under anarchy, uncoordinated competitive theft by 'roving bandits' destroys the incentive to invest and produce, leaving little for either the population or the bandits. Both can be better off if a bandit sets himself up as a dictator—a 'stationary bandit' who monopolizes and rationalizes theft in the form of taxes. A secure autocrat has an encompassing interest in his domain that leads him to provide a peaceful order and other public goods that increase productivity. Whenever an autocrat expects a brief tenure, it pays him to confiscate those assets whose tax yield over his tenure is less than their total value. This incentive plus the inherent uncertainty of succession in dictatorships imply that autocracies will rarely have good economic performance for more than a generation. The conditions necessary for a lasting democracy are the same necessary for the security of property and contract rights that generates economic growth."

Part III
Central Europe
The Visegrád Four

7   Waiting for change

Following the end of the post-war division of Europe between West and East, the Czech Republic, Hungary, Poland and Slovakia returned to be part of Central Europe. Although a rather elusive and controversial term, "Central Europe" is used here in a way similar to the practice of the European Union and various international agencies to identify a region that also includes other countries, such as Germany and Austria. This region is usually considered as part of what is defined in a very broad sense as Western Europe. In fact, the four countries were historically, culturally and politically an integral part of the West and economically they were rather strictly integrated with Germany.

Although their history was uneasy and turbulent, their link to the West and their uneasy or openly hostile relation first to Russia and then the Soviet Union was virtually uninterrupted. Yet their sharing of the Soviet-type system for years did introduce into their economic, social and political structures and systems some similarities with the Soviet Union and its successor countries. While transformation for the four countries was in a sense a return to their tradition, the path-dependent effect of their Soviet-type period should not be overlooked.

It is equally important to consider that these countries had different national histories and economic and social features throughout their history, along with some similarities. They were sometimes enemies and at other times allies. Two of these countries, the Czech Republic and Slovakia, formed a federation between 1918 and 1992, from their national independence through transformation, with the exception of the World War II years. During the Soviet-type period, their economic, political and military contacts, collaboration and integration were probably stronger than in any preceding period. Yet even within the "communist" (or "progressive," depending on the perspective chosen) camp, their relation was not always smooth and friendly. The main such event, though certainly not the only one, was the participation of Poland and Hungary in the 1968 invasion of Czechoslovakia.

The uneasy and changing mutual relations continued also during the years of transformation and into their EU membership. To be sure, their relation to the EU and the establishment of the Visegrád agreement definitely moved the emphasis in the direction of cooperation. Thus in the case of these countries, the external context had and has particular importance, certainly more so than in the case of Russia.

A short historical introduction

Czechoslovakia became independent in 1918, uniting Bohemia and Moravia, which were previously included in Austria, and Slovakia, a part of Hungary for nearly a thousand years.[1] Czechoslovakia's independence was officially proclaimed in Prague on October 28, 1918 and Slovakia officially joined the new state two days later. The formal international recognition of the new republic came with the Treaty of St. Germain of September 1919, and the Treaty of Trianon added Ruthenia in June 1920. The new state, a parliamentary democracy with Czech and Slovak as official languages, united two peoples with cultural and historical differences, and deep economic and social diversities. Moreover, the new state included sizeable minorities, mainly Germans (which constituted nearly one fourth of the entire population and were territorially highly concentrated) and Hungarians, and both groups were unhappy with the new territorial settlements.

The new country included most of the industry of the former Austro-Hungarian Empire. Most of the industrial area was concentrated in the Czech lands of Bohemia and Moravia and in particular in the German-inhabited Sudetenland, an area in which most large industrial conglomerates were controlled by Germans and German-owned banks. The economic development and social progress of the country were remarkable in the period between the two wars. Notable was also the solidity of the political system: after 1933, the country was the only democracy in Central and Eastern Europe.

The Munich Agreement of September 29, 1938 led to the cession of the Czech borderlands to Germany, with the consequent expulsion of the Czech population. Moreover, territories mostly inhabited by Hungarians in southern Slovakia and southern Rutenia were transferred to Hungary following the First Vienna Award on November 2, 1938. The so-called "Second Republic," renamed "Czecho-Slovakia," was reconstituted in late November 1938. It was made of three autonomous units: the Czech lands (including Bohemia and Moravia), Slovakia and Ruthenia.

While the Czech component of the new country was politically weakened by the events, the strong Slovak nationalist movement found an external support in Hitler's Germany. Slovakia separated from Czechoslovakia and declared independence on March 14, 1939. Two days later, German troops occupied Bohemia and Moravia, thus effectively putting an end to Czechoslovakia until the end of World War II.

Although Hungary recognized the independence of Slovakia and both countries were allied to Germany and Italy, a short border war broke out between them on March 23, 1939, following which further Slovak territory was annexed to Hungary. During World War II, Slovakia was a member of the Axis Pact and its army participated in the occupation of Poland and the war against the Soviet Union. Subsequently, the Soviet Army occupied the country in April and May 1945. The reconstituted Czechoslovak state (the so-called "Third Republic" of April 1945) accepted to cede Carpatho-Ukraine to the Soviet Union in June 1945, while the Sudeten Germans were expelled to Germany according to the provisions of the Potsdam Agreement. In addition, part of the Hungarian minority in Slovakia was expatriated to Hungary.

Hungary was federated to Austria in the Dual Monarchy since 1867 and until the end of World War I. The country became independent after the dissolution of Austria-Hungary in October 1918, following the armistice on November 3, 1918. Compared to its situation in the dual monarchy, Hungary came out of World War I strongly reduced in population and territory, occupied by the armies of the surrounding countries and going through a revolution in fall 1918 and the Republic of the Councils in 1919. After the defeat of the latter in August 1919 and the occupation of the country by the Romanian Army, the country was ruled by an authoritarian regime headed by Admiral Horthy. During World War II, Hungary was an ally to Germany and Italy and an enemy of the Soviet Union. Hungary recovered through the two Vienna Awards some of the territories lost with the Treaty of Trianon of 1920, to the disadvantage of Czechoslovakia and Romania. At the end of 1940, Hungary signed the Axis Pact and participated in the invasion of Yugoslavia, obtaining in exchange some territories of the former Yugoslavia. In 1941, Hungary directly took part in the invasion of the Soviet Union. While the German Army occupied Hungary in October 1944, the Soviet Army entered the country in September 1944 and occupied the entire country by early April 1945.

Poland regained its independence at the end of World War I, when the Polish territories formerly part of Austria, Germany and Russia were united in the independent Poland. This process was uneasy and included six border wars with Poland's neighbor countries in 1918–21, including a major Polish–Soviet War in 1919–21, following the Polish invasion of Soviet Russia. World War II started on September 1, 1939, with the German invasion of Poland, soon followed by the Soviet invasion of Poland on September 17. The country was occupied and divided by the two invading countries, in the framework of the Molotov-Ribbentrop Pact. The division lasted until June 1941, when Germany occupied the entire country as part of its invasion of the Soviet Union. This period was characterized by unutterable massacres of the population, including nearly all Polish Jews and much of the country's leadership. In the latter, the Soviets also played a part. The Soviet Army and the People's Army of Poland liberated the country in the second half of 1944 and early 1945. Although Poland was formally an ally to the Soviet Union, its liberation was half-hearted, following the bitter interwar relations between the two countries.

All the countries considered, then, had an uneasy historical relation with Russia and the Soviet Union. The Soviets initially considered them as occupied countries which could not be trusted, with the partial exception of Czechoslovakia. Another noteworthy issue was that each of the three countries had, during the war, expatriates to the Soviet Union. These were mostly members of each nation's Communist Party. Each nation also had regular (Poland) or irregular (Hungary and Czechoslovakia) armed forces that fought in their own countries against the German occupation and other forces abroad (in the Soviet Union) that fought on the side of or in strict cooperation with the Red Army.[2] These were the main bridges through which a cooperative relation, however asymmetric, could be built between the Soviet Union and the occupied countries. However, the split between the national communists and expatriated Muscovite communists was also established in this period. The split was the cause of the dramatic processes and purges against the former by the latter during the last years of Stalin's rule.

The political foundation of the Soviet-type system in Central Europe

When the war ended, all three countries experienced territorial and population changes and became pluralistic democracies. Hungary lost all the territories it had occupied right before or during the war. Slovakia was reunited with the Czech lands to form the new Czechoslovakia. The country regained the territories previously lost to Germany and to Hungary, but lost eastern Rutenia, which was included in Soviet Ukraine. Poland regained independence, but also went through dramatic territorial and population changes. Geographically, the country moved westward: it acquired large territories in former Eastern Germany (Prussia and Pomerania), from which the German population was expelled. At the same time, Poland lost vast territories in the east to the Soviet Union and part of the Ukrainian population previously living there. This was of overall advantage to the country, since the western territories were more developed and richer in natural resources and industry than the eastern territories. Equally important was that Poland acquired access to the sea on a long trait of cost with good ports.

After the post-war years of democratic regimes and national cooperation, with growing strength of the Soviet-backed communist parties, the beginning of the Cold War in 1947 changed dramatically the internal landscape. While the United States started a strategy of global containment (the Truman Doctrine), the Soviet Union consolidated its control over the countries of Central-Eastern Europe. The Berlin blockade from June 1948 to May 1949 represented the main international crisis of this period. This accompanied the takeover of political power in Eastern European countries by the communist parties and in due time the prevalence of Muscovite communist leaders over national ones.

The takeover was pursued through different means (Fejtő 1971). In Czechoslovakia, there was a communist *coup d'état* in early 1949. In Hungary, various parties were forced to join the People's Front in February 1949 under the leadership of the Communist Party. In Poland, the Communist Party led the Provisional Government of National Unity in Warsaw before the end of the war, in opposition to the London-based Polish government in exile. The Provisional Government had the backing of the Soviet Union. Using its control over the government and by means of political pressure over the opposition (which was practically outlawed in 1946), court trials and assassinations of opponents, the Communist Party consolidated its power. A pro-government Democratic Block, including left-wing parties under the leadership of the Polish Workers' Party, was formed in 1947 and won the successive elections, allegedly also through forged results. Poland thus entered into one-party dictatorship.

Following domestic events in Central-Eastern European countries and in the West, the Soviet Union promoted the establishment of Comecon[3] in 1949, in answer to the US Marshall Plan of 1947, and the Warsaw Pact, signed in 1955, as an answer to the establishment of NATO in April 1949. Having consolidated their domestic political power and based on the powerful presence of the Red Army, all three countries were ready to move towards an economic system similar to the Soviet one. All three countries nationalized their industries, collectivized agriculture and developed a central planning system. Yet there were important inter-country differences.

The Soviet-type economic system in Central-Eastern Europe

For Eastern Europe, the Soviet system (see above, Chapter 1) was an alien under-taking, when adapted to the countries that the Red Army occupied during World War II (and, for a short period, Yugoslavia and Albania) in the form of the Soviet-type system. It was an incomplete set of general principles and rules and related structures, that were based on coherent ideological principles and a coherent analysis of general power relations in politics and economics. However, along with its coherence, this economic system missed a set of fundamental economic issues and had two major problems for Central-Eastern European countries, together with its disregard of local circumstances.

In order to direct and control the economic apparatus, the central planning system required strong bureaucratization of the economy, which caused high transaction costs. Also coordination of economic activity, which could hardly rely on the direct interest of decision makers and executors, required a great deal of administrative activity. Informational flows in the economy were based in the central planning system: enterprises were required to inform central planners of their situation, while planners communicated their decisions concerning allocation and production targets to enterprises. In central planning, the latter communication had the form of plan commands (Grossman 1963). However, in reality, there was much bargaining going on between planners and enterprises and the latter could use their knowledge of the production process in a strategic manner, so to ease their situation and duties and increase rewards. This led to informational distortion and to many obstacles in the production and circulation of knowledge (Winiecki 2012).

The nature of the price system encapsulated the crucial questions of informa-tion distortion and the ineffective incentive system in the Soviet-type economic system. The price system reflected mostly political and social preferences, and not scarcity and production conditions. In this way, prices were a means of central planning, but hardly had any active role in orienting the decisions of producers and consumers. The conjunction between the conditions of production and the decisions to allocate resources, produce and consume were left to the wise judg-ment of central planners and, for basic decisions, to the leaders of the party.

The fundamental importance of incentives was clear to the founders of the sys-tem, who theorized the necessity of having a "new man" incorporating socialist political and social principles. The new man had to be altruistic and interested in social welfare and well-being, upon which individual well-being was dependent. For different reasons (from the failures of the system to the fact that it was implemented in mostly backward countries in a relatively minor part of the world), the new man did not materialize. Its proxy was pervasive political campaigns mobilizing economic actors and the population around simplified goals (Soós 1986). Although political campaigns played an important and successful role in some cases (the most important being the mobilization for the construction of the heavy industrial basis and for the war in the Soviet Union), overall they were a source of a waste of resources, including human resources. In fact, while the idea of the new man had clearly implied that the solution was to be found at micro-level, at the level of each individual and be therefore ubiquitous and continuous, campaigns could only be discrete and concentrate on particular objectives, to the disadvantage of the rest. Campaigns replaced the engine of self-interest typical of a capitalist economy, in an incomplete and ineffective way, although it reached remarkable results in selected fields at high human and economic costs. If moral and political incentives were ineffective, the little material incentives that were used were either ineffective or had perverse effects.

As to the specific problems of Central-Eastern European countries (CEECs), the first problem had to do with differences in the level of development. The Soviet system was tailored to the features of a country at a rather low level of development. As soon as economic growth was successful and full employment was reached, that system should have evolved into a system based on qualitative or "intensive" drivers of the economy: efficiency in the use of resources, technical progress, growing productivity. Central-Eastern European countries were generally at a higher level of development, had more sophisticated economies and (reasonably) well-working market institutions. An indirect proof of the importance of these factors is that overall growth rates were significantly higher in less developed countries (Bulgaria and Romania) than in the most advanced ones (Czechoslovakia and the GDR) during the entire period.

A second important issue was the proximity of the economic system to external countries. In most fields, there was a true autarchy and a complete separation from the rest of the world (Lavigne 1999). This concerned trade and financial relations, but also technology and technical progress were separated. This was at odds with the features of Central-Eastern European economies, certainly the ones considered here, that were traditionally open economies, integrated with Western European economies. They were not only economically more developed. All three countries were parts of larger countries before World War I: Austria-Hungary in the case of Hungary and Czechoslovakia, Austria, Germany and Russia in the case of Poland. Their economies were integrated with larger economies and all were economically integrated with western countries, primarily Germany.

The Soviet system was not only largely alien to the CEECs for ideological reasons. It also had many features that were tailored to Russian local circumstances. It was based on what was suitable for a large country, endowed with abundant labor and natural resources, but scarce in skilled and specialized resources, including technical personnel, sophisticated machines and equipment, and diffused transportation networks. Some fundamental institutions were typically Russian and alien to the CEECs. Agriculture was a case in point: before the October Revolution, Russian agriculture was privately owned and managed only in a small part (Wädekin 1973, 1982, 1990). Most of the land belonged to the tsar or to village communities. Under those circumstances, the socialization of land either in large state-owned farms or cooperatives was in a sense a continuation of Russian traditions in a different form. Quite different was the situation in Hungary, Poland and Czechoslovakia. In those countries, the private possession of land was pervasive and, while large estates were important, small land ownership was quite diffuse.

The greatest difference, though, was in the political and social regimes. While Russia was an autocratic political regime, whose features molded the new Soviet regime in many ways (see Part II on Russia, in this volume), Czechoslovakia had a democratic regime, while Hungary and Poland swung between authoritarian and democratic governments. In the economy, all CEECs had more (Czechoslovakia) or less (Poland and Hungary) developed market economies. Commands as means to manage an economy (Grossman 1963) were in line with Russian traditions, but alien to the CEECs.

In the organization of the economy, there were various causes for the problematic effect of Russian features and circumstances over the CEECs. For instance, Russian industry was territorially more concentrated in large firms and in few cities, while in the CEECs industry was more widely distributed throughout the territory (with the partial exception of Hungary). Firms had a much smaller average size, due to the presence of many small, even tiny, firms. Transport infrastructure in Russia typically linked the capital city with the rest of the country, while other cities and regions seldom had direct connections. The CEECs had more diffused direct connections among cities and regions, with the partial exception of Hungary.

The classical Soviet-type system was consequently highly centralized (Kornai 1959). Overcentralization was in the organization of the economy, but was also a distinctive character of economic management. The central planning system was the most typical instrument to this end, together with the central organs of the ruling party and the central government. All this reflected Russian traditions, but was very logical also in the frame of the system's general principles, its economic ideology. Central planning and centralization were in fact fundamental devices for the control of the economy and the activity of decentralized agents.

The fundamental type of planning—five-year plans—defined the fundamental economic variables and the features of development during the relevant period (Kornai 1992a, Lavigne 1974). Each plan was then broken down in yearly operational plans, that included detailed production targets for a number of products and for individual enterprises. These yearly plans met with growing problems as to the consistency of their targets with the available means, and their implementation was the cause of investment cycles (Dallago 1982). Consequently, they often had to be revised. The first five-year plans were adopted in Czechoslovakia in 1949 and in Hungary in 1950. Poland implemented a six-year plan in 1950. These plans had as their main goal to force industrialization and economic growth. The difficulties they met and the problems that forced industrialization and growth caused—in terms of weak adjustment, shortages and bottlenecks of production—were among the fundamental causes of social dissatisfaction and unrest that took place in the countries in the mid-1950s (Lavigne 1999, Winiecki 2012).

The system was also applied to international economic relations among socialist countries. These relied on the coordination among the economic offices of the parties in power, and the coordination of planning and direct deliveries that took place within Comecon (Kaser 1965).

Developments in the three countries were rather similar in this period. The basic elements of the new system were:

- the strong centralization of decision making and economic management;
- the public ownership of production means, except for marginal activities, and collectivization in agriculture;
- forced investment and growth in heavy industry, often with unrealistic preconditions and targets;
- transfer of resources from agriculture to industry;
- rapidly growing employment and stagnating wages and consumption;
- separation of consumer prices from production costs, and of production, from foreign trade;
- bureaucratization and political control of economic management; and
- lack of effective economic incentives to labor and production.

While material production increased significantly, the disregard for technical progress and quality made much of that production hardly exportable outside the socialist countries and also made problems for its domestic users. The economic model was nearly purely extensive, with scant regard for productivity. The disregard for services linked to production caused bottlenecks.

In Czechoslovakia, the first five-year central plan had as its fundamental components forced industrialization based on the accelerated growth of heavy industry; the collectivization of agriculture, along lines less coercive than in other countries;[4] nationalization of industrial and trade enterprises with more than fifty employees, as well as the land of large landowners. Private ownership of land was limited to fifty hectares. Independent farming and small-scale industrial activities were allowed on a provisional basis and for a temporary period. Forced industrialization privileged heavy mechanical industry and mining and proceeded by concentrating production in a low number (approximately 1,700 by 1958) of large units. Initially, the growth of industrial production and employment were successful overall, but were impressive in Slovakia. However, technical progress and productivity were ailing (Myant 1989, Teichova 1988).

Hungary implemented the Soviet-type system starting in 1949. Major changes included the collectivization of agriculture, which was thought to release resources to be transferred to forced industrialization, in particular the rapid development of heavy industry, which was a distinctive feature of all the new socialist countries.

In that period, heavy industry received more than 90 percent of the overall industrial investment. This model was at odds with the features of a country poor in raw materials and energy sources, that had to be largely imported, primarily from the Soviet Union. As in other countries, wage controls were enacted and consumer prices were disconnected from production prices and significantly increased. These measures caused the stagnation of agricultural production, bottlenecks in production and foreign trade, material shortages and popular dissatisfaction (Kornai 1979, 1980).

In Poland, the six-year plan of 1950 foresaw the organization and working of the economy along the line of a typical Soviet-type system. As in other countries, the core of the plan was forced industrialization, in particular the accelerated growth of heavy industry through massive investments and the transfer of labor forces from other sectors, and the collectivization of agriculture. However, the pace of the latter was slower than in other countries and a large private sector continued to remain in agriculture. Private industry and trade were nationalized. The first years of the new system brought significant results in terms of economic growth and employment (Kolodko 1988, 1989, Mizsei 1990), as in other CEECs.

Policies and reforms take place in the frame of the factors that inspire, influence, constraint and support them (Keeney 2004).[5] The fundamental components of the frame are the prevailing policy theories (which reflect the fundamental economic principles), the external (international) context, and local circumstances. Particularly important components of the latter are the existing institutions, the level of development and resource endowment, and the structural features of the economy, together with political and social relations. These factors, taken together, define which policies can be used, their effectiveness and their consequences.

The needs of the economy were oversimplified in favor of the absolute priority given to heavy industry and military production.[6] Priority was also given to quantity over quality, irrespective of the effective usefulness of production. In this, policies made use of the Material Product System (MPS) of accounting (Dallago 1993), that considered only material goods and disregarded most services when measuring production. Ideology, power relations within the Communist Parties and, in the CEECs, loyalty to the Soviet Union, were fundamental framing devices. Adaptation to local (national) circumstances was generally considered as a conservative deviation and a hostile move jeopardizing communist solidarity.

Policy framing was based on a clearcut and simple decision-making system: fundamental decisions belonged in the ruling party, typically in consultation with the Soviet Communist Party and other ruling parties. From the party, decisions went to ministries, which had to transform those broad decisions into detailed ones, typically broken down by sectors and by (large) firms. These detailed decisions were then implemented by firms, which formally could not take part in the definition of targets. Policy framing in the Soviet-type system was therefore a clear and apparently rational construction concerning thought and communication, whereby the latter had usually the character of an order.

Frames, with the support of politics and sometimes secret police, exercised a selective influence over perceptions of economic and political actors and through these over economic activity. Information supporting thought and communication frames in this system was under the influence of confirmatory biases. According to these, organizations and individuals had to rely on information and knowledge consistent with the official beliefs. Inconsistent information and knowledge had to be refuted as either irrelevant or politically dangerous. Confirmatory biases thus generated equilibrium fictions, a strong and persistent set of beliefs consistent with the information and the evidence submitted to the confirmatory bias. Under this surface, though, a second economy started to form, that flourished in the following period (Grossman 1977).

The centralized system based on central planning obtained some positive results in the reconstruction of the countries from war damages and in the development of heavy industry and full employment (Berend 1996, Berend and Ránki 1974, Lavigne 1974). Yet it mostly produced economic aberrations, a waste of resources, and some political discipline at the cost of economic apathy (Winiecki 2012). The growth of Soviet-type economies depended on the increase in the quantity of inputs, including natural ones, and much less on productivity growth. Growth required the mobilization of material resources through high investment in new plants and the creation of new jobs. The need to rebuild countries after wartime destruction and to create new industries, for both overcoming economic backwardness and replacing western imports, led to maximizing investment at the disadvantage of consumption. Employment soon reached full employment of first the male population and later on, around 1960 in most countries, also of the female population. However, wages stagnated and the gap between their standard of living and the West's increased progressively. This became the source of social dissatisfaction and, in some cases, unrest, starting from 1953 in Berlin.

Although the features of the Soviet system were rather similar in all countries, this situation remained relatively undifferentiated for only few years (1949–52). These years were important to construct the building blocks of the system, much less to have it fully working. Indeed, as soon as the system was in place, its irrationality and weakness were evident. Countries that started with very similar economic agendas began to consider variants of that system under the reorganization of national communists. Their aim was to build a system that was more in line with local features and circumstances. Politically, this move was made possible by the death of Stalin in 1953 and the political softening that followed in the Soviet Union, and by the East German revolt of 1953 and even more so those of Poland and Hungary in 1956.

Political and economic thaw

Evidence of the inefficiency and ineffectiveness of the Soviet and the Soviet-type economic systems soon appeared. While economic reform in the Soviet Union had to wait until 1965, some economic changes started along with political changes as soon as 1953, after Stalin's death. Further changes took place in 1956, following the 20th Congress of the Soviet Communist Party that initiated de-Stalinization in the Soviet Union. These mild moves had important effects in the CEECs.

The first, comprehensive change took place in Hungary with the government established in 1953 under the leadership of Imre Nagy (Berend 1990, Fejtő 1957). This government introduced various changes in the economic system, the most important of which was allowing farmers to leave agricultural cooperatives, which could also be dismantled. A massive exit followed, which put a virtual end to agricultural cooperatives in the country. More generally, the Nagy government decreased political interference in the economy and introduced some decentralization in economic management. These changes offered hopes and promises, yet the management of the economy was not up to what was needed, and obstacles were put in place by the party and central planners. In 1955, the Stalinists briefly regained full power under the leadership of Mátyás Rákosi, who had already been prime minister between 1949 and 1953 and general secretary of the party starting in 1945 and up to 1956.[7] For just over one year, the economy reverted to its previous centralized path. However, the dissolution of agricultural cooperatives remained an unsolved problem.

While the economic changes introduced between 1953 and 1955 were ephemeral, the economic consequences of the popular uprising of October 1956 were definitely more important and permanent. Some important changes were introduced by the new leadership under János Kádár.[8] As prime minister, Kádár announced a "Fifteen-Point Programme" that included, together with some political liberalization, important changes in the economy. Most important was the promise to improve the standard of living of the population. The standard of living of Hungarians improved progressively and soon became the highest among the members of Comecon. This situation was similar in regard to the relaxation of limits to personal freedom.

In 1959, the Kádár government began a large-scale collectivization of agriculture, ending in 1962 with the near-totality (more than 95 percent) of agricultural land under the cooperative system. This time, the government used incentives to convince peasants to join cooperative or collective farms. Collectivization was complemented by significant investments, large-scale mechanization and important increases of farm prices. These measures gave Hungarian agriculture an important boost, leading it to become the most successful among the socialist countries. A radical change of agricultural policies was also enacted, which included the abolition of compulsory deliveries. Important investments were implemented in industry, in particular engineering and chemical industries, whose production was mainly delivered to Comecon markets to pay for increasing imports of energy, raw materials and semi-finished goods. Small-scale private activity was liberalized in agriculture, handicraft and retail trade. Workers' management in plants was also promoted and central planning was made less mandatory. However, in spite of these important changes, political control over the economy remained firm, although through more indirect means.

Most important, the government and in particular the party recognized that the Soviet-type system, although liberalized and in spite of the residual growth and improvement of living standards it was still able to assure, was not up to the economic challenges that Hungary had to meet. In particular, by the early 1960s, the country had reached full employment and exhausted other sources of extensive growth, including the impossibility to import additional raw materials and semi-finished goods from the Comecon countries. What the country was missing most were the access to updated technology and the development of communication and transport infrastructure, necessary to improve the economy's efficiency. Improving efficiency was required so that the country could deeply reform its economic system and open to the West.

The situation started to change also in Poland in the same period, following workers' riots in Poznan in 1956 (Curtis 1992, Simatupang 1994). This prompted the Polish United Workers' Party (PUWP) to appoint Wladyslaw Gomułka, the leader of the so-called "national communist faction" within the party, as the first secretary in October 1956 with a program of reforms. The new government promised to change its development strategy and to increase and improve consumption, the main requests of national communists. There was also some decentralization in production and the investment rate was decreased. However, overall, these reforms were modest in their effect and short-lived. The only really permanent change was the decollectivization of agriculture, that remained in force until the end of the system. However, most farms were too small to be economically efficient and prosperous, and remained at subsistence level.

A new centralization followed these half-hearted reforms in early 1960s. Investments increased again to the advantage of a new wave of industrialization based on heavy industry to the disadvantage of consumption. However, the forced growth of priority sectors met with growing bottlenecks and structural distortion, caused by deficient planning and the stagnation of low-priority sectors. The standard of living also stagnated. On the plus side, this period avoided the accumulation of foreign debt.

In Czechoslovakia, de-Stalinization started later than in the two other countries (Myant 1989, Teichova 1988). No significant changes took place in the economic or political systems after the 20th Congress of the Communist Party of the Soviet Union (CPSU). The 11th Congress of the Czechoslovak Communist Party (CsCP) confirmed the conservative line in 1958. Things changed in the early 1960s, when the economy entered a period of stagnation, with the lowest growth rates among the socialist countries and the need to import food. The mood changed in 1963, when a critical debate started among economists, a debate that would lead to a project for a broader economic reform in 1965.

Reforms: the Hungarian New Economic Mechanism

After a long build-up, starting in 1961 with the establishment of a reform committee, the Central Committee of the Hungarian Socialist Workers' Party (HSWP) announced a program for a general reform of the economy on May 7, 1966 (Bauer 1983, Friss 1971). The reform, named as the New Economic Mechanism (NEM), was enacted since January 1, 1968. In spite of its reductive technocratic name, the Hungarian reform was the most radical, consistent, permanent and overall successful change of a Soviet-type economy. The general nature of the reform consisted in the attempt to overcome the inefficiencies and ineffectiveness of the Soviet-type economic system by reforming all sectors of the economy, the macroeconomic and the microeconomic management, the nature and role of the planning system and markets, prices and foreign trade. The NEM concerned both the structure of the economic system and the nature and working of economic policy.

Through the reform, the system of compulsory plan indicators was largely dismantled, except in the case of few strategic industries, and replaced by the decentralization of decision making. While the planning office defined *ex ante* the macro-aggregates of the economy, enterprises were generally free to take less critical decisions as to what they produced and how they produced it. They were motivated by a set of so-called "market indicators," including prices and profit. In principle, enterprises followed their interest to maximize their income within the frame of the indicators that planners defined. By changing the value of indicators (such as the interest rate or the share of income to be left to enterprises), planners were able to address enterprises to implement the macroeconomic aggregates defined in national plans. Enterprises were usually free to exchange goods and resources among themselves and adapt to prices. These facts led many observers to define the NEM as a market mechanism. In reality, prices had only limited allocative functions, while firms did not really maximize—what they tried to increase was not a true market profit, and financed investments from different sources.

Nevertheless, in the NEM, enterprises were much more active than before, had better incentives and their success was measured by their profitability. While in the Soviet-type system, enterprises were mere executors of central orders, in the NEM, they obtained wide freedom to make decisions regarding production and deliveries (sales) and also to establish economic and commercial relations with other firms, including foreign ones. They were also significantly free to source their inputs from various suppliers. This also concerned hiring workers and implementing investments, which did not require any formal information to be supplied to, or permit to be obtained from, the center. Overall, approximately half of investments were decided directly by the enterprises, the remaining half remaining the responsibility of the government. Public investments of major relevance were often coordinated with other socialist countries.

The NEM introduced major changes in the price system. The intent of the reform was to have flexible prices, reflecting the conditions of production and consumption and guiding the enterprises in taking efficient decisions. The active role for prices, though, had to avoid inflationary effects. This was a serious issue, since the Soviet-type system was usually in a situation of repressed inflation. Moreover, many enterprises were in a monopolistic situation and could exploit their new freedom by increasing prices. To avoid these changes, consumer prices were divided into three groups.

One group of prices were fixed and determined directly by ministries. These prices concerned basic materials, goods and services that were considered as critically important for production. Another group of prices had an upper, or an upper and lower, ceiling within which they could move freely. Limits were established by the government. This price type was used mainly in the case of products for which there was no substitute and were important for the standard of living, such as bread. Unfixed, that is, free pricing existed for the case of goods and services that were less important for consumers or were considered superfluous, such as luxury goods. This triple system of pricing was an important instrument in the hands of policy makers, since it allowed the economy not only to move towards a better reflection of production costs and the relation between demand and supply, but also to maintain market equilibrium and support a relatively egalitarian standard of living.

Important changes took place also in foreign trade. Hungary also had an open economy during the socialist period. When the NEM was implemented, trade relations with the West were important, but not in line with the country's needs and opportunities. Hungary traded primarily manufactured goods with its Comecon partners, although among imports raw materials were also important. The country's trade with the West was unbalanced: Hungary exported in similar quantities food, live animals and manufactured goods. However, nearly three-quarters of imports from the West were manufactured goods.

In order to improve the trade balance with the West, which was the traditional market for Hungary, the NEM radically changed the Soviet-type trade system. The latter completely isolated producers from foreign markets by means of specialized foreign trade organizations. While foreign trade organizations continued to exist, enterprises were often free to export. If they exported to the West, they were paid the correspondent sum in Hungarian forints of the foreign currency earned. This system gave enterprises further incentives to produce more and improve the quality of their production in line with the requests of western markets. This required also better use of technology.

Connecting enterprises, albeit mostly indirectly, to international markets required reforms also in the exchange rate and the banking system. It was typical of the Soviet-type system to have an administratively fixed exchange rate with the Comecon partner countries and with countries with non-convertible currencies. In this way and thanks to the monopoly of specialized foreign trade organizations, the domestic economy could be isolated from international markets, while the administrative exchange rate served purposes of foreign trade planning within the Comecon. The central management of enterprises and investment, whose activities were directly financed by the state budget in line with the central plan, did not require independent banks either. Banking activity was the domain of specialized sections within the central bank, dealing with such functions as financing investment or foreign trade activities.

Exchange rates and commercial banks were important in the NEM. Exchange rates were only internal and referred to the foreign trade of enterprises and tourism. Externally, the Hungarian currency remained non-convertible. The NEM also introduced a two-level banking system, according to which the specialized functions hosted in the central bank became independent commercial and investment banks.

Although remarkably consistent overall and in spite of Kádár's unchallenged leadership and political stability, economic events had an influence on the implementation of the reform. In spite of the worries that the Warsaw Pact invasion of

Czechoslovakia created, overall, the first years were successful in both economic terms, with good economic performance and exports to the West, and price stability, and reform implementation. However, the 1973 oil crisis represented a major negative blow and led to a serious deterioration of Hungary's terms of trade in the international market. In spite of this, policy makers responded by trying to accelerate economic growth. To do so, they significantly increased investments (gross investment increased from 34 percent of GDP in 1970 to 41 percent in 1978) and launched major investment projects, including in the energy and raw material sectors, to compensate for the deterioration of terms of trade. However, they also provided loss-making large firms, severely hit by higher energy prices, with subsidies financed by taxing profit-making enterprises, in particular those advantaged by higher world prices. This was possible only through the re-centralization of the economy, but it caused a deterioration in performance and efficiency of enterprises, and a halt to the reform.

Hungary had a processing economy, that required more imports of energy and raw material to support higher growth rates, being technical progress of limited relevance. This conservative strategy could not be sustained with only domestic resources. Trade balance in convertible currencies went into deficit and a growing one as time passed. Trade deficits were financed through loans obtained in the international market. Since foreign debt was reaching economically destabilizing levels (Mihályi 2013),[9] it was necessary either to improve the efficiency of the economy or give up openness to the West. Starting from 1978, the first option was chosen and the reform was revived, together with a stabilization program, in 1979. While the renewed reform introduced new changes in the economic system, policies were aimed at decreasing the weight of heavy industry, improving trade balance in convertible currencies (through import decrease and export increase), decreasing investments and keeping the level of consumption unchanged. The effect on foreign debt was positive in the short run and gross foreign debt decreased to 35.6 percent of GDP in 1982 (Mihályi 2013).

However, a new wave of negative events[10] worsened the international creditworthiness of Hungary and led to higher interest rates over its debt in convertible currencies. These effects resulted in a feedback loop in terms of further increasing gross foreign debt, which reached the value of US$17.7 billion by 1987 or 63 percent of GDP. To stabilize the country's situation, the government renewed a stricter stabilization program which further decreased investments and consumption, renewed the economic reform with new measures, increased prices, successfully applied to join the IMF and the World Bank in 1982, and obtained loans from these organizations for approximately US$2 billion. However, the economic situation remained difficult and the rate of growth decreased further.

Reforms: Poland and Czechoslovakia

Compared to the determination of Hungary to implement a comprehensive reform of the economic system, but not of the political system, Poland appeared indecisive and Czechoslovakia more interested in reforming the political system than the economy. In Poland, political and economic difficulties had been growing since the mid-1960s (Adam 1989, Hare 1987, Korbonski 1989).

Under Gomułka's leadership, prices were lowered, and wage increases and a major economic reform were announced. Inconsistencies between government measures, social protests, further measures contradicting the former continued for years. The end result was an ineffective economic system and an unbalanced economy. The Polish government was not averse to reforms, but gave priority to a program of modernization, which could succeed only after effective reforms were implemented. The development policy adopted in 1968 aimed at modernizing the economy, making it more competitive and, through this, increasing exports. The engine of this policy was technological modernization through the increase of investments, which happened at the expense of consumption. Gomułka's leadership was criticized, economic performance worsened and output stagnated. The situation was particularly difficult in agriculture and this motivated the government to increase significantly the prices of basic food items in December 1970. Protests followed, which led to Edward Gierek replacing Gomułka as first secretary of the PUWP.

The new leadership changed policy again. In the years 1971–73, the standard of living increased appreciably. Real wages rose 40 percent between 1971 and 1975. Compulsory deliveries in agriculture were abolished and peasants obtained higher prices for their products. However, the leading idea of this period was a new economic strategy, based on the massive import of western technology in order to modernize Polish industry. This, in turn, was intended to foster Polish exports to the West, which were expected to gain the resources needed to pay for the imported technology.

This strategy was made possible by the favorable conditions existing in the international financial markets and the East–West détente. The country could obtain massive loans at favorable conditions, estimated at around US$10 billion, that were used to finance the import of western equipment, machinery, licenses. A side effect of this strategy was that during the first half of the 1970s, Comecon's share in Polish foreign trade decreased significantly.[11] Some changes in the domestic economic system accompanied the strategy. In particular, industry was reorganized by combining state enterprises in big conglomerates. These were expected to enhance efficiency by means of economies of scale and improve the management of the new technology. However, the economic system remained virtually unchanged. This strategy ended in failure for different reasons (Dallago 1981). First, the unreformed economic system led to the inefficient use of the new technology or its simple waste. Consequently, the second part of the strategy—that is, massive increase of exports to the West—never materialized. Second, conditions in western economies and their financial markets changed abruptly and unfavorably in 1973, following the first oil crisis. In the West, inflation increased and economies went into recession. This caused a decline in the demand for Polish goods, particularly coal, and a sharp increase in the price of imported goods.

The overall outcome was high deficits of the balance of payments with western countries and rapidly growing gross foreign debt. The latter increased from

US$1.2 billion to US$8.4 billion between 1970 and 1975, and to US$23 billion by the end of 1980 (Boughton 2001). The bulk of this external debt in convertible currencies was owed to western governments and to some five hundred foreign commercial banks. This imposed a rapidly increasing and dramatic burden on the Polish economy: the service of debt corresponded to 12 percent of export earnings in 1971 and 75 percent in 1979. Due to the inability of the country to honor its debt, Poland obtained seven reschedulings of its commercial bank debt and five reschedulings of its sovereign debt between 1981 and 1990 (Cohn 2012).

The Polish government tried to keep control by decreasing imports, which caused further problems and bottlenecks in domestic production. Inflationary pressures accumulated and growth rates of the Net Material Product (NMP) slowed down and stagnated in the second half of the 1970s. In 1979, national income declined in absolute terms. Also following pressures by western creditors, the government attempted to fill the inflationary gap through price increases, accompanied by the administrative freeze of other prices in the late 1970s. However, this contributed to an acute shortage of the consumer goods, whose price was frozen. The simultaneous increase of nominal incomes created an increasing monetary overhang, that further destabilized the economy.[12] The NMP declined by nearly one-quarter between 1978 and 1982, after which a prolonged period of stagnation followed.[13]

The mounting dissatisfaction and militancy of the population led to a wave of strikes in 1980. The fundamental effect of these social movements was the establishment of the Solidarność union and a further change in the party leadership in September 1980. The signature of the Gdańsk Agreement between the government and Solidarność, included an increase, among other things, of minimum wages, pensions and welfare, the acknowledgment of the right of association in free trade unions and the abolishment of party control of industrial enterprises. The new first secretary of the PUWP, Stanislaw Kania, was appointed in September 1980 and served for slightly more than one year. During this period, he established a commission for economic reform, whose program was implemented since mid-1981. The reform program provided for the decentralization of economic management and gave enterprises wider competences and responsibility for their own economic and financial management. Following mounting economic and social problems and social unrest and afraid of Soviet intervention, martial law was imposed in December 1981. A period of international isolation of the country followed.

Czechoslovakia retained a traditional Soviet-type system longer than the two other countries. A new conservative constitution was approved in 1960. In this period, the country had also to accommodate a revival of sentiments in favor of Slovak autonomy, which Slovakia had lost in 1948. Slovakia was economically particularly successful compared to the Czech regions, also thanks to considerable investments in Slovak industry. This success apparently fueled autonomist sentiments.

More serious was the problem of economic stagnation that characterized the country during the 1960s. Stagnation triggered a politically critical situation and persuaded the CsCP to approve in 1965 a reform proposal for a "New Economic

Model," to be introduced from January 1, 1967. The reform foresaw some significant changes in the economic system, including

- limits to central planning to define the general production and investment targets;
- price and wages guidelines, leaving the precise definition to the matching of demand and supply;
- profitability goals for enterprises; and
- the transition to an intensive stage of economic development, with greater role for technical progress.

However, the practical consequences of the reform were modest, largely because of the opposition of the conservative political leadership.

The Central Committee of the CsCP appointed Aleksander Dubček to the post of first secretary on January 5, 1968. This was perhaps the single formal most significant factor leading to the start of the Prague Spring, signaling that the Prague Spring devoted much attention to political changes, along with economic ones (Bischof et al. 2009, Myant 1989, Teichova 1988, Williams 1997). In March 1968, censorship was abolished and the following month the CsCP published its reform program, the Action Program. The program pursued large-scale decentralization, introduced managerial autonomy, activated the market mechanism and legalized small-scale private economic activity, especially in services. The Action Program also transformed the country into a federation in 1967. However, Czechoslovak economic reform, just like its political reform, was short-lived. It was halted following the country's invasion by Warsaw Pact troops in August 1968.

The interplay of general rules and local circumstances

There is no doubt that economic reforms in all three countries foresaw as their common thread a greater adaptation to local features and circumstances, and a substantial weakening of the previous correspondence to the economic and political principles of the Soviet-type economic system. The reforms in the three countries were consequently different in their particular content, since each country had different economic, political and social features. A more daunting question is whether the economic reforms took into due consideration the fundamental economic principles and rules of good economic management.

While economic reform in Czechoslovakia did not have sufficient time to be properly defined and implemented and in Poland changes were quite contradictory, due to daunting problems and harsh implementation of individual measures, the case of the Hungarian reform is different. This was a carefully planned and properly implemented comprehensive reform. This is not to overlook the political problems that existed.[14] Hungary's economic reform was indeed the most consistent and comprehensive reform that was ever implemented in a European Soviet-type economy. Its importance went well beyond Hungary's borders, and it roused great interest and was studied carefully abroad, in particular in China.

The Hungarian economic reform of 1968 tried to pay attention to fundamental economic principles and rules as well as take into better consideration local features and circumstances. Among the latter were the reform of agriculture and cooperatives, liberalization of small-scale activities, greater autonomy for managers and decreased political interference, greater importance for consumption and consumers' preferences, economic openness of the country to the West, and reform of the banking system. All of these were important features of pre-communist Hungary and appropriate for its small, open and diversified economy. These reforms were important not only for making the economic system better correspond to Hungarian features and traditions, but also for decreasing transaction costs of economic activities and making incentives more effective.

Among the former were greater reliance on the market for both achieving a better balance between demand and supply and activating more effective incentives, although in modest part for allocating resources. Reforms were also important for granting a more active and greater role to prices and financial variables; greater autonomy to enterprises in determining investments, employment and wages; a role for profit in determining the situation of enterprises and their growth possibilities; a decreased role for the state budget in subsidizing enterprises, and weakened administrative central planning, largely replaced by indirect indicative planning on most issues.

It is clear that the Hungarian economic reform made a serious and consistent effort to streamline the economic system to local circumstances. At the same time, the new economic mechanism departed from the fundamental principles upon which the Soviet-type system was based. Yet NEM failed to assume the fundamental economic principles of a competitive market economy. These features gave the new system a remarkable strength and resilience, since it activated dispersed interests. Yet it failed to identify a system that could autonomously discipline and motivate enterprises to maximize social welfare without the government's continuing intervention. To the strength of the system, though, it should be stressed that the government's intervention was mostly indirect and was addressed at continually maneuvering the indicators that were supposed to lead enterprises.

Reforms were also potentially important for reframing policies. The aim was to reframe policies in such a way as to improve their correspondence to the country's features and needs, while better taking into consideration fundamental economic principles. The expected outcome was to decrease the costs for policy making and implementing and improving policy effectiveness. An important question was whether such reframing was to the disadvantage of policy coordination among socialist countries. There were two orders of problems. First, reforms and related reframing took place in some countries, but not in all. This ran the risk of having policies following different logics and with different approaches. Second, while a better consideration for fundamental economic principles should have made the international coordination of policies more effective, a greater attention to local circumstances was not a guarantee of greater effectiveness of coordination. This depended upon the structural features of the national economies. Since the economies of the CEECs were not structurally suitable to integrate effectively with their major economic partner, the Soviet Union, chances were that reforms could push countries away from deeper integration with non-reformed countries and towards market economies. This is indeed what happened with the reformed economies.

Outcomes of reforms and mounting problems: an assessment

During the Soviet-type period, Czechoslovakia, Hungary and Poland failed both to respect fundamental economic rules and to adapt to local circumstances. The former effect descended directly from the fundamental features of the Soviet-type system (central allocation of resources, administrative prices, ineffective incentives, etc.). The latter effect derived from the historical construction and evolution of the Soviet-type economic and political system, which incorporated many traditional Russian circumstances (Kornai 1992a).

Reforms created different problems in different countries, following the features and consistency of the reform programs and their implementation, and political and international circumstances. As mentioned, Hungary implemented what can be considered the most coherent and far-reaching reform. Changes were deep, rather consistent and continuous. In spite of some steps back, for example following the invasion of Czechoslovakia and again in the mid-1970s, the reform process regained vigor and speed each time. In 1982, there was a major and bold re-launch of the reform process (Dallago 1991, Kornai 1986), which started an important process of greenfield privatization and a good degree of genuine market liberalization. The Hungarian economy in 1989 was different from what it was before the reform: its institutions were remarkably changed, the structure of the economy and foreign trade were transformed, material incentives were effective, economic management was decentralized, central planning had a consistent indirect, non-mandatory nature and consumers behaved nearly as though they were living in a market economy. In many senses, the economic power moved from politics and the central government to enterprises and consumers.

One serious problem appeared: consumers' sovereignty improved slightly in the economy, and much more so in politics, albeit in a paternalistic form. This led the government to rely on an important inflow of foreign debt to purchase foreign goods for domestic consumers. Local production of "western" goods (such as blue jeans), although increased through a number of joint ventures, was insufficient to satisfy growing and increasingly sophisticated consumers' demand. The reform was better able to stimulate a more exacting demand than at activating supply.

A further, perhaps even more difficult, problem was the behavior of enterprises. While enterprises were freed from central commands and were largely free to pursue independent goals, they were still receiving massive budget subsidies and their budget constraint was soft (Kornai 1986). As a consequence, they had strong incentives to pursue gain, since salaries, in particular of managers but also wages of workers, depended in part upon the enterprises' economic results. However, these results came often from successful bargaining with central administrators and not from successful competitiveness. The consequence was that productivity was ailing, waste was serious and shortages spread, although for different reasons than in the Soviet-type system and at a superior quantitative and qualitative level of consumption and in part also production. In the reformed Hungarian economy, demand was constantly greater than supply (in both the production and consumption goods markets and the labor market), and the economy was in a permanent inflationary disequilibrium, that foreign debt only in part covered.

The situation in Poland was profoundly different. While reforms were often bold and radical on paper, what the country lacked was the coordination and consistency of reform efforts and, even more, a cohesive reformist leadership. Different pieces of reform were neither mutually coordinated, nor was the reform effort consistent through time. Changes of content and direction followed each other, often under the pressure of social movements and contrasts internal to the Communist Party (Kolodko 1988, 1989).

Overall, the most apparent feature of Polish reforms was a systemic vacuum. In fact, the dismantling of the political and administrative control over the economy were not replaced by effective market alternatives. In an apparent similarity with Hungary, Poland accumulated a huge foreign debt during the period of reforms. However, while Hungary consistently chose to honor the debt, Poland negotiated a reduction of its foreign debt with western public and private creditors. The most apparent outcome of internal economic and social instability and of repeated economic and political crises were recurrent and severe shortages in both production goods and consumer goods. The waste of resources was huge. This situation continued until 1989. During this period, large investments from the 1970s were halted, shortage of consumption goods became endemic and ration cards were introduced for buying food staples, the black market expanded, while foreign debt further increased due to high interest rates.

In Czechoslovakia, following the country's invasion by Warsaw Pact troops in August 1968, the economic system was reversed to a kind of Soviet-type system. Central planning was strengthened and forced industrialization was resumed. Czechoslovakia was more dependent upon trade with the Soviet Union and the other socialist countries than either Hungary or Poland.[15] One problem was that, being more distant from western economies, Czechoslovakia lacked investment in new technologies more than either Hungary or Poland. Although this deficiency prevented the possibility to export to western markets, nevertheless industrial output increased (Lavigne 1999, Myant 1989, Teichova 1988).

However, the standard of living of the population improved steadily, particularly in the early 1970s. Czechoslovakia did not attempt further reforms; the economic system was conservative, yet professionally well managed. As a consequence, the economy was characterized by balanced budgets and the absence of domestic and foreign debt. However, the inherent inefficiency of the Soviet-type system, particularly in the case of a rather developed and sophisticated economy like the Czechoslovak one, the effects of oil crises and the progressing stagnation in the Soviet Union and other socialist countries all had negative effects. As a consequence, the Czechoslovak economy entered into stagnation, particularly during the 1980s.

In a sense, and while Czechoslovakia was institutionally more conservative than either Hungary or Poland, economically the country was in a better position compared to the other two countries. At the same time, the fact is not irrelevant that economic actors were better disciplined than in either Hungary and Poland and had less opportunities to bargain with the state budget to obtain subsidies or other forms of help. They had stricter budget constraints, albeit of an administrative nature.

Overall, the three countries were in different situations and it is difficult to say which country began transformation from an advantageous position. What is worth stressing is that their choice of a transformation path was constrained in different ways. Hungary had the advantage of the better reformed economic system, its enterprises were more accustomed to dealing with western markets and competitors, and consumers were more selective and sophisticated in critically appreciating western goods and way of life. These factors gave the country the illusion that transformation would be easy, fast and successful, since institutional transformation had been largely accomplished. Yet Hungarian formal institutions often only mimicked market institutions and Hungary lacked enforcement.

Poland was in such a difficult situation that the essence of transformation was clear: stabilizing the economy. Although macroeconomic stabilization is not per se part of transformation, the need to begin with stabilization inevitably put enterprises, public administration, workers and consumers under stress. Institutions were bewildered, but enforcement was introduced from outside. Moreover, Poland enjoyed the support of western countries and international organizations, particularly in the rescheduling of debt, that the two other countries missed.

Finally, Czechoslovakia had apparently the most difficult task ahead, since institutionally it was the most unprepared country. Yet its economic situation was balanced and enforcement was effective. In a sense, Czechoslovakia had all the transformation choices available. However, and more than the other two countries, the internal composition of the country could be a strain and the uneasy relations between Slovakia and the Czech lands could be a liability.

Notes

1 For the history of Czechoslovakia, Hungary and Poland see the *Encyclopædia Britannica* online (http://www.britannica.com), Lukowski (2006), Molnár (2001), Polisensky (1991), Prečan (2013).
2 Poland also had an army fighting on the Western Front.
3 Comecon (or CMEA) was the Council for Mutual Economic Assistance, operating from 1949 to 1991. Its role was to coordinate economic planning and international economic cooperation among its member countries, which included the Soviet Union, Central-Eastern European countries and other non-European countries (Mongolia, Cuba and Vietnam) (Kaser 1965, Kiss 1969).
4 The Unified Agricultural Cooperatives Act, adopted in February 1949, opened the way to the voluntary foundation of cooperatives. However, different forms of discrimination were used to force farmers to join cooperatives. Although the formation of cooperatives was virtually completed by 1960 and enjoyed technical support with machines and fertilizers, the opposition by peasants to collectivization, the massive allocation of

labor force from agriculture to industry, and other problems resulted in a decrease in agricultural production.

5 Policy framing is a concept used in social sciences and public policy to analyze and explain the process by which actors, including policy makers, try to understand complex situations, make and implement decisions, and act. Framing is important, because different actors and decision makers may have different understanding and perceptions of the same situation. Framing includes devices that help in reducing the complexity and uncertainty that derive in such circumstances and in assigning roles to different actors. In doing so, framing also allocates decision-making power and the outcomes of decisions and actions.

6 Such priority derived from the Marxian analysis of capitalism and the priority of the development of Sector I (production means) over Sector II (consumption goods), as further developed by Stalin (1952).

7 Rákosi was general secretary of the Hungarian Communist Party (1945–48) and then general secretary of the newly formed Hungarian Workers' Party (1948–56). In this latter position, he was the *de facto* ruler of Hungary between 1949 to 1956. In August 1952, he also became chairman of the Council of Ministers. After the political changes in the Soviet Union following the death of Stalin and the mounting economic problems of the country, he gave up the position of prime minister in favor of Imre Nagy on June 13, 1953, while retaining the office of general secretary. Following mounting economic problems of the country and growing political attacks against his government, Imre Nagy was ousted by a unanimous vote of the National Assembly on April 18, 1955. However, due to the opposition of the Soviet leadership, the post of prime minister was assigned to András Hegedüs, who was a young political ally to Rákosi.

8 János Kádár, a former minister of interior in 1948–50 and a member of the Nagy government in 1953–55, was elected general secretary of the reorganized and renamed Hungarian Socialist Workers' Party (HSWP) on October 25, 1956, during the popular uprising. He kept this position until 1988. Following Soviet pressure, he was also appointed as prime minister on November 4, 1956, following the Soviet occupation of Hungary. He kept the latter position until 1958 and held it again between 1961 and 1965.

9 Gross debt was US$8.7 billion in 1981 in a country of 10 million inhabitants; most of it—more than 80 percent—was of short- or medium-term maturity, and its service absorbed one-third of convertible currency earnings. Compared to GDP, gross foreign debt amounted to 40 percent.

10 The most important such events were new increases of raw materials prices, which further worsened the country's terms of trade; the negative international effect of the foreign debt default and the establishment of martial law in Poland; the US embargo against Poland; Romania's insolvency, and a liquidity crisis in Hungary in 1982.

11 The share of overall exports to other Comecon countries decreased in all three countries. Conversely, the share of exports to Western countries increased. For Poland, the share of overall exports to the East was 56.6 percent in 1975 and that of imports from the East was 43.4 percent. These shares changed in the following years as follows (imports in parenthesis): 52.3 percent (63.2 percent) in 1980, 46.1 percent (54.3 percent) in 1986 and 34.8 percent (32.1 percent) in 1989. The corresponding shares for Czechoslovakia were: 65.4 percent (64.4 percent) in 1975, 63.4 percent (64.8 percent) in 1980, 55.1 percent (58.3 percent) in 1986 and 53.7 percent (54.8 percent) in 1989. In the case of Hungary, values were: 67.7 percent (62.7 percent) in 1975, 50.3 percent (46.9 percent) in 1980, 54.0 percent (50.8 percent) in 1986 and 41.0 percent (39.2 percent) in 1989 (Lavigne 1999).

12 Inflationary overhang identifies the purchasing power accumulated in the hands of the population that cannot be used because of shortages in the market.

13 According to official statistics, the net domestic material product fell by 2.3 percent in 1979, by 6.0 percent in 1980, and by 4.3 percent in 1981–83 (Fallenbuchl 1985,

Eberstadt and Eberstadt 1988). According to the IMF, GDP at constant prices increased by 3.8 percent in 1979 and decreased by 6.0 percent in 1980, by 10.0 percent in 1981 and by 4.8 percent in 1982 (World Economic Outlook data, IMF, http://www.econstats.com/weo/CPOL.htm).

14 As early as summer 1968, as a consequence of the invasion of Czechoslovakia by Warsaw Pact troops, there was a period of prudent reconsideration of some of the measures of the Hungarian reform, since the new political climate, internal and external alike, suggested prudence. Yet this reconsideration was brief, and did not derail the reform.

15 See note 3.

8 Central Europe on the eve of transformation

The topic moment in the transformation of Central-Eastern Europe took place in summer 1988. Mikhail Gorbachev, the general secretary of the Communist Party of the Soviet Union, announced an acceleration of *perestroika* at the 19th Party Conference on September 30. In his report to the Conference, that was published in *Pravda* on June 28, Gorbachev affirmed the freedom by the Central-Eastern European countries (CEECs) to choose their sociopolitical regime as a universal principle in the relation among allied countries.[1] The announcement amounted de facto to the repudiation of the so-called "Brezhnev doctrine" (Lévesque 1997).

The statement became a key concept of Soviet policy, both domestically and in the CEECs. The concomitant international agreements for the withdrawal of large numbers of Soviet troops from the CEECs only strengthened the value of the message and gave credibility to the end of the threat of Soviet invasion. These moves were the consequence of the definitive consolidation of the domestic political power by the reformists within the Soviet Communist Party. The new international stance of the Soviet Union, together with the intense international activity of the Soviet leadership and the pressure that this placed directly and indirectly upon the conservative leadership of the CEECs, made clear that those societies could take seriously the question not only of bolder economic reforms, but even of political reforms. Although initially the issue of international alliances was not on the table, this soon became an issue of discussion, decisions and action.

The changes in Soviet domestic and foreign policy raised much interest and hopes in the CEECs and very soon opened the way for the economic, political and social transformation of those countries. The first concrete consequence was the start of social and political movements for political reforms. This took place primarily in the politically most open countries, in particular Poland and Hungary, but others followed soon, including Czechoslovakia. Bolder economic reforms came also to the center of the stage. These were preceded by a general discussion of deeper economic reforms that the Hungarian party had organized in 1987 by setting up mixed reform committees with the participation of opposition economists. Added to these, opposition movements organized their own meetings and worked out reform programs.

This chapter presents a comparative view of these important events and the fundamental features of transformation programs and actions in Czechoslovakia, Hungary and Poland. It starts with a comparative overview of the economic situation in the three countries and an assessment of the most important economic problems.

The fading performance of Central-Eastern European economies

The economies of Eastern European countries entered the 1980s in a generally debilitated shape.[2] The high growth and full employment achieved in the 1950s and in part also during the 1960s belonged to a forgotten time, when social changes, the effect of the reconstruction period (Jánossy 1966, 1975) and the large-scale mobilization of previously unused human and material resources, and in part also technical resources, guaranteed a forceful growth of the economy and full employment (Figure 8.1). It is true that the quality of that production was generally poor, its technical level often backward, work was often poorly organized and work discipline was slack, and production went mostly to support accumulation to the disadvantage of consumption (Kornai 1992, Winiecki 2012). Nevertheless, in that period, achievements were evident, in particular in the military sector and the space sector. Some positive results were felt also in well-being and a middle class began to develop in some countries, particularly towards the ends of that period.

However, growing economic problems signaled that the Soviet-type economic system was increasingly unsuitable for supporting growth in increasingly sophisticated economies. In particular, it was unable to guarantee sufficient economic dynamism to economies that exhausted unutilized material and human resources and that aspired to trade with western countries. Reforms in the course of the second half of the 1960s and early 1970s tried to invert the course and modernize the economic system, by decentralizing part of decision making to enterprises, activating material incentives and opening up the economies to international trade.

Although these efforts were partly successful, in particular in improving the situation of consumers in Central European countries and to a more limited extent also in South-Eastern European countries and the Soviet Union, overall they were unable to improve economic performance. While generally the quality of production improved, other problems appeared, particularly in the form of external and internal deficits and debts. Although these were mainly the outcome of poor economic management and soft budget constraints (Kornai 1980), the political system prevented the implementation of more consistent and effective reforms. To be sure, these countries were unlucky in opening up at a time when also the dynamism of western economies was dramatically decreasing, economic crises were becoming a serious problem, "stagflation" was cured with austerity policies and the prices of energy and raw materials—of which most CEECs were poorly supplied—were growing fast.

These events—the modest effect of reforms and the instability in the world markets—gave strength to the conservative forces in the political and administrative structures. The second part of the 1970s was a time of economic centralization and slowing performance of the Soviet-type economies in most

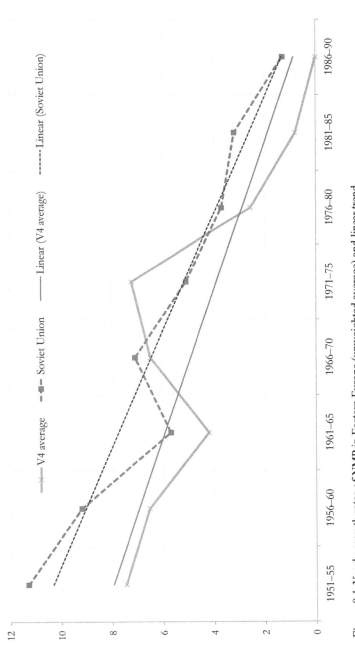

Figure 8.1 Yearly growth rates of NMP in Eastern Europe (unweighted average) and linear trend

Sources: own elaboration on data from Lavigne (1995)

countries. Growth slowed down in virtually all countries. Some, such as Poland, were in a prolonged stagnation. The situation worsened further in the 1980s, when this stagnation spread to most CEECs, including the Soviet Union (Aganbegyan 1988). Standards of living did not improve, thus breeding public dissatisfaction. The government's attempt to meet dissatisfaction with excessive wage increases in Poland and import of consumption goods in Hungary, while refraining from price increases, created budget deficits, external debt, a rapidly growing money supply in Poland and high external debt in Hungary. Inflation increased in both countries, but in Poland inflation scaled up to hyperinflation, with negative effects for output. Only in Czechoslovakia did economic and financial management continue to be orderly (Kornai 1992a).

It was this evidence of increasing economic ineffectiveness, together with the growing dissatisfaction of the middle classes and also of workers, traditionally the most loyal social and political basis of the system, that prompted the political leadership to open up to bolder reforms. An important goal was also to recover social legitimacy for the system and its leadership. The fundamental novelty of this time were developments in the Soviet Union.

With the weakening of the communist orthodoxy and the Soviet Union's grip over CEECs during the 1980s, social opposition movements started to organize and slowly acquire a political role. These moves were particularly important and spread in Poland and Hungary, much less so in Czechoslovakia. However, it was with the end of the threat of Soviet invasion that political change became overwhelming and with it economic transformation accelerated. The ground for this was prepared, at least in Poland and Hungary, starting in mid-1985.

Systemic crisis and the last attempts at reforms

Decreasing economic dynamism and the election of Mikhail Gorbachev as the first secretary of the Communist Party of the Soviet Union in 1985 jeopardized the legitimacy of the economic and political system in the CEECs and questioned the role of the Soviet Union as the political leader and guarantor of the system of socialist countries. These facts emboldened both reformers from within the system and opponents. Equally important, these facts isolated the guardians of orthodoxy and made them uncertain of the way to follow and their future. While attempts at stopping processes existed (e.g. Ligachev in the Soviet Union or Husak in Czechoslovakia), the debates and political arguments concerned increasingly the direction of either reform or systemic change.

Hungary

Once again, the Hungarian party was the most determined in attempting to keep the leadership of changes under its own governance, by establishing an increasingly bold economic reform agenda.[3] In 1982, a new wave of economic reforms was implemented (Adam 1987, Berend 1990, Dallago 1989, Hare 1987). These reforms, in particular, enlarged significantly the scope for non-socialized activities.

These were activities not directly controlled or planned by the government, but directly managed by their organizers or participants. These included the traditional private sector in small businesses, handicrafts and agriculture, the latter typically in symbiosis with agricultural cooperatives and state farms. More original and important were the so-called "work organizations." Of these there existed various types; their common denominator was that employees of a state-owned company could autonomously organize their after-work productive activity. They could use the machines, equipment and raw materials of their employer, usually for a fee, and produce goods and services that they could sell through the free market or, more usually, through their employer at market prices.

An important simplification of the administrative structure took place in the late 1970s and the 1980s, when the number of ministries was significantly decreased and the ministries' influence on managers was reduced. The number of branch ministries, the traditional backbone of Soviet and Soviet-type administration, were reduced to four (industry, agriculture and food, construction, and communications). Branch ministries became policy organs and lost much of their traditional authority over enterprises. At the same time, the competence and role of functional ministries—the Ministry of Finance and the Ministry of Trade in particular—were greatly strengthened. The former, in particular, was responsible for banking system supervision and for the definition and implementation of economic regulators, that reforms placed at the center of economic management.

The effort of reorganizing the economy to make it more effective and efficient also concerned enterprises (Lee and Nellis 1990). Large enterprises were broken up into smaller firms and the establishment of smaller, non-public types of firms was legalized and promoted in 1982 (see above). In 1983, state-owned enterprises, cooperatives, financial institutions and local governments were authorized to issue bonds to finance their activities. The governance of public companies was reformed in 1984 and 1985 with the introduction, among others, of self-management councils in about three-quarters of the 1,700 medium and large state-owned enterprises. The councils included elected representatives of the company's employees. A degree of political liberalization accompanied economic and administrative reforms.

These changes had the advantage of bringing new dynamism to the economy. Their disadvantage was that they introduced a clear division of the economy between the formal, socialized sector and the many forms of the non-socialized, quasi-private sector. The importance of the latter for the economy was relevant and growing (Dallago 1989).[4] However, the very success of this sector emptied the formal, socialized sector of much of its role and control over resources and made incentives in this sector nearly irrelevant, compared to the much more effective incentives in the non-socialized sector. Indeed, at the end of the 1980s, the economic and financial situation of Hungarian enterprises worsened further: investment funding was severely depressed, efficiency levels declined as much as profits did, and credit shortages were significant (Lee and Nellis 1990).

Confronted with the evidence of mounting problems and in search for more effective ways to improve companies' performance, the government adopted two important laws, whose effect went well into the transformation processes.

The Company Law of 1988 and the Law of Transformation of June 1989 allowed management and workers of state-owned companies to initiate the privatization process. Managers were ready to use the opportunities that these laws created and started processes of "spontaneous privatization." This meant that they either became the new owners of the companies' assets, or involved external (typically foreign) investors and became the highly paid managers of partially privatized firms (Lee and Nellis 1990, van Brabant 1992).

In a sense, institutional and economic success were achieved at the price of the disruption of the formal socialized sector. Central planning lost further importance and effectiveness, while market competition continued to be either non-existent or soft, since the formal sector protected the autonomous sector against competition by granting a captive market to it at favorable conditions. Moreover, the booming autonomous sector—in a sense, similar to the private cooperatives that were introduced in the Soviet Union during the 1990s (Malle 1992, Nuti 1992)—created a sizeable set of economic activities and people who were personally interested in enriching themselves and being independent, without paying the price of following the general rules of a well-working market economy. This further nurtured the illusion of the supposed magical properties of the private economy and the market system, to the disregard of the accompanying costs and hard institutions. In a sense, Hungary went excessively in the direction of privileging local circumstances to the disadvantage of general rules.

The unsustainability of the socialized system became increasingly evident also to the political leadership of the country. Political developments in the Soviet Union under the leadership of Mikhail Gorbachev further improved the chances for the powerful reformist component of the Hungarian Socialist Workers Party (HSWP), which tried to initiate a general reform process that would also involve some mild political liberalization. They attempted to coordinate the reformists within the party, opposition economists and various movements of the civil society around a process of general reform of the Hungarian economy and, to a limited extent, the political system.

An important event was the meeting of opposition intellectuals in Monori in summer 1985. The meeting was not authorized, but authorities tolerated it. The gathering was a very important one, since both main opposition lines were represented: the modernist, technocratic, so-called "urban" opposition and the traditionalist, nationalist and irredentist so-called "popular-national" opposition. The former looked at Western Europe, the latter at the traditional Hungary and the Hungarian population living in Hungary's neighboring countries. It was from the evolution of these two forces that the political landscape of post-transformation Hungary came. The importance of that gathering for the following events was twofold. First, it prompted the HSWP leadership to take action. Second, later on the ruling party also split along those lines. A second meeting, similar in composition but larger in participation, followed in Lakitelek in September 1987. This meeting requested openly the introduction of political pluralism in Hungary.

An important difference from Poland was that authorities tolerated these meetings, but did not take part in them. These were not round tables in which the existing

government recognized as a matter of fact that the social opposition was an equal partner, as in Poland. The party in power continued to govern change, or so it hoped, but accepted the pressure coming from an unrecognized opposition. In a sense, this approach included the seeds of paternalism, that was so typical of the Kádár regime and that continued also in the post-transformation period. Round table meetings came later, in summer 1989, when the party was dissolving.

In parallel with these external events, the HSWP congress in March 1985 approved a program for the revitalization of the economy. Following this and the foundation within the party of the Patriotic Front, the reformists in the party boosted a group of mostly young economists to analyze the situation of the country and work out a comprehensive reform program. This was worked out in a time when external debt was booming and Hungary became one of the most heavily indebted countries in the world in per capita terms (gross debt was at US$1,700 per capita in 1987, or 63 percent of GDP, according to Mihályi 2013). The program was published in 1987 under the title of "Turn and reform" (Antal et al. 1987). Its strong criticism of the existing political and economic system and related policies represented in a sense a technical admission of the necessity of change, with strong political implications.

The 1985 program played an important role in the acceleration of events that took place in 1988, since it deprived the ruling party and government of legitimization from within. In March 1988, János Kádár resigned as general secretary of the HSWP, thus ending his 32-year-long political power career. In the same year, the three main parties of what would become post-1989 Hungary were re-established, thus de facto transforming the country into a pluralistic one. In January 1989, the leader of the National Front within the HSWP, Imre Pozsgay recognized that in 1956 a popular uprising took place. In June 1989, Imre Nagy, the 1953–55 reformist prime minister, was rehabilitated and reburied in a public ceremony attended by a large crowd. This ceremony is often held as the moment when the old system died.

The year 1989 included other internal and external topic moments. In March, the opposition organized a round table, that ended with a division among the opposition forces. In May, the Hungarian government decided unilaterally to let down the iron curtain between Hungary and Austria and, in September, allowed East German citizens to cross the Hungarian border with Austria. During the summer, the opposition round table and the government met and agreed on the legal framework for systemic change. In October, the HSWP was dissolved in its last congress. The reformists formed a new party, the Hungarian Socialist Party (HSP), which played an important role in the post-transformation period. The formal moment of systemic change took place on October 23, 1989, the anniversary of the 1956 popular uprising, when the provisional Hungarian president, Mátyás Szűrös announced the birth of the new republic in front of the Parliament. At the end of the same year, the external gross debt of the country reached US$20 billion, or approximately US$2,000 per capita.

Systemic change reached its no-return threshold effects in 1990, with two major undertakings, both in March. On March 10, Hungary and the Soviet Union agreed on the withdrawal of Soviet troops. On the 25th, the first round of the first

democratic elections took place. In the meantime, privatization was taking place. Finally, at the end of 1991, Hungary abandoned the Warsaw Pact.

Poland

The fundamental feature of systemic crisis in Poland was the existence of a true, organized counter-power, Solidarność, which was established formally in September 1980. Its legitimacy derived from its 10 million members in 1981,[5] representing most of the Poland's employees, a membership larger than that of the party in power. This social movement had no match in any other socialist country. Another remarkable aspect of the Polish situation was that the government accepted de facto the existence of this counter-power, even if it did not recognize it de jure. Although the government occasionally used repression—in particular in the period of the imposition of martial law between 1981 and 1983—the government tried to reach a pragmatic settlement with Solidarność.

At the time, the standard of living was rapidly deteriorating in the country, inflation was rapidly increasing, shortages were endemic and the black economy was pervasive. The country was also fighting with a dramatic lack of convertible currency necessary to finance imports and pay back foreign debt[6] and with the effects of western sanctions. The government introduced ration cards for basic consumer articles, such as milk and sugar. This situation fostered social dissatisfaction and political instability.

In spite of martial law between 1981 and 1983 and the uneasy situation in following years, the Polish government tried to revitalize a very difficult economic situation with a pragmatic approach and a set of unconventional reforms. A process of decentralization of decision making in state-owned companies was attempted through the 1982 Law on State Enterprises (Lee and Nellis 1990). The law introduced worker's councils in most companies and increased enterprise autonomy. However, the performance of companies worsened and this contributed to the increase of economic instability.

A chain of Pewex state-owned stores was opened, selling goods in convertible currencies, as a device to obtain foreign currencies. More important, the scope for private activity was broadened, which led to a significant increase in the number of private businesses. Most important, state-owned enterprises obtained substantially greater autonomy, in particular through the 1988 law on economic activity. Fundamental principles of this reform were self-financing and self-management of state-owned enterprises (Nawojczyk 1993). The increased autonomy of state-owned enterprises and the disruption of the central planning system allowed managers to increase their control over companies through a kind of spontaneous privatization. While foreign investment was encouraged, the unstable political situation and the risky condition of the economy discouraged foreign investors.

The power dualism between the Polish United Workers Party (PUWP) and Solidarność proved to be costly to the country. In part, this was due to the growing uncertainty of the government amidst repeated economic failures and the growing radicalization of Solidarność, in which American and Western

European influence was rapidly increasing.[7] While Solidarność came out primarily of the mismanagement of the economy, social unrest—of which Solidarność represented the most important form and component— itself fostered further mismanagement through social resistance and other forms of boycott or external influence. This situation subtracted attention and efforts from the economy and diverted them towards political competition. It also increased political and economic uncertainty that further depressed economic activity and prevented the country from undertaking more orderly reforms and attracting foreign investment. At the same time, this situation weakened the government's management and control of the economy and gave managers greater independence from the central power. This played a significant role in the post-transformation years.

The situation looked hopeless to the government and the party, which accepted the idea that they lost control over the country affairs (Hayden 2006). Consequently, they set up 94 sessions of talks in 13 working groups with Solidarność (the "Round Table Talks") in April 1989. The talks ended with the agreement to move to a parliamentary political system and semi-free elections. Solidarność was legalized and could participate in the elections. The elections were semi-free, because non-communist candidates could compete for all the seats in the freely contested Senate, but for only one-third of the seats in the lower chamber of Parliament. The remaining seats were reserved for candidates of the PUWP, thus guaranteeing that the party was keeping transitorily political power. While the PUWP hoped to gain time to implement successful reforms, this time without social opposition, and thus improve its popularity, Solidarność's sweeping victory in the June 1989 election completely changed the situation and led to the formation of the first Solidarność government in September,[8] headed by Tadeusz Mazowiecki.

This government engaged soon in what became the first and, in a sense, classical transformation plan. The change to the Polish Constitution in December 1989 ended formally the socialist system in Poland. The formation of the new government was followed soon by the dissolution of the PUWP in 1990, from which the Social Democracy of the Republic of Poland (SDRP) was established.[9] The first fully free elections took place in October 1991. After the dissolution of the Warsaw Pact in 1991, an agreement was reached that Soviet troops would leave the country in 1993.

Czechoslovakia

After the invasion by the troops of the Warsaw Pact in August 1968, the country lived a period of intense "normalization" between 1969 and 1971 and a milder one that continued until 1987 (Bischof et al. 2009, Myant 1989, Teichova 1988, Williams 1997). Normalization consisted primarily in the return to the pre-Prague Spring situation in political power relations, in particular the restoration of the rule of the Communist Party of Czechoslovakia (CPCs). However, during this period some changes introduced in 1968 remained, in particular the reorganization of the country into a federation made of the Czech Socialist Republic and the Slovak Socialist Republic, with some of the ministries being organized on a

national basis and with independent national plans.[10] However, the CPCs remained a unified organ, which exerted the real control over the entire federation, and the federal plan had priority over national plans. Another difference was the dissident movement existing outside the party, that reached a certain relevance, in particular among intellectuals.

The normalization in 1969–71 started with the replacement of Alexander Dubček by Gustáv Husák as secretary general of the KSČ in April 1969. The main aspect of normalization was the consolidation of the new political leadership, that involved the removal of the reformers from leading positions and various other forms of political repression (Šimečka 1984). Other important steps included the removal or the modification of various laws (e.g. on press liberalization) enacted during the Prague Spring period, the strengthening of cooperation with the Comecon and Warsaw Pact members and stronger police power.

In the economic domain, the main consequence of normalization was the strengthening of the central control over enterprises, that had previously obtained substantial autonomy (Myant 1989). Also important were increased control over prices and stronger economic ties with Comecon countries, to the disadvantage of trade with western countries. The new government tried to gain popular support through higher economic growth and by improving consumers' situation, in particular in the first half of the 1970s. Net material product in the first half of the 1970s grew at an yearly average of 5.7 percent. The strategy was successful for a few years, but the economy's dynamism slowed down in the second half of the decade, averaging an yearly growth rate of 3.7 percent. Growth rates of personal consumption declined progressively, shortages increased and retail prices rose.

The first half of the 1980s was a difficult time for the Czechoslovak economy, as much as it was for western economies. Initially, in 1981 and 1982, the economy went through a slump and consumption declined. However, in the following three years, economic performance improved. It is to be noticed that western governments and banks decided to restrict credit to the CEECs following the introduction of martial law in Poland and the mounting indebtedness of various CEECs. Moreover, within the Comecon, the price of Soviet oil was tied to its international price through a mobile five-year average and oil exports to the CEECs were scaled back by 10 percent. When the international oil price started to decline in 1983, the formula kept Comecon's oil price increasing.

These difficulties prompted the Czechoslovak government to adopt reforms in industry and agriculture, entering into effect in 1981. Although limited in their goals, these reforms included some important measures, such as greater autonomy for managers of state-owned companies, in particular in investments, and material incentives for employees. The intention was to make enterprises more attentive to prices and costs and activate incentives to performance. However, central planning continued to be the fundamental means of economic management.

Throughout the 1980s, Czechoslovakia had the highest level of development among the CEECs and the highest standard of living. It also had a low external debt (US$2 billion in the second half of the 1980s) and balanced or surplus

budgets. In addition, the black economy was less widespread than in other socialist countries. The country, however, missed much of the information and communication revolution that characterized the world economy since the 1970s. In spite of the use of planning indicators emphasizing efficiency and quality, rather than gross output, the effect was modest due to weak incentives.

In particular, efficiency in the use of energy and raw materials was low in international comparison, and central planning was biased in favor of the production of producer goods and to the disadvantage of consumer goods. One reason for this was that the country had a stock of old equipment and machines, the consequence of extensive growth strategy, a stagnant resource base and growing dependence upon imports of energy and raw materials in a time of rapidly increasing international prices. As a consequence, the high level of industrialization and of national income did not translate into high standard of consumption or exports, comparable to those of western countries of a similar level of development. Moreover, the country increasingly was left behind—as with other CEECs—by western countries that in the early 1950s had had a similar level of development, such as Austria or Finland, and was overtaken by countries that were less developed, such as Italy and Spain (Table 8.1).

The problems that Czechoslovakia's economy was encountering increased the pressure to reform the economy, a pressure that was particularly strong after Gorbachev implemented reforms in the Soviet Union. A program of economic reform was announced in April 1987, to be started in 1991—too late. However,

Table 8.1 Economic development, East and West (per capita GDP at 1990 International Geary-Khamis dollar)

	1913	1928	1938	1946	1950	1972	1988	1990
Austria	3.465	3.657	3.559	1.956	3.706	10.771	15.754	16.895
Finland	2.111	2.707	3.589	3.683	4.253	10.448	16.088	16.866
Centre-North Italy	2.305	2.666	2.830	2.162	3.172	9.795	15.485	16.313
Ireland	2.736	2.737	3.052	3.052	3.453	6.663	10.234	11.818
Greece	1.177	2.234	2.677	1.386	1.915	7.400	9.784	10.015
Portugal	1.250	1.470	1.747	1.928	2.086	6.355	9.868	10.826
Spain	2.056	2.584	1.790	2.179	2.189	7.099	11.046	12.055
Czechoslovakia	2.096	2.977			3.501	6.858	8.709	8.513
Czech Rep.								8.895
Slovakia								7.763
Hungary	2.098	2.415	2.655	1.721	2.480	5.336	7.031	6.459
Poland	1.739		2.182		2.447	5.010	5.789	5.113
7 Eastern Europe	1.726				2.088	4.809	5.981	5.427
USSR	1.414	1.370	2.150	1.913	2.841	5.643	7.043	6.894
Russia								7.779
Ukraine								6.027

Source: New Maddison Project Database (http://www.ggdc.net/maddison/maddison-project/data.htm)

during the second half of the 1980s, deeper and bolder reforms were attempted, although some of them had only an experimental character. For instance, in 1987, some 120 state-owned industrial companies obtained greater autonomy in defining their production targets and profile, and managing their finances. They only obtained some basic targets from the central plan. More in general, the government pursued the improvement of the quality of production and technical progress and the transition to capital-intensive productions and techniques, which allowed them to decrease the use of energy and increase exports to western markets.

Economic and political legitimacy

One important issue, that received some attention at the time, concerned the legitimacy of the old system. Both the strength and weakness of the Stalinist system was the forced allocation of resources and forced growth (Kornai 1973). These worked until there were unused resources, albeit amidst enormous inefficiencies and high social costs. It is clear that the old ideological legitimacy, the one that supported the fight against "capitalist exploiters" first and forced industrialization later on, faded away with the death of Stalin. A new generation of Soviet leaders revealed the enormous social costs and crimes that Stalin's policy implied and its economic unsustainability, after full employment of resources was reached. In the CEECs, this change led to the change of the old Stalinist leadership, between 1953 and 1956.

The new course, in the second half of the 1950s and in a clearer and bolder way during the 1960s, looked for legitimation in the economic domain. The leading idea was to reach and overcome the most developed capitalist countries in both production and consumption levels. Both the space race and the military race provided initially some success. However, the inability to upgrade the economy's efficiency through mild reforms conflicted with the aim of improving consumption, given the systemic priority for heavy industry and the military sector. The price paid was the progressive irrelevance of central planning and the bureaucratization of the economy. Although it is undeniable that some improvement was reached in the situation of consumers, the working of the economy and the quality of production, a sort of "socialist" laissez faire spread to the economy in the form of diffused second economy (Grossman 1977, 1987) and forced adaptation in production (Kornai 1980, 1992a). The system lacked a proper coordination of economic activity and consistent incentives. Disorganization led to growing shortages and, in time, to progressive slowdown of economic dynamism. These problems were occasionally fixed through recurrent political economic campaigns (Soós 1986) and reforms. The latter were often timid and contradictory and failed to constitute an alternative source of legitimacy for the system. They were generally unable to give new motivation and effective incentives to replace the old ones. The general outcome was political and economic apathy.

Hungary was an important exception. The 1956 events shook up the system from its foundation. The political and economic elite looked for legitimacy through a kind of new social contract (summarized in Kadar's bold statement as early as 1961 that "those who are not against us are with us" [Berend 2009]) based on social tolerance (provided that the political system was not challenged) and personal well-being. Consumption improved and increased considerably and political tolerance created a favorable and often vibrant social and cultural climate. Some competition was introduced into the system and the quality of production improved. Shortage changed nature and structure, but continued to be pervasive and investment cycles became more prominent (Bauer 1981, Dallago 1982, 1987).

Seen from the post-transformation perspective, the real disadvantage of the Hungarian reform in terms of the renewed legitimacy of the system was that it was not economically sustainable. In fact, it was largely financed through massive credits obtained in western markets. Although the Hungarian economy was clearly in better shape than the Polish economy, its performance continued to fall short of the challenge which the need to repay the debt represented. Although it is true that the political successor of the HSWP—the renewed HSP—had some chances to do well at the first democratic elections, the serious indebtedness of the country and the illusion that the artificially generated well-being created in the population proved to be a shaky basis for the legitimacy of the new post-transformation system.

Neither Poland nor Czechoslovakia offered alternative ways to legitimize the old system. After the failure of the hopes that Gomułka's return to power and his "national communist" agenda created around 1968 and after the failure of Gierek's grand industrialization plan in the late 1970s, Polish society was characterized by a prolonged, at times acute confrontation between the power of the system and the counter-power of Solidarność. The economy suffered, the system had hardly any legitimacy, while social participation was strong and well-organized. A true counter-system was taking form. This active and organized participation to systemic change proved to be a strong basis for transformation.

Czechoslovakia could have represented a real alternative to legitimacy, had the 1968 general reform plan been allowed to develop. This plan also promised to deeply reform politics, along with the economy and the society. What remained, after the August 1968 invasion, was a conservative and centralized political and economic regime. Yet in this regime public administration, companies and consumers were well disciplined, with balanced budgets and no domestic and foreign debt. If the old system barely had any legitimacy, Czechoslovakia had undoubtedly the most disciplined economy in financial terms. This proved to be fundamental during transformation and the country had all their options open, in particular in the case of privatization. Moreover, even if firms were less autonomous from the central government than in either Hungary or Poland, they were nevertheless used to have a hard budget constrained, even if politically and administratively imposed.

Systemic collapse

Systemic collapse began in Poland in 1989, and continued into Hungary, East Germany, Bulgaria, Czechoslovakia and Romania. There were three main factors that promoted collapse: the countries' rapidly worsening economic performance, active social opposition, and the perspective of western support. The most important form of the latter was the perspective of entering the European Union. Three factors made change possible and perhaps inevitable: the Soviet Union's changed attitude opened the door, the loss of confidence of the old *nomenklatura* weakened resistance, and the illusions and misjudgment of the nature and costs of transformation created powerful motivations. With the partial exception of Romania, change had a peaceful nature.

Systemic collapse was initiated by social forces, whose action had rapid fundamental political effects. Soon after, the new democratic governments moved to change their economic systems. Poland was the most active in fostering systemic change (Kaminski 1991). The first crucial moment was on April 4, 1989. This was the day when the Round Table Agreement legalized Solidarność and announced partly free parliamentary elections to be held on June 4. Additional milestone events followed: on June 4, 1989, when Solidarność won overwhelming clear victory in the partially free election, and in summer 1989, when Hungary allowed East German citizens to cross over the iron curtain to Austria. Following electoral victory, Solidarność formed the first democratic government led by Tadeusz Mazowiecki. In 1990, Poland's president Jaruzelski resigned and was succeeded by the leader of Solidarność, Wałęsa, who won the 1990 presidential elections. On July 1, 1991 the Warsaw Pact was dissolved and, later on, various former members joined NATO and the European Union. On September 18, 1993 the last Russian troops left Poland.

In Hungary, following the replacement of János Kádár as general secretary of the HSWP on May 23, 1988, a new reformist government was appointed in November, headed by Miklós Németh. In January 1989, the Hungarian Parliament adopted various democratic measures, including freedom of association, trade union pluralism, free press, new electoral law and radical revision of the Constitution. Round tables between the HSWP and new opposition political parties began in April and ended in September with the signing of an agreement. The agreement included the reform of the Constitution, the establishment of a constitutional court, free political parties, multiparty elections for the Parliament to be held on March 25, 1990 and reform of the penal code and the law on penal procedures. In May 1989, Hungary took down the iron curtain along the border with Austria, while in June, Imre Nagy was rehabilitated and reburied. On June 19, 1991 Soviet troops left Hungary.

In Czechoslovakia, political changes came at the end of 1989 in a "soft" and rapid way, known as the "Velvet Revolution." Following street demonstrations in November, in parallel with the initial demolition of the Berlin Wall, the entire leadership of the Communist Party resigned and the party announced that it would dismantle the single-party system. The iron curtain with West Germany and Austria was pulled down in early December. Changes accelerated further in December, when the first largely non-communist government was appointed with the leadership of the Civic Forum, Alexander Dubček was elected speaker of the federal Parliament and Václav Havel as the new president on December 29. The first democratic elections were held on June 8, 1990 and one year later Soviet troops were withdrawn.

The three countries arrived at transformation in different economic and social conditions. Although they were considered as middle-income countries, remarkable differences existed in the level of their development (Table 8.2) and economic structures. The economic structures of the former socialist states differed in three essential ways: the share of industry, agriculture and services; the degree of monopolization; and the dependence on foreign trade. There were relatively large numbers of small enterprises in Hungary and Poland, most of which were private or non-socialized, and Hungary, in particular, had a sizeable services sector (Åslund 1992, pp. 5–6, Marelli and Signorelli 2010). Of the three countries, Czechoslovakia was the economically most developed, even if the country lost ground compared to other socialist countries. On the eve of transformation, Czechoslovakia had a highly industrialized economy, in which the industrial sector accounted for 60 percent of the net material product. The socialized sector accounted for the near-totality of production and employment.

The non-socialized sector was most developed in Hungary and Poland. An important part of these activities were not fully private, since fixed assets and often also the materials used and even the working time belonged to socialized companies and much of the production was sold to the latter, albeit usually at the private market prices. For this reason, it is not easy to calculate the real contribution of this non-socialized sector to the economy, while official statistics only consider activities in which property rights are formally private.

During the last years of the old system, reforms accelerated. The key issue in all countries was the governance of enterprises in the state and cooperative sectors and, in Hungary and Poland, the enlargement of the activity of private and non-socialized enterprises. Some fundamental laws on companies, joint ventures, taxation, trade and foreign trade were passed and some institutional reorganizations were implemented, such as the introduction of a two-tier bank system in Hungary. Also foreign trade with western countries was partially liberalized, particularly in Hungary.[11] In Poland, foreign trade liberalization was more limited (Curtis 1992) and in Czechoslovakia was nearly absent (LoC 1987). Private activities were liberalized in both Hungary and Poland, although various limits and constraints remained, such as on the number of employees, access to capital and the legal form. Such constraints prevented the development of strong, internationally competitive private enterprises (Dallago 1991). In spite of these limits, private activities expanded considerably, well beyond what appeared from official statistics (Dallago 1989).

Three countries

The three countries arrived at transformation in very different economic and institutional conditions. Czechoslovakia had an economically conservative, yet well-managed economy. It had neither domestic nor external debt. For this reason, it was free to choose the best path to transformation. The approach was

Table 8.2 GNP Levels: East-West comparisons (GNP per capita in US$, 1989)

| | Former Soviet-type economies | | | | Other middle-income countries | | | | | |
	Czechoslovakia	Hungary	Poland	USSR	Brazil	Portugal	South Africa	Mexico	Panama	Chile
GNP per capita, $	3,450	2,630	1,890	1,780	2,400	4,250	2,460	2,080	1,760	1,780
Geary–Khamis $	8,768	6,903	5,684	7,112	5,224	10,372	3,956	5,899	4,352	6,283

Source: World Bank Atlas 1991 (GNP per capita $) and New Maddison Project Database (http://www.ggdc.net/maddison/maddison-project/data.htm) (G-K $)

typically technocratic, without much social debate. The leading idea was a short-cut to a pure market economy via the dispersion of private property rights. It was expected that the outcome would be a highly diffuse ownership of firms, whose owners would start immediately to trade, thus establishing a competitive market for assets and competitive market prices for capital. This would spread markets to any sector. Unfortunately, this approach disregarded at least two idiosyncratic features. First, citizens who became owners were more oriented to consumption than to investment. Second, the financial sector (the banks) remained initially in the hands of the state. This prevented the development of financial markets, which kept privatized firms at bay for a while.

In Hungary, the boldest reformer before 1989, reforms created a quasi-market economy without private ownership of (large) firms and a booming non-socialized sector in small-scale activities. Economic management was decentralized, managers received responsibility, consumers obtained priority, perhaps the only Eastern European country to do so before 1989. However, external debt was among the highest in the world in per capita terms. This last fact determined the transformation path. Public assets were sold to "real" owners with sufficient capital. Self-privatization by managers apart, real owners could only be foreign investors. Thus privatization moved a substantial inflow of foreign capital, which appreciated the local currency. Foreign trade suffered as a consequence, in a country which was pursuing an export-led strategy.

Poland was the country which started transformation in the most difficult conditions. The government already implemented an export-led strategy in the 1970s, which was financed by abundant and cheap western liquidity. Foreign debt increased to high levels, yet the economy was unable to profit from the investment and the import of western machinery and equipment. The main reason were perverse incentives in Polish firms. Part of the debt (some 50 percent) was forgiven to the country before 1989 and Poland continued to enjoy a preferential treatment by the West. Among the reasons for this were the size of the country, its traditional uneasy relation with Russia/Soviet Union, and the high number of Polish expatriates in the West. When transformation started, Poland was the country that most needed external support, whose finances and economy were in the worst condition, under the risk of hyperinflation, and whose population was the most active and better organized in promoting transformation. Poland was the first and most consistent country to promote round tables between the government/Communist Party and the political and social opposition. It was also the first country to organize free elections, albeit weighted with many constraints. The initial transformation agenda was tailored on the Washington Consensus prescriptions (stabilization, liberalization, privatization) and the country was for a while a reference for other countries. Again, the disregard for important circumstances[12] created additional difficulties. The concern for further economic destabilization and political conflicts led to postpone for years the approval of a law on privatization.

In all the three countries the follow-up and outcome of transformation gave significantly different results compared to the original agenda. However, this was so in different ways. Poland was remarkably successful in the pragmatic pursuit of stabilization and reform, with remarkably positive outcomes. Hungary was a negative surprise, a country in which the economy and society became increasingly split, as the domestic sector fell behind in comparison to the successful foreign-owned sector and policies swung between opposite constituencies and aims. Czechoslovakia split into two countries soon after transformation began. The Czech Republic, more developed and apparently with stronger institutions, went through unexpected difficulties. Slovakia turned out to be a major positive surprise and the only country among the four that successfully adopted the euro.

Notes

1 "The concept of choice occupies a key place in the new thinking. We believe in the universality of this principle for international relations . . . In this situation, foreign imposition of a social system or a lifestyle through any method, and even more so through military measures, is a dangerous way of acting from the past" (Lévesque 1997, p. 80).

2 The Soviet-type economies achieved a 4.5 percent annual growth rate in per capita GNP during the 1950s, exceeding the 3.7 percent rate of growth of a comparison group of market economies (Gregory and Stuart 1997). While the comparison group of market economies averaged rates of growth of GNP per capita of 4.5 percent in the 1960s, 2.8 percent in the 1970s and 2 percent in the 1980s, the growth of per capita GNP of the Soviet-type economies is estimated to have decelerated to 3.6 percent in the 1960s, 2.8 percent in the 1970s and 0.8 percent in the 1980s (Svejnar 2002).

3 On the major events in the political and economic transformation in Hungary see http://tudasbazis.sulinet.hu/hu/tarsadalomtudomanyok/tortenelem/az-i-vilaghaborutol-a-ketpolusu-vilag-felbomlasaig/a-szocialista-rendszer-osszeomlasa/rendszervaltas-magyarorszagon.

4 Most of the jobs in the non-socialized sector were part-time and the sector included many pensioners. Dallago (1989) calculated the employment in the non-socialized sector in full-time jobs and found that these corresponded to approximately 45 percent of the jobs in the socialized economy. Given the lower productivity of the sector, its gross production corresponded approximately to 15 percent of the official one.

5 Encyclopaedia Britannica: http://www.britannica.com/EBchecked/topic/553374/Solidarity.

6 Long- and medium-term external debt with western countries was US$1.2 billion in 1971. This amount increased to US$20.5 billion by 1979 and to US$23 billion by 1980 (Nuti 1981). Debt service (amortization and interest) absorbed 12.4 per cent of export earnings in 1971, a share that reached 81.8 per cent in 1980. These figures do not include short-term debt, which by 1980 was around US$2 billion, nor do they include the debt to other socialist countries, which was estimated at another US$2 billion. If one includes short-term debt, the debt-service ratio to exports was around unity.

7 According to Judt (2005, p. 589), the United States provided Solidarność with as much as US$50 million financial support during the clandestine years.

8 This was the outcome of the two traditional PUWP's allies siding with Solidarność to form a coalition government. These were the ZSL (United People's Party) and SD (Alliance of Democrats).

9 The party was transformed into the Democratic Left Alliance (SLD) in 1999. The SLD was the leading government party in 1993–97 and again in 2001–05.

10 The federal government had exclusive jurisdiction over foreign policy, international relations, defense, federal strategic stockpiles, federal legislation and administration, and the federal judicial system. On other issues, republic governments shared responsibility with the federal government.

11 In June 1988, Hungary and the European Economic Community (EEC) signed a ten-year trade agreement, that provided for a reduction of quotas on about two thousand items by 1995. This agreement was the first of its kind between the EEC and a Comecon country. Another noteworthy development was the 1986 agreement between Hungary and West Germany on investment protection, under which German firms which invested in Hungary could repatriate their profits and were guaranteed against the nationalization of their assets (LoC 1989).

12 These included the liberalization of prices in an economy dominated by monopolies, the lack of domestic capital and savings, and the negative effect of macroeconomic stabilization for employment and consumption.

9   The many facets of transformation

The situation in the late 1980s in the CEECs and at the international level was novel and, for most of the cases, unforeseen just a few years earlier. It raised hopes within Central European countries and at international level. However, it also created serious problems outside the area directly concerned, mainly in Western Europe, not only for the geographical closeness and the uncertain political effects of the reunification of the continent. German unification apart, perhaps the most important issue for Western European governments was the evident goal of Czechoslovakia, Hungary and Poland to enter the European Union, a goal which the three countries put at the top of their transformation agendas.

Transformation of the type and scale involved was unforeseen and unknown. The only "reference" was the first transformation of Central and Eastern European market economies into Soviet-type economies two or three generations earlier, but this process involved totally different problems and approaches. It was clear that transformation had to do primarily with the nature of institutions and organizations and with policies based on general economic principles and rules.

While the general problem was clear, disagreement was both wide and deep as to which other problems needed priority treatment, how the problems had to be solved, by means of which approach and methods, and how fast. This opened the critical issue of adaptation to local circumstances and which place this should receive in the transformation process. The nature of the problems and the solutions implemented in each country were important for the outcome of transformation and the particular features and importance of path dependence. Problems and solutions were important in determining the economic and political performance of individual countries and their vulnerability to the international crisis. They were also important in determining the existence of independent causes of vulnerability and home-made crisis.

Starting conditions

Transformation opened various important questions: the macroeconomic balance of economies, social stability, institutions and markets; the structure of economies, and the nature and features of enterprises and the state. First, in some countries, the economy was deeply unbalanced. Both Poland and Hungary were in this situation, although Czechoslovakia was not. While both Poland and Hungary had sizeable foreign debts and domestic deficits, only Poland went through defaults in the 1980s. Both countries were under inflationary pressures, but only Poland was close to hyperinflation. Under these conditions, macroeconomic stabilization had high priority and had to be a precondition or an important part of transformation.[1]

Second, in both Poland and Hungary, there were also important problems of social stability. In Poland, a true counter-government existed in the form of Solidarność. The result of the first partially free elections was politically clear. Even if the PUWP obtained more votes than Solidarność (nearly 38 percent against 35 percent), it was clear that this was due to the constraints imposed upon the electoral system. Where competition was free, Solidarność obtained an overwhelming victory, which convinced the PUWP's former allied parties—United People's Party (ZSL) and Democratic Party (SD)—to take sides with Solidarność. This led to the formation of a coalition government under the undisputed leadership of Solidarność. Once the old leading party accepted the new reality, transformation became socially and politically simple: political power was fully transferred from the discredited and defeated PUWP to the new democratic government defined mainly by Solidarność.

In Hungary, the situation was more complex. In the 1990 elections, no party came out as the undisputed winner. The conservative Hungarian Democratic Forum (MDF) obtained less than one-fourth of the ballot and a number of seats in Parliament insufficient to form a government.[2] Next came the liberal pro-European Alliance of Free Democrats (SzDSz), with nearly 22 percent of votes. The conservative and populist Independent Smallholders' Party (FKgP) followed with 11 percent of the votes. The MDF, FKgP and the tiny Christian Democratic People's Party (KDNP) formed a coalition government, compelled internally to follow a contradictory policy, particularly in regard of agriculture and the European Union. The Hungarian Socialist Party (MSZP) won less than 11 percent of the votes. It was seriously defeated, but not crushed. This made defining a transformation strategy more complex and cumbersome and the outcome more contradictory.

The situation in Czechoslovakia was in a sense simpler, because of the traditional discipline reigning in the country and a long democratic tradition. The clear winner of the first free elections in 1990 were the Civic Forum (CF) and its Slovak counterpart, Public Against Violence (PAV), which together won 46 percent of the popular vote and a clear majority of the seats in Parliament. In spite of the clear majority, they chose to form a new liberal-conservative government together with the Christian Democratic Movement (CDM) and other unaffiliated members, under the premiership of Marian Calfa (PAV). The Communist Party, which kept a low profile and waged a moderate campaign, ended second with nearly 14 percent of the votes. The remarkable moderation of all parties and the favorable economic situation guaranteed a smooth political and systemic change. Macroeconomic stabilization in Czechoslovakia was not an important issue.

Third, the transformation proper was primarily about changing institutions. While the first institutions to change were political ones, it was clear that the revival of economic performance depended primarily upon economic institutions.

Attention and policy action was entirely concentrated on changing formal institutions and this revealed two problems, which were initially disregarded, under the illusion that they would be automatically solved. The first was that informal institutions were disregarded and there was confidence that they would adapt and change favorably once basic formal institutions were transformed. The second problem consisted in the socially unfavorable consequences of the change of formal institutions. The main issue was in the labor market:[3] the creation of unemployment was considered necessary in order to promote efficiency and discipline workers. Consequences for demand and human capital were considered to be short-lived and solved by the revival of the economy.

A fourth important issue was about markets. Mainstream economists, who had nearly a monopoly on policy making and policy advising, at least in the first years, considered that markets were natural to human societies and they would develop spontaneously. The opinion of Keynesian, Austrian and institutional economists was quite different. In any case, the development of markets received scant attention in the first years as efforts were concentrated on liberalization and privatization, from which well-working markets were considered to follow more or less spontaneously.[4] The problem was particularly acute in the case of markets that had not existed previously or that were distorted. The most important case was the financial markets. This disregard was a major drawback for transformation, one that extended its influence up to vulnerability to the international crisis.

A fifth important question concerned the economic structure. As noted in Chapter 8, these countries still had economic structures that were in part tailored to autarchic purposes, at least the part that served the domestic and Comecon markets. The structure also reflected low productivity, in particular of agriculture, and the scant interest in many services. As a consequence, economic structure reflected the excessive weight of industry and agriculture and the underdevelopment of services, particularly business services. There was also a serious problem with the size of enterprises, abnormally large in any sector and branch compared to similar market economies. Enterprises had also serious problems concerning their management styles, technology endowments and technical knowledge. The prevailing idea was to leave the solution of these issues to the new managers after privatization.

Finally, a fundamental issue was that of the nature and role of the state during transformation (Dallago 1996c, 2009). The standard approach was that the state was overgrown and had to be decisively downsized. This concerned not only functions that were to be dismantled, such as economic planning and police control. What was given insufficient attention was the fact that a well-working market economy requires effective and efficient public administration and other state functions, such as courts, business registration, fiscal system, statistics. The inability to grasp this fundamental issue since the onset of transformation caused many difficulties and distortions in the development and working of the new system. These difficulties and distortions extended the crisis and explain much of the vulnerability of these countries and also home-made crisis events.

This chapter reviews the most important economic features, problems and outcomes in Czechoslovakia, Hungary and Poland on the eve of transformation. The dissimilarities explain the different strategies that the three countries adopted. Then it goes on to consider the complex nature of systemic change and the critical relation between general economic principles and rules and local circumstances, and how these combined in the transformation strategies. Finally, the chapter deals with the three standard components of transformation and how these were implemented in the countries considered: macroeconomic stabilization, liberalization, and privatization.

The problems and issues on the eve of transformation

The three countries had different starting conditions concerning their macroeconomic situation. They also had different economic structures, levels of development, features of enterprises, management styles, features and size of the non-socialized sector, features of the state and the public administration. Macroeconomic stabilization was intended to have more balanced economies. Microeconomic reforms, including competition, were instruments for pursuing more efficient and competitive economies. Structural change of production and foreign trade and innovation had to contribute greater dynamism to economies. Market liberalization, freedom of enterprise and consumer sovereignty were meant to have more efficient allocation of resource and effective incentives; full employment and better wages were in pursuit of higher standards of living. Taken together, the success in implementing these objectives constitute a reliable measure in assessing the outcome of transformation.

The first issue is to assess whether the above objectives were mutually compatible or whether there were trade-offs between them. The standard approach was to consider that there was inevitably a period when trade-offs dominated, when production would inevitably decrease, but it was believed that this period would be sufficiently brief. This was sometimes defined as the "J-curve" effect of transformation (Lavigne 1999), and the issue was studied in particular in the case of the three countries considered here. The J-curve was linked to the transitory effect of reforms and restructuring, and the demand shock descending from stabilization programs. Alternatively, it was expected to descend from supply rigidities and a Schumpeterian effect of creative destruction which would reallocate resources from the old, unproductive uses to future, more productive uses (Gomułka 1991). After this period, the economy would take off and reach a more dynamic growth path, thanks to the superior features of the new system.

The reality was quite different and proved the existence of important and durable trade-offs which caused sizeable costs of transformation. In many countries, the growth curve turned out to be a prolonged recession or depression due to either demand shocks and excessively rigid macropolicies (Brada and King 1992), possibly credit crunch (Calvo and Coricelli 1993), supply-side shocks and supply rigidities (Linotte 1992), or excessively modest structural reforms (Bofinger 1993). Still worse and damaging in the long run, the costs hit the majority of the population and particularly specific social groups. This effect significantly increased inequalities (Milanovic 1998) and paved the way to vulnerability and home-grown causes of crisis. In general, and while the pre-transformation economic situation was difficult, economic performance during the first period of transformation was worse than expected in all countries (Table 9.1). Growth rates became negative, "transitional depression"[5] (Kornai 1994) was longer and deeper than expected, recovery weaker and bumpier than foreseen (Figure 9.1). As a consequence, unemployment was larger and more persistent than economically appropriate, let alone socially desirable. In spite of depression, inflation in some countries was higher and more persistent than expected. Predictably, public finances worsened, in spite of parsimonious welfare, certainly weaker than before transformation.

As a consequence of the unfavorable performance, the productive basis of various economies shrank and inequalities increased, sometimes considerably. Foreign debt also increased significantly in the first period of transformation and current accounts worsened (Table 9.2). Negative political and social consequences, such as the spread of political populism and poverty, followed. These negative effects increased the economic and social vulnerability of various countries, which continued into the international crisis.

The situation of individual countries was distinct. Czechoslovakia never had any serious problems with its foreign debt burden and continued to be better off than both Poland and Hungary when transformation started. Poland's foreign debt was the highest, both in its absolute value and related to the country exports, in spite of debt rescheduling in the 1980s. While in per capita terms Hungary was in the worst position, compared to exports the country debt situation was better off than Poland's.[6] After the dangerous increase in 1990, the country was able to bring debt under better control in 1991. Similar conclusions hold in the case of foreign trade (Rodrik 1994) (Table 9.3).

Transformation caused major changes in the labor market (Allison and Ringold 1996). Employment and participation rates started to decrease with the beginning of transformation and so continued for various years. Visible unemployment appeared as soon as economic transformation started and grew rapidly between 1989 and 1993. This was due to both restrictive policies that characterized macroeconomic stabilization and the consequent output collapse,

Table 9.1 Inflation, unemployment and budget balance, 1990 and 1991

	Percentage change in real GDP			Inflation, % change, end period		Unemployment, %, in December		General government balance, % of GDP	
	1989	*1990*	*1991*	*1990*	*1991*	*1990*	*1991*	*1990*	*1991*
Czechoslovakia	0.7	−0.4	−16.4	18	54	1.0	6.6	0.1	−2.2
Hungary	−0.2	−4.0	−7.5	33	34	1.7	8.5	0.5	−4.3
Poland	0.2	−12.0	−8.0	249	60	6.5	11.4	3.5	−7.2
Soviet Union	3.0	−2.3	−17.0	6	152	0	0	−8.0	−26.0

Source: IMF, European Commission for Europe and national statistics

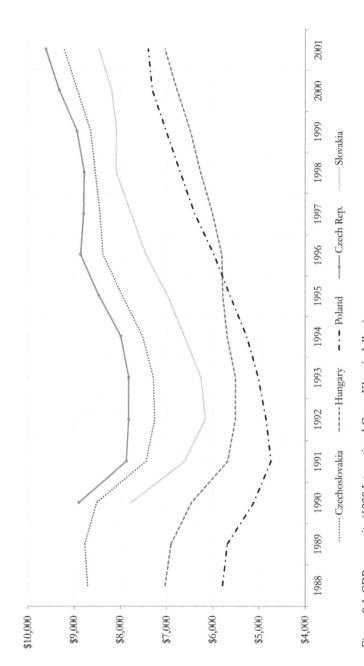

Figure 9.1 GDP per capita (1990 International Geary-Khamis dollars)

Source: New Maddison Project Database (http://www.ggdc.net/maddison/maddison-project/data.htm)

Table 9.2 External debt, 1989–91 (in billion US$)

	Gross debt			Net debt			Net debt/exports (%)		
	1989	*1990*	*1991*	*1989*	*1990*	*1991*	*1989*	*1990*	*1991*
Czechoslovakia	7.9	8.2	9.9	5.7	7.1	6.7	106	120	81
Hungary	20.4	21.3	21.9	19.2	20.2	18.0	195	316	194
Poland	40.8	48.5	48.4	38.5	44.0	44.8	453	364	350
Soviet Union	54.0	63.0	n/a	38.8	54.3	n/a	92	117	n/a

Source: IMF, OECD and national statistics

and to the change in technologies, that tended to be a substitute for labor while also requiring more skilled labor.

On the supply side, the labor force decreased because many workers were discouraged or not required, since they were unskilled or had skills that had become useless in the new economic system. However, most of the changes took place on the demand side. Harder budget constraint for state-owned enterprises and greater competition led companies to dismiss employees and to avoid hiring new ones. As a consequence, the size of the labor force contracted. Long-term unemployment grew steadily and was an important proportion of total unemployment. It was strongly correlated with growing poverty.

Along with minorities (the Roma population in particular), the main losers were school-leavers and young workers, and those close to retirement, although the latter could participate in early retirement and disability pension arrangements. Also, women were more likely than men to be dismissed from employment, and many women voluntarily left the labor market. High unemployment rates and long-term unemployment explain much of the significant growth of inequality and put the welfare system under stress. Given that previously welfare was linked to jobs, unemployment also meant loss of welfare, since time was needed to set up the new welfare system.

At the same time and in spite of these problems, labor market adjustments accompanied and supported economic restructuring and liberalization. A further important change was the significant increase of employment in the private sector, that compensated the loss of jobs in the public sector. Moreover, the sectorial

Table 9.3 Budget, trade and current account balance, 1989–91

Country	Budget balance, % of GDP			Trade balance, bln USD			Current account balance, bln US$		
	1989	*1990*	*1991*	*1989*	*1990*	*1991*	*1989*	*1990*	*1991*
Czechoslovakia	−2.4	−0.3	−1.9	n/a	n/a	n/a	n/a	−0.1	1.7
Hungary	−1.3	−0.1	−4.6	0.8	0.9	−1.2	n/a	0.1	0.3
Poland	−6.1	0.7	−3.5	1.7	5.7	−0.6	n/a	0.7	−1.4
Russia	n/a	n/a	n/a	n/a	n/a	8.0	n/a	−6.3	2.5

Source: Lavigne 1999, p. 284, based on ECE/UN data

and branch profile of employment also changed, as the traditional socialist sectors (heavy industry, mining, agriculture) declined and employment grew significantly in the service sector. This meant important changes of required skills, but also losses for those regions where the old socialist industry was concentrated. Since these were traditionally the most backward regions, the transformation of the labor market went hand-in-hand with the increase of territorial disparities.

Countries differed also in the case of the labor market (Figure 9.2). Hungary lost a significant amount of employment between the start of transformation and 1997, after which recovery was slow but consistent. In Poland, the loss was more significant and longer, since the decrease of the participation rate ended only in 2007, after which there was an important recovery. The latter was particularly significant, since it took place in the years of the post-2007 international financial crisis. Also significant was the increase of the participation rate in Hungary during the same years. Poland maintained a significantly higher participation rate than Hungary for the entire period.

The case of Slovakia and the Czech Republic is particularly interesting. In the latter, the participation rate was stable through the 1990s. It only decreased mildly between 2000 and 2008 and increased slightly after 2011. Being Slovakia, that is, the part of former Czechoslovakia where much of the socialist heavy industry was concentrated, the rapid and significant decrease of the participation rate between 1991 and 1994 was only obvious. What is remarkable is the stability that followed, at a level of participation similar to that of the Czech Republic.

Soviet-type economies had a highly egalitarian income distribution. With transformation, distributive disparities increased strongly in various countries, including Russia and other post-Soviet countries. However, in Hungary, Poland and Czechoslovakia (and then the Czech Republic and Slovakia), distributive disparities continued to be relatively mild, although higher than before transformation. The Gini coefficient was on average 0.23 in the CEECs in the mid-1980s (Flemming and Micklewright 1999). The index was 0.20 in Czechoslovakia and close to it (0.21) in Hungary. Poland had the highest degree of inequality, 0.25, still well below the average of OECD countries, which was 0.30 in the same period.

With transformation, the picture changed (Table 9.4). Distributive inequalities increased in each country. However, while in both Czechoslovakia and its two constituent republics, the Czech Republic and Slovakia, and Hungary, the increase was moderate and remained below the OECD average, in Poland it surpassed this average. This effect was due in particular to the welfare and fiscal systems (data after taxes and subsidies), which in Czechoslovakia and Hungary were better structured to keep a fair level of equality in incomes (Garner and Terrell 1998). The case of Russia (and other post-Soviet countries) is different. In these cases, inequality reached levels that were typical of Latin American countries (Commander et al. 1999).

The increase of inequalities, together with a prolonged depression of the economy and the fall of employment decreased significantly the basis for domestic consumption. To this the decrease of public expenditure should be added, as a

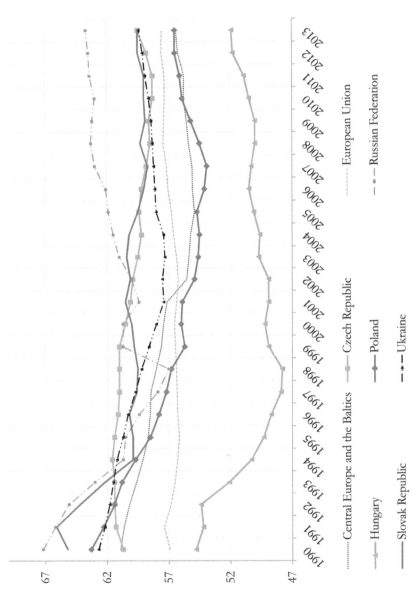

Figure 9.2 Labor force participation rate, total (% of total population ages 15+) (modeled ILO estimate)

Source: World Bank, World Development Indicators

Legend:
········· Central Europe and the Baltics
━■━ Hungary
━━ Slovak Republic
━■━ Czech Republic
━◆━ Poland
━▲━ Ukraine
――― European Union
━·━ Russian Federation

Table 9.4 Income inequality (Gini coefficients)

	Late 1980s		Early 1990s		Late 1990s	
	Year	*Gini*	*Year*	*Gini*	*Year*	*Gini*
Czech Rep.	1988	20.0	1992	23.0	1996	26.0
Hungary	1987	24.4	1992	26.0	1998	25.3
Poland	1987	25.0	1993	29.8	1998	32.7
Slovakia	1988	19.5	1993	21.5	1996	26.3
Russia[a]	1991	26.0	1993	39.8	2000	39.9
Russia[b]	1992	54.3	1994	45.5	1996	51.8

Source: Commander, Tolstopiatenko and Yemtsov (1999)

Notes
a based on Goskomstat data;
b based on survey data

consequence of macroeconomic stabilization and the new economic refrain of small public sectors and balanced public budgets. The strong decrease of demand that resulted from these events was only attenuated by the increase of exports, that were anyway initially modest in many transformation countries. Under these conditions and in spite of the need to restructure enterprises for competing in the new circumstances, it was difficult to find reasons for strong investment activity. The inevitable outcome was a prolonged and deep recession and, in some countries, depression.

Along with deep economic changes, transformation brought about important novelties also in human life and social circumstances. A number of social indicators suggest that average living standards improved during the transformation in Central Europe, improved slightly in the Baltic countries, remained about the same or declined slightly in the Balkan countries not involved in wars, and declined in the CIS (Svejnar 2002). Life expectancy at birth between 1989 and 1999 increased significantly in the Czech Republic, by nearly three years (from 71.66 to 74.62), by more than two years in Poland (from 71.04 to 73.19) and by nearly two years in Slovakia (from 71.03 to 72.70). In Hungary, life expectancy at birth increased by more than one year (from 69.50 to 70.62).[7] These trends continued previous trends of the 1980s.

While life expectancy in Central Europe improved, other social aspects witnessed the signs of social stress and in particular, the consequences of economic and life uncertainty. Fertility rates (total births per woman) decreased significantly in all transformation countries and this they did by much more than in Western Europe, let alone the United States.[8] Marriage rates declined strongly and divorce rates slightly increased or remained stable.[9]

Poverty increased dramatically during the decade following the start of transformation. According to the World Bank data, Eastern Europe and Central Asia were the only areas in the world where poverty (defined as the share of population living on less than US$1 a day) increased, although starting from very low levels (from 1.5 percent of the population in 1990 to 5.1 percent in 1999).

In a 2007 study on the compliance with the Lisbon Strategy, Ederer et al. (2007) used calculations of the European Human Capital Index[10] to conclude that a continuation of the good economic performance and rise in prosperity in Central and Eastern Europe was not to be taken for granted and was not even likely, in particular because of adverse demographic developments and under-utilization of human capital, as well as a persistent brain-drain and inadequate investment in education and skills. The best-placed country was the Czech Republic, whose score was similar to those of Ireland and France, in an intermediate position within the EU. Hungary and Slovakia had similar scores, slightly worse than Germany's. Finally, Poland had the lowest score, on a par with Spain's.

Ederer et al. (2007) also measured human capital endowment, meant as the level of five different kinds of investment in skills used in the economy: informal parental education, formal school education, formal university and higher education, formal and informal adult education, and informal learning on the job. The value thus obtained was subsequently depreciated to account for obsolescence and forgetting in the existing knowledge base. The Czech Republic had the highest level of human capital endowment among the countries considered here together with Hungary, although both countries still lagged behind Western European levels. Poland had a middle level, while Slovakia trailed behind with low public investments in education and consistently poor showing in international educational achievement.

The Europe 2020 Strategy of the European Commission replaced the Lisbon Strategy starting in 2010. The Commission defined eight indicators to monitor the implementation of the Europe 2020 strategy. These include, among others, tertiary education attainment and gross domestic expenditure on R&D, which are grouped as the first main pillars of the Europe 2020 strategy: the Smart Growth Index. Other indicators are the employment rate of the population aged 20–64, early leavers from education and population at risk of poverty or exclusion, which are grouped in the Inclusive Growth Index.

Pasimeni (2016) developed a synthetic composite index—the Europe 2020 Index—to quantify, measure and monitor the progress achieved by countries towards the objectives of the strategy and using the above indexes. The Europe 2020 Index overall score provided results consistent with those of Ederer et al. (2007):[11] the Czech Republic had an average score within the EU average, Poland and Hungary a rather weak score and Slovakia had one of the lowest. Over the years, although on absolute level all countries improved their score, the trend relative to other EU member countries improved for the Czech Republic and Poland, stagnated for Slovakia and worsened for Hungary.

It is also interesting to assess the countries' scores and relative position within the EU in the case of the two indexes that have to do with human capital: Smart Growth and Inclusive Growth. The Czech Republic and Slovakia had a slightly worse ranking in the case of Smart Growth than for the synthetic Europe 2020 Index. However, both countries fared much better in the case of the Inclusive Growth index. Hungary and Poland kept their position as to the former index and slightly improved (Poland) and worsened (Hungary) their ranking in the case of the latter index. This means that the main relative advantage was for the Czech Republic and Slovakia in social indicators, while in the case of education and research the average ranking of the four countries was slightly worse than the average of EU member countries.

Systemic change and transformation strategy: general rules and principles and local circumstances

In a sense, transformation was moved by the desire and the necessity for former Soviet-type economies and socialist countries to go back to sound general economic rules and principles. The Soviet-type economic system, an economic system alien to the features and circumstances of Central European countries such as economic structure and culture and based on rules that did not promote efficient and effective management of the economy, ended in economic failure.[12] Moreover, economic reforms, which can be interpreted as a step towards sounder general economic rules and principles and also towards better adaptation to local circumstances, were unable to improve upon the situation and in some cases even worsened it.

The origin of the new entrepreneurs may be useful to clarify the issue.[13] In those countries which had strong pre-war traditions of private entrepreneurship, such as Czechoslovakia, Hungary and Poland, a number of entrepreneurs during the transformation period originated from former entrepreneurial families. These were either self-employed in the second economy, or occupied leading positions in state-owned companies during the socialist period (Smallbone and Welter 2001). In the four countries considered here (the V4),[14] "family history" was quoted by the 9 percent of surveyed business owners as one of the factors that influenced their decision to start a business. The situation of Poland was particularly telling: "family tradition" was the most common reason for start-ups by firms initiating business before 1981, according to the survey of three hundred manufacturing SMEs undertaken in 1995. This factor was mentioned by 42 percent of respondents. However, for those businesses which started after 1991 the factor was nearly negligible and mentioned by only 4 percent of respondents. At the same time, in a 1997 survey in Ukraine, Belarus and Moldova, only a handful of respondents mentioned "family background" as a factor behind their start-ups.

The radical move to systemic change was often presented as a case of transition, a linear process of transformation departing from a clear starting situation and moving toward a well-defined final objective through a fundamentally straight and smooth process. Unforeseen obstacles and transitory difficulties could be removed by political determination to reform and external support. International organizations, such as the IMF, the World Bank and the OECD saw the issue in this way. The same was true for leading western governments, the US and German governments in particular. Yet this approach overlooked two serious problems, thus causing many of the difficulties and divergent paths that those countries encountered.

First was the fact that the transition approach overlooked completely the role and effect of local circumstances. According to this approach, there was only one blueprint for change: the Washington Consensus. The term "Washington Consensus" refers to a set of ten economic policy prescriptions with an orientation towards a market-based approach.[15] The reference is to the Washington-based institutions, where the consensus was formed: the IMF, the World Bank and the US Treasury Department (Williamson 1989, 1990, 1999, 2004). The Consensus is considered as the standard reform package that national governments were suggested to implement and the international institutions required for extending their support. With time, the term came to assume a broader and popular meaning and became confused, both popularly and also in policy making, with neoliberal or even market-fundamentalist policies. In more recent years the consensus has evolved towards an approach more attentive to, among other things, local circumstances (Stiglitz 1998).

Second is the role of informal institutions. Informal institutions embrace uncodified attitudes, which are embedded in a society, and which act as regulators on individual behavior and interpersonal relations (Smallbone and Welter 2012). Examples of important informal institutions are routines, trust, traditions, social norms, moral values, interpersonal and social relations, governance traditions, management styles, the economic role of families and genders, and political attitudes. Informal institutions are generally of a qualitative type, as are many differences among countries (Jütting et al. 2007). One problem with policies based on the original Consensus, i.e. the one that dominated policy making when transformation first started, was that adaptation to local circumstances was of a quantitative character, if any. Yet quality also matters. Indeed, local circumstances have much to do with informal institutions.

Given their pervasive importance, it is important to incorporate informal institutions in development strategies and policy making. This is particularly important in countries that are struggling with development and systemic change, and which have disrupted public structures. In fact, changing formal institutions in these countries is insufficient and often ineffective, and the role of the state and its governance and its enforcement capability are also ineffective (Dallago 1996c, 2009). Moreover, informal institutions evolve as a culture-specific, collective and individual interpretation of formal institutions and, as a consequence, influence the effectiveness of the latter.

It is important to adapt strategies and policies to local realities and conditions, in order to maximize their positive impact on development and transformation (Knight 1992, Nee 1995, North 1990, Olson 1982, Williamson 2000, Zenger et al. 2000). There are at least two reasons for this. First, policy objectives and instruments for transforming informal institutions having negative effect on economic performance need to consider the existing power balance in order to gain maximum support of different political actors for transformation (Jütting et al. 2007). Second, relying on informal institutions is also important in order to strengthen the effect of new formal institutions, thus mitigating the risk of their ineffectiveness and the negative effect of the institutional void that may be created due to the time needed to implement and enforce the new formal institutions.

The critical question is: how to incorporate informal institutions into transformation strategies and policies, without having the former blocking or derailing the latter? This is a point that also international organizations came to recognize after years of subscription to an approach that was generating more problems than it was helping to solve (Burki and Perry 1998). Solving the conundrum clearly required that the new democratic governments had a detailed knowledge of their economy and society upon which base pursuit of their transformation objectives, among which a better implementation of sound general economic principles was prominent. This also meant that there could not be a "one size fits all" strategy and policy, and that inevitably transformation paths had to vary.

Transformation countries had distinct informal institutions that derived from their history and culture, including the peculiar features of their experiences during the socialist era. However, the Soviet-type system gave a recognizable imprint to these countries, which had some common traits. Moreover, the V4 countries also had an important common past as part of the Austrian and Austro-Hungarian empires. These experiences and some cultural similarities highlight that this is a group of countries that also shared some institutional similarities, upon which some common traits of transformation strategies and policies could build (e.g. cultural and political orientation to the West and in particular to Germany, and great importance attributed to education and culture).

These institutional features created a context that was alien to the nearly *dirigiste* approach that international organizations suggested and supported. Various new democratic governments, backed by international organizations and western governments and organizations, forced the new agenda in this context, using the political and administrative power of the state. Additional informal problems that had importance also in V4 countries were a certain inclination to egalitarianism, and a disinclination to risk-taking and self-determination. The presence of these and other informal institutions, at odds with what was required for a well-working competitive capitalist system, highlights the importance of learning and adaptation processes, and therefore the need for time and consistency of processes and policies.

The conflict thus created between the enforcement of new formal institutions and the existing informal institutions opened opportunities for personal gain through the exploitation of privileged positions in the transformation process and interpersonal and social relations among privileged groups (Dallago 1996b, Pejovich 2006). The most advantaged were usually people who had a role in the new government and state structure, who were in control of state-owned enterprises going through privatization, who had a role in the privatization process.[16] Countries where these consequences were important, such as Hungary (Stark 1996), were ill-suited to perform successfully in an open and competitive world. Their performance was weak and their economy became more vulnerable to the international crisis.

Thus one important consequence of the mismatch between formal and informal institutions was that this generated path dependence—i.e. that the set of decisions one faces and the outcome obtained from such decisions or other events and changes is limited or influenced by the decisions taken, the achievements obtained and the events in the past, even though past events and circumstances may be remote and no longer relevant (David 1985, Arthur 1994). Such a mismatch strengthened moral hazard and principal-agents contrast, increased transformation costs, made enforcement ineffective and incurred important transaction costs.

Cognitive psychology has highlighted various important mechanisms that inhibit long-term social rationality, mechanisms that were important during the first period of transformation. One such important mechanism is mistakes in interpretation due to lack of sufficient knowledge of the environment, and the effect of social stereotypes, usually coming from past experiences or different contexts (Bonini and Hadjichristidis 2009). These factors, together with the inconsistency of individual preferences and uncertainty about one's own interest in a changing context, create uncertainty and inconsistency of individual rationality and mismatch with social rationality.[17] Under these circumstances, signaling is also particularly complex or incorrect or distorted, which contributes to misinformation and unrealistic expectations and the creation of illusions (Andor 2010). This is likely to create informational conformism (Bocchiaro 2009), which is typical of ill-defined circumstances and is important in critical situations inhibiting the full utilization of logico-analytical capabilities, typically delegated to "experts." Moreover, decision making and preferences suffer from the underestimation of costs, typical in unknown and ill-defined events and circumstances.

While, under normal conditions, these mistakes may smooth away each other through the interaction of numerous individuals with different information, knowledge and preferences and through the activity of organs with different roles and specializations, during transformation, the situation may be different. The speed and the internal and external pressure, the strong expectations and the interpretation and policy uniformity (because of the virtual lack of alternative interpretations), dramatically increase the chances that consistent and even self-strengthening mistakes are incurred.[18] Under these conditions, the best individually rational behavior—for those who are in the circumstances to do so—is to maximize rents through the appropriation of valuable assets in the short run, under the constraint of uncertainty concerning the future behavior of political and legal authorities. Any other approach requires investments with returns postponed in time, a behavior that is risky in uncertainty.

Table 9.5 summarizes and compares the main features of transformation in Central Europe and Russia.

On the reasons for path dependence and the new elites

Actors able to influence the variability of particular attributes of transformation were able to influence the distribution of income, wealth and opportunities to their own advantage. In particular, they could influence the allocation of property rights, and the income flow that assets produced. Consequently, it was easier and less costly to capture those assets for those advantaged in the ownership or political

Table 9.5 The main components of transformation

	Hungary	Poland	Czechoslovakia (until 31/12/92)	Russia
Macroeconomic stabilization	Restrictive monetary, budgetary and income policy, launched in 1990	Restrictive economic policy, launched on 01/01/1990	Restrictive economic policy, launched on 01/01/1991	Stringent monetary policy, based on high interest rates and budget expenditure cuts
Price liberalization	Gradual since 1975	January 1990	January 1991	02/01/1992 for 90 percent of consumer prices and 80 percent of producer prices
Demonopolization (anti-trust laws)	Anti-monopoly law in force since 01/1991	Anti-monopoly office created in 1991	Law on protection of competition (02/1991), Commercial Code (01/1992)	Law on Competition and the Restriction of Monopolistic Activity in the Commodity Markets in 1991
Privatization (Restitution to former owners)	Partial compensation	Very limited compensation	Yes. Laws 11/1990; 02/1991	Decree on privatization on 29/12/1991
Large-scale privatization	Began in 09/1990	Began in 1990, slow	Began in 1991 (law in 10/1990; law in 02/1991)	Began in 1992 with a voucher scheme
Banking reform	Since 1987; banking laws end 1991	Since 1987–8	Since 1990. Banking law in 1991	Since 1991
Setting up capital markets	Budapest Stock Exchange opened in 06/1990	Warsaw Stock Exchange opened in 04/1991	Prague and Bratislava Stock Exchanges opened in 04/1993	Moscow Stock Exchange in 1997
New laws on foreign investment	1989, amended in 1990	1988, amended in 1991	1988, amended in 1992. Commercial Code	1999

Source: Adaptation from Lavigne 1999, pp. 122–28

structure, in the use of violence, and in the control of information. These were, for instance, the new and outgoing politicians, officers responsible for the privatization process, managers, and irregular or criminal actors. There were various cases and examples of this kind of behavior: the value-decreasing effect of the activity of the old system agents is well known in both market economies (e.g. the so-called "paradox of privatization") and transformation economies (e.g. de-capitalization of enterprises and inter-enterprise arrears).[19]

Transformational distribution consisted of the redistribution of property rights over existing assets (like the ownership of firms and real estate) or new system-specific assets (like positions in the new government, political parties, or privatization agencies). There are many examples of this kind of behavior in Central and Eastern Europe. Many managers of state-owned enterprises and also middle- and high-ranking party officials became owners by utilizing their bargaining power, social and professional networks, knowledge, and skills accumulated in the old system.[20] This was in particular the case of the already mentioned spontaneous privatization that preceded transformation in Central Europe and of insiders' privatization in Russia, Ukraine, Serbia, Croatia and Romania. Other relevant cases were those of former state administrators who entered privatization agencies and of previous administrators or managers who were able to obtain legally or illegally the funds necessary to establish their own private businesses before abandoning their old jobs. This was a widespread phenomenon that explains the origin of a great number of post-transformation owners and entrepreneurs.[21] However, transformational distribution was not necessarily and entirely negative. In fact, it gave powerful incentives to implement systemic change, although it influenced the features of the new system.

Specific structures were set up to govern the distribution of costs and gains. This was the case of round tables between the old government and representatives of the opposition, such as in Poland. The management of such structures and the implementation of the agreements required intermediaries. This role was played by such organizations endowed with enforcement authority, such as the Church, or the European Union. On other occasions, judiciary bodies played a similar role, for example the Constitutional Court in Hungary.

Other problems during transformation were absent, incomplete, or incorrect knowledge, and information asymmetry. Consequently, the costs of measurement, enforcement and control were much higher than they would be in normal conditions, and the implementation and outcome of these functions were particularly weak.

These problems highlight that spontaneous processes were insufficient to guide systemic change to socially productive results and stress the fundamental role of good institutions and the state during transformation. The state is a fundamental structure to reduce uncertainty, amplify the domain of public information, extend the actors' time horizon, and govern collective action during transformation. It is only within this framework that transformation processes could have productive effects. In transformation countries, from the very beginning, this was clear only in exceptional cases (in particular in Czechoslovakia). In other countries, it was only in the early 1990s (generally 1993–94) that it became evident. Unfortunately, in other countries—in particular, various post-Soviet republics—the near-demise of the state enormously increased transformation costs and depressed opportunities for productive transformation. The adaptation to these circumstances was the establishment of a paternalistic or authoritarian state via path-dependent adjustment, as the chapters on Russia and Ukraine in this book clearly prove.

These processes strengthened path dependence as a rational response which rendered some specific solutions less difficult and less costly and therefore more likely to prevail than others. However, path dependence gave no guarantee of socially superior outcomes. The restructuring of economic elites during transformation provides a good illustration of the above. A comparative study of the fate of the old elites during transformation found that by 1993 the former cadre elites in Hungary and Poland had a 2:1 chance to belong to the new elites in a managerial or professional position of at least similar level to their previous one, while their chances to remain in a party or state administrative position were small (Wasilewski 1998). Most of them (approximately two-thirds) moved to business and to managerial and professional roles, taking advantage of the privatization process and its initially loose conditions that privileged insiders. The situation in Russia was quite different, with greater chances for the old party and state elites still to be in party and state positions by 1993 and a smaller proportion moving to managerial or professional roles. The Russian case shows clearly the strength of path dependence.

An intertemporal comparative research based on a 1994 survey and a 2003–04 survey (Lane et al. 2007) found that initially the new Czech economic elites consisted mainly of former middle-ranking managers in the socialist sector, many of whom were previously members of the Communist Party. Over time, this elite was transformed and replaced by a new, younger elite. Privatization played an important role in fostering the internal change. Few of the new members of the economic elite belonged in the old elites or were close to the old political elites. The Czech case shows an interesting evolution away from path dependence.

The Hungarian case is different and, in a sense, was half-way to path dependence. Here, asset appropriation was rather important and took place through spontaneous privatization and the privileged position of insiders during privatization. It is noteworthy of Hungary that, thanks to repeated economic reforms, the transformation of elites started well before systemic change, in particular during the second half of the 1980s. After transformation began, in the 1990s, elite change slowed down, as much as intergenerational mobility: at the end of the decade approximately half of the new elites were former party members. More often, members of former elites moved through organizations to new elite positions.[22] The Polish situation is apparently between the Czech and the Hungarian cases, although closer to the latter.

A further important aspect of the social difficulty of transformation and its problematic social context is given by the low level of social capital.[23] Although it is difficult to assess how much social capital decreased during transformation and whether this was due to the pre-transformation disruption, or to transformation choices, the rapid and significant increase of unemployment, the disruption of social services and other negative outcomes, it is clear that social capital in transformation

Table 9.6 Social capital indicators, 2000

	Trust	Membership	Press	Labor union	Police	Parliament
Czech Rep.	25	48	37	22	33	13
Hungary	22	21	30	23	43	33
Poland	18	13	48	34	56	34
Slovakia	16	49	49	43	44	43
1. Average V4	20	33	41	31	44	31
2. CEE-CIS	22	25	39	29	43	26
3. W Europe	37	48	39	40	70	43
1-2	-2	8	2	2	1	5
1-3	-17	-15	2	-10	-26	-12

Source: Own elaboration on d'Hombres et al. (2006)

countries is low (d'Hombres et al. 2006, 2010). The situation is particularly nega-tive in the CIS countries, but is bad also in the V4 countries (Table 9.6).

For instance, the mean degree of individual trust in others is equal to 22 percent in the transformation countries, and is respectively 37 percent, 24 percent and 33 percent in the US, Africa and Asia. However, there are significant national dif-ferences. The level of trust is at a bare 16 percent in Slovakia and at 18 percent in Poland, but is at 22 percent in Hungary and 25 percent in the Czech Republic. The score of Slovakia and Poland is at the average level for Africa, while that of Hungary and the Czech Republic corresponds to the average level of the US.[24] The position of V4 countries changes according to the indicator: except for trust and confidence in police, Slovakia scores above the others. Yet all these coun-tries have a significantly lower score than the Western European average, except for confidence in the press. While this situation is the outcome of the economic, political and social consequences of transformation, the thinness of social capital is in itself an important obstacle to the success of transformation.

The Visegrád Group and European integration

The four Central European countries shared and continue to share many impor-tant aspects that place them apart in the world of transformation countries. This particular situation was in many senses a privileged one, that made the countries themselves and also most observers expect that these countries would fare best of all the CEECs undergoing transformation. The most important features that these countries shared and that favored them were:

- the relatively high and similar level of development and sophistication of their economies;
- the fact that before socialism they were either highly economically developed (Czechoslovakia) or fairly so (Hungary and Poland);

- the democratic past, in spite of authoritarian regimes for part of their history (Hungary and Poland between the two wars);
- their sharing important experiences and institutions as part of the Austrian Empire;
- their closeness to Western Europe and its large markets, and the reforms and openness to western capital and trade (Hungary, but also Poland) and the good administration (Czechoslovakia) that they also implemented during the Soviet-type period.

Although these aspects were distinct in each country, overall, they gave a picture of these countries' greater readiness to successfully transform their economies into modern, open capitalist economies. Their common strengths were an implicit realization of the importance to follow sound principles of economic management. Their distinctiveness also stressed the importance to adapt to local circumstances. A further advantage of this cooperation is economic weight: as a group, they accounted for nearly 65 million people and would be fifth in the European Union for their overall GDP.

These countries, in spite of the distinct political stance of the new democratic governments, shared a willingness to play an active part in rebuilding a Central European space of democracy, economic and social progress, and stability. There was a genuine and laudable belief at play: these countries wanted to accelerate the "return to history," i.e. reactivate their roots as a fundamental part of western culture and traditions. They also wanted to assert their geopolitical unity and distance themselves from the former Soviet space, which they considered to be not only militarily and politically threatening, but also culturally alien, economically backward and a new source of instability. There was also some kind of opportunism at play: these countries were convinced that they would enter the European Union in a few years, before the others.[25] In order to improve their chances, speed up the process and obtain the most favorable conditions, it was important that they distinguished themselves from the rest of the transformation countries.

It was also for these reasons, and for the EU informal pressure, that Czechoslovakia, Hungary and Poland established the so-called "Visegrád Group" (V4) in 1991. After the division of Czechoslovakia on January 1, 1993, the Czech Republic and Slovakia entered as successor countries. The aims were to promote free trade liberalization and to present those countries as a "Central Europe" distinct from the other post-communist states. Later on, common projects and coordination in different fields—from energy (including nuclear energy) and transport infrastructure to security and military issues,[26] from culture and science to education and youth exchange[27]—integrated the agenda.[28] In spite of its modest actual importance, in particular after these countries joined NATO in 1999 and the EU in 2004 (Brazova et al. 2013), the founding of the Visegrád Group in the Hungarian town of Visegrád was one of the most important formal steps in the regionalization of transformation countries outside the former Soviet area.[29]

The V4, however, was under the negative influence of national interests. It worked reasonably well as an interest group during the talks with NATO and the

EU until 1993. After this, national interests started to prevail in order to obtain the maximum national advantage from accession and membership. In addition, their economic strategies, policies and development paths began to diverge, making cooperation more difficult and less advantageous. As a consequence, the role of the group weakened. In recent years, cooperation resumed and the V4 also worked as a pressure group within the EU. However, the member countries' different position vis-à-vis the recent tension with Russia has also created tension within the group.

The establishment of the Visegrád Group can be considered as a precondition for the ultimate goal and fundamental undertaking of these countries: EU membership, which came in 2004. The first formal step in this direction was the conclusion of the Europe Agreements in December 1991, with an identical structure for all three countries.[30] The ground was prepared at the end of 1989, when the Strasbourg European Council of December 8–9, 1989 declared that it intended to create an association with the Central and Eastern European countries that were beginning their transformation. The European Commission presented an initial outline for future European agreements to the Council and European Parliament in April 1990 and further refined the project into a general framework in August 1990. On December 18, 1990, the Council authorized the Commission to open negotiations, beginning December 20–22, 1990, with Czechoslovakia, Hungary and Poland.[31]

The Agreements created an association between the EU and the signatory countries in Central and Eastern Europe. Their meaning was both political and economic: the Agreements defined both the framework for political interaction and the promotion of economic and trade relations among the parties and created the basis for EU technical and financial assistance.[32] The Agreements provided for the free movement of goods by introducing preferential treatment and aimed at establishing free trade arrangements between the Community and V4 countries.[33] While the Agreements were based on the principle of reciprocity of concessions granted for liberalizing trade in industrial products, Czechoslovakia, Hungary and Poland obtained a longer period for liberalizing their markets vis-à-vis the Community. The Agreements also provided for financial cooperation and freedom of financial transfers arising from commercial transactions, for European assistance under PHARE, for better conditions for the movement of workers, establishment and services, payments and capital, and competition. Particularly important was the commitment that the three associated countries undertook to adapt their legislation to Community legislation.[34]

Most important, the Agreements were recognized as the first step towards the gradual integration of the signatory countries into the European Union. The Agreements were submitted to preconditions: the EU signed them when it recognized that the partner countries made important progress in transforming their economies and establishing pluralist democracies and when their economies were well integrated with EU economies, which became their main trade partner and provider of foreign aid.

The Europe Agreements were the basis for the declaration, at the meeting of the European Council in Copenhagen in 1993, that "the associated countries in

Central and Eastern Europe that so desire shall become members of the European Union." Consequently, the European Council in Copenhagen decided to further enlarge the market access for V4 countries. Individual countries then submitted their application for membership: Hungary on April 1, 1994, Poland on April 5, 1994, Slovakia on June 27, 1995, and the Czech Republic on January 23, 1996.

Following these applications, the European Commission formulated an Opinion on each application. The Luxembourg summit of the European Council in 1997 accepted the Commission's opinion and invited the Czech Republic, Hungary and Poland (together with Slovenia, Estonia and Cyprus) to open talks on their accession to the EU. The negotiation process began on March 31, 1998. The case of Slovakia was kept separate, due to political difficulties (see Chapter 10). Slovakia was invited for negotiations on joining the EU at the European Council summit in Helsinki in December 1999. Formal negotiations began in March 2000 and Slovakia soon joined the first group of countries.

Accession negotiations ended for all V4 countries in December 2002 at the Copenhagen summit and the Treaty of Accession was signed in Athens on April 16, 2003 between the then fifteen EU member countries and the ten acceding countries.[35] National referendums followed during 2003, which approved the accession.[36] The V4 countries became EU members on May 1, 2004, together with six other countries (Cyprus, Estonia, Latvia, Lithuania, Malta, Slovenia). Taking into consideration the significant expansion of the Union, the Treaty amended previous EU treaties by providing, among other things, for a new system for qualified majority voting in the Council of the European Union.[37] All the V4 countries also joined the Schengen Area, which oversees the abolition of border controls between adhering countries and common visa policies.

Joining the common currency

The most ambitious EU undertaking was the introduction of the euro as common currency.[38] The adoption of the euro was the outcome of a long process of treaties setting common rules and monetary and financial convergence (Dallago 2016, De Grauwe 2014). The most critical problem of the common currency, in spite of its long-lasting and technically careful preparation, was that it lacked previous political unification and a common government of the economy (Nuti 2015).

The basis for the euro were established with the foundation of the Economic and Monetary Union (EMU) as part of the Maastricht Treaty signed in 1992. The following years saw fundamental steps to the implementation of the common currency, including the implementation of the single market and the establishment of the European Central Bank, in three stages. In the first stage, implemented on July 1, 1990, all internal barriers to the free movement of goods, persons, services, and capital among member states were abolished. In the second stage, fiscal discipline and the convergence of national economic and monetary policies were enforced, including the Stability and Growth Pact (SGP), and the predecessor of the European Central Bank (ECB) was created. This took place on January 1, 1994 in the form of the European Monetary Institute (EMI). The ECB was established in

June 1998. The third and last stage was the irrevocable definition of the conversion rates of national currencies on January 1, 1999. The euro was introduced as the single currency by eleven member countries on that date, although it only started to be circulated physically starting on January 1, 2002. Other countries followed in the following years. The overall number of countries which have adopted the euro is presently 19.[39]

The adoption of the common currency meant that there is one monetary policy common to all Eurozone member countries and the competence for this policy belongs in the Eurosystem, the monetary authority of the Eurozone. The Eurosystem includes the ECB and the central banks of the Eurozone countries and pursues the primary objective of maintaining price stability.[40] Monetary policy is defined by the ECB and implemented by national central banks. At the same time, fiscal policies continue to belong in the competence of national governments, albeit under the rules and the constraints established by the convergence criteria and the SGP. This distinction was originally conceived to allow national governments to react to asymmetric shocks according to the peculiar situation of their own country, while common monetary policy was meant to take care of symmetric shocks (Buti and Sapir 1998). Following the international crisis of 2007, the Union started to move in the direction of a European banking union.[41]

The distinction of competences for monetary policy and fiscal policies appeared soon to be unsustainable, both because of the significant differences existing among national financial situations and even more so during the crisis. There was a double adaptation. First, the Eurosystem was put in charge of acting also as a leading financial authority safeguarding financial stability and promoting European financial integration. Second, all member countries were pushed to support the convergence of their economies to the common criteria.[42] This requirement was particularly stringent for the Eurozone countries and for the countries willing to adopt the euro.

Like any other country which wants to enter the European Union, Slovakia committed to adopt the euro as part of the Accession Treaty. Such commitment implies an obligation for any country (except for the United Kingdom and Denmark), but it is without a fixed time limit and is submitted to full compliance with the conditions defined in the convergence criteria. However, Slovakia pursued the introduction of the euro as quickly as possible in parallel with EU accession negotiations. The country entered ERM II in 2005.[43] The Dzurinda government set January 1, 2009 as the target date for adopting the euro. The following Fico government confirmed the commitment. The country having complied with the convergence criteria by spring 2008, the Commission recommended that Slovakia be accepted into the Eurozone. The decision was made on May 7, 2008 and the conversion rate was fixed set at 30.1260 Slovak crowns to the euro starting May 29, 2008. Slovakia was accepted in the Eurozone at the Brussels summit on June 19, 2008 and adopted the euro on January 1, 2009.

So far, Slovakia is the only V4 country which has adopted the euro.[44] This was definitely an unforeseen event during the first period of transformation, when all the odds were against this outcome and the other countries were considered the frontrunners. There are different reasons why the Czech Republic, Hungary and Poland have repeatedly postponed their adoption of the euro and not entered ERM II thus far. They all moved between different forms of pegged and free floating exchange rates, following the convenience or the need imposed by the external situation.[45] They repeatedly set deadlines, which were regularly postponed. The most puzzling case is probably Hungary, a country which back in 1989 was considered the frontrunner, thanks to the far-reaching reforms that were already in place and the openness of the country to the West. As of early 2016, Hungary had no plan to join the euro. The ongoing European crisis is certainly a part of the explanation, as much as are the revealed faults of the euro construction. However, some of the reasons pre-date the crisis and are internal to Hungary and the other countries, as explained in the following chapters.

So far, five Central-Eastern European countries have adopted the euro. Along with Slovakia (in 2009), the others are Slovenia (2007), Estonia (2011), Latvia (2014) and Lithuania (2015). All these countries entered the EU in 2004, and ERM II either in 2004 or 2005. Slovakia was the last country to enter ERM II, in November 2005. Before entering ERM II, these countries kept their national currencies pegged to a strong currency for years: Estonia to the DM and then the Euro between 1992 and 2002, Latvia to the SDR[46] between 1993 and 2005, Lithuania to the US\$ between 1994 and 2002. Slovenia and Slovakia adopted managed floating of their currencies (Marer 2016).

Why did Slovakia decide to go resolutely and rapidly towards adopting the euro? There are reasons of different nature behind this decision. According to Marer (2015), there were "the economic philosophy and unusual political and economic expertise of key persons in the new government, a determined wish to irrevocably break with recent past policies, and the fervent desire to catch up to and perhaps leapfrog the Czech Republic." The country adopted the euro as a fundamental part of a comprehensive package of economic reforms. Political determination appears as the fundamental factor for both further linking the country to the EU and capturing the political and economic advantages of monetary integration.

Conclusions

If the case of Slovakia is so noteworthy and successful in adopting the euro, why did the other three V4 countries fail to do so and apparently distance themselves further from the common currency? There are similarities among the countries behind this, but also idiosyncratic reasons. Each country manifested repeatedly and in different forms the intention to adopt the euro and even published clear deadlines for doing so. In part, the lack of determination was the outcome of the vicissitudes of the common currency: determination was stronger when the euro had appeared more desirable, particularly before 2008. When the crisis revealed the faults and dangers of the common currency, these countries chose to step back. This was obviously an implicit recognition of the perceived weakness of the three economies. This position does not mean that these countries have reached a final determination not to adopt the euro. Indeed, as members of the EU, they have an obligation to adopt the euro, but they prefer to wait for the proper time and the proper external and domestic conditions.

The Czech Republic offers in a sense the oddest case. Thanks to the traditional prudent and balanced management of the country's finances and monetary issues, inflation and interest rates are under control and similar to those of the Northern European countries. This makes the adoption of the euro theoretically easier and less risky than for any other V4 country. Yet also the advantages, including external credibility or the need to decrease inflation and exchange rates, are less important. If a country is capable of reaching price and interest-rate stability at low levels on its own, a further important reason for adopting the euro, such as macroeconomic stability, appears to not be determinant. Moreover, the advantages in the real economy that were expected from the adoption of the euro were not particularly apparent and this made an important appeal vanish. What remains is the importance of the euro in protecting a country against external shocks and thus in reducing macroeconomic volatility. However, the common currency deprives the national government of two fundamental policy instruments: the exchange rate and monetary policy. Both are fundamental in case of asymmetric shocks and their loss would increase macroeconomic volatility. The economic models used in the Czech Republic apparently do not reach a clear-cut conclusion on the advantages in terms of macroeconomic stability that would be obtained from the introduction of the euro (Hurník et al. 2010, Marer 2016). There is also a further political reason behind the Czech prudence: the opposition by one of the leading and most influential politicians, Václav Klaus, and his supporters to the entire European construction.

The case of Hungary is distinct from the Czech one and in a sense opposite to it. Hungarian economic and financial performance was weak, as shown above. The country had serious problems in complying with the convergence criteria and had the highest debt-to-GDP ratio among the V4 countries. It also reached the highest deficit-to-GDP ratio in the past decade. Due to its unbalanced financial situation and the economy's weak performance, Hungary was closed to sovereign debt default in 2008 and needed a quick bailout loan of US$25.5 billion provided jointly by the EU, the IMF and the World Bank. Perhaps the most important obstacle is the lack of political determination. Indeed, the present government is against the perspective of joining the euro and even opposed adopting the policies that would be necessary for doing so (Marer 2015, Neményi and Oblath 2012).

Poland is again in a different situation. By 2015, the country fulfilled four convergence criteria: the deficit, the debt, the inflation rate, and the interest rate criteria. As a consequence, in June 2015, the EU lifted the Excessive Deficit Procedure under which Poland had been since 2009. Moreover, the Polish economy is sound and it was the only EU economy that avoided recession during the crisis. Yet it did so also because its government was free to pursue an independent monetary policy and keep a flexible exchange rate. Weakening the złoty was an important instrument for regaining competitiveness. Moreover, opinion polls in the second part of 2014 and the first part of 2015 show that most Poles (between 50 percent and 75 percent) oppose Poland adopting the euro. At the same time, the country has gained a remarkable influence within the EU and adopting the euro would strengthen this influence. Overall, it seems that the country is not really refusing the common currency and the real debate among experts and policy makers is apparently around the timing for doing so. Since economic considerations are not particularly inclined on either side of the decision, the political debate is particularly important in determining decisions (Foy 2015, Marer 2016).

Notes

1 Fischer and Gelb (1991) prudently considered that the transformation process was both complex and intertwined with political factors and idiosyncratic features of each country. For these reasons, no single detailed road map could be provided to guide systemic change. After the first years of transformation, Fischer et al. (1996) reconsidered the issue, concentrating in particular on the relationship between stabilization and growth. They found that stabilization was critically important for the success of transformation and growth. In particular, lower fiscal deficits led to lower inflation and higher growth; pegged exchange rate regimes were more effective in reducing inflation and thus raising growth; structural reforms played a vital role in reviving growth and reducing inflation.

2 The leader of the party and the first democratically elected prime minister, József Antall made a controversial statement in 1990 as soon as he was elected, that had serious foreign policy consequences in the years to come. He stated that he intended to be the prime minister of 15 million Hungarians "in spirit and feelings." One-third of those people were living in surrounding countries, not Hungary.

3 On the nature and features of unemployment during transformation, see OECD (1994).

4 See Kornai (1990) for an important criticism and a reasonable alternative to the mainstream approach.

5 Other definitions include "transitionary recession" by Fisher et al. (1996).

6 This was due to the fact that Hungary had a more open economy than Poland. The degree of openness (exports plus imports as a share of GDP) in 1990 was 64.1 percent in the Czech Republic, 46.0 percent in Poland, 58.5 percent in Hungary (in 1991) and 58.3 percent in Slovakia (World Bank, World Development Indicators).

7 In the same period, life expectancy at birth increased by about two years (from 75 to 76.9) in the United States and from 76.5 to 78.5 years in France and by one to three years in most central European countries. It increased slightly in the Baltic countries and declined slightly in Albania, Bulgaria and Romania. The case of the CIS countries was different: in Russia, life expectancy at birth declined by 2.5 years between 1989 and 1999, by over three years in Ukraine and almost four years in Kazakhstan. This negative trend in CIS countries was largely due to the early deaths of middle-aged males (Svejnar 2002).

8 Between 1989 and 1999, fertility rates decreased from 1.87 to 1.17 in the Czech Republic, from 2.08 to 1.37 in Slovakia, from 2.08 to 1.40 in Poland and from 1.78 to 1.32 in Hungary. In the same period, fertility rates declined slightly in Western Europe: from 1.79 to 1.77 in France, from 1.42 to 1.35 in Germany, from 1.80 to 1.71 in the United Kingdom. In the same periods, the fertility rate in the United States increased from 2.01 to 2.06 (Svejnar 2002).

9 In 1999, compared to 1989, marriage rates per 1,000 inhabitants fell to half in the Czech Republic (from 8.6 to 4.3), by nearly a similar proportion in Poland (from 6.8 to 3.6), by one third in Slovakia (from 7.6 to 5.0) and from 6.3 to 4.6 in Hungary (Svejnar 2002). Trends were similar in other transformation countries, including the

CIS, but were stronger in the Baltic republics. These declines were much stronger than the previous decade in the same countries and in Western Europe and the United States.

10 The Index measures a country's ability to develop and nurture its human capital in four separate categories: human capital stock, human capital utilization, human capital productivity, and demographic outlook. A score is assigned to each category in each country, and each score is aggregated together in a composite ranking. The ranking can be used to compare human capital development across countries. Zero is the best possible score; 48 is the worst (Ederer 2006).

11 Calculations were made for the period 2003–12. The overall index includes, along with the Smart Growth and Inclusive Growth indexes, also the Sustainable Growth index, which rates greenhouse gas emissions, the share of renewable energy in gross final energy consumption and energy intensity of the economy.

12 Behavioral psychology and behavioral economics demonstrated that economic decision making and behavior may be under the influence of systematic misperceptions (Kahneman et al. 1982, Kahneman and Tversky 1984, 2000, Tversky and Kahneman 1981). Such decision making and behavior do not correspond to the standard principles of rationality, yet they may be predictable, since biases are consistent and systematic. The transformation process provided various examples of systematic misperceptions. Such was, for instance, the disregard for the foundation of new competitive enterprises due to the nearly absolute priority given to the privatization of large state-owned companies, except in Poland.

13 See also the different origin of the new elites in Lane et al. (2007) and the section on "On the reasons for path dependence and the new elites" in this chapter.

14 In the following, the Czech Republic, Hungary, Poland and Slovakia are identified as V4 or the four member countries of the Visegrád cooperation (see the section "Joining the common currency" in this chapter).

15 The consensus, according to Williamson (1989), included ten rather broad policy recommendations. These were: fiscal discipline; redirecting public spending from subsidies toward broad-based provision of pro-growth and pro-poor services (primary education, primary health care, investment in infrastructure); broader tax base and moderate marginal tax rates; moderately positive real interest rates determined by market processes; competitive exchange rates; trade liberalization; liberalization of inward foreign direct investment; privatization of state-owned enterprises; deregulation with prudential oversight of financial institutions; and well-defined and secure property rights.

16 On the privatization approach, recommendations to transformation countries and the conditionalities attached to support by international institutions see IMF (2001) and World Bank (2005).

17 See Ferge (2010, p. 45) for the interesting case of opinion polls in Hungary in 1988.

18 This is not to say that no alternative interpretations or strategies and policies existed. Indeed, these did exist (Lavigne 1999). However, for years, these did not receive the attention that they deserved, let alone be seriously considered as feasible policy alternatives.

19 On the role of criminal actors during transformation, see Grossman (1995). On such phenomena as de-capitalization of enterprises and inter-enterprise arrears in transformation economies, see Coricelli (1996).

20 "In becoming private owners, they [the new fused economic-political elite] used their privileged access to information, their dense networks of ties, and their knowledge of how the system worked to consolidate a dominant position in the new capitalist economy. The new elite, with roots in the old Communist *nomenklatura* as well as in the private sector that began to prosper under Gorbachev, was immune to control from above and below" (McDaniel 1996, p. 164). "although in many ways 'private', the new economic elite that had begun to assert itself in the late Gorbachev period was not . . . really a

capitalist class in the classical sense. Its rights were still defined as much by its political power as by its ownership of property. It did not have to act by market principles but could continue the closed monopolistic practices inherent in the Communist system" (ibid., p. 171). Something similar also took place in Central Europe on the eve of transformation, when round tables between the government/party in power and the social opposition were organized and when "spontaneous" privatization took place. As a result of these agreements, the old holders of power were granted or directly captured some privileges. A typical case was spontaneous privatization. Managers, politicians and directors in the old administrative and political machine used their control over assets to convert it into ownership of industrial assets. The state, workers and the population were consequently expropriated of the property rights they enjoyed in the past (Voszka 1996).

21 Cf. the examples quoted in (Dallago 1997).

22 Bekker (1995) applies Janossy's (1966, 1975) analysis of development processes to evaluate the short-term and long-term economic prospects of systemic change after 1989 and warns of the possible traps of being quasi-European or carrying out quasi-changes in the course of systemic transformation.

23 Social capital is the expected social and/or economic value from interpersonal or collective (social) networks and cooperation in terms of greater productivity of individuals and groups or lower transaction costs of social interaction. According to the OECD, social capital are "networks together with shared norms, values and understandings that facilitate co-operation within or among groups" (*OECD Insights: Human Capital*, downloadable at http://www.oecd.org/insights/37966934.pdf). The World Bank defines social capital as referring to "the institutions, relationships, and norms that shape the quality and quantity of a society's social interactions" (http://web.worldbank.org/ WBSITE/EXTERNAL/TOPICS/EXTSOCIALDEVELOPMENT/EXTTSOCIAL CAPITAL/0,,contentMDK:20185164~menuPK:418217~pagePK:148956~piPK: 216618~theSitePK:401015,00.html). Thus social capital is the glue that holds institutions together and that creates social cohesion, a critical factor for societies to prosper economically and for development to be sustainable.

24 African countries considered are Algeria, South Africa, Zimbabwe, Uganda, Tanzania, Egypt, United Arab Republic, Morocco, Nigeria. Western European countries are Luxembourg, Austria, Belgium, Germany, Denmark, Finland, France, Spain, the United Kingdom, Greece, Ireland, Italy, Malta, the Netherlands, Portugal, Sweden, Iceland. American countries are Canada, Chile, the United States, Venezuela, Puerto Rico, Peru, Mexico.

25 One of the authors (Bruno Dallago) recalls here various informal talks he had, primarily with economists of those countries, between 1988 and 1990. Nearly all of them were convinced that their country would become a member of the European Union within a very few years, provided that their country was the first to move. This view was shared by non-specialists whom he had the chance to talk with.

26 The Visegrád Battlegroup was established in 2011 and is to become operational in 2016. While initially the goal was to hold regular exercises under the auspices of the NATO Response Force and to include also Ukrainian forces, following tensions with Russia over Ukraine in 2014 the Battlegroup integrated better into the EU military strategy.

27 The Group established the International Visegrád Fund in 1999 in Bratislava with an annual budget of €8 million (2014). The Fund's aim is to award grants, scholarships and research fellowships, and artist residencies.

28 On the Visegrád Group activity, see the official website (http://www.Visegrádgroup. eu/). The historical chapter of the website (http://www.Visegrádgroup.eu/about/ history) enumerates four factors of decisive relevance in the formation of the Visegrád Group: (1) the desire to eliminate the remnants of the communist bloc in Central Europe; (2) the desire to overcome historic animosities between Central European countries; (3) the belief that through joint efforts it will be easier to successfully

accomplish social transformation and join in the European integration process; and (4) the proximity of ideas of the then ruling political elites.

29 Neumann (2001) examines the relationship between democracy and regionalization in Eastern Europe and supports the view that regionalization in former Eastern Europe has been a by-product of the membership applications to the European Union.

30 The Europe Agreements with Poland, Hungary and Czechoslovakia were ratified by all of the Parliaments of the previous twelve member countries by the end of 1993. The effect of the Agreements in terms of EU market access and other economic consequences materialized on March 1, 1992. After the dissolution of Czechoslovakia, Europe Agreements with the Czech Republic and with Slovakia were signed on October 4, 1993 and came into force on February 1, 1995.

31 See http://europa.eu/rapid/press-release_IP-91-1033_en.htm?locale=en.

32 See http://europa.eu/rapid/press-release_MEMO-94-7_en.htm. The political dimension and the cultural cooperation component were included in this kind of agreements for the first time.

33 Visegrád countries were also recommended to implement the Central European Free Trade Agreement (CEFTA), which took place on December 21, 1992 in Kraków and entered into force in July 1994. The Agreement was successively amended and joined by other countries in South-East Europe (http://www.cefta.int/). Lately, most countries withdrew from CEFTA, which as of 2015 included seven countries of South-East Europe (http://www.cvce.eu/en/obj/the_central_european_free_trade_agreement_1992_2015-en-43ff12bc-7d97-4bca-9986-215d7146bfaa.html). For relevant documents see http://www.cvce.eu/en/collections/unit-content/-/unit/02bb76df-d066-4c08-a58a-d4686a3e68ff/201e6e1f-b36b-4f9a-978f-401942c778a6/Resources#43ff12bc-7d97-4bca-9986-215d7146bfaa.

34 The basis for this was the *Acquis Communautaire*, which contained some 3,000 directives and 100,000 pages in the Official Journal of the European Union. In the accession process, the provisions of the *Acquis* were divided into 35 chapters and the progress of each country was assessed against each of these chapters. The score went from "generally already applies the acquis" to "situation totally incompatible with EU acquis." A country was accepted for membership when its situation responded positively to the 35 chapters. Given the detailed nature of these chapters, EU membership was often considered as the critical sign for the end of transformation. The 35 chapters were: (1) Free Movement of Goods, (2) Freedom of Movement for Workers, (3) Right of Establishment & Freedom to Provide Services, (4) Free Movement of Capital, (5) Public Procurement, (6) Company Law, (7) Intellectual Property Law, (8) Competition Policy, (9) Financial Services, (10) Information Society & Media, (11) Agriculture & Rural Development, (12) Food Safety, Veterinary & Phytosanitary Policy, (13) Fisheries, (14) Transport Policy, (15) Energy, (16) Taxation, (17) Economic & Monetary Policy, (18) Statistics, (19) Social Policy & Employment, (20) Enterprise & Industrial Policy, (21) Trans-European Networks, (22) Regional Policy & Coordination of Structural Instruments, (23) Judiciary & Fundamental Rights, (24) Justice, Freedom & Security, (25) Science & Research, (26) Education & Culture, (27) Environment, (28) Consumer & Health Protection, (29) Customs Union, (30) External Relations, (31) Foreign, Security & Defence Policy, (32) Financial Control, (33) Financial & Budgetary Provisions, (34) Institutions, (35) Other Issues.

35 The accession meant that the country was considered to comply with the fundamental Copenhagen Criteria or Accession Criteria for EU membership, which the European Council had approved in Copenhagen in 1993. The Criteria are the essential necessary conditions for a candidate country to become a member of the EU. These are political criteria (stability of institutions guaranteeing democracy, the rule of law, human rights and respect for and protection of minorities), economic criteria (a functioning market economy and the capacity to cope with competition and market forces), and administrative and institutional capacity (to effectively implement the *Acquis* and

ability to take on the obligations of membership) (http://ec.europa.eu/enlargement/policy/glossary/terms/accession-criteria_en.htm). See also Koyama (2015).

36 The referendums took place between April and June 2003. All had a positive outcome and the large majority of voters supported accession, albeit the turnout was rather modest. In the Czech Republic, the referendum was held on June 13 and 14, 2003. Turnout was 55.2 percent of those having right and 77.3 percent of voters approved the proposal. Corresponding date and figures for Hungary were April 12, 2003, 45.6 percent turnout and 83.8 approval; Poland June 7 and 8, 2003, 58.9 percent and 77.6 percent, and Slovakia on May 16 and 17, 2003, 52.1 percent and 93.7 percent.

37 The Council of the European Union (often referred to as the Council of Ministers, or sometimes just called the Council) is a decision-making organ of the EU including the 28 national ministers with similar functions and competences, one per each member country. The Council meets in ten different configurations, according to the issue under consideration. In economic issues, the most influential is the Council for Economic and Financial Affairs (Ecofin), which is composed of economics and finance ministers of the member states. The presidency of the Council is taken by one of the national ministers according to a rotation system of six months, with the exception of the Foreign Affairs Council, which is chaired by the Union's High Representative. Fundamental decisions are taken by unanimous voting, while in most issues qualified majority voting is used. The Council should be distinguished from the European Council, which is the fundamental common decision-making organ. The European Council consists of the heads of state or government of the member states, the European Council's president and the president of the European Commission. The European Council defines the EU's general political direction and priorities.

38 On preparing for the euro and related documents, see http://ec.europa.eu/economy_finance/euro/adoption/preparing/index_en.htm; on convergence criteria before adopting the euro, see http://ec.europa.eu/economy_finance/euro/adoption/who_can_join/index_en.htm.

39 In early 2015, the following countries adhere to the Eurozone: Austria, Belgium, Cyprus, Estonia, Finland, France, Germany, Greece, Ireland, Italy, Latvia, Lithuania, Luxembourg, Malta, the Netherlands, Portugal, Slovakia, Slovenia and Spain. Greece became the twelfth member of the euro area on January 1, 2001. Slovenia entered in January 2007, Cyprus and Malta in 2008, Slovakia in 2009, Estonia in 2011, Latvia in 2014 and Lithuania in 2015. All EU member countries are obliged to adopt the euro once they meet the relevant criteria, with the exception of the United Kingdom and Denmark.

40 Price stability is defined as "a year-on-year increase in the Harmonised Index of Consumer Prices (HICP) for the euro area of below 2%." The ECB Governing Council has clarified that its aim is to maintain inflation rates below, but close to, 2 percent over the medium term.

41 Following the international crisis, the EU strengthened prudential requirements for banks and depositor protection and adopted more stringent rules for managing banks in distress. These rules form now a single rulebook for all financial actors in the 28 member states. The single rulebook is the foundation for the developing Banking Union in the Eurozone. As a first step in this direction, the EU agreed to establish a Single Supervisory Mechanism and a Single Resolution Mechanism for banks.

42 The Lisbon Treaty (TFEU) defined a number of convergence criteria that EU member countries have to comply with before adopting the euro. These are: (a) not be subject to a procedure for excessive budgetary deficit; (b) price stability and low average inflation rate; (c) low long-term nominal interest rates, not exceed by more than 2 percent that of the three best performing member countries in terms of price stability; (d) stable exchange rates with the other Eurozone countries for at least the last two years; (e) national legislation compatible with EU norms and treaties. Convergence criteria, which are meant to avoid tensions within the EMU, complete the Maastricht

criteria, that served the preparation of the euro, and strengthen the SGP, which is meant to assure the compliance with the criteria after the euro is adopted, regarding in particular government deficit and government debt. The SGP was adopted at the Amsterdam European Council in June 1997. The Maastricht criteria, originally defined in Maastricht in 1992, foresee price stability (not exceeding the average of the three countries with the lowest inflation by more than 1.5 percent), low public deficit (the general government deficit must not exceed 3 percent of GDP) and public debt (the total public debt must not exceed 60 percent of GDP), low and not diverging interest rates (the nominal long-term interest rate cannot exceed that of the three countries with the lowest inflation rate by more than 2 percent in the year preceding the entrance decision), and stable exchange rates (participation in the exchange rate mechanism of the European monetary system without any break during the two years preceding the examination of the situation and without severe tensions or devaluation against the currency of any other member state).

43 The convergence criterion on exchange rate stability requires participation in the Exchange Rate Mechanism (ERM II). ERM II, that succeeded ERM on January 1, 1999, is aimed at ensuring that exchange rate fluctuations between the euro and other EU currencies do not disrupt economic stability within the single market, and to help non-Eurozone countries prepare themselves for adopting the euro. The Slovak koruna joined ERM II on November 28, 2005, and observed a central rate of 38.4550 to the euro. It was then revalued twice: on March 19, 2007 to 35.4424, and on May 29, 2008 to 30.1260. During this entire period the koruna maintained the standard fluctuation band of ±15 percent. Slovakia adopted the euro on January 1, 2009 (http://ec.europa.eu/economy_finance/euro/adoption/erm2/index_en.htm).

44 Marer (2016) provides a thorough analysis of Central-Eastern European countries vis-à-vis the euro.

45 The Czech Republic's koruna was pegged to a basket of currencies between 1993 and 1995. Between February 1996 and May 1997, ±7 percent fluctuations of the exchange rate were allowed. The exchange rate regime changed again following the 1997 Asian crisis, when the koruna had to switch to managed floating to counteract speculative attacks. Later in the year, the country returned to managed floating with inflation targeting. Hungary adopted an adjustable peg between 1990 and 1994, switched to a crawling band between 1995 and 2001, and adopted a euro target zone allowing for ±15 percent fluctuations against the euro between 2001 and 2008. Hungary changed to managed floating with inflation targeting in 2008. Poland had a fixed exchange rate against the US$ until May 1991 and then against a basket of five currencies, but had to abandon it after a sharp devaluation of the złoty. In October 1991, the country adopted a crawling peg until May 2005, after which a crawling band system was adopted, with fluctuation band increasing from ±7 percent to ±15 percent. A free-floating exchange rate system with inflation targeting was adopted in April 2000 (Bańbuła et al. 2011, IMF 2014c).

46 Special Drawing Rights used by the IMF. The SDR is an international reserve asset, created by the IMF in 1969 to supplement official reserves of its member countries. SDRs can be exchanged for freely usable currencies. Its value is based on a basket of four key international currencies.

10 Transformation at work

Systemic change started without a reliable and shared theory of transformation and hardly any previous experience which could act as a reference. The diversity of situations in different countries should have suggested that alternatives be considered and how they might fit into the diverse circumstances. In such undefined situations, vested interests could play a significant role. Economic difficulties and political disagreements pushed the new governments to hurry with implementing transformation along general rules and principles while disregarding the need to adapt to local features and circumstances. Transformation agendas relied initially on incomplete blueprints and paid scant concern to the complex changes and the complementarities and trade-offs among the different components.

The mainstream approach, based on general rules and principles, came to identify three fundamental components of transformation: macroeconomic stabilization, liberalization, and privatization.[1] Two issues received particular attention in the debate over transformation and in policy making. These were the issues of sequencing and timing. The former was about which component of the three had to come first. The second had to do with the speed of approach to the implementation of reforms and policies: through the fastest possible action or in a gradual way? This dichotomy reflected the different analyses of economic processes, while consideration for local circumstances hardly played a role, except possibly in Hungary.

Fast action or "shock therapy" (or "big bang," as it was also termed in Poland) was devised to implement an abrupt separation of the new system from the old one, which had to be disrupted in the fastest way possible. The separation was addressed to sever links with the past and to interrupt conservative links among people and organizations and between these and the state budget (Lipton and Sachs 1990). It was also implemented to introduce new formal institutions that would be irreversible (i.e. privatization), new organizations (i.e. competitive firms), new positive and negative incentives (i.e. wages linked to productivity, unemployment and bankruptcy, and taxation). The term "shock therapy" itself was chosen to communicate the idea of a medicine, bitter yet necessary, to cure a sick economy and debilitated society. Shock therapy was based on the consideration of markets as the natural condition of a free society and efficient economy. Once freed from the unnatural constraints that the old system imposed upon them and provided that macropolicies stabilize the economy, markets would develop spontaneously.

Well-functioning markets may well need some structures and resources to operate (e.g. information structures, qualified labor, capital accumulation), but these would develop spontaneously through the interaction of self-interested economic and political actors.

This view was very much in line with the popular version of the Washington Consensus and with the popular reading of the idea of efficient markets. Perhaps more important, the fundamental goal was to catch the "window of opportunity" (Gaidar and Pöhl 1995) that events had created and act before the communists and in general the enemies of change could reorganize. This approach required the fast and perhaps harsh hand of political power, a solution that led some scholars to define the promoters of this approach as "market Bolsheviks" (Reddaway and Glinski 2001).

Although the term "shock therapy" was applied also to macroeconomic stabilization, the true core of the approach was privatization:[2] give away or sell public assets to private owners, thereby creating a class of owners strongly interested in defending the new system. To this end, liberalization and competition could be sacrificed, if necessary. And in most cases, the sacrifice appeared to be necessary, or at least convenient, either to speed up privatization or to maximize the sale price of public assets. Regrettably, privatization policies did not include the foundation and growth of new private enterprises, a process that was usually labeled as "greenfield" privatization. As a matter of fact, the implementation of transformation based on the shock-therapy approach increased the chances for path-dependent developments.

The alternative approach of a slower, gradual and broader-based transformation was labeled as "gradualism." Gradualism was based in the idea that change can only take place in a gradual and evolutionary way, and that it is important to make time for new formal institutions to develop and gradually replace old institutions and for informal institutions to adapt and start interacting with the new formal institutions (Murrell 1992). The term was willfully mildly pejorative, since this approach was accused of being proposed in the interest of old elites and aimed at allowing them to retain their power. It may be useful to distinguish two alternative kinds of gradualism. One kind certainly had the flavor and often the substance of foot dragging. More important, there was another strong type of gradualism that was based on evolutionary and Austrian theories, with some support by Keynesian economists.

According to evolutionary and Austrian scholars, institutions and markets can only evolve gradually ("*Natura non facit saltus*") through the co-evolution of a wide set of changes and events (Murrell 1992, Roland 2000). Policy makers can foster these processes with proper institutional policies and reforms, but cannot replace the innumerable changes, learning and adaptations that organic processes require. According to this view, the transformation process requires a coherent, coordinated and consistent action of institutional reform and policy making. Self-interested actors and social coordination will do the rest.

Although positions in the debate were clear-cut, the reality of reforms and policy making was much less sharp. This obliged reformers and policy makers

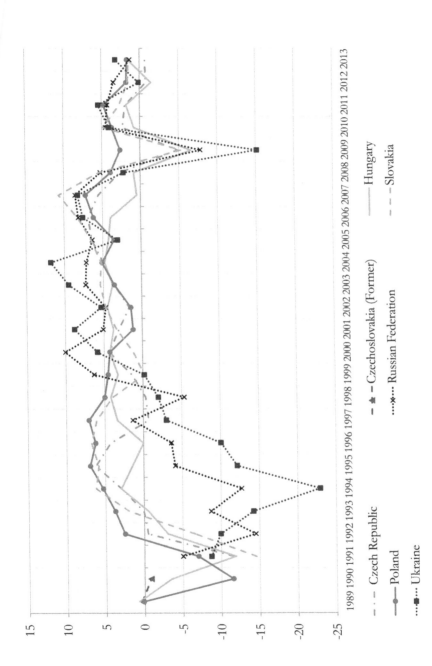

1989 1990 1991 1992 1993 1994 1995 1996 1997 1998 1999 2000 2001 2002 2003 2004 2005 2006 2007 2008 2009 2010 2011 2012 2013

- - - Czech Republic - ▲ - Czechoslovakia (Former) ——— Hungary

——— Poland ·····×···· Russian Federation - - - Slovakia

·····■···· Ukraine

Figure 10.1 Growth rate of GDP at constant 2005 prices in percent

Source: United Nations database (http://unstats.un.org/unsd/snaama/dnlList.asp)

to compromise and change or adapt their decisions and implementation, following negative events and effects. Moreover, the active opposition of the losers, their protests and their support for parties with alternative programs obliged governments to modify reforms and policies or governments were replaced. As a consequence, all countries followed a mixed path and the general debate faded away. More interesting and useful was to understand where shock therapy was useful and where gradualism was a better choice.[3]

The Central European countries had rather similar political and economic general blueprints of becoming pluralist liberal democracies and competitive market economies. However, their political and economic situations were distinct, concerning in particular their macroeconomic equilibrium and external accounts. From this came a distinct need for and role of macroeconomic stabilization, which heavily impacted upon the kind and speed of privatization that was preferred. In turn, privatization choices impacted upon the fate of liberalization. From these differences, dissimilarities of economic performance and a lack of synchronization of the business cycle descended (Figure 10.1).

Transformation at work: Poland

The economic situation was particularly critical in Poland. The Polish economy had been in a permanent crisis since the late 1970s (Figure 10.2). Transformation thus hit an already debilitated economy. Moreover, the Polish economy was also under the threat of hyperinflation and had a high foreign debt of more than US$41 billion at the end of 1988, corresponding to nearly two-thirds of the country's GDP (Kolodko 1991, Kolodko et al. 1992, Kolodko 2000). Average consumer prices increased by 251 percent in 1989 (IMF World Economic Outlook database). However, in the first month of price liberalization introduced by the Balcerowicz plan, January 1990 compared to the previous month, CPI inflation jumped to nearly 80 percent and the index for the year reached 586 percent.

It is rather obvious that, under these conditions, the new Polish government had no choice but to implement macroeconomic stabilization as a top priority. This goal was part of the Balcerowicz Plan, from the name of the then finance minister and vice prime minister Leszek Balcerowicz. The plan, approved in 1989 and enacted in January 1990, was based on what came to be labeled as "shock therapy."

The Plan was much more than simple shock therapy to cool down inflation, though. It was implemented by means of ten Acts which covered a number of critically important issues, including hardening the budget constraint of state-owned companies and protecting workers against dismissals during privatization. The Plan forbade the national central bank to finance the state budget deficit, introduced the possibility for state-owned companies to go bankrupt, abolished the possibility for state-owned companies to obtain preferential access to credit, introduced the same taxation rules for all companies, tied interest rates to inflation, and introduced the possibility for foreign investors to invest and export their profits. Moreover, the Plan foresaw austerity measures aimed at cooling down the economy, including a tax limiting wage increases in state-owned companies,

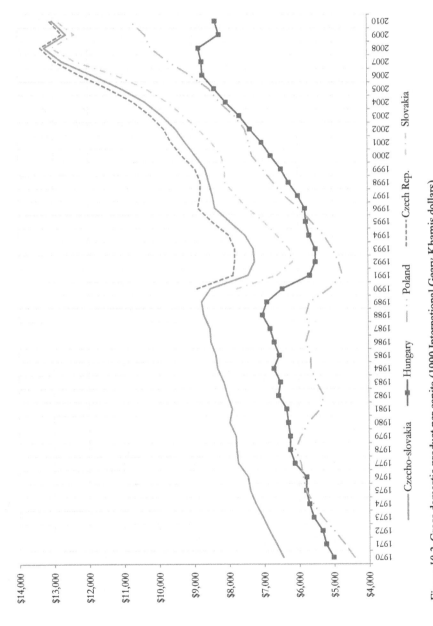

Figure 10.2 Gross domestic product per capita (1990 International Geary-Khamis dollars)

Source: New Maddison Project Database (http://www.ggdc.net/maddison/maddison-project/data.htm)

tempered with the protection of workers of state-owned companies against mass dismissals, and introducing unemployment benefits and unemployment agencies.

Finally, the plan liberalized foreign economic relations, including the external conversion of the złoty, abolishing the state monopoly in international trade, creating a uniform customs rate for all companies. The outcome was fast and successful reorientation of trade relations from Comecon to western countries, which absorbed four-fifths of Polish exports by the end of 1992. Through openness, liberalization and favorable conditions, including a very liberal foreign investment law approved in 1991 and high import tariffs on particular goods (cars), the country was also fairly successful in attracting foreign direct investments (FDI), particularly in the auto industry, although initially much less so than Hungary, in part due to a degree of political and social instability. The end of Comecon, the curtail of subsidies to companies, the liberalization and reorientation of trade to western markets and the association agreement with the EU brought a dramatic and fast structural change. The main victims were companies in the heavy industries and exporting to the Comecon markets and companies unable to survive the competition of western companies, including mining, textiles and electrical engineering. The outcome was unemployment and redeployment of workers and investments.

The Plan's measures were supported internationally. The European Union set up the PHARE program[4] in 1989 as a pre-accession program for supporting transformation in Central European countries. The IMF granted Poland a stabilization fund of US$1 billion and an additional stand-by credit of US$720 million. The World Bank granted additional credits for upgrading exports. Bilateral support by various governments was also important and relieved the country of half of the burden of its debt capital and the interest rates cumulated to 2001.

The effects of the Plan were mixed. It is important to note that the Plan aimed at stabilizing and liberalizing the economy and at reducing the weight and the role of the state. However, it did not include any privatization measures. While this could appear as a shortcoming of the Plan, in reality and perhaps unwillingly this fact contributed to the success of transformation in Poland by leaving ample room for the establishment of new private businesses. Among the positive outcomes, the most relevant in the short run was undoubtedly the stabilization of prices. Indeed, inflation decreased to 4 percent per month in March 1990 over the previous month. In the following years inflation decreased consistently (Figure 10.3).

On the plus side of the Polish transformation policies, one should also mention the rapid decrease of the state's influence over the economy, with a correspondingly rapid increase of the role of the market. The balance of the state budget improved rapidly thanks to the drastic decrease of subsidies to prices and companies. However, the number of workers who lost their job increased rapidly and unemployment rate rapidly rose above 10 percent, the highest rate among the Central European countries, together with Slovakia (Allison and Ringold 1996, Svejnar 1999). The situation with unemployment worsened further and reached the top in the early 2000s, after which it decreased (Figure 10.4).

What is perhaps most interesting, in the case of Poland, is that a success story came out of the most difficult situation at the start of transformation. After the

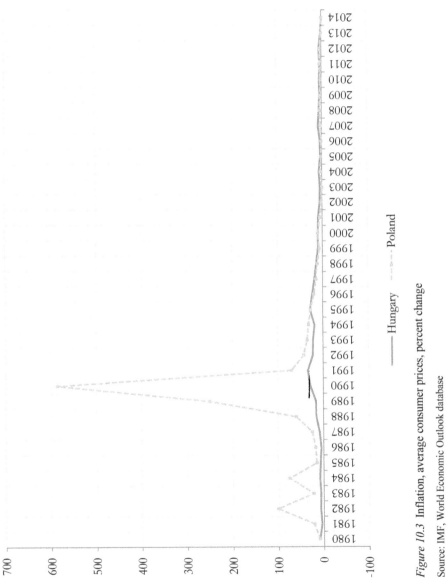

Figure 10.3 Inflation, average consumer prices, percent change

Source: IMF, World Economic Outlook database

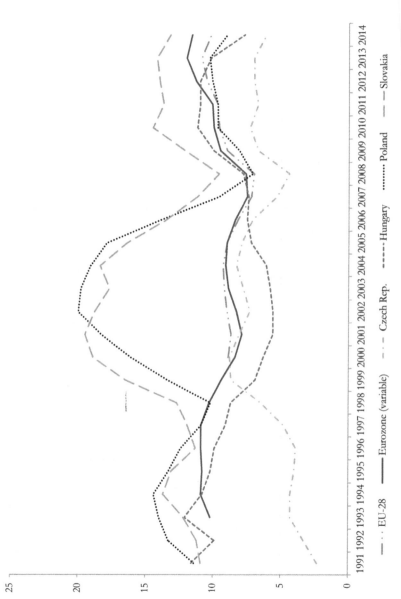

Figure 10.4 Unemployment rate, annual average, in percent

Source: Eurostat, World Bank (World Development Indicators for the following years: Czech Republic 1991–92, Hungary 1991–95, Poland 1991–96, Slovakia 1991–97)

1991 1992 1993 1994 1995 1996 1997 1998 1999 2000 2001 2002 2003 2004 2005 2006 2007 2008 2009 2010 2011 2012 2013 2014

— · · EU-28   —— Eurozone (variable)   — · · Czech Rep.   – – – – Hungary   · · · · · · Poland   — — Slovakia

first difficult years, a dynamic growth took hold in the country, that not even the 2007 world financial crisis interrupted (Table 10.1). Poland was the first transformation country to reach the level of pre-transformation GDP. Looking at per capita GDP in Geary-Khamis dollars, Poland reached the bottom in 1991 and surpassed the 1988 level in 1996 (Table 10.1). Comparable years for Hungary were 1993 and 2001. In the case of Czechoslovakia, the corresponding years were 1992 and 2000.

One problem with assessing Poland's performance is that GDP per capita before transformation was the highest in 1978. In the following decade, there was a serious GDP drop in early 1980s and stagnation followed. Taking 1978 as a reference, the Polish economy recovered that level in 1997. It is fair to recognize that an economy that had such a long period of crisis accumulated a growth potential in terms of human, material, technological and knowledge resources that is much higher than in countries whose economy expanded, albeit at a slow pace. However, it should also be stressed that, if the revival of the economy was so clear and constant, reforms and policies during transformation must have helped. The descending part of the J curve, which had to be short-lived and mild in the intention of reformers, was definitely worse even in Central European countries, yet less than in other CEECs. More important, the ascending part of the curve was faster than in other countries and uninterrupted.

Social costs in terms of lost income and lost jobs were significant. Yet, though there were more than one million jobs lost in the state sector, the booming private sector soon created many employment opportunities. By 1992, there were more

Table 10.1 GDP per capita (1990 International Geary-Khamis dollar)

	Czechoslovakia	Hungary	Poland	Czech Rep.	Slovakia
1988	8.709	7.031	5.789		
1989	8.768	6.903	5.684		
1990	8.513	6.459	5.113	8.895	7.763
1991	7.439	5.676	4.738	7.865	6.606
1992	7.254	5.510	4.842	7.818	6.158
1993	7.282	5.506	5.011	7.814	6.251
1994	7.517	5.687	5.265	7.985	6.612
1995	7.956	5.781	5.623	8.464	6.977
1996	8.374	5.802	5.970	8.859	7.445
1997	8.439	6.001	6.388	8.793	7.762
1998	8.543	6.263	6.704	8.780	8.089
1999	8.643	6.482	7.008	8.937	8.084
2000	8.930	6.772	7.309	9.320	8.188
2001	9.219	7.035	7.399	9.616	8.466

Source: New Maddison Project Database (http://www.ggdc.net/maddison/maddison-project/data.htm)

than 600,000 private enterprises supplying approximately 1.5 million jobs, most of them the outcome of greenfield investment. One important aspect of Poland's transformation was in fact the critically important role that new private enterprises had in driving growth revival.

In Poland, priority was de facto obtained by the creation of new private firms. Also, so-called "small" privatization—the privatization of retail and catering—was swift and successful. At the same time, the stages of privatization law for large companies were difficult and slow, with years of debates and uncertainty. Privatization of state-owned enterprises in Poland moved slowly and relied first on "commercialization" (Błaszczyck et al. 1999).[5] Under commercialization, firms remained in state ownership, but they were placed under private law and were run by independent supervisory boards rather than directly by the state.

In the first two years of transformation, privatization consisted mostly of so-called "liquidation" privatization, i.e. the direct sale, rent, or leasing of assets of small- and medium-size state-owned enterprises. Large-size enterprise privatization was slow and consisted mostly in the commercialization of companies or their public offering to strategic investors, forming the so-called "equity" privatization. The latter acquired greater importance after 1992, while the dominant method of privatization in various large companies in 1994 became the debt-to-equity swap.

Thus far, the country lacked a mass privatization policy and such a policy's related law.[6] A Mass Privatization Project was actually in discussion during summer 1990 and a Law on Privatization of State-Owned Enterprises was adopted in July 1990. Large-scale privatization started at the end of the year. Due to political difficulties, the Law on the National Investment Funds and their privatization was adopted by the Parliament only on April 30, 1993 and started to be implemented at the end of 1994.

In the Polish variant of mass privatization, the state set up fifteen National Investment Funds to which the 60 percent of the shares of 512 medium and large companies to be privatized were transferred (Hashi 2000). Polish citizens could not acquire shares in the privatized firms' stock, but they were entitled to become shareholders of the Funds. In the attempt to solve the issue of monitoring the monitors, each Fund was governed by a management consortium gathering foreign and Polish banks and audit agencies. The management consortium was given the explicit objective of increasing the value of the asset portfolio held by the Fund.

In spite of these difficulties and delay, the development of the private sector proceeded rapidly. By 1995, the private sector was estimated to produce approximately 60 percent of GDP. As said, the main contribution did not come so much from privatized large companies, as in other transformation countries, but by newly established small- and medium-size enterprises. Amidst political and privatization uncertainty, but based on policies supporting private business and pro-growth policies, new private enterprises boomed. In addition, the lack of a law that would force the privatization of large companies gave managers the opportunity to restructure companies. As a consequence, also many state-owned companies improved their efficiency and became competitive.

Transformation at work: Hungary

Privatization in Hungary started very soon. Indeed, the process started before transformation, in particular following the 1988 company act (Act VI of 1988 on Business Organizations). The act started to streamline Hungarian legislation to the EU legislation, but also gave the managers of state-owned companies discretionary powers in managing, restructuring and even selling parts of companies. The State Privatization Agency (SPA) was established in January 1990 to manage the process of privatization. Its task was delicate and strategic, since privatization had to create the resources necessary to fix the massive US$21.2 billion foreign debt in 1990.[7] Predictably, the process was ridden with accusations of corruption. However, it was technically successful, since privatization provided important revenue for financing the country's foreign and domestic debt (Mihályi 2010).

While major privatization involved most of the large companies, public utilities were also privatized. These included giant companies such as the national telecommunications company Matáv, the national oil and gas conglomerate MOL, and electricity supply and production companies. Extremely important was also the privatization of the banking sector, although the largest bank, the National Savings Bank (OTP), remained in public ownership for years. The sale of most banks to foreign owners raised heated debates and problems in the years to come and some observers considered the banking sector's difficulties as one of the important causes for the lack of modernization and growth of the SME sector.[8]

Successful as it was, privatization had at least two important drawbacks. First, it attracted significant amounts of FDIs which, along with being beneficial to the country in different ways, also pushed the appreciation of the exchange rate of the forint. Appreciation discouraged high-priced elasticity exports, which were typically those of the traditional SMEs owned by Hungarian businesspeople. Moreover, significant fiscal subsidies and advantages and the infrastructural investment tailored to the needs of foreign investors gave the advantage to large companies. As a consequence and also due to the higher efficiency that FDIs brought to large companies, domestic SMEs found difficult to expand and upgrade (Dallago 2003). This contributed to the development of a dual economy. One important consequence was that many SMEs were able to survive only through tax evasion, which contributed to the sizeable expansion of the irregular economy (OECD 2008).[9]

The problem with SMEs in Hungary had been serious since the onset of transformation (OECD 2008). While SMEs had a recognized great potential, this remained largely undeveloped. Their presence in the economy is outstanding still today: they account for nearly 70 percent of employment and over half of the sales and value added. Due to this, their potential for job creation and for innovation makes the improvement of their performance fundamental for the development of the economy. However, SMEs are generally weak as a propulsive factor: their average size is particularly small and their productivity is low. Most Hungarian SMEs are not innovative or internationally competitive, due to the under-qualification of their human resources and their inadequate R&D skills. Also significant are structural differences among SMEs across regions. However, the situation with SMEs result-ing from the greenfield investments of foreign investors is different.

Privatization in Hungary included other components, which were at times under the influence of ideological biases. This was, for instance, the case of agriculture. Hungarian agriculture was mostly organized around cooperatives, which were overall successful under the liberalization of their activity during the 1960s and even more so the 1980s. Members of the cooperatives were generally satisfied with their situation, since they could pursue lucrative production on their family plots attached to the cooperative or state farm and had overall incomes higher than workers' in industry. However, the first democratic government of 1990–94, led by the conservative Hungarian Democratic Forum, proceeded to disrupt agricul-tural cooperatives to please its junior partner, the Independent Smallholders' Party. Cooperatives were split up and their assets, including land and machinery, were given back to their former owners and members. Sometimes, these were members of the cooperative, but in many cases they had moved to cities and had abandoned agriculture, or emigrated. To continue production, cooperatives had to lease back land, often through short-term contracts with the new owners. The ensuing disrup-tion and uncertainty converted a successful sector, with an important foreign trade surplus, into an ailing sector for years.

The same government also intended to proceed to the physical restitution of the assets that were expropriated at the end of the 1940s to their former owners. Due to a ruling by the Constitutional Court, though, the restitution law[10] only offered vouchers to previous owners. These vouchers could then be exchanged for land managed by agricultural cooperatives and could be used to buy the home where the owner was living. These vouchers could also be traded and for years were an important trading item in the Hungarian stock exchange.

Similar to the other countries, small-scale privatization was successful and smooth in Hungary as well. Small retail and catering businesses were privat-ized between 1990 and 1994, although they soon had to fight for survival due to the powerful competition from the large international retail chains that flooded the country.

In spite of its apparently favorable starting situation, Hungary's transformation was less successful than expected and ridden with unwanted consequences and unforeseen difficulties. Of these, four stand out for their importance and long-term effects. The first was the indebtedness of the country, that in per capita terms was similar to that of Poland in 1989. Unlike Poland, Hungary never went through default and preferred to rely on its own resources to solve external indebtedness. The high level of the debt and its high interest rates, however, drained the coun-try's resources for years,[11] as well as the rather soft fiscal policies in the years before and after transformation (Mihályi 2013).

Negative demographic trends were a second unfavorable occurrence. While Poland was a country with dynamic population growth and high numbers of people entering the labor force for years and while Czechoslovakia had a bal-anced age structure, the age pyramid in Hungary had a rapidly shrinking base. Each year, the number of those entering the labor force was less than those exiting, an imbalance that immigration could not compensate.[12] This fact had important and negative consequences for the economy. The lack of young age classes is known to hamper innovation and productivity and consequently is seen as a drawback on the country's development perspectives. The dependency ratio (share of people under the age of 15 and above the age of 64 in the total population) grew constantly, from 64.6 percent in 1980 to 66.2 percent in 1990 and to 68.7 percent in 2011 (Mihályi 2012).There are two aspects of the Hungarian labor market that are particularly problematic. The first is the employment rate, which suffered a particularly negative shock in the first years of transformation (HCSO 2010). By 1996, only 3.6 million people were employed, 1.3 million less than before transformation. Employment rate fell accordingly, from around 64 percent in 1990 to 52 percent in 1996.

The shock was entirely due to restrictive transformation policies and reforms, including privatization, that led to the expulsion of elderly workers and women from the labor market. However, the employment rate had improved since the second half of the 1990s and up to the 2007 international crisis, after which it decreased again. In spite of this improvement, the unemployment rate in Hungary continued to be relatively low, approximately 10 percent by 2010, lower than the EU15 average. Moreover, the labor market remained rigid and made little use of such flexible solutions as part-time employment. Indeed, within the EU, Hungary is second only to Greece for the number of hours that employees work on average per year (OECD database). Thus the overall supply of labor in Hungary is lower than in the Czech Republic, Poland and Austria, but it is higher than in France or Italy (Eurostat database and Mihályi 2012).

Although demographic trends and labor market features are unfavorable to Hungary, they are not sufficient to explain the low dynamism of the Hungarian economy. More important is low productivity (Figure 10.5).

Productivity is low in Hungary due to the excessive fragmentation of domestic enterprises, that have, on average, diminutive dimensions when compared internationally (Dallago 2003), and also due to the significant territorial differences among regions of a country that lacks important geographical barriers (Mihályi 2012). Given the rather traditional international specialization of Hungary, which sees the significant presence of traditional industries, the tiny average size of enterprises is an important drawback that prevents a proper exploitation of scale economies. This drawback is particularly significant in the service sector and in the building industry.

While one of the standard components of transformation was the radical decrease of the average size of enterprises,[13] the excessively small average size of SMEs causes several problems to the economy (OECD 2008). Small domestic enterprises have difficulties and weak incentives to invest and to grow. Many small enterprises have low profit rates and lack the resources for investment. Moreover, it is a well-known problem that small enterprises, which are generally family businesses, suffer from the problem of control and intergenerational succession. Both problems lead the founder to keep low dimensions and diversify assets to other uses, in particular to real estate. Moreover, small enterprises have difficulties in accessing the capital

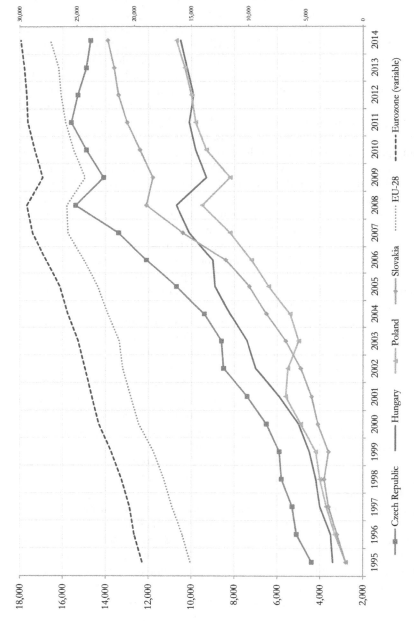

Figure 10.5 Gross domestic product at market prices, current prices, euro per capita

Source: Eurostat

market and external finance. In fact, they usually lack internal expertise in preparing business plans. Small enterprises also present fiscal problems and are more prone to evade taxes and employ irregular labor. They are also typically unable to play an important role in vocational training, both because of their limited size, and because they tend to have a traditional profile.

Territorial disparities are significant in Hungary, surprisingly so in view of the small size of the country and the relatively homogeneous geography. Territorial disparities are a drawback for the economy, since they depress economic activity, go with problems in infrastructure, shrink demand and investment opportunities, and cause congestion in the developed part of the country; they explain an important part of inequalities. It is noteworthy than FDIs in Hungary are concentrated in a tiny part of the country, mostly in Budapest and the axis connecting the capital city to Vienna.

The fourth economically unfavorable event was costly social policy and the drive to consumption. Generous social policies, relative to the level of development of the country, are both a boon and a drawback for the economy. They are a boon because they keep demand high and avoid excessive disparities among social groups and attenuate the negative effects of territorial disparities. They are a drawback because they absorb resources that cannot be invested in the economy. Costly social policies must be financed through taxation, including social security contributions. Both taxation and social security contributions were indeed high in Hungary in international terms, a situation which discourages investment and hiring employees (Kornai 1992b, 1997b).

The low level of investment is the other side of what happened with consumption. Hungary began its transformation period with a particularly high share of GDP spent in consumption. This was the consequence of the "goulash communism" policies of the 1970s and the 1980s, and the illusion that systemic change meant first and foremost higher consumption.

Generous social policies and a drive to consumption in a country with low productivity growth, high debt, high tax evasion and negative demographics put policies under pressure. By 1995, the fiscal situation had deteriorated and FDIs had decreased. Current accounts also worsened, due to high import demand. Lajos Bokros, of the center-left government led by Gyula Horn, introduced an austerity package in March 1995, as soon as he was appointed as the new finance minister. The "Bokros package" included cuts to welfare, a limit on the growth of wages in the public sector, higher custom duties, depreciation of the forint, and accelerated privatization. Austerity policies were deeply unpopular, but were successful in improving the financial situation. A reform of the pension system followed in 1996, which introduced a two-pillar system involving private pension funds, replacing the previous fully state-based system.

Along with problems, transformation in Hungary also experienced successes. The country was successful in upgrading its infrastructure, also thanks to the appropriate use of EU funds. A successful feature of the Hungarian transformation was the significant inflow of FDIs, particularly in the first half of the 1990s, when nearly half of FDIs to European transformation countries went to Hungary alone. The country also enjoyed an important advantage over other transformation countries, derived from the openness to economic relations with western countries which had already started, well in advance of transformation, in the 1980s. In the following years, the inflow decreased and the outflow of profits increased. However, Hungary had cumulative foreign direct investments totaling more than US$60 billion in the decade following 1989 (CIA 2008), corresponding to over one-third of all FDIs in Central and Eastern Europe, including the former Soviet Union. Attractive factors were the country's skilled and relatively inexpensive labor, tax incentives, modern infrastructure, and a good telecommunications system. Also important were accommodating monetary and fiscal policies, with important tax benefits for foreign investors, and the flexible exchange rate policies.

One important reason why FDIs initially privileged Hungary so much more than other transformation countries was the privatization program. Due to the difficult situation of Hungarian finances and in particular the high foreign debt of the country, privatization was used to raise money from foreign investors. The choice had a two-pronged strategic motivation. First, foreigners were the only investors with real capital and the method was effective in raising revenue for the state. Domestic investors had insufficient resources for buying the high-value assets that were on sale and for investing valuable resources to restructure and modernize privatized enterprises. Second, foreign investors were seen as carriers of effective corporate governance and as an important vehicle for placing Hungarian enterprises into international value chains. Both goals were achieved, in spite of scandals and evidence of the use of transfer prices by foreign investors, and attracted sizeable amounts of FDIs.

An important drawback was that most foreign investment went to buy existing companies. This was important, because those companies were restructured and upgraded and soon became the driving sector of exports. Yet the centrality of large companies, the resources that governments had to spend in preparing those companies for privatization, the advantages that foreign investors obtained in terms of low taxes and subsidies, left modest resources for supporting genuinely greenfield investment and enterprises and submitted economic policies to the interest of foreign investors. Moreover, the sizeable inflow of foreign resources pushed the value of the domestic currency, the forint, to excessively high values, to the disadvantage of exports by domestic firms. In the long run, these occurrences proved to be costly to the country development.

In spite of the costly relief brought about by the Bokros package, the financial situation soon worsened again. The state budget deficit increased above 10 percent by 2005. While the knowledge of the true situation was concealed for a while in view of the April 2006 electoral campaign, after the elections the new center-left government headed by Ferenc Gyurcsány enacted a new package of austerity measures, with the goal of reducing the budget deficit to 3 percent of GDP by 2008. As a consequence of austerity, the economy slowed down and the financial situation remained difficult. When the international situation became difficult in 2008, the country had to require a quick rescue package of US$25 billion, granted by the EU, the IMF and the World Bank.

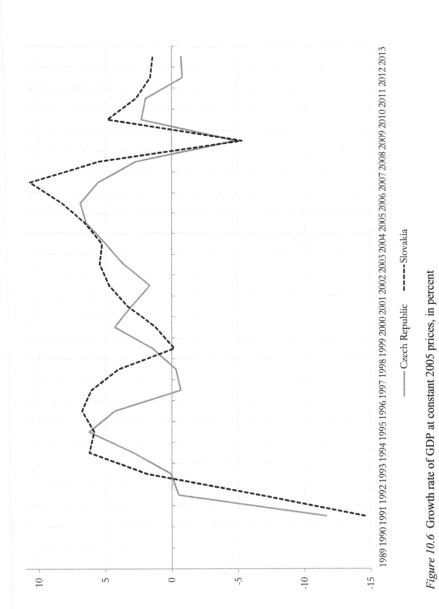

1989 1990 1991 1992 1993 1994 1995 1996 1997 1998 1999 2000 2001 2002 2003 2004 2005 2006 2007 2008 2009 2010 2011 2012 2013

——— Czech Republic   ----- Slovakia

Figure 10.6 Growth rate of GDP at constant 2005 prices, in percent

Source: United Nations database (http://unstats.un.org/unsd/snaama/dnlList.asp)

Transformation at work: the Czech Republic and Slovakia

The first policy package for transforming the Czechoslovak economy was introduced on January 1, 1991. Although the government inherited an economic situation that, overall, was balanced and stable, it proceeded with the fast liberalization of prices, wages and trade, to be followed by rapid privatization. As a result of these policies, the recession was deeper in Slovakia than in the Czech Republic in 1991: the fall of GDP was respectively 11.6 percent and 14.5 percent (Figure 10.6).[14] However, the Slovak economy recovered soon and overall achieved a better economic performance than the Czech Republic for the rest of the 1990s and, with the exception of 1999 and 2000, up to the time of writing.

Unemployment was much higher in Slovakia: in 1993, the unemployment rate in Slovakia was 14.7 percent compared to only 3.8 percent in the Czech Republic. In the Czech Republic, there was initially a dramatic upsurge of inflation well above the Slovak level (see below and Figure 10.7). Consequently, real wages significantly decreased in both republics (Table 10.2).

The first wave of reforms were implemented by the federal government in a still unified country. Price liberalization was a fundamental part of the first package implemented in 1991. The outcome was a dramatic increase of the inflation rate, similar in the two republics: 36 percent in the Czech Republic and 34 percent in Slovakia. Liberalization was accompanied by restrictive monetary and fiscal policies and a stable, pegged exchange rate, which ensured that inflation fell rapidly. However, the consequences of policies were negative for the real economy and Czechoslovakia also went through a deep recession in 1991–92 (Figure 10.6).

Privatization was implemented in three components in the years 1990–92. First, real estate assets that had been nationalized or confiscated since 1948 were restored to the original owners or their descendants. The major part of these restitutions (affecting real estate, farm land and shares in some industrial enterprises nationalized after February 1948) was completed in 1990–91.

Second, small retail outlets and other small-scale enterprises were sold rapidly, generally through public auctions open only to domestic bidders, typically insiders,

Table 10.2 Real wages: international comparison, 1990–93

	Real wages (% change over previous year)				1993 as percentage of 1989
	1990	*1991*	*1992*	*1993*	
Czech Republic	−5.4	−23.7	10.1	4.1	82.7
Hungary	−3.5	−6.8	−1.5	−4.0	85.0
Poland	−24.4	−0.3	−2.7	−1.8	72.0
Slovakia	−5.9	−25.6	8.9	−3.9	73.3

Source: from Kornai (1997a), p. 135

Note: The figure for 1990 refers only to the category of workers and employees, excluding workers in agricultural cooperatives; from 1991, they are included.

and organized by district privatization committees. This so-called "small-scale" privatization involved about 23,000 small-scale activities. In addition, state assets transferred to municipalities and cooperatives were transformed into businesses.

Third, large companies were privatized through the so-called "voucher" privatization, which took place in two waves (Carlin et al. 1995, Djankov and Pohl 1997, Schütte 2000). This privatization involved more than 60 percent of the companies that the state decided to privatize. It had the aim of creating a highly diffused ownership of privatized enterprises, owned by the entire adult population, who could obtain such ownership as a free right and against a modest fee. This was possible thanks to sound public finances, which did not need to use privatization as a revenue source. Voucher privatization had also the advantage to avoid the keen problem of establishing a price for companies that did not operate in a market context and that were going through a radical change. The free trading of vouchers and their conversion into shares, it was expected, would establish both prices for capital and a capital market.

However, voucher privatization resulted in the overwhelming majority of ownership shares owned by investment funds, to which most citizens gave their vouchers. Yet most of these investment funds were owned or controlled by banks, still in public ownership. Moreover, the lack of sufficient control allowed funds to make use of "tunneling," a term used first in reference to the Czech Republic (Johnson et al. 2000).[15] This form of asset stripping consists of decisions, made by a group of people controlling but not entirely owning a company, to transfer its assets or profitable activities to another company that they own or control entirely, so that this group can then dispose freely of such assets. Due to legislation loopholes and the lack of control institutions and proper enforcement, tunneling grew to significant importance in the Czech Republic and Slovakia and caused noticeable damage to the economy as a whole and to many minority owners, undermining public trust in the whole process.

Czechoslovakia had additional problems when confronted with these outcomes, which put cohabitation of the two republics at risk. Policies were uniform, since they were decided and implemented at the federal level. However, the effects were uneven in the two republics, because of their different economic structure and situation. The consequences for Slovakia were initially worse than for the Czech Republic for both GDP and unemployment (Beblavý 2010, Wemer 2013). Slovakia depended more on the fading Comecon markets and its large heavy industry production found difficulties in other markets. At the same time, western investors were much less interested in Slovakia than in the Czech lands: overall, 3,000 joint ventures were established with western investors in 1991, but only 600 of these were based in Slovakia (Wemer 2013).

Voucher privatization proved to be more popular in the Czech Republic than in Slovakia, whose citizens were more sensitive to state ownership and employee and management buyouts. In fact, they kept more accurate memories of the socialist period, a time when Slovakia was the target of resource transfers and development programs. Perhaps more important, unemployment in Slovakia reached the level of 12 percent in 1992, which was more than three times the Czech level.

The path to transformation in Czechoslovakia was deeply affected by the split of the federation into two entities on January 1, 1993: the Czech Republic and the Slovak Republic. Although opinion polls showed that the large majority of citizens in both republics were in favor of keeping the federation, two strong future national prime minister, Václav Klaus[16] in the Czech Republic and Vladimír Mečiar[17] in Slovakia, agreed on the divorce. On February 8, 1993, the monetary union was dissolved and both countries implemented fully independent policies.

The dissolution of the federation had initially negative consequences for Slovakia, which had to strive to activate democratization while building a nation state amidst unfavorable conditions (Szomolányi 2004, Wemer 2013). Indeed, Slovakia suffered from a deeply distorted industrial structure and foreign trade structure, a lack of state institutions and administrations for managing the economy and financing the state budget, and the near-absence of foreign confidence and FDIs.[18]

While the two countries shared the same state and government for decades, since the end of World War I, their economic structures had been deeply different. Among the reasons for this was the industrialization strategy of socialist Czechoslovakia. Slovakia inherited much of the heavy and arms industries of former Czechoslovakia. Moreover, most of the Slovak industry was organized in large companies (Koyame-Marsh 2011). Quite different was the situation of the Czech Republic, which had developed light and tourism industries and markets which were more open to the West. Moreover, Slovakia was less developed than the Czech Republic: Czech per capita GDP was 15 percent higher than Slovak GDP. Due to this situation, expectations were that the Czech Republic would flourish and Slovakia would lose strength.

Thanks to its more balanced industrial and trade structure and the solid state administration, the Czech Republic proceeded with bold and fast reforms. Slovakia encountered problems that would have resulted in much higher output fall and unemployment had the country embarked on some kind of harsh stabilization. The loss of fiscal transfers from the richer Czech Republic, greater trade losses from the disruption of the Comecon market, losses in the Czech market, lower credibility and worse conditions in international financial markets, and lack of sound state administration were all factors that made the Slovak situation more problematic. Moreover, the population was less favorable to the fast transformation to capitalism.

Since the so-called "velvet divorce" of 1993 that led to the separation of the two republics, the two countries have followed different transformation paths. The Czech path was more standard and more promising in the light of dominant mainstream views and policy recipes. Yet expectations were somehow disappointed: after years of political difficulties, Slovakia became one of the most successful transformation countries. At the same time, the Czech Republic met unforeseen problems. Why was this so?

There were major differences between the two countries. One important difference was in governments and the policies they followed. The Czech government was dominated, in the critical period of the 1990s, by Václav Klaus, himself an economist and a supporter of shock therapy and laissez-faire policies. The strong man of Slovakia was Vladimír Mečiar, who was known abroad more for his autocratic government style and repressive stance to the press than for the achievements of his government.

Further major differences were in their transformation strategies and economic policies. While the Czech government proceeded with rapid liberalization and privatization, particularly of large companies, the Slovak government was definitely more prudent and hostile to the standard transformation policies and reforms. The Slovak government followed a non-standard transformation path that in the end proved to be effective.[19]

While it is clear that the 1990s were fundamental years for transformation, opinions and analyses are deeply split as to why, in spite of negative odds, Slovakia ended so much better off than the Czech Republic. And it did so by adopting the euro, the only Central European country to do so thus far. While it is difficult to find analysts who praise the Mečiar government's policies, positions are split on the effect of these policies and reforms. According to some, those policies were negative and the country flourished those policies notwithstanding, mainly thanks to what the following Mikuláš Dzurinda's governments accomplished (Szomolányi 2004).[20] According to others, Mečiar's years were a period of prudent economic, political and social consolidation that prepared the ground for the standard Dzurinda policies in a country that could not have survived were these policies implemented when it became independent (Csaba 1995, Wemer 2013).[21]

Price liberalization was accomplished in the unified Czechoslovakia as part of the first reform package of 1991. Inflation (measured by GDP deflator) jumped to 36 percent in the Czech Republic and 34 percent in Slovakia. The federal government used tight monetary policy to cool inflation down, although inflation remained well above 10 percent until 1995 (Figure 10.7).

A particularly evident difference between the Czech Republic and Slovakia was in their privatization and enterprise restructuring processes. A common feature of the two countries, in spite of the different privatization methods used, was the low amount of revenue for the state and the modest involvement of foreign investors compared in particular to Hungary.[22] Small business privatization went on rapidly and smoothly in both republics, as in the other Central European countries. In the Czech Republic, new small- and medium-size firms experienced strong growth and attracted a fair amount of FDIs.

Major differences existed in the privatization of large state-owned companies between the two republics. Three main privatization methods were extensively utilized in transformation countries (Carlin et al. 1995, and Djankov and Pohl, 1997) for large companies. These are direct sales to outside owners, management-employee buy-outs (MEBOs) and mass privatization. Each method has advantages and disadvantages in terms of rapidity, revenue for the state and effectiveness of restructuring and corporate governance. In general, direct sales are typically slower, but have advantages over the others in terms of revenue for the state, effectiveness of corporate governance and restructuring. In particular, if the new owners are foreign investors from more developed countries, they also have better access to capital and skills. Mass privatization and MEBOs have the advantage of speed

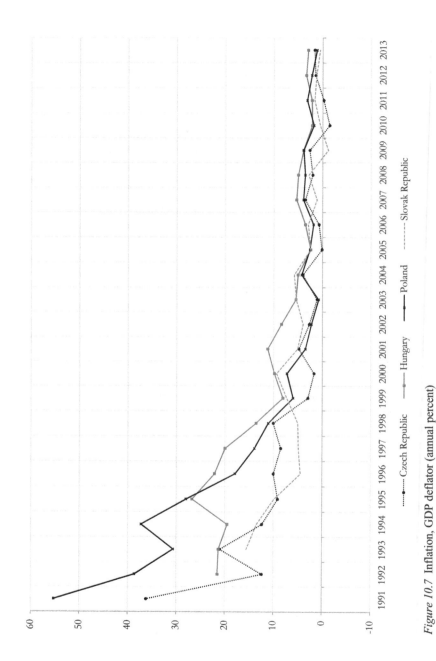

Figure 10.7 Inflation, GDP deflator (annual percent)

Source: World Bank, World Development Indicators

and of softening social and insiders' opposition to privatization, but generally have weaker outcomes in terms of governance and restructuring.

Both the Czech Republic and Slovakia inherited the voucher privatization that was started in Czechoslovakia. After separation, the Czech Republic continued consistently with voucher privatization, albeit amid problems in the relation between investment funds and their owners, the banks. Technically, the process was fast and effective in transferring companies out of state control. Indeed, the Czech Republic was outperforming all other transformation countries in terms of privatization achievements and the weight of the private sector in GDP, mainly thanks to voucher privatization. While the private sector accounted for 2 percent of GDP in 1990, this share increased to 70 percent in 1995 and 80 percent by 1999 (EBRD 2000, World Bank, 1999).

However, the country paid a price in terms of the privatized companies' growth. Indeed, the system created initially dispersed ownership and owners without the necessary capital to restructure companies. Since small owners were more interested in acquiring an income from their vouchers, they sold the shares obtained through vouchers to large investment funds. These were interested in getting the shares and consequently lacked the capital needed for restructuring. Some 70 percent of the vouchers were purchased by investment funds, which thereafter redeemed them into shares. Moreover, the majority of these funds (seven out of the ten major ones) were owned by banks, which were still in state ownership (Myant 2003). As a consequence, voucher privatization failed to improve governance, harden the budget constraint of companies or improve managerial behavior. Wages and salaries grew faster than productivity, thus worsening competitiveness, and firm restructuring proceeded slowly. However, FDIs were overall successful and higher than in Slovakia, although less than in Hungary (Figure 10.8)

The consequences of the rapid voucher privatization bear an important lesson for transformation: institutions matter. In principle, this conclusion was clear at the start of transformation.[23] The formalism of much praised transformation choices, such as the voucher privatization in Czechoslovakia or, later on, in Russia, offers a further example of the difficult penetration of findings in policy making or, if one prefers, of the power of political convenience over knowledge.

The problems that privatization and other policy measures brought to the Czech economy were tackled between 1996 and 1997 with a new package of reforms and policy measures. These measures addressed in particular the effective build-up of market institutions, including financial institutions, improved the regulatory and legal environment of business activity, encouraged company restructuring, and streamlined the Czech economy to EU requirements.[24] However technically successful and rapid voucher privatization was, it turned out that "the speed of privatization is not the single criterion, not even the most relevant one" (Mertlik 2000).

Slovakia pursued a different privatization path after its independence. Voucher privatization was abandoned and the preferred privatization method became direct sales to domestic outside investors through auction. After the 1994 elections, the third Mečiar government dramatically changed privatization strategy

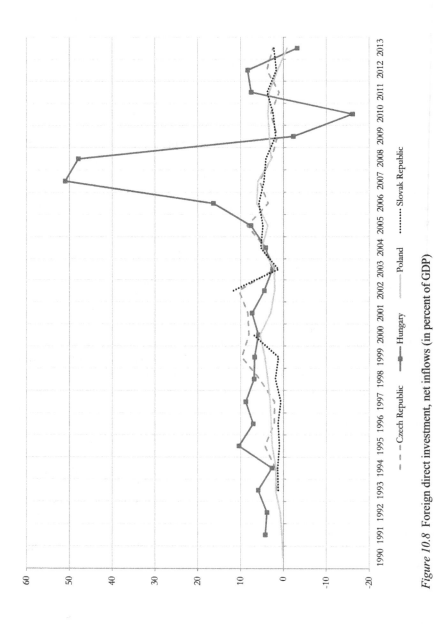

Figure 10.8 Foreign direct investment, net inflows (in percent of GDP)

Source: World Bank, World Development Indicators

(Beblavý 2010). In the new strategy, large industrial companies, particularly those critically important for exports, were sold to domestic investors. These were generally insiders, in particular top managers and businesspeople with close political ties to the government. While foreign investors had the possibility to acquire partial ownership of companies, MEBOs soon became the dominant method. This led to the dominant ownership by insiders. This kind of privatization had mixed effects on the necessary restructuring of these companies. While restructuring proceeded, this was considered to be insufficiently effective and failed to involve foreign capital (OECD 1999).[25] Nearly all the main companies were later resold to strategic foreign investors. Problems also mounted in the bank sector: their prevailing public control helped to curb inflation and to finance investments, but also led to misallocation of capital.

MEBOs are often accused of being used to protect entrenched insiders and discourage restructuring. However, in Slovakia, this kind of privatization did not obstruct the restructuring of companies. Based on 21 case studies of Slovak firms, with detailed financial information for 1991–96 and interviews with top management, Djankov and Pohl (1997) found that the majority of firms successfully restructured without the help of foreign investors or government restructuring programs.[26] This happened in spite of the fact that much of the sample surveyed were of firms initially classified as "nonviable lossmakers." Djankov and Pohl also found that MEBOs did not hamper restructuring and the new owners/old managers did what an interested owner would do: invest in new technology, lay off part of the workforce, look for foreign partnerships, and sell controlling stakes to outsiders in return for fresh financial resources. Even voucher privatization was followed by a rapid consolidation of ownership and thus did not result in weak corporate governance.[27]

Other scholars, however, offer a different perspective. According to Beblavý (2010), insiders' privatization was not accompanied by strong restructuring and growth, nor by the conquering of new markets. Moreover, the banking system was under state ownership and political management, which caused a misallocation of capital. These problems were aggravated by the lack of foreign direct investment. The contagion from the August 1998 Russian crisis pushed firms and industry into a difficult situation and unemployment rapidly increased. With the change of government in 1998, a new industrial strategy was implemented. The years up to 2002 were years of strong restructuring in both industry and the financial sector. Large state-owned banks and many utilities were consolidated and privatized. Institutional reform was accelerated, in particular in the fields of bankruptcy and corporate governance and the corporate income tax was cut from 40 percent to 25 percent in several steps. As a consequence, FDIs accelerated significantly between 2000 and 2002 (Figure 10.8).

Macroeconomic stability was high on the agenda of the federal government after price liberalization. Restrictive monetary and fiscal policies and the introduction of a stable, pegged exchange rate in 1991 helped to control and cool down inflation. After independence, the Czech Republic continued to follow prudent fiscal policy with balanced budgets—this continued until 1998. Indirect help also came due to the end of fiscal transfers to Slovakia following independence.

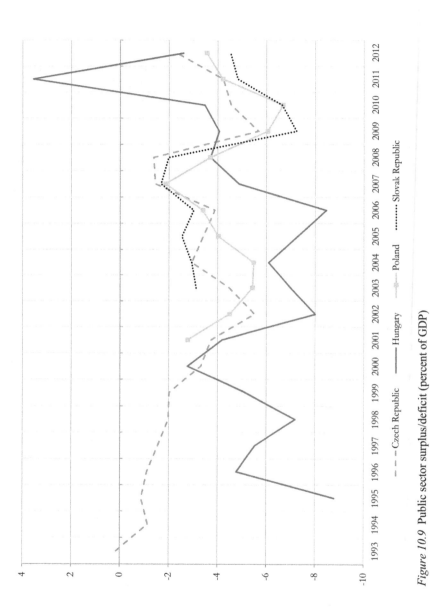

Figure 10.9 Public sector surplus/deficit (percent of GDP)

Source: World Bank, World Development Indicators

However, after 1998 and until 2006, public-sector budget deficits in the Czech Republic rose significantly, in particular in early 2000, when deficits moved between 4 percent and 6 percent of GDP (Figure 10.9).

The softer budget policy and the decision to float the koruna in May 1997 were the consequences of the recession of 1997–98. While GDP slowed down, the inflation rate accelerated again in 1998 to 11 percent (GDP deflator). Unemployment also increased significantly from the low level of the years up to 1996 (around 3 percent) and reached 9 percent at the end of the decade (Figure 10.4). After the recession, Czech economic performance continued to be weak for years, at least until 2002. The general slowdown of the European economy in concomitance with the Asian and Russian financial crises had a role in explaining this outcome. The stagnation of the Czech economy had also structural causes (Louzek 2014). Among these, high public spending, governmental regulation, subsidies and instability of the legal system played important roles.

Although Slovakia also inherited the Czechoslovak macroeconomic stability and fiscal prudence, it decided to abandon it by the mid-1990s in favor of a more active fiscal policy. Public expenditure was increased in order to stimulate the economy through massive infrastructural investments and wage increases. The strategy was successful in terms of GDP growth and moderate inflation. However, also due to the negative effect of the Russian crisis, unemployment started to increase, fiscal deficit grew to between 5 percent and 10 percent and the current account balance moved from 2 percent surplus in 1995 to 10 percent deficit in 1996 and there it remained until 1998 (Beblavý 2010).

In the years from independence to the change of government and policy strategy in 1998, the Slovak economy had an unstable and unbalanced evolution. During this period and after the economic shock of independence in 1993, years of good export-led growth, low budget deficit and low inflation (1994 and 1995) were followed by negative growth and high fiscal and current account deficits from 1996 to 1998. Twin deficits were the outcome of policies aimed at reviving the economy via extensive infrastructural investment and real wage increases. Similar to the Czech economy, the Slovak economy was suffering for the slowdown in Western Europe and the Asian and Russian crises.

The Slovak government tried to control increasing macroeconomic imbalances due to expansionary fiscal policies through severe monetary policy, which caused soaring real interest rates. The central bank used a fixed exchange rate to pursue price stability. Similarly to what happened in the Czech Republic in May and June 1997, the central bank had to give up the fixed exchange rate and, on October 1, 1998, adopted floating exchange rates. This caused a serious breakdown of the economy and a significant increase in unemployment.

The lack of international confidence in the Slovak government, the tense political atmosphere and the loss of economic stability led foreign investors to desert Slovakia and to international difficulties. Slovakia could not gain OECD membership, missed the first round of NATO enlargement and was not admitted to EU accession negotiations. The negative performance of the economy and international isolation led to changes of government and economic strategy, ensuing the

1998 elections. The period that followed, up to the next elections in 2002, started with further serious deterioration of the economic situation. The new government's determination to address the economy's imbalance initially caused even further deterioration and the revival of inflation.

In the years 1998–2002, some fundamental events and policy implementation took place that changed the situation of the Slovak economy and deeply improved its international perception. The evident unsustainability of the previous industrial system led to vigorous industrial restructuring, and the consolidation and privatization of large state-owned banks and many utilities. These were also years of dramatic institutional changes. The legal frame of bankruptcy and corporate governance were improved and corporate income tax was decreased from 40 percent to 25 percent in several steps. The pension, education and health care systems were reformed with the goal of increasing the efficiency of public expenditure and strengthening the sustainability of public finances.

While the 2002 elections confirmed the government in office and policy continuity, several important changes and events took place. In particular, the second Dzurinda government paid more attention to fiscal consolidation and structural reforms. The approaching 2004 deadline for EU accession provided an important incentive to this end. The revived international reputation played an important role in the strong renewal of economic growth (Figure 10.1). In fact, growth was driven primarily by massive FDI inflows to industrial investments and inflows of EU funding, which supported construction and household consumption.

In the years 2002–03, the government paid much attention to fiscal consolidation and in 2004, it implemented a package of new far-reaching structural reforms, including the adoption of the flat tax system at 19 percent. The acceleration of policy adjustment and related structural reforms had as a goal compliance with EU convergence criteria by 2006. This was aimed at adopting the euro. Slovakia entered ERM II in November 2005, to prepare itself for the adoption of the euro in 2009.

New elections were held in 2006 and a new social-democratic majority headed by Robert Fico replaced the conservative Dzurinda majority, which had governed between 1998 and 2006. While high economic growth, macroeconomic stability, low inflation and increasing employment continued, the new government aimed at improving social policies and supported the improvement of living standards. The new government changed its privatization policies, criticizing in particular the sales of utilities. It also blocked any further privatization and cancelled privatization transactions that were incomplete, while relying on public-private partnership (PPP) and public investment. It was this government that adopted successfully the euro in 2009.

Looking at the entire period from independence to the 2008 international crisis, one finds a surprising outcome: growth in Slovakia was stronger than in the Czech Republic. The yearly average growth of real GDP in Slovakia was about 5 percent for the entire period, but was about 8 percent between 2005 and 2008. The corresponding figure for the Czech Republic was definitely lower in the period 1993–98, at just 1.8 percent and was closer to Slovakia during the following decade, at approximately 4.

One of the remarkable features of both countries is that transformation took place amidst a significant degree of economic equality. Indicators of inequality, although worsening, remained more favorable compared to both Hungary and Poland and was among the lowest in the entire European Union. What was remarkable is that public expenditure aimed at social protection was substantially decreased in Slovakia in the years 1999–2005 from 20 percent of GDP in 1999 to 16.9 percent in 2005, while it remained stable in the Czech Republic and increased in both Hungary and Poland (Beblavý 2010). In spite of this unfavorable picture, both income inequality and risk of poverty[28] remained rather favorable and clearly better than in both Hungary and Poland. The same conclusion holds for income distribution. Both the Czech Republic and Slovakia had lower degrees of inequality both before and after social transfers, meaning that their economies produced less and lower inequality and their social security systems was better developed.

Conclusions

The World Bank (2002) maintained that there was a broad consensus that reforms and policies should include the following components: macroeconomic stabilization, price and trade liberalization, hard budget constraints on banks and enterprises, privatization, reform of the tax system, restructuring public expenditure, legal and judicial reform, and reform of public sector institutions. While there was broad agreement among experts and policy makers on these components, other aspects, such as sequencing, speed of implementation and the specific design of reforms and policies were debated and remained debatable. In the end, it was left to national governments to choose, largely in the function of local circumstances. What appeared to be of the greatest importance was the level of commitment and the determination of reformers and policy makers in implementing the chosen strategy and policies and their flexibility in adapting to changed and unforeseen circumstances.

The years elapsed since the start of transformation and up to the 2008 crisis presented outcomes at odds with initial expectations in Central-Eastern Europe. These surprises raise a set of questions. Why did previous frontrunners meet with so many difficulties and why did they turn out to be, in a way, laggards? Why did countries that started transformation in difficult circumstances and with negative odds of success surprisingly end up doing so well? Was this due to the quality of the institutions and the policies implemented, or to external and lucky circumstances? Was it the outcome of what happened during transformation, or was it the poisoned effect of pre-transformation situations and choices? Are present successes and difficulties a solid and permanent outcome, or could they be reversed in the years to come?

Based on the experiences of the first decade of transformation, Kolodko (2001) identified twelve major policy conclusions. The most important one is that the institutional arrangements are the most crucial factor for progress towards durable growth. Institution building is by its nature a gradual process that must be carefully governed, in order to avoid having informal institutionalization filling the systemic vacuum. The size of government is not particularly important for supporting these developments, but the quality of policies and the way in which government makes changes are fundamental. New policy domains are also important: the reform of the judiciary system to serve the needs of the market economy, the shift of competence and power from the central government to local governments, income policy and government concern for equitable growth, the development of NGOs, opening and integrating with the world economy. Moreover, international organizations should support further regional integration and cooperation and even more so, in general, should reconsider their policies towards transformation economies. Finally, it is important to consider that interactive processes of learning-by-monitoring and learning-by-doing continue and will last for several years.

At the beginning of transformation, the mainstream idea was that speed and soon reaching a critical mass of changes were of the utmost importance. It was considered that muddling through or prolonging reforms would give strength to the old vested interests and would maintain major distortions. This in turn would incite people and organizations to seek privileges and subsidies,[29] would deter investment and innovation and would work poorly (Fischer and Gelb 1991, Lipton and Sachs 1990, Shleifer and Vishny 1998). Unfortunately, also ill-conceived or harsh changes proved to lead to similar results. *Ex post* it is easy to see the many reasons that the so-called "gradualists" had for their transformation proposals (Murrell 1992, Roland 2000).

International organizations and western governments, based on the mainstream view, supported the transformation governments willing to adopt mainstream policies and reforms. After nearly a generation of transformation, from 1989 to the 2008 crisis, the transformation landscape in the V4 countries is mixed. Countries that started as champions of the shock therapy approach, Poland in particular, ended up being effective and fast in fostering the economy's greenfield privatization. Countries that were the epitome of rapid privatization, the Czech Republic in particular, were embroiled in difficult governance issues, with the state returning to a leading role through the investment funds. Countries that were advanced in liberalization and competition before transformation, Hungary in particular, were returning to selective protectionism and price controls and subsidies. Countries that had to start nearly from scratch in building a state and related administration, that were engulfed with old-style heavy and weapons industry, that were under the strong influence of political populism and internationally isolated, Slovakia in particular, ended up being the true positive surprise of transformation.

One of the problems in explaining these outcomes is that reform blueprints, prepared by domestic experts and international organizations, were biased towards general rules of economic management. As soon as those blueprints became reform plans and policies and were implemented, governments had to come to terms with local circumstances. Some countries did this better than others, sometimes for the wrong reasons. Unfortunately, the need to adapt reforms and policies to local circumstances, after a more consistent general version was attempted and met difficulties or failed, opened the door to vested interests and foot dragging.

Not every delay went sour, however. In Poland, the Parliament was unable to find a majority to ratify a privatization law for years. This gave time and opportunities to new businesspeople to invest in new initiatives and find the necessary resources to do so, without the competition of large-scale privatization over resources and over government support. Moreover, state-owned firms had the time and the pressure to restructure and become competitive. The size of Poland's economy, the largest among the V4, also helped. One interesting aspect of Poland is that it is the V4 country in which inequalities reached the highest level. However, this does not seem to have prevented the development of the country, apparently because mobility was high and opportunities existed for many, including through emigration. The weak side of the Polish success is probably its inability to upgrade sufficiently its international specialization and its reliance on competitiveness based on cheap labor.

In Slovakia, the first years were a time of uncertain reforms and policies, and of trials and errors, with policy changes following negative feedbacks from previous moves. The populist rhetoric did not help much in finding a way out, yet perhaps it was useful in preparing the ground for the reforms that came later.[30] Perhaps more important, it gave the opportunity to understand which were the Slovak local circumstances and how these could supplement and support general rules and sound economic principles. Slovakia's determination to adopt the euro helped to find a common ground compatible with the hard rules necessary in a monetary union. In a sense, it appears that Slovakia was able to enter a positive sum game.

The cases of the Czech Republic and Hungary are different and distinct. Both countries were considered to be in the best position among all transformation countries at the start. Hungary was certainly the frontrunner in reforms. Yet it had two drawbacks that acquired increasing importance through time: a population eager to start transformation for increasing and improving consumption, while taking their generous welfare system for granted, and a sizeable foreign debt, that the governments chose to fully honor. Moreover, productivity was low in the domestic sector and the demographic situation was the most unfavorable among the V4. The latter, together with the generous welfare system, put public finances under stress.[31] Ideological populism also caused significant damages, particularly the badly managed privatization of land which worsened significantly the situation of agriculture, an important sector in Hungary. The situation of agriculture was, together with the drive to consumption, one of the most important causes for the sizeable deficit of foreign accounts. Even what appeared to be one strong advantage of Hungary—her leadership in attracting FDIs particularly through the sale of companies—turned out to have important negative consequences: appreciation of the forint, distortion of the fiscal and subsidies system, competition from higher wages and for resources and markets to the disadvantage of the domestic SMEs sector, which was unable to become competitive. The success of foreign-owned companies was not sufficient to save the economy from entering a prolonged instability. These features added to serious failures in the field of human capital and R&D, which suffered from underfunding.

Finally, the Czech Republic devoted its efforts and energies in the first years of transformation to a basically formal undertaking: privatizing state-owned enterprises through the voucher system. While the idea was brilliant, in that it avoided the intractable problems of giving a price to companies before privatization and the lack of domestic capital, as well as promising to be deeply democratic, its promises however in terms of efficiency and effectiveness were not well placed. Also, in the Czech Republic, most citizens proved to be uninterested in becoming owners and acted as interested consumers when they chose to give their vouchers to investment funds. Lacking sufficient domestic capital, these funds could only be set up by state-owned banks and foreigners of uncertain origin and substance. The outcome was to blur and complicate the governance of privatized companies. While the problem was somehow solved in the following years, this process was costly and time consuming.

Overall, it appears that Poland and Slovakia were better able, albeit for different reasons and in different ways and at least in the long run, to couple the respect for sound economic rules and principles with adaptation to local circumstances. Since this is essentially a problem of development, it takes time, but it produces superior and stable results. Conversely, the Czech Republic chose to follow formal principles. In a sense, it implicitly considered that a market economy develops spontaneously once the economy is privatized and the government follows a laissez-faire approach. As to Hungary, it had to submit much of its policy sovereignty to the interests of foreign investors, however important these may be, and to the disadvantage of the quality and role of domestic SMEs. Another important flaw of the Hungarian approach was the weak management of its finances, which jeopardized the respect for sound economic rules and principles.

What came out of nearly two decades of transformation was a rather inconsistent and surprising V4 pattern, one including promising countries with others taking risks to enter a European semi-periphery. It is amidst these situations that the countries entered the period of international and European turmoil.

Notes

1 Marer and Zecchini (1991) is an important reference, although their approach is considerably more complex. For a broad systemic view, see Csaba (1995). By taking a comparative, historical approach and looking at late-twentieth-century economic reform experiences in different countries, Ahrens (1994) identifies a number of key challenges for the success of transformation: political stability, social consensus, a commitment not to backslide, a popular acknowledgment of the hardships entailed, and reasonable expectations concerning future rewards.

2 On privatization in transformation countries, see Bornstein (1994). On the lessons of Western experiences, see Dallago (1999).

3 Popov (2000) looks for an alternative explanation for the dynamics of output during transformation. He finds that over 60 percent of the differences in the economic performance of 28 countries in transformation can be explained by uneven initial conditions (an important component of local features and circumstances), such as the level of development and pre-transformation disproportions in industrial structure and trade patterns. Together with variations in inflation rates and institutional capacities of the state (as measured by the change in the share of government revenues in GDP and/or by the ratio of the rule of law to the democracy index), Popov explains over 85 percent of differences in GDP change. The conclusion is that the debate between shock therapists and gradualists, however interesting, was to a large extent incorrectly focused and misguided and disregarded the primary issue of transformation: the strength of institutions.

4 Poland and Hungary Assistance for the Restructuring of the Economy (PHARE).

5 For an interesting database on privatization, see http://www.privatizationbarometer.net/.

6 For an introduction to mass privatization in transformation countries, see Adam (1994). On mass privatization in Poland, see Klich (1998) and Rider and Zajicek (1995).

7 Gross foreign debt was US$20.4 billion in 1989 and increased up to US$31.7 billion in 1995 (Stark 2009), which actually meant a slight decrease as a percentage of GDP, from 69.9 percent to 67.1 (Mihályi 2013).

8 On the role of the financial sector for SMEs growth, see Csaba (2003).

9 Blagojević and Damijan (2013) investigate how the efficiency of the business environment and corruption (i.e. informal payments and state capture) affect the microeconomic performance of firms as a function of the type of firm ownership in 27 transformation countries in 2002–09. The authors find that private firms (domestic and foreign-owned) are more involved in both informal payments and state capture. Foreign-owned firms are likely to benefit from informal payments, while state-owned firms are more likely to experience negative effects on productivity growth. However, the involvement of firms in corrupt practices diminished after 2004 and their negative impact on firm performance declined.

10 "Law XXV of 1991 on Partial Compensation for Damages Unlawfully caused by the State on Property owned by Citizens in the Interest of Settling Ownership Relations": see Comisso (1997).

11 Debt service in convertible currencies as a share of GDP, which was 11.5 percent in 1989, increased to 20.4 percent by 1996, decreased progressively to 8.5 percent by 2002 and increased again to 10.4 percent by 2005. Debt service jumped to 21.3 percent by 2009 and 22.4 by 2011 (Mihályi 2013).

12 Emigration from Hungary did not increase significantly, in particular after the country joined the EU in 2004. While Polish emigrants provide the country with significant remittances (€2.7 billion in 2009), the balance for Hungary is slightly negative (incoming remittances minus outgoing remittances from immigrants to Hungary were minus €50 million in 2009) (Mihályi 2012).

13 With transformation, the average size of enterprises decreased significantly, since one of the structural features of Soviet-type economies was the oversize of enterprises. In Hungary, the average number of employees per enterprise in 1980 was 2,162, which decreased to 380 employees by 1990 (Amsden et al. 1994, p. 93).

14 United Nations database (http://unstats.un.org/unsd/snaama/dnlList.asp).

15 Johnson et al. (2000), define the term "tunnelling" to describe "the transfer of assets and profits out of firms for the benefit of those who control them" (p. 22). See also Djankov et al. (2008).

16 Václav Klaus was the second and last prime minister of the federated Czech Republic from July 1992 until the dissolution of Czechoslovakia. He was then the first prime minister of the independent Czech Republic from January 1, 1993 to January 2, 1998. He later served as the second president of the Czech Republic from March 7, 2003 to March 7, 2013. Klaus was also the founder of the center-right Civic Democratic Party.

17 Vladimír Mečiar, the leader of the People's Party-Movement for a Democratic Slovakia (ĽS-HZDS), served three times as prime minister between 1990 and 1991, 1992 and 1994, and from December 13, 1994 to October 30, 1998. Mečiar was also president of Slovakia between January 1, 1993 and March 2, 1993 and again between March 2, 1998 and October 30, 1998.

18 Between 1989 and 1997, Slovakia received a bare 1.8 percent of the total FDIs to transformation countries. Comparable figures for the Czech Republic and Hungary were respectively 12.2 percent and 25.2 percent (Wemer 2013).

19 This was recognized also by the World Bank (1999) and the OECD (1999).

20 Mikuláš Dzurinda was prime minister between 1998 and 2006, presiding over two governments. He was also the founder and leader of the Slovak Democratic Coalition (SDK) and then the Slovak Democratic and Christian Union.

21 According to Wemer (2013, a closer look at macroeconomic data demonstrates an impressive economic record. Mečiar slowed down the privatization process, retained

control of key industries, and maintained the social safety net. By doing so, his government was able to soften the blow of economic transformation and prepare the groundwork for later market reform.

22 According to the World Bank (1998, p. 30), only around 5 percent of the cumulative revenue from privatization came from foreign investors in the Czech Republic by the end of 1995. The corresponding figure was around 13 percent in Slovakia, compared to nearly 60 percent in Hungary and to 25 percent in Poland.

23 Important economists stressed the fundamental role of institutions in determining the working of economies and organizations. Some of them were awarded the Nobel Prize for economics well before or at the start of transformation: Gunnar Myrdal and Friedrich August von Hayek in 1974, Herbert A. Simon in 1978, Ronald H. Coase in 1991, and Robert W. Fogel and Douglas C. North in 1993.

24 Pavel Mertlik, the then governor of the Bank for the Czech Republic, stated the following at the Annual Discussion Boards of Governors in 2000: "The real critical aspect of the transition is the second-generation reforms, namely building of the institutional underpinnings of a market economy under the circumstances of a lack of market skills and experience, of attitudes and perceptions different from those prevailing in countries with a long and uninterrupted experience of a market economy. If the structural and institutional reforms have not been completed, the macroeconomic stability is not sustainable. It is not difficult to create institutions of a market economy *in the nominal terms*—i.e., laws, codes, and organizations that *look like* the ones in traditional market economies or carry identical names. The challenge is to create institutions that *function like* in stable market economies, that produce the same, predictable outcomes. It should be a lesson for the Bretton Woods institutions, too: fulfilling institutional conditions in the nominal terms (such as approval of certain laws or the foundation of institutions of a certain name) does not automatically mean that from the first day, the society will benefit from outcomes that could be expected from such institutions in traditional market economies" (Mertlik 2000, original emphasis).

25 "There is a critical mass of enterprises that have been through the crucial initial steps of restructuring through major adjustments in productivity, products and markets. The remaining core of problematic enterprises is relatively well identified, notably those connected with the previous armament industry . . . The financial situation of the enterprise sector has deteriorated rapidly, notably with the mounting of inter-enterprise arrears, increasing non-performing loans in the banks' balance sheets and tax arrears. Progress in the effective implementation of bankruptcy and competition policy has still to be made. The actual trade openness of the economy contrasts with the perception on the part of foreign investors that the authorities and enterprises have had a strong preference for domestic ownership and control": OECD (1999), pp. 109–10.

26 For a comparative view of restructuring during transformation, see Djankov and Murrell (2002).

27 "This was the true success of the Mečiar economic program: by delaying full privatization of the Slovakian economy, as mandated by 'shock therapy,' Slovakia avoided the economic hardship and unrest which would have followed until the country successfully consolidated and accepted capitalism as their economic model of choice": Wemer (2013), p. 109.

28 The risk of poverty defines the share of the population that has a total income of less than 60 percent of the national median.

29 Åslund (2002) maintains that transformation is best understood as strife over subsidies. See also Hellman (1998).

30 "The transition of Slovakia from heavily industrial socialism to advanced capitalism was one of the most radical in Eastern Europe, but it only occurred because it was one of the slowest": Wemer (2013), p. 111.

31 Kornai (1992b) explains that Hungary, together with other transformation countries, became prematurely social welfare states, which caused excessively high taxes and social transfers and prevented economic growth.

11 The crisis

From imported to home-made

The strength of an economic system can be best seen when the economy is under stress, such as in the case of unforeseen shocks. It is under these circumstances that an effective institutional frame and a policy set are fundamental for giving the economy resilience and effectiveness in maintaining economic equilibrium, guaranteeing the employment of resources and pursuing development. These conditions require that the economy and its management comply with sound economic rules and principles, but also adapt to local features and circumstances, build upon complementarities and foster positive spillovers between the two sets of rules and circumstances.

Since the time when the V4 countries started their transformation and strove to converge to the European Union, the respect for sound economic rules and principles took primarily the form of complying with the EU's convergence criteria. These are formal, standard and short-run criteria whose primary aim is to preserve financial stability in a club of countries which are under the coordination and surveillance of an incomplete set of common institutions and organizations. Although keeping fundamental balance of each economy is important for the common economic stability, it is evident that the EU's main concern is to avoid that some country has to pay the bill of imbalances in other countries and discourage "free riding" among member countries. This aim is a hard objective within the Eurozone, and it could not be otherwise under the present circumstances. As Mario Draghi, the president of the European Central Bank, stated, the Eurozone was not built for subsidizing some countries to the expenses of others.[1] For doing so, some kind of political union would be necessary, but this union is not yet foreseen.

While the aim seems plain—discipline for everybody, so everybody plays by the same rules and this guarantees a level field and virtuous outcomes—in reality it is not. Indeed, and in spite of the long preparation that a country must go through before being accepted as a member of the Eurozone, countries are different and start from different conditions. In particular, some countries are economically vulnerable while others are resilient. This distinction is particularly important within the Eurozone (Dallago 2016), but it is important more generally within any kind of integration among different partners.

Economic vulnerability is usually considered to be measured in the amount of exposure and reaction of an economy to exogenous shocks and international market fluctuations (Briguglio et al. 2009, Cariolle 2011, Cordina 2004, Guillaumont 1999, 2009).[2] It is in particular a country's structural features that influence the size and likelihood of shocks and the exposure to these shocks, which may result in economic vulnerability. The causes of vulnerability are therefore both endogenous (structural features and internal shocks) and exogenous (external shocks). The opposite to vulnerability is resilience, which is determined by a country's possibility and ability to implement economic policies that guarantee an effective defense against shocks. Resilience is the policy-induced ability of an economy to withstand or recover from the effects of such shocks.

The classical case that is considered in the literature on vulnerability is one of shocks arising out of economic openness and export concentration. This is usually the case of small economies that are, to a large extent, shaped by forces and processes most outside the country's control. Other reasons for vulnerability exist: production and foreign trade are not diversified; exports are characterized by high income and price elasticity; imports are rigid and not easily substitutable; transportation costs are high and the attractiveness for business and investment are low due to geographical remoteness; markets are not competitive; the size of the public sector's activity is large compared to the size of the country; and/or the absorption capacity for technology, investment and international development initiatives are low.

The case usually dealt with in the literature is not exactly the same as the case of V4 countries. Differences refer in particular to the causes of vulnerability, while effects are similar. While there are general reasons for vulnerability and resilience, other reasons are idiosyncratic. In the case of V4 and other transformation countries, the transformation process they went through and the adaptation to EU institutions, policies and practices caused more vulnerable structures and less effective governments and intervention instruments. When hit by external shocks, these countries either cannot freely use policy instruments to withstand or recover from the effects of such shocks (e.g. if they are members of the Eurozone), or they may be too weak to withstand external shocks (e.g. if the reform of their economic system and policy instruments are not completed or effective, or their economy is imbalanced in consequence of transformation or specialization in particular goods, such as raw materials). A country in a vulnerable situation, which is being a member of a supranational organization depriving it of some of its competences,[3] is one that needs to recover resilience in ways that are different from the case of countries that can use sovereign policies (Gretschmann 2016).

The crisis in the United States

Until the mid-1990s, the Western European and Japanese economies were converging to the performance and productivity level of the US economy (Faini 2006). However, in the following decades, the distance between the US's productivity level and that of the Western European and Japanese economies returned to widen again. Apparently a prolonged period of convergence was followed by a period of divergence. However, this second period witnessed the catch-up of a new group of emerging countries, including some of the most populous countries, the so-called "BRIC" countries (Brazil, Russia, India, China), as well as other smaller countries, including Korea and Taiwan.

There are various problems with this standard reading of the situation. One problem has to do with demographics: while Western European countries were aging, their population stagnating and the age-dependency ratio was growing,[4] the United States kept a better age balance, thanks to immigrants, and their population was growing.[5] These different dynamics of population influence favorably productivity measures based on the population (e.g. GDP per capita) in the case of Western Europe. Perhaps more important, employment increased more in Western European countries than in the United States. Thus, productivity measured as output per person employed gives a more favorable result for the United States than Western Europe. Finally, the number of worked hours in Western Europe decreased more rapidly than in the United States in the 1990s and 2000s, in particular in Germany, France and other Northern European countries. The decrease in the number of worked hours relative to the United States also happened in emerging countries. Thus, productivity per hour worked gives a better relative picture of Western Europe compared to the United States.

Given these institutional and organizational differences and dynamics, it is not easy to reach an irrefutable conclusion as to the catching-up process. What remains clear is that average long-term growth of labor productivity slowed down in western economies since 2000, but accelerated in emerging and developing economies (Chen et al. 2010). These dissimilar productivity dynamics in different regions of the world explain a good part of national economies' different rates of competitiveness and their vulnerability or resilience when confronted with the 2007–08 crisis.

The three decades preceding the crisis witnessed considerable financial innovation and restructuring of industry, often through mergers and acquisitions led by financial and fiscal considerations. These processes were particularly significant and sizeable in the United States and led to innovation, economic growth and the accumulation of financial and real bubbles. Growing bubbles led to financial distress in the United States, where the crisis started in 2007–08.

In the decade preceding the crisis, the world economy expanded at a remarkable rate of 3–4 percent per year. However, from 2007, developed western economies went through a "great contraction" (Rogoff 2011, Stiglitz 2010). While the overall situation was one of shared and prolonged economic difficulties, it is important to highlight that the situation and the unfolding of events was dissimilar, although interacting, in different countries. This warning also refers to the differences between the situation of the United States and that of Europe and, within the latter, among different countries. V4 countries are not an exception in this perspective.

Compared to the United States, the countries of the European Union, in particular those of the Eurozone, were economically and institutionally more prudent in the years preceding the crisis. In spite of this, and in spite of the fact that the crisis originated in the United States, there were within Europe causes of the crisis that were in part similar to, or even more serious than, those in the United States.

For instance, European banks were much more leveraged than US banks (Bologna et al. 2014).[6] The consequence of these endogenous factors was to diminish the resilience of national economies to external shocks and to generate asymmetric effects in different countries. This happened even when external shocks were largely symmetric. In both the European Union and the Eurozone, common institutions and policies were not only ineffective in counteracting these factors and events, but often they contributed to growing vulnerability (Dallago 2016).

Various factors and events eased the progression of bubbles into a major international crisis. The most immediate cause was excess credit, both private (easy credit, subprime mortgage) and public (excessive deficit expenditure in time of private credit expansion) (Razin and Rosefielde 2011, Stiglitz 2010). However, excess credit was caused by a set of processes whose origin dated back to the late 1960s, when the post-war capital-labor bargain (Reich 2007) ended and stagflation took over. There were four major processes that led to this outcome: slowing productivity, deregulation and financialization introduced to activate markets, growing inequalities, and soft public and private financial discipline. These processes started a causation cycle where each element reinforced the others, albeit with idiosyncratic features and developments in different countries.

Although the crisis was caused by private financial problems originating in the banks (Blyth 2013), the crisis was ultimately embedded in real problems: the inability of the financially most developed and active countries—the United States and United Kingdom in particular—to maintain the traditional standard of living for the middle and the lower classes without inflating the financial economy and running unbearable current account and/or budget deficits. The problem was that financialization was an unstable and weak substitute for the demand that used to come from a prosperous middle class and relatively well-off lower classes of consumers. Indeed, financialization led to financing excessive and risky credit and inflated prices. The overheating of the economy also resulted from the extremely high cost of the Afghanistan and Iraq wars (Orszag 2007, Stiglitz and Bilmes 2008). These events led to substantially higher interest rates,[7] with serious negative consequences for the solvency of many subprime borrowers. As a consequence, derivatives issued on those subprime mortgages and other claims rapidly lost value and financial institutions holding them in their portfolios went into distress.

At this point, a set of regulatory and policy failures transformed the crisis into a "great contraction." There were three fundamental events: the implosion of the financial and real bubbles, particularly the real estate bubble; diffused uncertainty and pessimism; and restrictive regulation and policies. The consequence of these factors was a dramatic decrease of global financial flows.[8] The contraction followed the great expansion during the pre-crisis decades, when large global banks, institutional investors and transnational companies with their international financial activities dominated the scene.

The fundamental importance of financial activities in developed economies had extremely important real consequences. Financial and related real bubbles fostered high demand and prices and fueled economic expansion and employment.

It was primarily the burst of the housing bubble that prompted the crisis, as it extinguished an important part of economic activity. Moreover, the burst made the costs of economic activities doubtful, which discouraged buyers and created uncertainty over the value of assets and liabilities and the ability of debtors to repay their debts. Business uncertainty increased dramatically, pessimism diffused and the time horizon of economic actors shortened. In particular, highly leveraged banks went to the brink of insolvency, had their governments not bailed them out to the cost of sovereigns' budgets. Their increasingly prudent attitude strengthened further the depressive effects.

The US government intervened to avoid the worst, albeit late in the game and with much hesitation and ambiguity. The rescue of one part of the economy, the private financial sector, dramatically worsened the public budget. Massive resources were used to keep banks and financial organizations afloat. While this move to fight the crisis was technically successful, in political and economic terms it was a near-failure (Blinder 2013) and ended up in a great distribution of income to the advantage of the private financial sector (Blyth 2013). Indeed, policies were extremely costly for public finances and they failed to solve the crisis. This was for two fundamental reasons. First, banks and financial organizations became extremely prudent in their business activity after they were rescued and decreased sharply their lending operations. Second, they imposed upon risky borrowers to repay their debts. Both moves starved the economy of credit and accelerated the depressive effects of the bubble's implosion.

The rescue put public finances under stress: public debt soared, taxation increased, but fiscal revenues often decreased and public expenditures decreased. While disposable income decreased and unemployment grew, taxpayers and consumers became more prudent and decreased their consumption. This in turn had negative effects for demand, investment and employment. One further problem was that the crisis hit social groups in different ways and contributed to significant increases in wealth and income inequalities.[9] This was due in particular to the high leverage of middle-class families and the high share of homes in their portfolios (Pfeffer et al. 2013, Wolff 2014). However, in relative terms it was the disadvantaged groups—minorities, the less educated, the young, and pre-recession poorer groups—that suffered greater declines in wealth and income. In the end, the 2007–09 financial crisis in the United States caused huge losses of economic output and financial wealth, increased government expenditures, had severe psychological costs and caused a loss of skills due to extended unemployment.[10]

The crisis crosses the Atlantic

The financial crisis in the United States expanded rapidly to the real economy and ended in a great recession. Although the crisis started in the United States, the size of the US economy and the strict financial and real linkages (finances, trade, investments, transnational companies, military cooperation, policy coordination) between this economy and those of Europe transmitted a major financial and economic shock from the former to the latter. Within the European Union, an additional, critical effect was soon evident: the crisis of the common currency, the euro. The external shock emanating from the United States revealed the institutional fragility and the economic vulnerability of the Eurozone.

The Eurozone crisis was thus the effect of an external contagion, imported from the United States, and then of a subsequent internal contagion. The former was important both for its direct effects and indirectly for having triggered the internal European crisis. It is thus important to understand why this happened, in spite of the greater financial prudence that characterized European financial regulation and organizations compared to the US situation. It is also important to see whether such prudence characterized V4 countries' behavior.

Prior to the 2007–08 crisis, the European Union and, in particular the Eurozone, had serious home-grown problems. These problems were the outcome of the uneasy process of integration, submitted to continuous compromises with national governments. In spite of the apparent soundness of the European construction on paper, this construction suffered from the lack of fundamental governance power and conflicting interests between the EU organs and national governments. Commonly held organs barely had any decisive governance power, except in secondary matters. This led "Eurocrats" and EU institutions to accumulate an enormous amount of formal rules (the *Acquis Communautaire*) that extended to detailed matters, without being able to adopt a true common governance. In spite of these efforts and achievements, national governments continued to keep the golden share. The only (partial) exception became with time the European Central Bank, the only nearly sovereign European governance organ.

This structure depicts a situation of incomplete institutional architecture and missing governance. However, the external context was calm and Europe did not generate tensions from inside[11] (Dallago and McGowan 2016). The tensions that occasionally broke out took place far from the EU and were under the responsibility of other governments and markets. The burdensome institutional architecture of the EU and its unbalanced and incomplete governance structure were sufficient, together with the action of national governments, to take care of the problems effectively.

The situation changed completely when the contagion of the US crisis reached Europe. While there were already tensions and imbalances within the EU, countering this new contagion and its effects required resolute and proper policy action. However, while the US administration was bold enough, albeit with uncertainty and internal contrasts, in stabilizing the situation using a policy mix that was extremely costly but effective, the EU and even the Eurozone were unable to do so. The reason was not the inability of Europeans to devise and implement effective policies. The main culprit was the institutional incompleteness of the monetary union. Together with a lack of trust among member countries of the Eurozone and the democratic deficit of the European construction (Blokker 2015, Piattoni 2015, 2016), the EU architecture made policy choices grossly incomplete.

Policy choices came down to the least common denominator, i.e. policies whose implementation would discipline countries in the short run and avoid contagion and inter-country distribution of income. Although such policies were sufficient to avoid financial disasters, they hardly were effective in relaunching economic growth and employment. The effect of policies and the financial turmoil worsened dramatically the situation of the real economies. This permanently depressed demand and, through the fiscal multiplier (Blanchard and Leigh 2013), worsened public finances. Public finances were actually under a double blow: the direct one, coming from the choice of rescuing financial institutions in distress, and the indirect one, coming from the fiscal multiplier. Moreover, within the Eurozone, there was also the choice to give priority to rescuing financial institutions belonging to Eurozone countries different from the particular Eurozone member country in distress. This was especially the case with French and German banks, which were heavily involved in the financial activities of Cyprus and Greece and which were rescued by means of common funds or public funds of other Eurozone countries, although they had to accept a degree of devaluation of their credits. Private distress and debt were transformed into public distress and debt.

Among V4 countries, the crisis and policy ineffectiveness of the Eurozone were directly important only for Slovakia.[12] As a member of the Eurozone, Slovakia was directly influenced by the currency crisis. Moreover, it suffered because of the monetary union's institutional and policy incompleteness, which prevented the free use of monetary policies (the interest rate was fixed by the ECB), as well as the lack of the currency policy (national depreciation was impossible in the monetary union) and the strong value of the euro. At the same time, Slovakia suffered because of the inability to use freely fiscal policies as a member of the Eurozone.

Also the other three countries were negatively influenced, both directly through the currency channel (both Hungary and the Czech Republic had their currency somehow linked to the euro for years—see section "Conclusions" in Chapter 9) and as members of the European System of Central Banks which required them to follow a monetary policy coordinated with that of the Eurozone. As prospective members of the EMU, these countries were bound to respect convergence criteria, a clearly disadvantageous situation, since compliance with convergence criteria in a period of crisis prevented the use of anti-cyclical policies. Finally, the recession of the Eurozone impacted heavily upon V4 countries, since Eurozone countries were and are their main economic and financial partners.

Thus the European crisis was moved by the US contagion through important economic and financial linkages between the US and EU, but was fueled by deep home-made problems. Moreover, most European economies were deeply imbalanced for various reasons and were independently breeding grounds of crisis that would have burst anyway, albeit perhaps later and in a somewhat milder form.

The main channel of contagion was through the housing bubble burst which caused the fall in the value of mortgage-backed securities. Since many important European banks had considerable amounts of subprime securities in their portfolio, the dangerous effect of the US bubble burst spread to Europe. Other channels acted through the consequences of policy decisions and market reactions in the United States, such as the increase in interest rates and the effect of restrictive credit policies. Other channels were the fall of US demand for European exports (by 18 percent in 2009), the effect of the weaker dollar on the competitiveness of European goods, and the general business uncertainty that spread worldwide.

The first European country to be hit was Iceland. It was not an EU member country, but was associated to the EU, a condition Iceland renounced in 2015. Its heavy systemic bank crisis started in October 2008 and continued through 2011. All three main privately owned commercial banks collapsed after failing to refinance their short-run debt and withstand a run on deposits. Iceland needed urgent IMF assistance and was the first developed country to do so in 30 years. The consequences of this financial crisis were heavy: the krona fell by more than 80 percent against the euro in 2008 and the GDP fell by a combined 9.3 percent from 2008 through 2010 (Hart-Landsberg 2013). The unemployment rate increased from 1 percent in 2007 to 8 percent in 2009, real wages fell by 4.2 percent in 2008 and 8 percent in 2009, and the stock market lost 75 percent of its value.

Next, the crisis spread to EU member countries which had kept their national currency. The United Kingdom was the first EU country which encountered difficulty. This happened in 2007, when the government had to intervene to rescue Northern Rock, which was the first large commercial bank that, following the US crisis, required emergency government funding. The British economy is strictly linked to the US economy and the government implemented restrictive policies to try to stabilize the financial situation. The credit crunch that followed depressed house prices and diminished consumer spending. The UK entered into recession in the second quarter of 2008.

Common elements and divergent paths in the V4 economies

Some of the causes, steps and effects of the crisis were similar in V4 countries and resembled what happened in other EU member countries (Sobják 2013). However, other aspects were typical of former transformation countries and still others were typically national. Among the crisis features that were common to transformation countries, there was the fall in GDP, the decline of production in manufacturing and the building industry, a considerable decrease in exports and a massive outflow of foreign capital. In part, these effects were the consequence of the recession in Western Europe, where demand for imports from V4 countries decreased.

Although V4 countries present common features, events and trends, it is also important to be aware of the differences existing among them. One striking initial difference is in GDP growth (Figure 11.1). In the long run, since the mid-1990s, the European Union, considered as an aggregate economy (EU-28), had a descending annual trending growth rate, from 3.4 percent at the beginning of the period to 0 percent by 2013. The trend for the Eurozone (in changing composition of member countries) was very similar, but slightly lower than the EU at 28 member countries.

Overall, V4 countries presented a more favorable trend, with important national differences. The trend was clearly higher in both Poland and Slovakia over the entire period. The difference in the annual trend growth compared to the

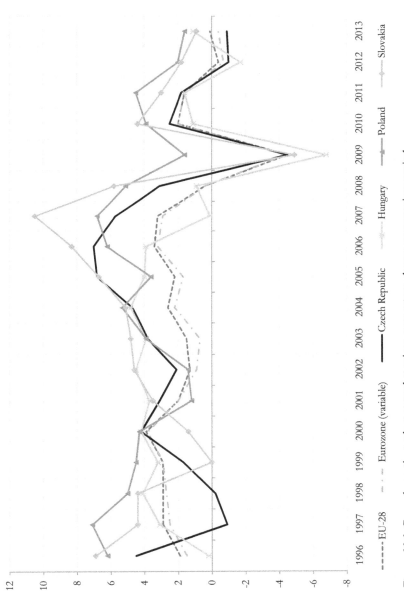

Figure 11.1 Gross domestic product at market prices, percentage change over previous period

Source: Eurostat

- - - - - EU-28   - - - Eurozone (variable)   ——— Czech Republic   .... Hungary   —▲— Poland   —◆— Slovakia

EU-28 was around 2 percent at the beginning of the period for Poland and slightly less for Slovakia. The difference was around 3 percent at the end of the period, meaning that both countries improved their relative performance compared to the average performance for the entire EU. Both countries had a descending trend through the years, but the slope is gentler than in the average of the 28 EU member countries: −0.137 in the case of Poland and −0.113 in the case of Slovakia (although Slovakia has significantly higher yearly variations in the rate of growth) compared to −0.185 for the EU-28. The trend is clearly and strongly influenced by what happened during and after the most critical years of the crisis and is testimony to better performance before the crisis and better reaction to the crisis and more rapid recovery. Poland and Slovakia can be considered two successful economies, both among V4 countries and within the EU.

The cases of the Czech Republic and Hungary are definitely less successful, yet these two economies present mutually different situations and trends. The Czech economy's trend is roughly parallel to that of Poland and Slovakia, yet in coincidence with lower yearly growth rates, close to 2 percent lower rates per year. The slope of the regression is −0.11 for the entire period, very similar to Slovakia's, although also in this case yearly variations in the growth rates are rather large. While the Czech economy had a relatively weak performance within the V4, it performed fairly well compared to the EU-28. While at the beginning of the period, in mid-1996, the Czech trend showed yearly growth rates similar to those of the EU-28 average, by 2013 the Czech economy trend was definitely better, around 1.5 percent better per year.

The case of Hungary is the most problematic. While the performance of the Hungarian economy was not distinctly worse than that of the other V4 countries until 2006 included, the situation changed dramatically and for the worst since 2007. As a consequence, Hungary, which had trend yearly growth rates better than the Czech Republic at the beginning of the period, ended up with definitely the worst performance among the V4 countries. Indeed, the trend growth rate at the end of the period was negative by approximately −0.3 percent. Hungary's performance was clearly worse than the EU-28 average from 2007 (with the exception of 2008) until 2012. However, 2013 saw a recovery, which accelerated in 2014.

The period since the mid-1990s witnessed a clear convergence of the V4 countries' GDP to that of the EU (Figure 11.2). The V4 countries began from a lower level of GDP, but growth rates were higher than the EU average. The convergence was strong and fast in the case of Poland and Slovakia. Poland was also the only EU member country whose growth rates were always positive, even in 2009, the *annus horribilis* of the world economy and the EU in particular. Convergence continued afterwards and still goes on. After negative performance in 1997 and 1998, the Czech economy returned to converge, until 2008. Since then, the convergence process stopped and the Czech economy moved in parallel with the EU-28 economy. In 2014, the Czech GDP was still slightly lower than the level reached in 2008. This is true also for Hungary, in spite of recovery in 2013 and 2014. The convergence of the Hungarian economy was fair until 2006. However, the collapse of Hungarian GDP in 2009 and again in 2012 was the worst among

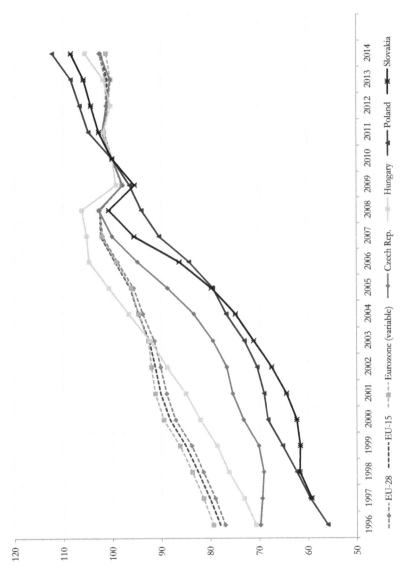

Figure 11.2 Gross domestic product at market prices (chain-linked volumes, index 2010 = 100)

Source: Eurostat

- - ◆ - - EU-28   - - - - EU-15   - -■- - Eurozone (variable)   ━◆━ Czech Rep.   Hungary   ━▼━ Poland   ━✳━ Slovakia

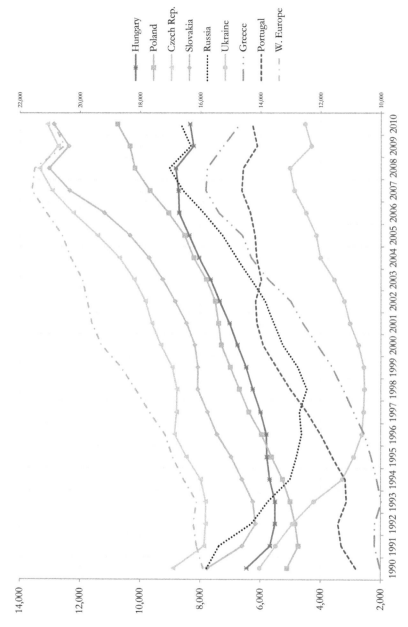

Figure 11.3 Gross domestic product per capita (1990 International Geary-Khamis dollars)

Source: The Maddison-Project, http://www.ggdc.net/maddison/maddison-project/home.htm, 2013 version

Note: Western Europe includes 30 countries. Right axis for Western Europe, Portugal and Greece.

the V4 and clearly worse than in the EU-28. Moreover, GDP growth between 2006 and 2008, and again 2010 was the weakest among the V4.

On average, the level of development of the V4 countries improved compared to that of the EU-28 countries. However, this does not hold in the case of per capita GDP calculated using international dollars (Figure 11.3). Among the V4 countries, only Slovakia was catching up to Western Europe from 1990 onward, while Poland roughly kept the pace. Hungary lost the most. Clearly the situation within the V4 group is variegated and relative positions significantly reshuffle through time. In particular, Hungary started in a better situation than Poland but ended up in a clearly weaker position. The Czech Republic also saw its relative position slightly worsen compared to Poland and, in particular, Slovakia. However, this outcome was largely the effect of transitional recession. If the years 1990–92 are excluded, only Hungary diverged in per capita GDP compared to Western Europe.

The complexity of the situation is highlighted also by other indicators, such as public finances, inflation, unemployment and social indicators, particularly those referring to inequalities. As members of the European Union, these indicators are crucially important for both the stability of the integration process and the V4 countries' participation in it, as defined in the convergence criteria, and in view of the social and development objectives of the Union, as defined in the Europe 2020 strategy.

GDP growth was, in all the V4 countries, more the result of successful exports than of growing domestic private or public demand. All four countries were successful in increasing their market shares, in a period when all Western European countries (except Luxembourg) saw their own world export shares decrease, some of them significantly (Table 11.1 and Figure 11.4). Hungary had the best performance over the period until the international crisis: compared to 1995, Hungary's world export share of goods and services increased by 2.3 times (from 0.28 percent of world exports in 1995 to 0.64 percent in 2008). However, the performance of

Table 11.1 Increase of export market shares (increase of the country's percentage of world total, goods and services)

	2014/1995	*2008/1995*	*2014/2008*	*2014/2010*
Czech Republic	1.92	2.03	0.95	1.00
Hungary	1.89	2.29	0.83	0.93
Poland			1.05	1.06
Slovakia			0.95	1.08
Estonia	2.25	2.00	1.13	1.13
Latvia			1.14	1.14
Lithuania			1.21	1.31
Romania			1.21	1.21
Slovenia	1.00	1.19	0.84	0.94

Source: Own elaborations on Eurostat database

the Czech Republic was also noteworthy, with a more than twofold growth (from 0.38 percent in 1995 to 0.77 percent in 2008).

The situation changed with the international crisis, in particular for Hungary. The country's share of world exports, in fact, decreased remarkably and has recovered only in part since then. By 2014, the share remained lower than in 2008 (0.53 percent of world market exports in 2014, down from 0.64 percent in 2008), when the country registered its best achievement. Recovery in Hungary started only in 2013, after its share of world exports went down to 0.49 percent in 2012. Different is the case of the Czech Republic, which recovered faster from a milder fall of its market share (from 0.77 in 2008 to 0.70 in 2013). Recovery of the world market share only started in 2014 and the country is still below the level reached in 2008 (0.73 percent in 2014). Slovakia is similar to the Czech Republic in that the decrease was milder than in Hungary (from 0.41 percent in 2008 to 0.36 in 2010), but the recovery afterwards was not yet a full one (0.39 percent in 2014).

Unfortunately, data on world market shares published by Eurostat for Poland and Slovakia only began in 2004 and 2008 respectively. This makes impossible to compare the four countries over the entire period. Poland had the best performance in the post-crisis period among the V4 countries: indeed, by 2014, the country had a higher market share (1.09 percent) than it had in the most successful year, 2009 (1.05 percent). The crisis caused overall a rather mild decrease of the world market share (to 0.99 in 2012).

Current account in the V4 countries was constantly in deficit since 1996 and over the period up to the crisis. In some of the years, the deficit was quite significant, more than −6 percent of GDP, the limit that the EU considers to be problematic. Until 2006, Slovakia was below or at this limit, except in 1999 and 2000. Hungary was constantly in the same situation during 2000–08. Poland fared better and had mostly a milder deficit, except in 1999 and again in 2007 and 2008. In most years, the Polish current account deficit was between −2 and −4 percent of GDP. The Czech Republic was slightly above the −6 percent deficit only in 1996 and at that value in 1997 and 2003. In the remaining years, the Czech current account was around −5 percent deficit between 2000 and 2002 and again in 2007 and at −2 percent deficit or lower in the remaining years. Following the crisis, exports recovered better than imports, thus leading to a general improvement of current accounts. Hungary's current account improved dramatically and since 2010 was converted into surplus. Slovakia went into surplus starting in 2012 and the Czech Republic in 2013. Only Poland continued to keep current accounts in deficit, although a mild one (around −1 percent of GDP since 2013).

Financial account and FDIs feature in part a mirror image of current accounts. In fact, in the years between 1995 and 2010 the balance of payments for the entire V4 group was overall only slightly negative. In the years from 2011 and 2013 the balance of payments of all countries improved significantly and was positive. Poland was the exception, since the situation in this country only improved starting in 2014. Particularly impressive was the performance of Hungary, whose balance of payments was constantly in surplus since 2009 and reached extremely high surpluses of around 10 percent of GDP, particularly in 2012 and again in

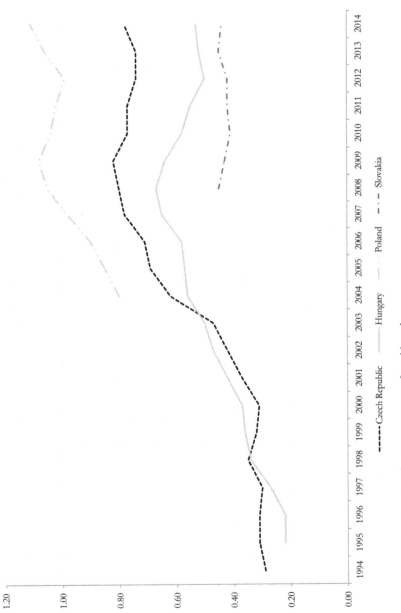

Figure 11.4 Export market shares, percentage of world total

Source: Eurostat

----- Czech Republic ——— Hungary ····· Poland —·— Slovakia

1994 1995 1996 1997 1998 1999 2000 2001 2002 2003 2004 2005 2006 2007 2008 2009 2010 2011 2012 2013 2014

0.00 0.20 0.40 0.60 0.80 1.00 1.20

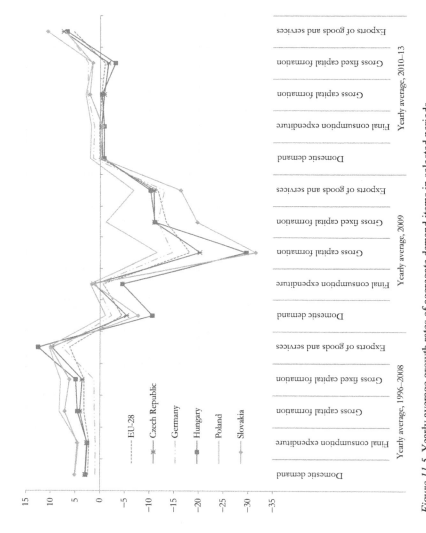

Figure 11.5 Yearly average growth rates of aggregate demand items in selected periods

Source: Own elaborations on Eurostat database

2014. However, this performance was largely due to the significant amount of EU transfers, mainly capital transfers (HCB 2015).

Looking at the components of aggregate demand and considering the average growth rates in selected periods, it is interesting to notice that, on average, exports were the most dynamic component in all periods, except in 2009 (Figure 11.5). Export performance of each of the V4 countries was better than the EU-28 average in all periods, except for Slovakia in 2009. The worst performance during 2009 was of gross capital formation, in particular in Slovakia and Hungary, while in Poland the fall of gross capital formation was relatively mild, also in comparison with the EU-28 and Germany.

The growth of final consumption expenditure was stronger in all the V4 countries compared to the EU-28 in the period 1996–2008, particularly so in Slovakia and Poland. The situation in 2009 witnessed a mild decrease in the EU-28 average and a mild increase in the V4 countries. However, Hungary is a remarkable outlier that experienced a significant fall of final consumption expenditure. In the period 2010–13, final consumption expenditure continued to be slightly negative in all the V4 countries, with the exception of Poland.

Overall, the years since the crisis were difficult for the V4 countries, with some bright spots. Most important among these were exports, which recovered quickly and well from the deep depression of 2009. In the case of domestic demand, Poland—and Slovakia until the crisis—clearly did better than the EU average, and the Czech Republic and Hungary.

European convergence criteria

While only Slovakia adopted the euro, the Czech Republic, Hungary and Poland, as members of the European Union, also were under the convergence criteria within the Stability and Growth Pact (SGP). In fact, the Pact applies to all EU member countries. The Union defined and implemented these criteria to make economic and financial cooperation possible and free of risks for other countries. Convergence criteria are in line with the precepts of ordoliberalism and the German social market economy and provided the basis for European policies (Bonefeld 2012, Ptak 2009, Schnyder and Siems 2013).

In order to pursue these goals, any EU member country is required to meet a series of conditions, which include a set of convergence criteria and the compatibility of national legislation with the *Acquis Communautaire*, i.e. the existing EU legislation. The latter regards the independence of the national central bank, its objectives, and its integration into the European System of Central Banks.[13] At least once every two years, the European Commission and the European Central Bank prepare a convergence report to the Council based on these conditions and assesses the progress made by the member countries in complying with the criteria.[14]

There are four fundamental convergence criteria: price stability, government finances, exchange rates, and long-term interest rates. Price stability in a country is defined as an inflation rate no more than 1.5 percent higher than in the three best-performing member countries in terms of price stability during the year preceding the assessment. The reference aggregate is the Harmonised Index of Consumer Prices (HICP). As to government finances, member countries should have a ratio of annual government deficit to GDP at market prices that does not exceed 3 percent, measured at the end of the preceding financial year. Moreover, the ratio of gross government debt to GDP at market prices must not exceed 60 percent at the end of the preceding financial year. Exchange rates must remain stable compared to the currency of any other member country during the two years preceding the examination of accession and should be free of severe tensions. Finally, the nominal long-term interest rate must not exceed by more than 2 percent that of the three best-performing member countries in terms of price stability during the year preceding the examination. The reference aggregate is the average yield for 10-year government bonds in the previous year.

Strictu sensu, convergence criteria apply only to the members of the Eurozone. Among the V4 countries, this is the case only of Slovakia. However, all EU member countries must adhere to the Stability and Growth Pact (SGP). The SGP consists of a set of rules and procedures that are based on the convergence criteria and that are designed to ensure that member countries pursue sound public finances and coordinate their fiscal policies. In case a country does not comply with the rules and their limits, a set of procedures is foreseen to correct excessive budget deficits or excessive public debt. These include a preventive arm, a corrective arm and an excessive deficit procedure.

The preventive arm binds EU governments to pursue sound fiscal policies and policy coordination by setting each one a budgetary target defined in structural terms,[15] the so-called "Medium-Term Budgetary Objective" (MTO). MTOs are defined in a Stability Programme in the case of Eurozone member countries and in a Convergence Programme for countries keeping their national currency. These Programmes and the country's compliance with them are assessed by the European Commission and Council. The corrective arm makes use of the Excessive Deficit Procedure (EDP) to ensure that the necessary correction of excessive budget deficits or excessive public debt levels is undertaken in a step-by-step approach.

Convergence in price inflation was generally slower in the V4 countries than it was in countries that entered the EU earlier. Also price growth rates in other former transformation countries converged faster downward to the EU average, with the exception of Romania and, to a lesser extent, Bulgaria. However, convergence was successful and ended in 2014, a year when inflation was close to zero, spanning from −0.1 percent in Slovakia to +0.4 percent in the Czech Republic, lower than in the EU-28 average (+0.6 percent) (Figure 11.5). In any case, the achievement was remarkable, particularly so in Hungary and Poland, countries in which the inflation rate in 1997 was respectively 18.5 percent and 15.0 percent in the same year. In the average of the then 15 EU member countries, HICP was at 1.7 percent. Slovakia also had an inflation rate of 12.2 percent in 2000. In the Czech Republic, price inflation was more moderate, yet even in this country it was at 8.0 percent in 1997. European integration, integration of markets and competition were effective in stabilizing the inflation that dominated the V4 countries, in particular Hungary and Poland, since the 1980s.

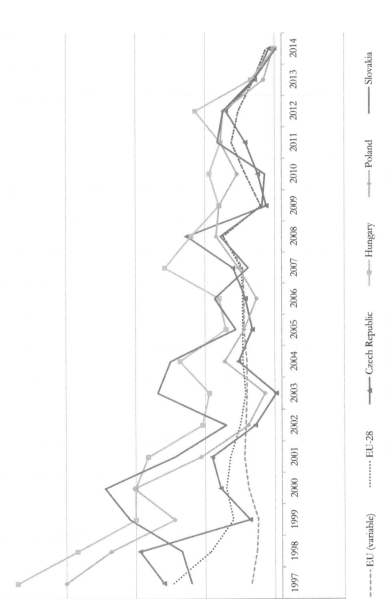

Figure 11.6 Harmonised Index of Consumer Prices (HICP), all-items, annual average rate of change

Source: Eurostat

208   *Central Europe: the Visegràd Four*

Current public finances were an Achilles heel for the V4 countries after the period of transitional depression was over (Figure 11.7). Even the Czech Republic, which during pre-transformation had particularly disciplined public finances, since 1995 had deficits above the required 3 percent for most of the years up to 2005. Net borrowing of general government as a percentage of GDP was generally above the limit of 3 percent defined in the SGP in all countries. It was only in 2013 and 2014 that all countries, except Poland, complied with the requirement.

Hungary was the most problematic country, not only because in most of the years the deficit was above the limit, but also because the excess was quite significant, between 6.4 percent and 9.4 percent, in the seven years between 1995 and 2006. It is interesting to note that between 2009 and 2012, Hungary was the best performer among the V4 countries, except in 2011. Slovakia was similar to Hungary in that the general government's budget deficit was between 6.2 percent and 12.1 percent in the six years between 1995 and 2012. However, since 2003 and up to 2008, Slovakia was the best performer among the V4 countries, with only 2006 slightly above the limit. The Czech Republic had a similar positive performance between 2004 and 2008 and again since 2011 (with the exception of 2012). Poland generally followed a more moderate path, avoiding high deficits, except in 2009 and 2010, when it was the worst performer, together with Slovakia. In no year since 2004 was Poland able to place itself within the 3 percent limit. Compared to the EU average, the V4 countries had weaker performances until 2008. However, starting in 2009, their average performance was constantly better than the EU average. This is a remarkable result, after several financially difficult years.

In spite of difficulties with budget deficits, the V4 countries had an enviable record with public debt (Figure 11.8). On average, these countries had a much better performance than the EU average. The Czech Republic, Poland and Slovakia in no year between 1995 and 2014 had public debt above the limit of 60 percent to GDP. The debt increased since 2009, as effect of deficits and of the crisis on GDP, but in 2014 debt returned to decrease in all three countries. The case of Hungary is different: except the years 1999–2004, when the debt was at or below 60 percent of GDP, in all other years, Hungary had a debt larger than the required limit. However, since 2011, the Hungarian debt has consistently decreased. This is the second time Hungary decreased its debt, the first one being the years after the Bokros package up to 2001. During this period, the debt decreased by more than 32 percent of GDP, from 84.5 percent of GDP in 1995 to 51.9 percent in 2001. This was a particularly successful period, because interests payable on public debt registered an impressive fall, from around 9 percent of GDP at the beginning of the period to 4 percent in 2002, a level that was kept ever since.

Slovakia also had a very successful period of debt reduction, between 2000 and 2008, when the debt decreased by more than 20 percent of GDP, from 49.6 percent to 28.2 percent. Interests payable on debt accompanied these swings with a dramatic increase to 4 percent of GDP in 2000, up from 2.5 percent in 1998. In 2008, interests payable on debt amounted to only 1.2 percent of GDP.

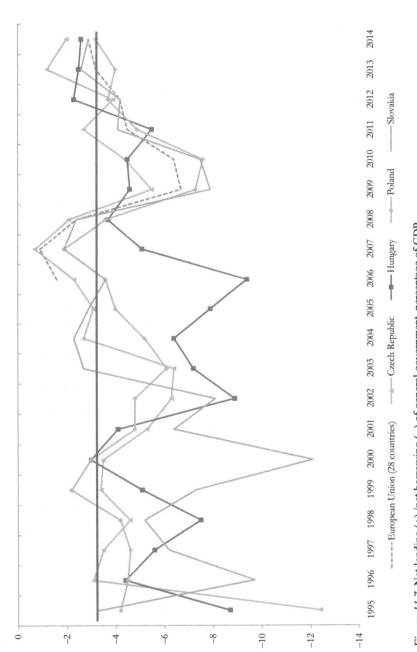

Figure 11.7 Net lending (+) /net borrowing (−) of general government, percentage of GDP

Source: Eurostat

Note: The solid grey line at 3 percent deficit represents the EU benchmark.

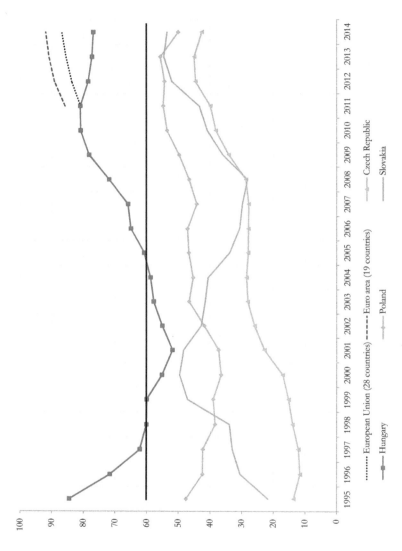

Figure 11.8 General government consolidated gross debt, in percent of GDP

Source: Eurostat

Note: The black line corresponds to the stability parameter for public debt.

As an effect of the crisis and the growing debt, interests payable increased again to 1.9 percent of GDP in 2014. Poland and the Czech Republic had a more stable level of debt: in Poland rather stable around 50 percent, and in the Czech Republic in constant growth, from slightly above 10 percent in the mid-1990s to around 45 percent in the 2010s. Interests payable on the debt increased slightly in the Czech Republic during the entire period, but remained very low, around 1 percent. In Poland, they decreased from 3 percent in 2000 to 2 percent in 2014.

A third convergence criterion is the stability of exchange rates.[16] The stability of exchange rates is defined when compared to the currency of any other member country during the two years preceding the examination of accession. Exchange rates should also be free of severe tensions. The reference country of exchange rate stability is obviously Germany, which is the main trading and economic partner of all the V4 economies.[17] The only V4 country which kept the stability of the exchange rate was Slovakia after the country joined the euro in 2009. Given the determination of the Slovak government to fiscal consolidation and to join the euro, which dates back to 2002, the Slovak exchange rate started to appreciate until the euro was adopted.

Poland also kept a fair stability of the exchange rate since 2009, after the Polish złoty strongly depreciated in 2009. The case of the Czech Republic is somehow different: the Czech koruna appreciated after independence and continued to do so until 2008. A period of stability followed until 2011, when the currency started to depreciate. The case of Hungary is at odds with the criterion. The Hungarian forint strongly depreciated between 1994 and 2000, then appreciated in 2001–02. Years of relative stability followed until 2008. This is the period when it looked as though the country would join the euro soon. With the crisis, the exchange rate of the forint started to depreciate again.

The stability of long-term interest rates forms the fourth convergence criterion.[18] The reference interest rate is the average yields for 10-year government bonds in the previous year, which must not exceed by more than 2 percent that of the three best-performing member countries in terms of price stability during the year preceding the examination. Once again, Germany is used as a benchmark (Figure 11.10). German long-term interest rates converged consistently towards a very low level, slightly above 1 percent by 2014. The stability of this path and the size of German financial markets[19] made the 10-year bond the reference bond over which interest rate spreads are calculated for other countries. Given the evolution of international money markets, interest rates decreased in all the V4 countries. However, important differences exist among individual countries.

Since 2001, the path followed by Czech interest rates has been the most consistent one. Czech long-term interest rates followed German rates rather well, with a spread well below 1 percent between 2002 and 2008 (Table 11.2). It was only with the 2009 crisis that the spread increased to 1.62 percent and remained slightly above 1 percent until 2012, after which it decreased to around 0.5 percent. What is remarkable about Czech stability is that the country had a significantly better performance than the Eurozone average in the years 2010–14. The performance of Slovakia was weaker than the Czech Republic's, except in 2009 and

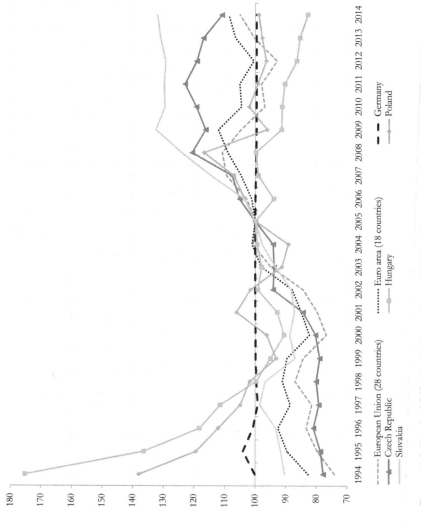

Figure 11.9 Nominal Effective Exchange Rate with 37 trading partners, index 2005 = 100

Source: Eurostat

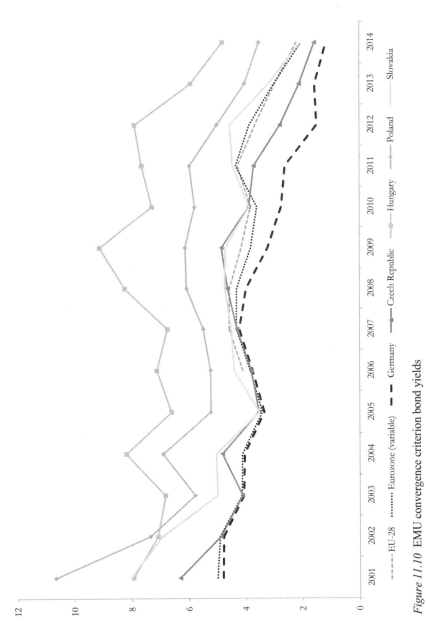

Figure 11.10 EMU convergence criterion bond yields

Source: Eurostat

Table 11.2 EMU convergence criterion bond yields: spread over German yields

	2001	2002	2003	2004	2005	2006	2007	2008	2009	2010	2011	2012	2013	2014
EU-28						0.34	0.35	0.58	0.93	1.08	1.67	2.16	1.39	1.05
Eurozone (variable)	0.20	0.13	0.07	0.08	0.07	0.08	0.10	0.33	0.60	0.86	1.73	2.36	1.42	0.88
Czech Republic	1.51	0.10	0.05	0.78	0.19	0.04	0.08	0.65	1.62	1.14	1.10	1.28	0.54	0.42
Hungary	3.15	2.31	2.75	4.15	3.25	3.36	2.52	4.26	5.90	4.54	5.03	6.39	4.35	3.65
Poland	5.88	2.58	1.71	2.86	1.87	1.47	1.26	2.09	2.90	3.04	3.35	3.50	2.46	2.36
Slovakia	3.24	2.16	0.92	0.99	0.17	0.65	0.27	0.74	1.49	1.13	1.84	3.05	1.62	0.91

Source: own elaborations on Eurostat

2010. The spread of Slovak long-term interest rates in 2012 went above 3 percent, a sign of serious tensions in the money market. Poland and even more so Hungary had clearly more problematic situations. While Polish interest rates followed an uncertain, yet descending path, Hungarian long-term interest rates moved around 8 percent until 2012 and only in the last two years did they decrease to below 5 percent. The spread over German rates was consistently high over the entire period, most of the years well above 3 percent and even around or higher than 6 percent in 2009 and 2012.

In part, the situation is different when real long-term interest rates are considered in order to account for differences in inflation rates (Figure 11.11). While German real interest rates were always positive and as high as 4.6 percent in 2009 and as low as 0.5 percent in 2013, Hungarian real rates changed dramatically from year to year and were also in negative territory (−1.2 percent in 2001 and again in 2007). Also Czech real interest rates were negative twice and by larger amounts than Hungary's: in 2008 and 2012 (respectively −2.3 percent and −2.0 percent). Slovak rates were negative in 2003 and 2004 (respectively −3.4 percent and −2.5 percent). Only Polish rates moved constantly in positive territory, between around 5.5 percent in 2001 and 2002 and 1.4 percent in 2012. In the case of real interest rates, the spread over German rates decreased to below 1 percent for the Czech Republic and to slightly above 1 percent for Slovakia. Only in Poland and Hungary did the spread remain significant (Figure 11.12).[20]

Interest rates, in particular, long-term interest rates related to state bonds, are fundamental for assessing the sustainability of a country's participation in the common currency. The need to maneuver interest rates for assuring financial and economic stability depends in part upon the size of the public debt compared to GDP and is linked, in open markets with highly mobile capital, to the exchange rate and consequently to the price competitiveness of a country's goods and services in the world market. It may be too risky for a country with economic imbalances that cause unstable and high interest rates to join the common currency. This is apparently the situation of Hungary and also Poland, but not of the Czech Republic.

Although not a formal part of the convergence criteria and the SGP, foreign indebtedness is nevertheless an important parameter to assess the sustainability of a country's economic and financial situation. In the case of the V4 countries, this is particularly important, since in both Hungary and Poland foreign indebtedness was a fundamental cause of their critical situation. Conversely, neither in the case of the Czech Republic nor of Slovakia was foreign debt an issue of some relevance. Foreign debt was generally on the rise as a share of GDP after the years of transformational stabilization (Figure 11.13). This observation concerns in particular Poland and Hungary, the two countries which had very high foreign debts during the last years of socialism and also in early 1990s.

Poland went through 14 episodes of debt restructuring between 1981 and 1994, the only V4 country to have needed restructuring, including two episodes of reduction of debt face value in 1985 and 1994 (Das et al. 2012). As a result, foreign debt decreased significantly below 40 percent of GDP. Polish foreign debt

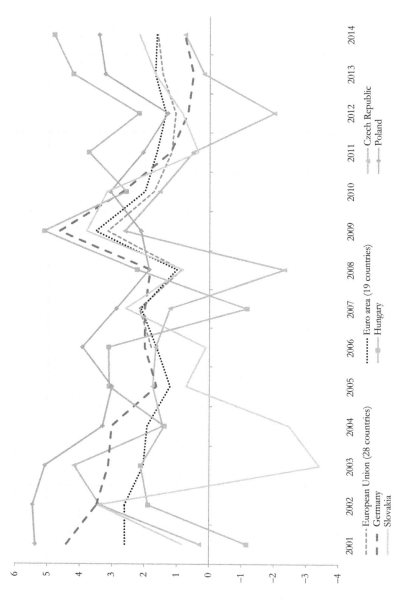

Figure 11.11 Real long-term interest rates

Source: own elaborations on Eurostat database

Note: Annual average rate of change of all-items HICP is subtracted from EMU convergence criterion bond yields.

European Union (28 countries)
Germany
Slovakia
Euro area (19 countries)
Hungary
Czech Republic
Poland

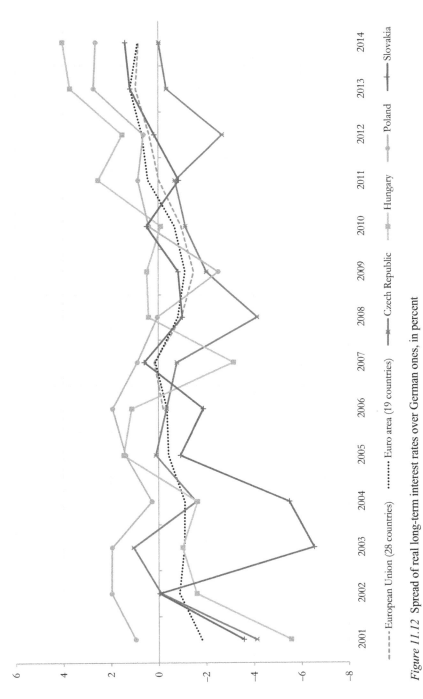

Figure 11.12 Spread of real long-term interest rates over German ones, in percent

Source: own elaborations on Eurostat database

---- European Union (28 countries) ········ Euro area (19 countries) ——— Czech Republic ——+— Slovakia

——■— Hungary ——●— Poland

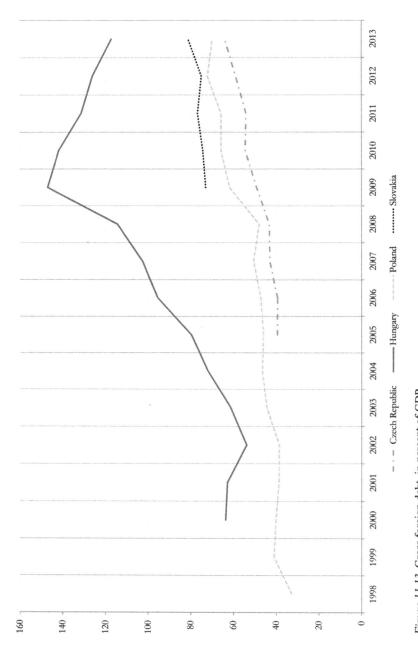

Figure 11.13 Gross foreign debt, in percent of GDP

Source: own elaborations on Eurostat database

- - - Czech Republic ——— Hungary - - - - Poland ········· Slovakia

started to increase slowly again since 2002 and until 2008. With the crisis, in 2009 foreign debt increased by nearly 4 percent of GDP, after which it kept rising slowly. In 2013, Polish debt decreased slightly.

Foreign debt increased slowly also in the Czech Republic and Slovakia. By 2013 and compared to GDP, foreign debt was at 70 percent and 81 percent respectively. The most problematic case is again Hungary. The country always chose to honor its foreign debt without going through any restructuring. Although debt remained high as a consequence, stabilization and careful management during the 1990s decreased foreign debt to below 60 percent of GDP by 2002. Afterwards, the debt kept rising significantly and consistently until 2008, when it reached 114 percent of GDP. It then jumped to 147 percent in 2009, following the IMF–EU–World Bank bailout. The crisis prompted Hungary to tackle the problem of its foreign debt and decrease it to the pre-crisis level (117 percent) by 2013 (Eurostat database).

The transformation countries' attempt to catch up with Western Europe had an important component in households' debt. The Czech Republic, Hungary, Poland and Slovakia experienced rapid growth of debt in the household sector, similar to other transformation countries which are now members of the European Union. Debt levels in the V4 countries were catching up with levels observed in the old member countries of the EU. One troubling aspect of this debt was that it was in foreign currencies. When domestic currencies, in which households' income was mostly expressed, started to depreciate against foreign currencies, households risked default.

With the start of the century, borrowing in foreign currencies became popular in various CEECs to capture what appeared to be lasting benefits: lower mortgage payments thanks to lower interest rates on foreign currencies, in particular the Swiss franc. This attitude was particularly spread among households, but was also important for businesses. Although there was a risk that, in the case of depreciation of the national currency, the value of mortgages would increase correspondingly, that event appeared unlikely. Capital was flowing abundantly into most CEECs, making those currencies strong. These were the years when various CEECs were planning to join the euro within a short time. This would have done away with the risk and getting into debt in a stable foreign currency now anticipated a future gain.

Hungarians were particularly eager to borrow in foreign currencies, particularly in Swiss francs since 2004, both because the national currency was strong and because the government decreased subsidizing mortgage loans in national currency (Norris 2014, see also Barrell et al. 2009). The problem became particularly serious, for both the level of such indebtedness and when the forint progressively weakened.[21] In Hungary, households were eager to assume their debt in foreign currencies, particularly in Swiss francs, to take advantage of the particularly low interest rates on the latter. Stimulated by lender banks, households aimed at saving on the high interest rates that they had to pay on loans in the national currency. They also foresaw the possibility to gain by repaying their debt in a weakening currency (the Swiss franc) out of their income in a strengthening currency (the Hungarian forint). Although a similar situation existed in Poland, better bank regulation significantly diminished the risk in this country.

According to the Hungarian government, half of the households took loans in foreign currencies. In fact, banks—many of which were affiliates of large foreign banks—promoted aggressively the desire of households, since this provided them with extremely lucrative opportunities and bank regulation was lax. Unfortunately for borrowers, in 2008 the forint started to depreciate both against the euro and, in larger measure, against the Swiss franc. To relieve a situation that was at risk of getting out of control, the government used a variety of measures to alleviate the borrowers' situation, including compensation that banks should pay in 2015 to those borrowers who were damaged by unfair contracts and an extraordinary bank tax. Borrowers also gained the possibility of converting outstanding foreign currency mortgage loans back into forints. Although there is evidence that banks often misused this opportunity to the disadvantage of poorly informed customers, these measures also worsened the banks' situation. These measures contributed to convert the banking sector from a profitable and well-capitalized sector into one where most banks needed capital infusion and have low rating. A consequence was mutually feeding the credit crunch and the scramble for liquidity (Sobják 2013).

Unemployment and inequalities

With the unfolding of transformation, the labor market was the first to change. From a situation with no unemployment and a labor shortage in the form of a high number of job vacancies and slack employment, the labor market was converted into a market with rapidly growing unemployment as early as spring 1990. Since then, unemployment has remained an intractable issue in most CEECs. However, the V4 countries' situation is variegated in this case also, and it is not easy to find a consistent pattern. It is useful to distinguish employment into its different forms and age classes and unemployment.

In general, the Czech Republic comes out with the most balanced and effective labor market. The Czech employment rate at 65 percent until 2010 and at 69 percent in 2014 is by far the highest among the V4 countries and consistently higher than the average employment in both EU-28 and the Eurozone (Figure 11.14). Of the other three countries, Poland dramatically improved its low employment rate of the pre-crisis level and since 2008 has increased it above 60 percent. In Hungary, the rate hovered around 55 percent until 2011, then it increased rapidly to nearly 62 percent in 2014. Slovakia was slightly more stable than both Poland and Hungary, with a rate hovering around 60 percent for the entire period.

The employment rate includes different types of employment. It is particularly important to look at the quality of employment and consider the percentage of employees with temporary contracts. In Slovakia, Hungary and the Czech Republic, this kind of employment was stable at low levels (between 5 and 9 percent) until 2009 (Eurostat data). Since 2010, the share has increased to around 10 percent. All these countries kept the proportion of temporary contracts well

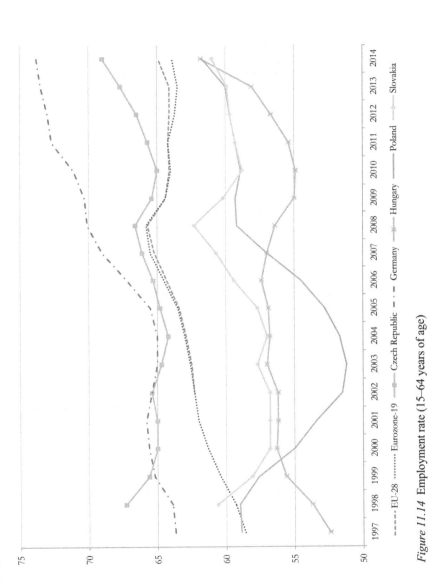

Figure 11.14 Employment rate (15–64 years of age)

Source: Eurostat

below the average of both the EU-28 and the Eurozone, and also well below that of Germany, where the figure moved between 12 and 15 percent. Quite different is Poland's situation. The country started from a low share of around 5 percent until 2000, and then dramatically boomed to 28 percent by 2007, where it remained in the following years.

Another indicator of the quality of employment, the share of part-time workers in total employment, is less significant. In fact, all the V4 countries made consistently less use of part-time contracts than in the EU. In the case of Poland, this share, which was around 10 percent, decreased to 8 percent since 2005. In the three other countries, the figure moved between 2 and 7 percent. Low levels of part-time work are probably a sign of a certain degree of rigidity of labor markets and low levels of choice left to employees. Moreover, there is probably a kind of replacement effect between part-time and temporary contracts in Poland, since the decrease of the former is roughly coincident with the stabilization of the latter.

Unemployment figures in Poland and Slovakia behaved oddly between 1998 and 2008 (Figure 10.4). While the two countries were not particularly different from the EU average or Hungary in previous years, their unemployment rate increased dramatically to 20 percent by the early 2000s. These were years of decreasing employment rates in both countries (Figure 11.14). Then the rate decreased rapidly to below the starting level, a level coincident with that of the EU average in the case of Poland, at around 7 percent. Since then the Polish rate moved slightly below the EU average, while that of Slovakia remained significantly above. In the case of Hungary, the unemployment rate was below the EU average in the years 1997–2006 (a period of increasing employment rates), it moved slightly above the latter until 2012, then moved resolutely downward. The Czech Republic was clearly the best performer for most of the period: its unemployment rate moved from 4 percent until 1996, around 8 percent between 1999 and 2005, and around 6 percent afterwards, even in the crisis years. Only Hungary did better between 1999 and 2005. Youth unemployment (those under age 25) in all countries moved in a fashion similar to overall unemployment, with rates slightly more than twice as high, coinciding with rapidly decreasing employment rates. Youth employment rates started to increase in 2012, while remaining at two-thirds of the EU average.

The problem of inequality is only partially linked to unemployment. Another important influence comes from incomes, including the remuneration of labor, and the ownership and remuneration of capital. Gini coefficients give evidence of two different situations within the V4 countries.[22] The Czech Republic, Hungary and Slovakia had and have a more egalitarian income distribution compared to the EU average, a fact due primarily to a developed and rather generous welfare system. Only in Hungary did the Gini coefficient increase by some 3 points following the crisis. Conversely, Poland had and has a Gini coefficient constantly higher than the EU average and even more so of the other three countries. However, income inequality in Poland was constantly decreasing, although at a very low pace since around 2010.

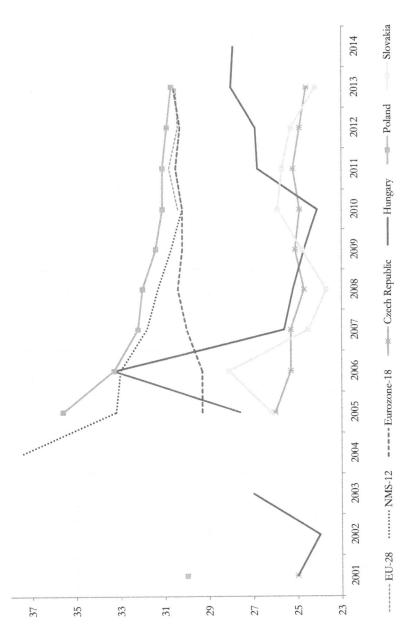

Figure 11.15 Gini coefficient of equivalized disposable income

Source: Eurostat

Finally, the process of the V4 countries' net earnings catching up when accounted in euros to the EU average—an important indicator for foreign investors—continued through the entire period. However, the process has smoothed out since the crisis and differences remained stable at between around 30 percent (depending on the kind of earner considered) in the case of Hungary and Poland and above 40 percent in the case of the Czech Republic. Slovakia is at approximately 30–35 percent of the EU average level. These relatively low levels of earnings, when accounted in euros, suggest that standards of living in these mostly very open economies are still far from the EU average. However, they also suggest that the area is still an interesting site for investment by Western European countries.[23]

Industrial and financial integration

One important feature of economic development, particularly in the 1990s and afterwards, was the development of global value chains (Ash 2015). After the start of transformation, the V4 countries also entered these chains, as part of their increasing European integration. These economies were and are strictly linked to Western European supply-and-production chains, in particular to German ones (Aiyar et al. 2013). The V4 countries produce components of German goods, but they also produce finished goods whose production was delocalized from Germany. Industrial integration gave a strong contribution to the development of bilateral trade linkages with Germany since the 1990s. Large inflows of German FDIs supported the set-up and development of supply and production chains, also through greenfield investment, and were more important than portfolio investment and cross-border bank flows. The FDIs contributing to supply chains, and in particular to the manufacturing sector, were a particularly important share of overall FDIs in the case of the V4 countries, in a proportion that was much larger than in the case of other transformation countries.

Participation in supply chains was important for the V4 countries in various ways. Participation led to important technology transfers and technology absorption. This in turn fueled the rapid expansion of the V4 countries' exports in knowledge-intensive sectors and had important spillovers for the domestic industry, a fact that supported income convergence.[24] The complementarities between domestic production and supply chain activities strengthened the synchronization of the business cycle among the countries participating in the chains. The importance of the participation in global chains prompted the V4 governments to follow policies supporting their participation and enhance the competitiveness of their industry, including upgrading labor skills.

Few data suffice to illustrate the outstanding importance of this sector in all V4 countries (Table 11.3). Foreign-controlled enterprises have a presence and a role in the V4 countries that is much higher than in the EU average.[25] Employment in foreign-controlled enterprises as a share of total domestic employment is nearly five times higher in the V4 countries than in the EU average. Value added in foreign-controlled enterprises as a share of total value added is 4.3 times higher. Employment in the V4 countries is more than one-fourth of total employment,

Table 11.3 Employment and value added in foreign-controlled enterprises as a share of total domestic employment and value added

	Employment*	Value added**	Value added/employment
Czech Republic	27.27	42.94	1.57
Hungary	25.79	51.89	2.01
Poland	25.38	35.07	1.38
Slovakia	25.02	38.23	1.53
EU-27	5.21	9.83	1.89
Average	25.87	42.03	1.62
V4/EU	4.96	4.28	

Source: Own elaborations on Eurostat database

Notes:
* Employment in foreign controlled enterprises as a share of total domestic employment
** Value added in foreign controlled enterprises as a share of total value added

compared to barely 5.2 percent in the EU average, and the share is similar in each V4 country, with the Czech Republic slightly above the other countries. In value added, the situation is different and inter-country differences are important. While in Slovakia and Poland, the share is below 40 percent and in the Czech Republic slightly above it, in Hungary, more than half of value added produced in the country comes from foreign-controlled enterprises.

The main characteristics of foreign-controlled enterprises reveal some interesting differences among both the recipient countries and the controller country. Considering the number of people employed per enterprise, one would expect that this is the highest in Poland, being this by far the largest V4 country. While this is so with, on average, 203 employees per enterprise in 2012, it may be surprising to find the smallest country, Slovakia, in the second place with 155 employees on average.[26] The Czech Republic follows with 70 employees. Hungary has by far the smallest number: 35 employees. There are also significant differences referred to countries where the controller is registered. Controllers registered in the United States control the largest enterprises (measured in number of persons employed per enterprise) in all the V4 countries except Slovakia. In this latter case, controllers of the largest enterprises are registered in the Netherlands. On average, investors registered in the United States govern the largest foreign-controlled enterprises in the V4 countries (159 employees on average). Next come controllers registered in the Netherlands, followed by the United Kingdom and Germany. On average, controllers registered in Austria, followed by Italy, control the smallest enterprises.

Labor productivity (measured as gross value added per person employed) is relatively even in the foreign-controlled enterprises in the V4 countries. It is the highest in Hungary, with €38,000 and is due in particular to enterprises controlled by US (€58,200) and French investors (€43,800), with Italian investors obtaining the least (€24,800). The lowest outcome is in Slovakia (€34,600). The extremes in Slovakia are represented by controllers registered in Italy (€66,000) and in Germany (€31,500). The Czech Republic and Poland are generally placed between these extremes. The case of foreign-controlled enterprises in Hungary is particularly interesting: they are on average the smallest ones and at the same time have the highest labor productivity.

There is one significant aspect of this kind of integration that is important to appreciate for assessing the effects of the global crisis. The V4 countries' greater trade openness through their participation in supply chains aimed at increasing exports worldwide, increased their exposure to shocks and policy actions originating outside Europe. The same did not hold for the exposure to German final-demand spillovers and the effect of German fiscal policies, which remained relatively small for the V4 countries. In fact, German-V4 bilateral trade is mostly in intermediate goods and this softened the effect of both shocks in German final demand and German fiscal policies. However, the role of Germany was important in absorbing global shocks: the soundness of the German economy's fundamentals guaranteed for the V4 countries that global shocks were smoothed out through supply chains. Overall, deep integration with the German economy guaranteed that global shocks were weakened by the time they reached the V4 countries, compared to what happened to less integrated countries, such as small Southern European countries.

Production and trade integration with Western European countries, and in particular with Germany, gave the V4 countries greater resilience when the US contagion reached them. Orlowski and Tsibulina (2014) examined integration of the financial markets and the banking sectors in Central and Eastern Europe and the Eurozone. They studied co-movements between government bond and equity markets of Germany and those of Poland, Czech Republic, Hungary and Slovakia (plus Slovenia). They found that the V4 countries were split into two groups. There was high correlation of government bond yields of the Czech Republic and Poland with German yields. Such correlation did not hold in the case of Hungary and Slovakia. In the case of equity returns, those of the Czech Republic, Hungary and Poland exhibited high correlation with German returns, while those of Slovakia showed no correlation. Integration of the banking sectors with the Eurozone was higher in the case of the Czech Republic and Poland than in the case of Slovakia, while Hungary lagged behind, being under the influence of country-specific shocks.

One of the general effects of the crisis was the collapse of both net and gross financial flows across the world. While before the crisis, the EU had a stable and sizeable capital account surplus, in parallel with its overall current account deficit, during the crisis the EU registered capital account deficit, except for few quarters (Darvas et al. 2014). The Eurozone, which had had an approximately balanced net financial account before the crisis, continued to do so after the crisis broke out. However, the Eurozone witnessed a dramatic decrease of capital flows during the crisis years (Lane 2013). When the Eurozone showed clear signs of instability in 2011 and the euro came under attack, the Eurozone experienced considerable capital outflows and current account surpluses. This trend persisted in 2013–14, in spite of the greater stability of the Eurozone. Net capital outflows continued, while gross flows were significantly reduced compared to the pre-crisis years and remain lower.

The situation of V4 countries was different in this period (Darvas et al. 2014). Net flows decreased, but on average they did not turn negative. While FDI liabilities continued to be particularly important, the net financial account position (including foreign direct investment, portfolio equity, portfolio debt and other investments) registered a significant inflow in Poland also during the crisis and until the first quarter of 2013, after which outflows dominated. In Hungary, capital inflow was prevalent until the first quarter of 2013, although at a lower level and with a more unstable profile than Poland. Capital inflow continued also in the Czech Republic, while Slovakia had mild capital outflow or equilibrium between early 2012 and mid-2013. Before and after this period, capital inflow was significant in Slovakia.

Microeconomic features

Transformation had to do more with the microeconomic features and setting of the countries than with their macroeconomic situation. Indeed, performance and competitiveness[27] of an economy in open and integrated markets depend basically upon the quality of its institutions, its human capital and its enterprises, although the macroeconomic situation may put a constraint upon, or support, microeconomic potential. Moreover, a country's resilience to the international crisis has much to do with the ability of its enterprises to compete. The massive inflow of foreign capital into the V4 countries after transformation is an indirect proof of successful microeconomic transformation, related in particular to the conditions for greenfield investments and the integration into global value chains. It is important to have a more detailed and refined picture of microeconomics in the V4 countries to better understand the effects of the crisis and the countries' adaptation. In what follows below, efficiency issues, competitiveness and the conditions for enterprising are considered.

Labor costs in the tradable sector is a fundamental measure to assess the competitiveness of enterprises and countries. Starting from very low levels, labor costs in the V4 countries converged rapidly to the EU level (Figure 11.17).[28] Starting from 2009, convergence stopped abruptly and slightly decreased. In 2000, total labor costs in the unweighted average of the V4 countries was at 21.4 percent of the EU-28 level. This share had increased to 37.1 percent by 2008 and then decreased to 35.4 percent by 2014. Individual countries behaved somewhat differently in the pre-crisis period. Convergence was most rapid in the Czech Republic, but also retreat was fairly significant in the crisis years. Convergence was fast also in Slovakia, but the peculiarity of this country, the only one to do so among the V4 countries, is that in the post-crisis years convergence simply slowed down. Poland slightly increased divergence in the first part of the 2000s, then rapid convergence followed until 2008, mild divergence until 2012, and then again mild convergence since 2013. Hungary had a somewhat slower convergence until the crisis and then

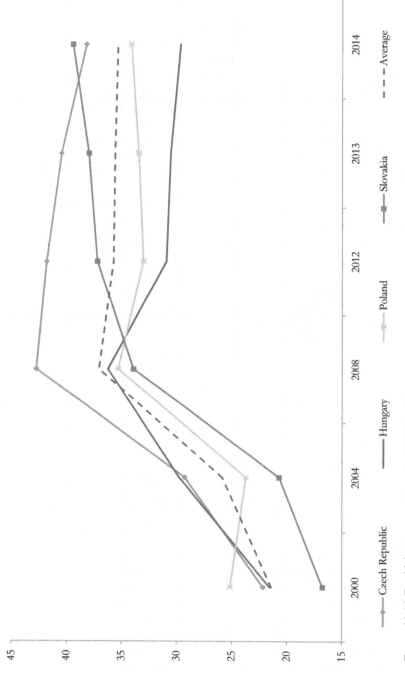

Figure 11.16 Total labor costs compared to EU-28 = 100

Source: Own elaborations on Eurostat database

Note: Industry, construction and services (except public administration, defense, compulsory social security) had the fastest and most significant fall of labor costs among V4 countries. In 2014, Hungary had the lowest relative labor costs and Slovakia the highest one.

Real effective exchange rates (REERS) give a good measure of the change in a country's price competitiveness.[29] REERs take into account the change in costs or prices relative to other countries. A rise in the value of REERs, then, indicates a loss of competitiveness due to either higher inflation or higher labor costs or other costs. REERs in different EU countries measured against unit labor costs diverged rather seriously and continuously (Eurostat database). Before the crisis and since 2001, when the euro was already the common currency and ready to start circulating, REERS in both the EU and the Eurozone started to grow after years of descent. After the crisis, internal devaluation policies were successful in helping countries regain competitiveness and depreciate their real effective exchange rates, particularly for the vulnerable countries that lived through the most severe crisis. However, the situation was uneven among countries. This effect can be observed also in the V4 countries, in different ways in different countries (Figure 11.17).

Hungary's REER increased constantly until 2008, particularly starting in 2000, and decreased more than in the EU and other V4 countries since then. In the Czech Republic, the surge was the strongest and continuous since the mid-1990s; the descent started only in 2012. In Poland, the pattern was less well-defined: REER increased until 2001, then decreased significantly through 2004, then increased again until 2008. After the crisis, in 2009 the fall was particularly strong, but then remained unchanged at a level similar to 2005. In Slovakia, the rate appreciated until 2009, strongly from 2006; then, in 2010, it decreased mildly and then remained approximately unchanged at a much higher rate than before the crisis.

It is also interesting to compare REERs calculating different deflators: unit labor costs and consumer price indices (Figure 11.17).[30] In the EU-28, the appreciation of REERs was guided more by labor costs than by consumer prices between 2001 and 2008. Depreciation until 2012 was moved principally by consumer prices, while the following appreciation in 2013 and 2014 was led by labor costs. The pattern was similar in the Czech Republic and Hungary until 2004, the year of EU membership. In this period, appreciation was caused primarily by labor costs. Then in both countries (in 2007 in Hungary, 2008 in the Czech Republic), depreciation was led again by labor costs. In both countries, then, it was labor costs that determined the economy's competitiveness, which is in line with the situation of countries hosting an important component of foreign enterprises.

In countries that entered a regional integration and opened up significantly their economies to the world market, prices are under the strong effect of international competition, while labor costs reflect much more local circumstances, in particular institutions and technology. In Hungary, the devaluation in the post-crisis period was particularly significant. Conversely, in both Poland and Slovakia, it was consumer prices which had led appreciation before the crisis, although after 2004 both deflators moved roughly in synchrony in both countries. After the crisis, depreciation was caused mainly by labor costs.

Overall, during the crisis period, Hungary was particularly determined and successful in depreciating its REER and this it did mainly through decreasing

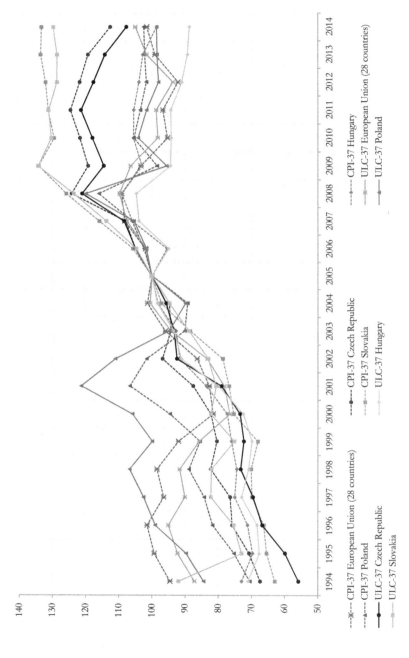

Figure 11.17 Real Effective Exchange Rate, CPI and ULC deflators, 2005 = 100

Source: own elaboration on Eurostat database

Note: Deflator—unit labor costs (ULC) and consumer price indices (CPI) in the total economy, 37 trading partners

--×-- CPI-37 European Union (28 countries)
--▲-- CPI-37 Poland
—●— ULC-37 Czech Republic
ULC-37 Slovakia

--●-- CPI-37 Czech Republic
--■-- CPI-37 Slovakia
ULC-37 Hungary

CPI-37 Hungary
--※-- ULC-37 European Union (28 countries)
ULC-37 Poland

labor costs. Similar, but less prominent, was the performance of Poland. Both countries were able to significantly depreciate their REER compared to the level this reached before the crisis. Slovakia kept the level it had reached in 2008, while in the Czech Republic the REER remained basically unchanged until 2011, but then decreased effectively, led by labor costs.

Institutional reforms and organizational improvements are fundamental for the effectiveness of an economic system and the competitiveness of its economy. Indeed, transformation moved largely around these issues. A further major under-taking in the V4 countries were reforms and changes implemented in the perspective of joining the EU. While these broad systemic changes are fundamental for freeing the creative forces of an economy, also fundamental is fostering and developing entrepreneurial abilities (Baumol 1993) and enterprises' competitiveness.

The Doing Business database and publications of the World Bank provide use-ful hints regarding these elusive issues.[31] The Doing Business project provides a set of different measures of business regulations for local firms in 189 economies and selected cities at the subnational level starting in 2004. Although the methodology was modified through time, this time span allows for a degree of intertemporal comparison of reforms and changes and their effects. The fundamental considera-tion of the project is that the quality of business regulation and the institutions that enforce it are a major determinant of an economy's development. Within this, the project focuses in particular on the regulations and institutions affecting small- and medium-size domestic registered firms, since these constitute the bulk of firms and employment in nearly all countries.

The Doing Business database aims to highlight and measure the influence of different kinds of regulations on opening and running local small- and medium-sized businesses. The database measures and trails changes in regulations in eleven areas in the life cycle of a business.[32] An important advantage of a stand-ardized approach is to make data comparable across countries. However, there are also important limitations, such as the disregard of important issues (e.g. an econ-omy's proximity to large markets or the quality of its infrastructure services) and the subjective nature of the expert assessment upon which results are obtained. Other limits derive from the nature of what is measured: the project is based on the concept of a representative small- and medium-size business, generally a local limited liability company operating in the largest business city. While this is fair in Hungary and tolerable in Slovakia and the Czech Republic—countries in which the capital city hosts an outstanding share of business activity[33]—the method is more problematic in Poland, a country with much more territorial dispersion of business activity.

Doing Business measurement provides an interesting complement to the find-ings presented above and adds some evidence on the multifaceted situation of different countries (Figure 11.18). First, it is confirmed that the V4 countries were overall rather successful in their institutional and organizational development. Their average general score, i.e. the "ease of doing business" rank, would place the V4 in forty-second place in the overall ranking. This is on a par with Belgium and a better ranking than Italy and Luxembourg. Second, the best-ranked V4 country,

Poland, is next to France and better than Spain. The worst-ranked, Hungary, is better placed than Italy. Second, the aggregate outcome is the result of great disparity of the rankings in the different indicators. The indicator in which the V4 countries excel both on average and also individually is getting credit. Quite good is also the average ranking in the case of registering property and resolving insolvency, while in the case of enforcing contracts, the countries are only slightly better placed than their overall average of doing business. The worst results are in dealing with construction permits, getting electricity and paying taxes.

Important complementary information comes from the "distance-to-frontier" score, a score that is calculated for each indicator in the Doing Business database (Figure 11.19). This score helps to assess the absolute level of regulatory performance and how it evolves over time. The score is built along a scale from 0 to 100, where 0 represents the lowest performance and 100 the highest, i.e. the frontier. The absolute value of the score shows the gap between a particular economy's performance and the best performer (typically Singapore) at any point in time. The change of the score over time evaluates the absolute change in the economy's regulatory environment.

In the years following the crisis, for which Doing Business scores are available for all the countries, all the V4 countries have improved their distance-to-frontier score both in absolute terms and compared to the average score of the EU (excluding the V4 countries). Poland implemented the greatest improvement: starting from last place in 2009, with a distance of more than 10 points to the EU average, Poland reached the first place among the V4 with less than 1 point difference to the EU average. The next positive performance is the Czech Republic's, which gained 6.5 points. Hungary and Slovakia improved their distance from the EU average respectively by 1.5 and 1 point. It should be noticed that in this period, the average score of the EU improved by nearly 2 points. Even greater was the improvement of Ukraine and Russia, which improved their score relative to the EU average respectively by more than 19 points and nearly 10 points over the period.

The data confirm a general process of convergence of V4 countries to the EU average also in institutional and organizational issues. Data also confirm that the most effective performer was Poland, followed by Slovakia. However, Slovakia is a country which lost momentum. Conversely, the Czech Republic accelerated convergence, although starting from a lower level, while Hungary continued its uneasy path.

The main reason behind the dissimilar effectiveness of convergence to the frontier are reforms and restructuring activity. An important achievement for establishing an enterprise was the general implementation in all V4 countries of the one-stop shop, the system by which prospective businesspeople can implement all the files and procedures they need to establish their business at one office.[34] This was implemented in Slovakia in 2009 (which further improved the registration system in 2015), in the Czech Republic in 2009, in Hungary in 2010 (online registration, with registration confirmed one hour after application), and in Poland in 2010. Various other enhancements and some deterioration took place. Among

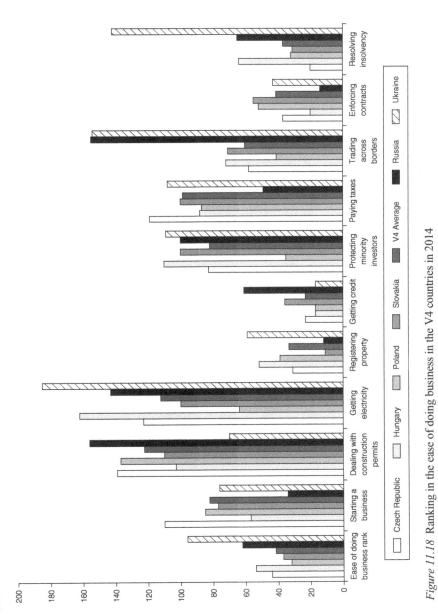

Figure 11.18 Ranking in the ease of doing business in the V4 countries in 2014

Source: World Bank, Doing Business database, 2015

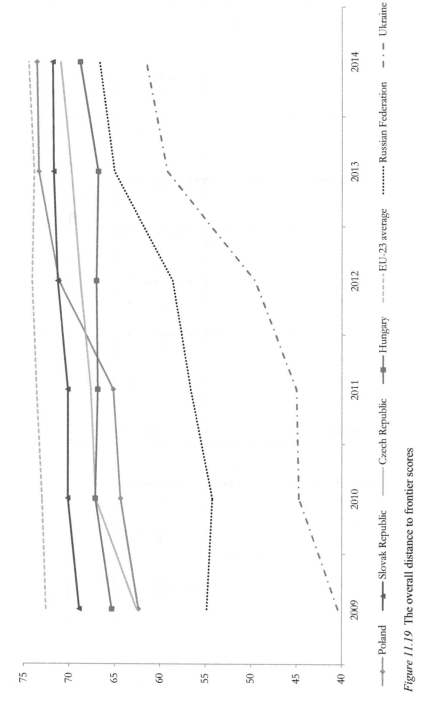

Figure 11.19 The overall distance to frontier scores

Source: World Bank, Doing Business database, 2015

Note: Malta is not considered in the EU average, since the database is incomplete for the entire period

the most important ones countries made starting a business easier by reducing the minimum capital requirement: Hungary in 2009 (though in 2015, Hungary increased the paid-in minimum capital requirement), Poland in 2010, the Czech Republic in 2015.[35] Improvements were often faster and more effective than in most other EU member countries and this gave the V4 countries a competitive advantage that was useful in both improving the situation of their enterprises and attracting foreign investors.

Notes

1 "We should not forget that the stakes for our monetary union are high. It is not unusual to have regional disparities in unemployment within countries, but the euro area is not a formal political union and hence does not have permanent mechanisms to share risk, namely through fiscal transfers. [Cross-country transfers between euro area countries exist as part of the EU cohesion policy. These funds are however in principle temporary, as they designed to support the "catching-up" process in lower income countries.] Cross-country migration flows are relatively small and are unlikely to ever become a key driver of labour market adjustment after large shocks. Thus, the long-term cohesion of the euro area depends on each country in the union achieving a sustainably high level of employment. And given the very high costs if the cohesion of the union is threatened, all countries should have an interest in achieving this" (Draghi 2014).

2 The United Nations Committee for Development Policy has worked out an Economic Vulnerability Index (EVI) which includes seven indicators. These are grouped into factors of exposure (population size, remoteness from markets, export concentration, share of agriculture, forestry and fisheries in GDP) and factors determining the size and likelihood of shocks (share of homeless population due to natural disasters, instability of exports of goods and services, instability of agricultural production). EVI has been used since 2000 as one of the criteria utilized, in addition to GDP per capita and the human capital (measured by the Human Asset Index), in order to identify Least Developed Countries (LDC) (Guillaumont 2011, see also http://www.un.org/en/development/desa/policy/cdp/ldc/ldc_criteria.shtml).

3 There is a fundamental and significant difference here between a country which is part of a monetary union—such as Slovakia—and a country which is part of a less strict organization—such as the other three V4 countries. The former lost a large part of its policy sovereignty (directly in the case of monetary policy, indirectly in the case of fiscal policy) in exchange for the advantages of the common currency (Marer 2015). The effects of such an institutional setting over its vulnerability depend upon the structural situation of the national economy and on the working of the monetary union.

4 The age-dependency ratio is the ratio of people younger than 15 or older than 64 (dependents) to the working-age population (those of age 15–64, who are typically in the labor force).

5 This was true particularly since the start of the century. According to World Bank data (World Development Indicators), the age-dependency ratio in the United States remained fairly stable, while it kept growing fast in Western Europe. The ratio was 52.5 percent in the United States in 1995 and 48.5 percent in the Eurozone. The ratio kept rising in the Eurozone, at an accelerating pace, and reached 52.5 percent by 2013. In the United States, the ratio decreased constantly to 48.7 percent in 2007, after which year it increased to 50.4 percent by 2013 (http://data.worldbank.org/indicator/SP.POP.DPND/countries?display=default).

6 According to Bologna et al. (2014), the leverage ratio in a sample of European banks decreased from its peak in December 2008 from 50.5 percent to 26.1 percent (ratio of total assets on the bank's balance sheet to common equity). In the ten largest US banks

the fall was larger, from 32.8 percent to 14.1 percent. European banks in the sample include the 43 largest banks of the 64 banks involved in the transparency exercise carried out by the European Banking Authority (EBA) in December 2013. The banks in the sample account for 94 percent of the total assets of the original EBA sample and for about 79 percent of the banking systems' assets in their own countries.

7 The discount rate in the United States was 1.25 percent from November 2002, but was increased to 6.25 percent in August 2007. Interest rates on federal funds grew from 1 percent from June 2004 to 5.25 percent in September 2007.

8 Cross-border financial flows increased from 4 percent of GDP to 21 percent of GDP between 1980 and 2007, from US$470 billion to US$12 trillion (Manyika et al. 2014). This growth was faster than any other kind of flows. By 2012, financial flows had collapsed to 5 percent of GDP, or US$3.9 trillion. The fall of cross-border lending was from US$5.8 trillion in 2007 to US$235 billion in 2012, a bare 4 percent of the pre-crisis level.

9 Income inequality in the United States rose sharply before and during the crisis, but consumption inequality fell below its 2000 level by 2009 and remained lower afterwards (Meyer and Sullivan 2013).

10 Various estimates exist of the cost of the crisis in the United States. A Federal Reserve study estimates direct costs at between US$6 trillion and US$14 trillion (Atkinson et al. 2013). This corresponds to US$50,000–120,000 for every US household and to 40–90 percent of one year's output. By adding to these costs the effects of lost consumption, national trauma, and other negative consequences, more than one year's output was probably lost. The US Government Accountability Office estimates the overall cost at more than US$22 trillion (GAO 2013).

11 The 1990s were a successful time for the European Union, which was only mildly influenced by external crises. The EU was the origin of only one unconventional financial and monetary crisis, the crisis of the European Exchange Rate Mechanism (ERM) in 1992–93. The crisis originated in the rapidly growing interest rates in Germany, following that country's unification, that led Italy (temporarily) and the UK (permanently) to leave the system. In spite of its seriousness, the crisis remained isolated and the European monetary system recovered rather quickly.

12 Slovakia joined the euro in 2009, but was under the common monetary discipline for years in advance.

13 The European System of Central Banks (ESCB) includes the European Central Bank (ECB) and the national central banks (NCBs) of all 28 member countries of the European Union, independently of the currency they adopt. The Eurosystem comprises the ECB and the NCBs of the Eurozone countries, i.e. the member countries that adopt the common currency.

14 The Convergence Reports examine whether the member countries satisfy the conditions foreseen for adopting the euro. Since all member countries, except the UK and Denmark, must in principle adopt the euro, the Reports are prepared also for the countries which keep provisionally their national currencies.

15 Being defined in structural terms, budget deficit (or surplus) targets take into consideration the effect of business cycle on output and filter out the effects of one-off and other temporary measures.

16 Nominal effective exchange rates (NEERs), which are used in this description and in Figure 11.9, measure changes in the value of a currency against a trade-weighted basket of currencies. A rise in the index means a strengthening of the currency. The NEER of a country or currency area, which is also determined as "trade-weighted currency index," aims at tracking changes in the value of that currency relative to the currencies of its principal trading partners. It is calculated as a weighted geometric average of the bilateral exchange rates against the currencies of competing countries. In the Eurozone, the NEERs of individual member countries differ slightly because of the different composition of the principal trading partners.

17 Aiyar et al. (2013) show that the V4 trade links with Germany grew much faster than in other European countries and strengthened considerably since the mid-1990s, largely reflecting the V4's increased integration into the supply chains. However, Poland's trade with Germany grew more slowly than in the case of the other three countries. Also the share of German value added embodied in the V4 countries' exports expanded much more rapidly than in the case of other countries, thanks to large-unit labor-cost differentials and adequate labor skills to support supply chain activities, geographic proximity, cultural similarities, and an analogous sectoral structure. Rahman and Zhao (2013) compute an "industrial similarity index" relative to Germany, and show that the V4 countries had strong similarities with Germany even before they integrated into value chains with Germany.

18 The parameter used within the EU is long-term interest rates, used as a convergence criterion for the European Monetary Union, based on the Maastricht Treaty. These are interest rates for long-term government bonds denominated in national currencies. Data are based on central government bond yields on the secondary market, gross of tax, with a residual maturity of around ten years.

19 Germany has the largest public debt—general government consolidated gross debt— within the European Union at €2,170 billion in 2014, since 2009 higher than Italy's €2,135 billion. As shares of national GDP however, Italy's debt remained substantially higher at 132.1 percent of GDP compared to 74.7 percent of GDP in Germany (Eurostat database).

20 In the Czech Republic, the average spread was 0.7 percent in the entire period 2001–14. It was 0.4 percent in the years before the crisis (2001–08) and moved to 1.0 percent in the years of the crisis (2009–14). Correspondent data for Slovakia were 1.4 percent, 1.1 percent and 1.7 percent; for Poland were 2.7 percent, 2.5 percent and 2.9 percent. Finally, for Hungary were 4.0 percent, 3.2 percent and 5.0 percent.

21 According to Mihályi (2013, p. 131), household debt remained stable at around 3,000 billion forints, or 30 percent of all household debt, between the beginning of 2005 and the end of 2011. Conversely, debt in foreign currencies jumped to around 6,000 billion forints or close to 70 percent. In 2012, these proportions changed slightly from debt in foreign currencies to debt in forints.

22 Other measures of inequality, such as income quintile share ratio, give a similar picture. All data are from Eurostat.

23 This conclusion depends upon the level of taxation and social contributions on labor incomes. According to the Eurostat database, the share of employers' social contributions and other labor costs paid by employers in the V4 is rather high, except in Poland (data refer to the structure of labor costs in the business economy, in enterprises with ten employees or more). This is so, compared to both Western European member countries and to the other CEECs. Poland is in both cases close to the average. However, it should be considered that labor costs are much lower than in Western European countries on an absolute level, so that a relatively higher share corresponds to a much lower cost.

24 The OECD calculates the participation index to global value chains in OECD countries (OECD 2012; see also De Backer and Miroudot 2013, 2014). The participation index at the country level indicates the share of foreign inputs and domestically produced inputs used in third countries' exports. In 2008, foreign inputs and domestically produced inputs used in third countries' exports, as a share of gross exports, in the V4 countries was among the highest: Slovakia was third among OECD countries after Luxembourg and Korea with 64 percent, followed by Norway and Hungary with 63 percent. The Czech Republic was seventh with 62 percent. Only Poland, a larger economy, was in the middle of OECD countries, with 53 percent. These effects are particularly significant in the automotive industry, but are important also in the electronics industry. In the motor vehicles' industry, also Poland—together with Slovakia, Hungary and the Czech Republic, all countries with important car-assembly activities—have large participation indexes. The three smaller countries (Slovakia, Hungary and the Czech Republic)

also have high indexes measuring the distance to final demand, meaning that they have companies that are on average located at the higher levels in the supplier networks of automotive industry. That is, the intermediate goods that they produce are exported to other countries and included there in more downstream production activities. These intermediate goods are only shipped to a limited number of nearby countries, in particular to Germany.

25 According to Eurostat, a foreign-controlled enterprise is an enterprise resident in the compiling country which is controlled by an institutional unit not resident in the compiling country. Control means that the controller has direct or indirect command over more than half of the shareholders' voting power or more than half of the shares of the controlled enterprises and thus has the ability to determine the general policy of an enterprise and choose appropriate directors.

26 The source of date is Eurostat database.

27 It is difficult to define precisely a composite concept like competitiveness (Durand and Giorno 1987). Competitiveness is generally used in a comparative sense to define and analyze the general performance of an economy, with particular concern for international trade. Competitiveness depends upon various factors. Price competitiveness depends upon the relation between domestic prices and international prices, which can be modified through the exchange rate. However, competitiveness also depends upon non-price factors, mainly qualitative factors. Among these, particularly important are technical innovation, the quality of the products in which the country is specialized and other aspects linked to quality, such as customer care and after-sale services, payment terms and conditions, the reputation of the producer and the country. Higher quality of the exported products improves the terms of trade of a country and thus strengthens its international position. Competitiveness is also directly linked to productivity levels and their improvement. Improving productivity decreases the cost of products and, in a competitive environment, their price, which usually boosts exports. Many of the above factors are difficult to measure. For this reason, competitiveness is often measured by comparing levels and changes of international costs or price differentials. These measures of competitiveness are certainly more precise, but unfortunately disregard factors that are fundamental in explaining the overall competitiveness of an economy. This is particularly important in the long run, when qualitative and institutional factors may change significantly and thus influence strongly competitiveness. For these reasons, international comparative analyses take often a broad approach to competitiveness. The World Economic Forum (WEF 2014) defines competitiveness as "the set of institutions, policies, and factors that determine the level of productivity of a country" (p. 4).There is general agreement that innovation is the most strategic factor of competitiveness. Competitiveness has a direct relation to productivity, while productivity has a direct relation to efficiency in its various meanings of allocative, technical and organizational efficiency. Pursuing efficiency means complying with general principles and rules in economic activity, which guarantee the soundness of economic management and consequently ensures that economic activity is profitable and sustainable. However, adaptation and use of local circumstances—such as proper and effective economic use of natural endowments, social capital, human resources—guarantee that production and transaction costs are minimized and incentives are effective. Adaptation and use of local circumstances are particularly important in defining many of the factors, particularly qualitative ones, that are so important for the competitiveness of economies and their international specialization.

28 Eurostat data are in euros. Apart from Slovakia, which adopted the euro in 2009, labor costs data also reflect exchange rates. The Czech koruna appreciated significantly against the euro in the years preceding the crisis, so Czech labor costs in euros were inflated by the appreciation of the national currency. Since the crisis the koruna depreciated by 11 percent, thus contributing to decreasing labor costs. Although the Hungarian forint and the Polish złoty had significant swings during the years before

the crisis, their average exchange rates to the euro remain rather stable. After the crisis, the Polish złoty remained overall stable; conversely, the Hungarian forint depreciated significantly, thus explaining much of the fall in labor costs.

29 The real effective exchange rate is the nominal effective exchange rate, which is a measure of the value of a currency against a weighted average of the currencies of its trade partners, divided by a price deflator or index of costs, such as labor costs.

30 Eurostat publishes various calculations of REERs. The following observations refer to a comparison between REERs deflated by unit labor costs and by consumer price indices in the total economy against the weighted average of the currencies of the 37 most important trade partners.

31 The Doing Business data-collection cycle starts from the submission of 48,000 questionnaires to different stakeholders (including close to 10,000 local private experts), goes through data verification and on-site visits and data analysis and government feedback to data coding. Data are based on expert assessments, considering that experts (e.g. notaries or corporate lawyers registering several firms every year) have cumulative experience of relevant regulations and cases. The annual data-collection process adds each year to an existing stock of information and knowledge and thus is an exercise in updating the existing database.

32 These are: starting a business, dealing with construction permits, getting electricity, registering property, getting credit, protecting minority investors, paying taxes, trading across borders, enforcing contracts, resolving insolvency, and labor market regulation.

33 The share of GDP at current market prices by NUTS 3 regions in the capital cities was 38.1 percent in Budapest, 27.3 percent in Bratislava and 24.7 percent in Prague, but was 12.9 percent in Warsaw (Eurostat database).

34 A similar concept is the single-window system typical of international trade. The United Nations Economic Commission for Europe defines a single window as "a system that allows traders to lodge information with a single body to fulfil all import- or export-related regulatory requirements": UNECE 2003. See also Young Choi 2011.

35 For the Doing Business database on reforms see http://www.doingbusiness.org/reforms.

12 Transformation and crisis in Central Europe

An assessment

There were important differences among the V4 countries in the outcomes of transformation and the crisis. These differences in success witness the role of different starting conditions, the differences deriving from distinct institutional systems, and the governments' different ideologies which contribute to an explanation regarding the different policies that were implemented.[1] More generally, it appears that the countries that were better able to conjugate—by will or by chance—general principles and local circumstances had in general better results than those which followed more ideological paths. Poland and Slovakia were more pragmatic in their policies and reforms and implemented them by taking better notice of local circumstances without giving up the fundamental respect for general rules, in particular regarding the Stability and Growth Pact (SGP). It may well be that this was so because these two countries were disadvantaged by their difficult starting situation, with the odds against their success. Conversely, Hungary and the Czech Republic were considered to be reform leaders, either because they had inherited a deeply reformed economy from the socialist era (Hungary), or because they did not need macroeconomic stabilization, already having a balanced economy and a government determined to proceed with rapid privatization (the Czech Republic).

With their situation apparently so safe and advanced, Hungary and the Czech Republic were not alert to the warnings coming from disregarded local circumstances. For instance, Hungary implemented very harsh bankruptcy and liquidation procedures with its 1991 law, which created serious damages to the economy.[2] However, the Hungarian pendulum tended to swing excessively in the direction of local circumstances. In the Czech privatization process, a medley was created between enterprises and state-owned banks through investment funds, which caused many problems and attracted policy priority in the following years (Fitzsimmons 2002, Kočenda 2003, Pistor and Spicer 1998). The result was that many banks became both lenders and shareholders in newly privatized firms, while the development of investment funds into effective governance actors was hampered by a lack of regulatory oversight and investor protection.

In Poland and Slovakia, a correct and in part, lucky, mixture of stabilization, liberalization and privatization done at the right moment, as well as the more sober attitude of the population, helped to dramatically improve the situation.

The timing of reforms and policies was also more realistic: changes were not implemented in a hurry, but when the economy and the society were ready to accept them. Outcomes were surprisingly positive in both cases, although problems persisted, as the European Commission highlighted in its convergence reports (EC 2014). It is therefore useful to assess how different transformation approaches and EU membership helped or hampered these countries to reach a remarkable resilience or, alternatively, vulnerability to the international crisis and how this changed their situation.

The effect of EU membership

Overall, the effect of EU membership was important and beneficial to the V4 countries under any heading, although it was not an easy undertaking from the perspective of the crisis (Koyama 2015). Income convergence was important, measured both at commercial exchange rates and at the PPP. GDP per capita increased from 49 percent of the EU-15's in 2003 to 65 percent in 2013, when measured in purchasing power standards (Jedlička et al. 2014a). An important part of this progress was due to EU membership: the ERSTE Group's researchers estimated that EU membership increased the annual average growth in V4 countries by about 1 percent from 2004. The Czech Republic, Slovakia and Poland also registered an impressive improvement in the quality-of-life ranking, and the Czech Republic even surpassed Italy and the UK.

The effect of EU membership on foreign trade was even more impressive and was in a win-win perspective (Jedlička et al. 2014a). Since joining the EU in 2004, the V4 countries' exports grew three times faster than exports of the EU-15 (the EU member states before the 2004 enlargement), thus converting the Czech Republic, Hungary and Slovakia into three of the top five open economies in the EU-28. The success of exports was also qualitative; particularly important was the shift of technology-rich exports to Western Europe in the case of the V4 countries (IMF 2011). Progress was impressive in the most prominent export-oriented industry: car manufacturing. Presently the V4 countries, with a population similar to that of France, are the second largest car producer in the EU after Germany, having surpassed in the past decade France, Spain, the UK and Italy. However, it should be noticed that this progress took place primarily thanks to foreign capital, while the domestic sector lagged behind, particularly in Hungary and with the partial exception of Poland. It is also important to stress that such progress in trade went to the advantage of exports from old member states to the V4 countries. These exports increased twice as fast as the total exports of old member countries. EU membership guaranteed also the possibility for people to migrate to more developed and wealthier countries, with beneficial effects for their skills. Particularly important was the possibility to study abroad, which many more students from the V4 countries exploited as compared to the past (Jedlička et al. 2014b).

This spectacular progress is proceeding towards its limits. Prices and capabilities are changing in the V4 countries. There are problems with connectivity and cross-border infrastructure. Capital markets are still small and insufficiently integrated and liquid. The state of investment in R&D, innovation, and the quality of education provide important challenges in the years to come. V4 societies are aging and suffering from demographic decline. As a consequence, labor-force shortages are bound to hurt potential GDP growth, unless the countries are successful in attracting skilled immigrants. In order to avoid this success trap, the V4 countries need to move up the value chain of production (CEPI 2014, Jedlička et al. 2014b).

Successes and incoming problems apart, as members of the EU, the V4 countries must comply with the convergence criteria's requirements. In its latest convergence report, the European Commission took a negative stance to the three countries which had not adopted the euro thus far (EC 2014). The report considers all those factors that should be in place before joining the euro. The conclusion is straightforward for all the three countries: neither the Czech Republic, nor Hungary, nor Poland fulfill the conditions for the adoption of the euro. Although such conclusion is without practical consequences, since none of the three are planning to join the euro soon, nevertheless the Commission's negative judgment stresses the existence of serious institutional and policy problems.

The features and effects of the international economic crisis

The international crisis had differentiated effects in the V4 countries. This group hosts the only EU member country which never had negative growth during the crisis: Poland. The Polish economy was the fastest growing economy in the Union, with an average yearly growth rate of 3.1 percent over the years 2008–13 and of 2.7 percent in the period 2009–13 (Table 12.1). Slovakia was second in the EU over the first period (1.8 percent average yearly growth) and fourth over the second (1.0 percent), due to the −4.9 percent fall of GDP in 2009. The two other countries, the Czech Republic and particularly Hungary, had much worse performances: the Czech Republic ranked respectively eleventh and eighteenth, while Hungary ranked twentieth and twenty-second. Both countries had an average negative growth between 2009 and 2013, not limited to what happened in

Table 12.1 V4 countries' GDP at market prices (percentage change over previous period) and ranking within the EU-28

	2008	2009	2010	2011	2012	2013	Average 2008–2013 Growth	Rank	Average 2009–2013 Growth	Rank
Poland	5.1	1.6	3.9	4.5	2.0	1.6	3.1	1	2.7	1
Slovakia	5.8	−4.9	4.4	3.0	1.8	0.9	1.8	2	1.0	4
Czech Republic	3.1	−4.5	2.5	1.8	−1.0	−0.9	0.2	11	−0.4	18
Hungary	0.9	−6.8	1.1	1.6	−1.7	1.1	−0.6	20	−0.9	22

Source: own elaborations on Eurostat database

2009: the Czech Republic's income fell also in 2012 and 2013. Hungary's GDP had a serious fall (−6.8 percent) in 2009 and 2012, although it increased since 2013. These data expose the existence of a split in the group, between two successful countries in terms of growth, and two other countries which show evident signs of difficulty.

However, when more refined data are used, the V4 countries' performance appears weaker, although not necessarily bad (Table 12.2). One useful indicator is the gap between actual and potential gross domestic product, expressed as a percentage of potential GDP. In this case, Poland was also the best EU performer in the 2009–14 period, with a positive gap of 0.64 percent. The other V4 countries had a negative gap: of −1.6 percent the Czech Republic, −1.9 percent Slovakia and −3.0 percent in Hungary (authors' calculations on Ameco database). Indeed, Hungary was among the worst performers in the EU (ranked 24), with the Czech Republic in the eighth position and Slovakia in tenth. Poland had the best performance among EU-28 countries.

Average scores and ranking are much weaker in the case of productivity indicators (Table 12.3). In the case of GDP per person employed, the best performing V4 country continues to be Poland, but its ranking is just nineteenth in the EU-28 when accounted in commercial euros (seventeenth at the PPS). The rankings of Czech Republic, Slovakia and Hungary are respectively twentieth (twentieth), twenty-fourth (twenty-first) and twenty-sixth (twenty-second). Compared to the pre-crisis period (1995–2008), what is clear is particularly the much better performance of Poland during the crisis. While the Czech Republic and Slovakia

Table 12.2 Different rankings for V4 countries compared to EU-28 average, 2009–14

	Gap between actual and potential GDP at 2010 reference levels (% of potential gross domestic product at constant prices)		GDP at current prices per person employed		GDP at current prices per person employed	
	Average %	*Rank*	*Average* 1000 EUR	*Rank*	*Average* 1000 PPS*	*Rank*
Poland	0.64	1	31.96	19	47.19	17
Czech Republic	−1.64	8	30.91	20	44.42	20
Slovakia	−1.93	10	24.50	24	41.96	21
Hungary	−3.02	24	24.10	26	41.57	22

Source: own elaborations on Ameco database

Note

* Purchasing Power Standards (PPS) are a weighted average of relative price ratios in respect to a homogeneous basket of goods and services, both comparable and representative for each country. PPS are fictive 'currency' units that remove differences in purchasing power, i.e. different price levels between countries

slightly improved their relative standing, Hungary worsened its position when accounted in commercial euros and improved it when accounted in PPS.

The explanation for the relatively weak performance of V4 productivity was that the average number of hours worked annually per person employed was much higher in the V4 countries (in Poland and the Czech Republic) or higher (in Slovakia and Hungary) than in the EU average.[3]

Microeconomic performance was also mixed (Table 12.1), with Poland and Slovakia outperforming the Czech Republic and Hungary, and with good ranking particularly in getting credit and registering property. However, in other cases (in particular, paying taxes and trading across borders, but also protecting minority investors, starting a business and dealing with construction permits), the V4 countries' rank was quite weak on average. Although these countries achieved important improvements, much has to be done to make these economies really fit for international competition.

Performance in inflation was equally mixed, but downward price convergence to the EU average was strong and by 2014 nearly complete (Figure 11.6). In the case of public finances, the situation during the crisis was again mixed (Figure 12.2). While the situation with public debt remained better overall than the EU average (Figure 11.8), public deficits in the Czech Republic were generally better than in the EU and the V4 average. The situation of Hungary was also better, except in 2012. Conversely, the situation of Poland was worse, except in 2012. Generally, Slovakia performed better, except in 2011 and, compared to the V4 average, in 2012.

Also distinct was the situation of external debt within the V4 group of countries (Table 11.13). Hungary had a peculiar and important growth of external debt. The growth had already started in 2008 and was due more to the country's difficult financial situation than the effects of the international crisis. In the other three V4 countries, foreign debt did not register any particular variation during the crisis.

Unemployment, both total and youth unemployment, was also not particularly out of line compared to the EU average (Table 12.3). Two countries, the Czech Republic and Poland, had significantly lower unemployment rates. Slovakia had a significantly higher unemployment rate during the entire period, while Hungary had a higher rate until 2012, but a lower one since then.

Table 12.3 V4 countries' rankings for GDP at current prices per person employed

	1995–2008		2009–14	
	€	PPS	€	PPS
Czech Republic	22	21	20	20
Hungary	23	24	26	22
Slovakia	24	22	24	21
Poland	25	25	19	17

Source: own elaborations on Ameco database

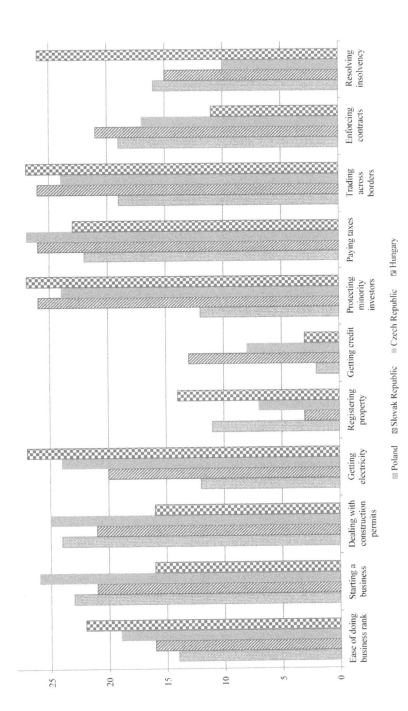

Figure 12.1 The V4 countries' rankings within the EU-28 in the ease of doing business (2015)

Source: World Bank, Doing Business database, 2015

Table 12.4 Intra EU-28 export (in percent of total export)

	2000	2005	2010	2014
European Union (28 countries)		68.0	65.4	63.3
Czech Republic	86.5	86.1	84.3	82.1
Hungary	84.2	82.3	78.4	79.8
Poland	81.4	78.9	79.3	77.1
Slovakia	90.3	87.6	84.7	84.4

Source: Eurostat

From 2008 when the international crisis broke out and onward, individual V4 economies displayed different performances and trends. In a sense, they followed their long-term post-transformation trends, significantly influenced by their financial situation. The most important difference in performance, both before and after the crisis, was the distinction between two economically successful economies, the Polish and Slovak economies, and two less successful and even problematic economies, the Hungarian and Czech economies. Although the distinction was clear along real variables—including growth rates, unemployment, and microeconomic features—it was less so when more detailed indicators are used.

A rather clear difference existed for each country between aggregate and per capita performance. Although the V4 countries improved their economies' efficiency, their performance was strongly dependent upon a more extensive use of labor resources. This also serves to compensate for the relatively low employment rate, with distinctions. First, the Czech Republic had an employment rate constantly higher than the other three countries for the entire period and also higher than the EU average (Figure 11.14). Second, employment rates decreased in the V4 countries in 2009, except in Poland, but from 2011 on, rates increased significantly in all the V4 countries. This was roughly in line with GDP growth, which derived again from extensive sources. Third, the number of worked hours per year slightly decreased, except in the Czech Republic.[4]

Compared to the EU-28 average in the period following the mid-2000s, the V4 countries had constantly better performance of GDP, employment and productivity (Eurostat database). The difference was particularly significant in productivity, both per person employed and per hour worked. The only exception was employment in 2010. Employment in the V4 countries attenuated the effect of GDP fall, thus causing a greater decrease in productivity per person employed. The recovery following in 2010 and 2011 was fueled by the revival of productivity, while employment continued to decrease or stagnate. Conversely, the 2014 expansion was driven by the remarkable increase in employment. Compared to the average of EU-28 and with the exception of 2010, the V4 countries relied more on employment and this, together with the good productivity performance, allowed them to achieve higher GDP growth.

However, the V4 countries were not all the same. In employment, the Czech Republic had a more stable performance in line with EU-28, but typically only slightly better. In the other countries, yearly swings were stronger, but generally

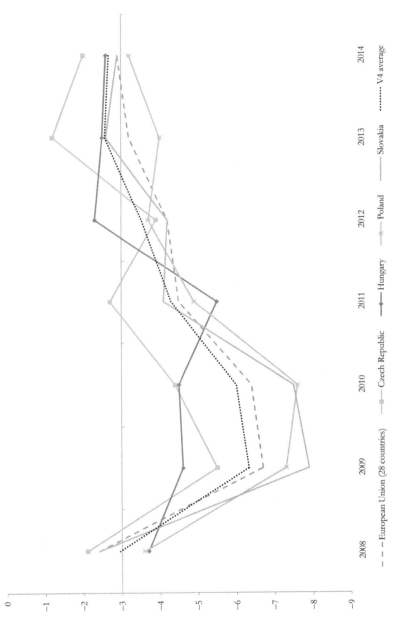

Figure 12.2 Net lending (+) /net borrowing (−) of general government, percentage of GDP

Source: Eurostat

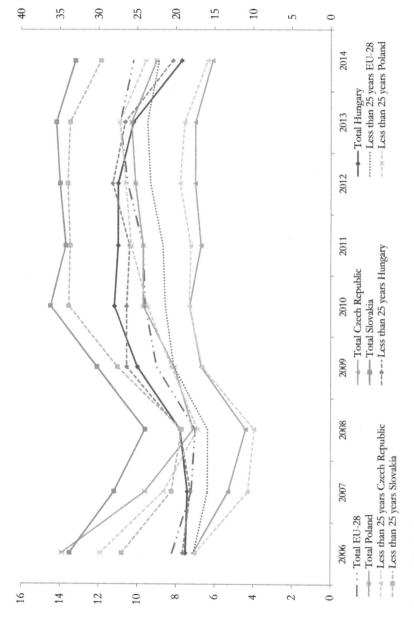

Figure 12.3 Total unemployment rate by age groups, annual average, percent

Source: Eurostat

better than the EU-28 average. Only Hungary until 2009, Slovakia in 2009 and 2010 and Poland in 2010 had worse employment performances than EU-28. In all other years, their performances were much better. Noteworthy was the significant increase of employment in Hungary from 2012.

Intercountry dissimilarities and differences with the EU-28 average were even larger in productivity. In 2009, all V4 countries had worse performances than the EU-28 in both real labor productivity per person employed and per worked hour. In the case of both indicators, Poland and Slovakia performed better than the other two V4 countries in most years. The Czech Republic and Hungary had worse results, except for productivity per hour worked in Hungary from 2012, which was on a par with the best performers.

It can therefore be concluded that Poland and Slovakia owe their superior performance to a certain improvement in productivity, much higher in both cases than the EU average in the post-crisis years. The consequence of ailing productivity in Hungary was that labor costs (nominal unit labor cost) grew much faster than in the other V4 countries and the EU average, particularly since 2012.[5] However, in Hungary more than in other countries, there was a deep dualism between the highly productive sector dominated by foreign investors and the more traditional and less efficient domestic sector.[6] The contribution of the foreign-owned sector to added value in Hungary was more than twice its contribution to employment, compared to approximately 1.6 times in the Czech Republic, 1.5 times in Slovakia and 1.4 times in Poland (authors' calculations based on Eurostat database; see also Table 11.2). Indirectly, these data confirm that the domestic economy in Poland was more productive than in other countries in relation to the foreign-owned sector, followed by Slovakia and that this dualism was most pronounced in Hungary. It should be remembered, though, that in absolute value total labor costs were much lower in the V4 countries than in the EU average (Figure 11.16).

Labor costs are an important determinant of prices and the competitiveness of an economy. Together with nominal exchange rates (Figure 11.9), they determine real effective exchange rates (REERs) (Figures 11.18 and 11.19), the main indicator of price competitiveness. Obviously, this only partly concerned Slovakia, since this country adopted the euro in 2009, the year when the crisis began, and thus suffered for the euro's strength, particularly through the end of 2012. Among the three countries which kept their national currencies, the Czech Republic had the strongest appreciation right before the crisis. In Poland, the nominal effective exchange rate (NEER) depreciated in 2009 to the 2005 level and remained unchanged thereafter. In Hungary, the exchange rate depreciated through the entire period of the crisis. The real effective exchange rate, deflated with unit labor costs, brought little change compared to the nominal rate.

The financial situation

Along with the effects on real economies, the international crisis had significant financial consequences. Overall, the V4 countries appeared to be financially solid during the crisis, with the exception of Hungary.

Hungary was not the only country in Central-Eastern Europe that had its own structural and financial weaknesses as it entered into deep crisis in 2008. The Baltic countries, which at that time still held their national currencies and enjoyed high growth rates between 2004 and 2007, had nevertheless accumulated tensions in the economy (Kattel and Raudla 2013, Mačys 2012). These included double-digit inflation, housing bubbles, real exchange rate appreciation, rapid wage increases, fast-growing net foreign liabilities, and mounting current account deficits. These domestic financial and real bubbles burst in early 2008, following the credit supply slow-down and the tightening of credit conditions. Negative real effects soon followed: domestic private and public demand fell and exports shrank. A dramatic contraction of GDP followed in 2009: by 14.3 percent in Estonia, 14.8 percent in Lithuania and 17.7 percent in Latvia. Unemployment around 18 percent was the highest in the EU at that time.

However, Hungary was the first among the former transformation countries that the crisis hit heavily. Hungary had followed expansive fiscal policies, which caused high budget deficits for five consecutive years, between 6.4 percent of GDP in 2004 and 9.4 percent in 2006 (Figure 11.7). The country also accumulated large gross foreign debt, which had been rapidly growing since 2002 and which in 2008 was above 114 percent of GDP (Figure 11.13). General government-consolidated gross debt was at its minimum in 2001 at 52 percent of GDP, but increased to 72 percent by 2008 (Figure 11.8). Domestic and external imbalances turned Hungary into one of the most financially vulnerable countries in Europe (EEAG 2012, Valentinyi 2012). The seriousness of the crisis obliged Hungary to turn to an IMF-administrated international bail-out, the first EU country to do so. The IMF guaranteed a support package of US$25.5 billion in 2008, with the contribution of the EU and the World Bank.

Under the negative effects of the crisis, the V4 countries adopted quite severe legal frameworks for managing the public debt, in the form of constitutional ceilings (Addo Awadzi 2015). Hungary did so before the Fiscal Compact was adopted at EU level in 2013.[7] In both Hungary and Poland, the debt ceiling was established under each country's Constitution,[8] thus giving it a permanent character and a nature superior to law. The price for this was to give rigidity to economic policies that could be disadvantageous in times of crisis. In Slovakia, the ceiling was adopted as part of a law.[9] The Czech Republic was consistently prudent in placing the public budget under rigid rules, considering the country's enviable record in fiscal discipline. In early 2015, the Czech government approved a constitutional amendment setting the debt ceiling at 55 percent of GDP, lower than outlined in the EU's SGP. It was also foreseen that measures to slow down the debt growth would be taken when the debt goes beyond 45 percent of GDP.

One of the potentially devastating risks for the V4 countries was that they hosted a large number of foreign-owned banks, which controlled an important portion of credit. However, lending by foreign banks included a relatively high share of domestic savings and interaction with local banks, which made their activity in the V4 countries relatively stable and their strategy a long-term one (Aiyar et al. 2013, Epstein 2013, 2014, OECD 2012). In Hungary, the share of cross-border bank flows was much larger than in other countries. Moreover, Hungary hosted a particularly important amount of FDIs, which proved to give greater resilience to the economy. In fact, FDIs financed production and thus followed a longer-term strategy. They proved to be stable during the crisis and had a stabilizing effect on the economy, whereas portfolio inflows in the pre-crisis period had created a consumption bubble. A problem with FDIs in production, though, came from the relatively small size of three of the V4 economies, compared to some of the investing companies. This exposed those countries to the risk of importing external shocks through FDIs, against which flexible exchange rates offered only a limited protection.

The present situation and perspectives

The Czech Republic had strong economic fundamentals, in particular a balanced financial situation and external position, a credible monetary and exchange rate policy and a healthy bank sector. This was important to withstand the crisis, but not to foster economic growth. The Czech government implemented fiscal consolidation in 2011 in order to foster recovery after the crisis (Sobják 2013). The measures were concentrated in public expenditure and consisted of public-sector wage cuts and elimination or reduction of social benefits. In 2012, after a long debate, health care and the pension system were reformed. On the revenue side, the tax system was reformed, and tax exceptions and allowances were eliminated. These austerity measures had a negative effect on domestic demand (both government and household demand) and consequently on the economy. By 2011, austerity had slowed down the recovery started in 2010 and led the economy into recession in 2012 and 2013 (Figure 11.1). Ailing exports, due primarily to the crisis in Europe, added to the recession, which ended only in 2014, when domestic demand and strong exports supported the economy.[10]

Because of these overall unsatisfactory developments, the Czech Republic was under the corrective arm of the Stability and Growth Pact. According to this, the country should preserve a sound fiscal position in line with the medium-term objective of its convergence program (EC 2015a). According to the European Commission (EC 2015b), the Czech Republic complied with some of the Commission's recommendations, including increasing growth-enhancing investment, improving tax compliance, and strengthening the fiscal framework. However, the country is criticized for being late with other reforms, including reducing taxation on labor, reforming the pension and health care systems and reinforcing the fight against corruption.

The Hungarian economy was the first one among the V4 to meet very serious difficulties as early as 2006, well before the international crisis, and entered stagnation in 2007. The country also needed an IMF-led bailout in 2008, the only country in the group to do so. In spite of this support, Hungary witnessed the worst recession in the V4 in 2009. The following recovery was the most anemic in the group. Consolidation policy implemented in 2011 notwithstanding, the country went back to recession in late 2011 and 2012. The three major rating agencies cut Hungary's credit rating to junk level. The government started negotiations with the IMF for a financial rescue package, but suspended negotiations one year later. The financial situation of Hungary is the weakest in the V4. With a public debt of around 80 percent of GDP since 2009 and a public deficit well above 3 percent, the country was under an excessive deficit procedure since 2004 and until 2013. The financial situation improved afterwards.

This situation constrained policy freedom. The center-right government established in 2010 started to make use of "unorthodox" policies to manage the crisis.[11] These included the nationalization of private pension funds and a significant reduction of public and private debt, particularly private debt incurred in foreign currencies, to the disadvantage of banks (see Chapter 11) in order to stabilize finances. Major reforms on the revenue side were the implementation of a flat personal income tax of 16 percent, a banking tax, and temporary sectoral levies on financial transactions and other items. VAT was increased to 27 percent from 25 percent, the highest in the EU. The government also re-nationalized companies and the private pension pillar, a move that reversed the 1998 reform.[12] The revenue from these companies was used to consolidate public finances.

Reforms were also implemented to improve the efficiency of the public administration and of the loss-making public transportation companies. The country entered into serious political conflict with the EU over different issues, including the independence of the Hungarian Central Bank, and over policies also with the IMF. The Hungarian government was surprisingly successful in resisting the EU's and IMF's pressures and continued with its unorthodox policies.[13]

The spectacular success of exports, and the country's ability to absorb significant amounts of EU funds and stabilization policies had the effect of improving growth. While until 2012 Hungary was the worst performer of the V4 in growth, the situation started to change in 2013. In 2014, the growth rate of real GDP was 3.6 percent, led by domestic demand (IMF 2015a) and the massive inflow of EU funds. Although growth is foreseen to slow down in the coming years, nevertheless unemployment decreased significantly, inflation declined to around zero, investments increased and public deficit has remained well below 3 percent since 2012. The European Commission considered this revival of the Hungarian economy to be fragile, criticized some features—in particular the continuing external imbalances—in spite of recent progress, and the high public debt (EC 2015b, 2015c, 2015d). The Commission also stressed the need to improve on various aspects and to take decisive policy action and monitoring. Additional problems that require monitoring and intervention include the high regulatory burden on the financial sector, the high level of non-performing loans making deleveraging difficult, the flaws in the tax system, the unstable regulatory framework and the lack of transparency in decision-making procedures.

Poland provided the most spectacular success in the V4 and the EU to withstand the crisis. Even in 2009, its GDP growth rate was 1.6 percent, while in 2010 and 2011 growth was at 4 percent. However, growth slowed down to below 2 percent in the following two years, but revived in 2014 to 3.4 percent (EC 2015e). There were different reasons for this initial success. Poland entered the crisis with sound financial and banking sectors. Moreover, the złoty was free to float, not being pegged to the euro, and its significant depreciation upheld the competitiveness of exports and the value of EU funds flowing into the country. Poland, due to its larger size that better isolated the economy from external shocks, had a lower degree of openness than the other V4 countries,[14] and was slightly more open to outside the EU (Table 12.4). Depreciation, together with the robust domestic demand allowed the country to survive the worst period of the crisis unscathed.

Under these favorable conditions, policy making could concentrate on an effective program of fixing public finances (Sobják 2013). This was obtained by increasing taxes and reducing tax allowances, postponing retirement age and tightening the eligibility criteria for early retirement and disability pension schemes. Policies also took care of improving the working of markets and the microeconomic structure by solving barriers to entrepreneurship, increasing working-time flexibility and job subsidies. However, growth decelerated in 2012 and 2013, due in part to slowing exports. Foreign debt increased and public deficits remained constantly above 3 percent of GDP from 2008 and was particularly high in 2009 and 2010. However, overall, forecasts remained positive, with continuing robust economic activity led by solid domestic demand, supported by improving labor market conditions and strong investment activity. Public finances also improved gradually.

There remained some less bright spots on the Polish scene, however. Poland was subject to the corrective arm of the Stability and Growth Pact since July 2009. However, the excessive deficit was expected to be corrected by 2015 (EC 2015e). In its review of the Polish situation, the Commission established that the excessive deficit situation in Poland was corrected and requested that the Council abrogate the Excessive Deficit Procedure (EC 2015f).

Other problems remain. According to the European Commission and the IMF (EC 2015g, IMF 2015c), there remains some structural challenges, especially in relation to the efficiency of public spending and tax compliance. Several structural weaknesses also characterize the Polish labor market, such as labor market segmentation and geographic and vocational mobility. Moreover, the country relied so far on low labor costs and disregarded the need to boost its innovative capacity and move up the value-added chain. Other problems include bottlenecks and deficiencies in transport, energy and information and communications networks, a burdensome and complex fiscal system, weak coordination among different government levels, and an inadequate capacity of regional and local governments to implement and monitor policies. Moreover, the IMF (2014a) recalled the critical role that the rise in geopolitical tensions in neighboring countries can have for the country and its economy.

Slovak GDP expanded at rates above 4 percent per year since 2004, after having reached a growth rate of 10.5 percent in 2007 and nearly 6 percent in 2008. GDP fell by 4.9 percent in 2009, but recovered at 4.4 percent in 2010, after which performance decelerated, but remained second only to Poland. One advantage of Slovakia before the crisis was its stable financial sector and balanced public finances. Being the smallest V4 economy as well as an open economy, Slovakia suffered significantly from the fall of foreign demand caused by the crisis in 2009. This was an important reason for the fall of GDP and the growth in unemployment in that year. Another important reason for the 2009 recession was the euro, which Slovakia had adopted in the same year. Although the common currency improved monetary stability, the country suffered from a strong currency, which depressed competitiveness, while its V4 neighbors had 20–25 percent depreciation. One problem with the euro was the cost that the financial crises in some of the member countries imposed upon the other countries, which had to participate in financing the rescue funds. In particular, the risk that Greece posed to the Eurozone finances was a cause of fragility for Slovakia.

Two factors were the engine for recovery as soon as 2010: strong labor productivity growth, especially in manufacturing, and wage moderation in 2009 and the following years. The country's economic and financial bases were strong and balanced, thanks to the structural reforms implemented in the early 2000s, including the reforms to the fiscal system, pensions, the labor market and health care. Fiscal policies became strongly expansionary in 2009 and 2010, when yearly public deficits moved close to 8 percent, thus causing a significant growth of public debt as a percentage of GDP: from 28.2 percent in 2008, to 52.1 percent in 2012 and to 54.6 percent in 2013 (Figures 11.7 and 11.8). A number of reforms were implemented to stabilize the situation, including changes to the second pillar of the pension system and the revision of the labor code.

Fiscal consolidation implemented after the crisis consisted mainly of tax increases on labor, companies and banks. These measures increased unemployment and slowed down growth, which by 2012 was 1.8 percent and was driven almost entirely by the expansion of the export-oriented automotive industry. Growth in 2013 was 1.4 percent. Domestic demand continued to be weak, reflecting the persistently high rate of unemployment until 2013. At the same time, the growth of foreign demand also weakened. A mild recovery to 2.4 percent followed in 2014, driven by domestic demand supported by a decrease in unemployment. On the plus side, fiscal consolidation decreased budget deficits below 3 percent since 2013. Wages increased from 2012 and inflation continued to be low, and in 2014, it turned slightly negative.

The European Commission and the IMF (EC 2015h, IMF 2014b, 2015d) considers the situation of Slovakia rather sound, but with many unsolved problems. The Commission recommends that the country pursues growth along three main economic and social policy pillars in 2015: investment, structural reforms, and fiscal responsibility. Although the long-term prospects of public finances improved, there remained inefficiencies in tax collection and tax administration, while according to the Commission the health care sector continues to be a drag on the long-term sustainability of the public budget. In the labor market, despite some recovery, unemployment remains high, and long-term unemployment persists as a major challenge. Investments are low and their performance poor, as is reflected in the relatively low quality of infrastructure, particularly in Slovakia's central and eastern regions. Public administration and the justice system are still inefficient and tax collection and administration retain various inefficiencies. Competitiveness is restrained by lack of improvements in the ease of doing business.

A comparative assessment

After the crisis, the V4 countries appear to have recovered from the deep problems that emerged most intensively in 2009. Three countries applied a different mix of standard reforms, which improved their financial equilibrium, but this came to the disadvantage of growth. Due to austerity policies, the Czech Republic went into recession in 2012 and 2013 and was placed under the corrective arm of the Stability and Growth Pact until 2014. Poland continued its good performance and left the corrective arm in 2015, with some structural problems. The country continued to depend excessively upon cheap labor and failed so far to upgrade in the value chain. Slovakia had a good recovery in 2010. However, fiscal consolidation implemented after the crisis slowed recovery and contributed to growing unemployment. After the crisis, when exports were the leading sector, demand became the main engine of growth.

The fourth country, Hungary, entered into an extremely difficult economic and financial situation well before the crisis. Its unorthodox policies, used since 2010, led to a fair revival of the economy and to decreasing imbalances by 2014, after years of difficulties. However, public debt remained high and the sustainability of the policies and the economic revival are dubious.

In a sense, after more than a quarter-century since the start of transformation, the V4 region is unified, yet is internally diversified and even split. One fundamental feature that draws attention is that the two countries that were initially considered to be in the best situation—Hungary in particular, but also the Czech Republic—turned out to go through rather disappointing events and obtained weaker results. The two countries which initially appeared to be more problematic, Poland and Slovakia, were positive surprises.

The crisis, which reached its deepest point in 2009, confirmed this pattern. Poland was the only EU country to keep positive growth rates through the crisis and Slovakia, in spite of the deep fall in 2009, was the first to recover. It is therefore increasingly difficult to consider the region as a homogeneous area. In 2009, a further change happened: Slovakia adopted the euro, which further differentiated the area. This is a major and probably long-term difference, since the other three countries apparently do not intend to adopt the common currency in the foreseeable future. The present deep difficulties of the Eurozone make that event unlikely for years to come. If the Eurozone is able, after the Greek crisis, to recover and avoid other major crises—an event that presently cannot be excluded—the Eurozone may become better and more deeply integrated. If so, the destiny of Slovakia may be increasingly attracted by other Eurozone countries and the country will be hardly considered as part of the V4 anymore if such future materializes.

A similar divisive effect can come from the already significant differences in the level and features of institutional and structural reforms and consolidation that

were introduced during the last years. Policies and political regimes are also factors that can push countries apart. It is true that the region keeps important trade
links, but these may not be sufficient to keep the countries strongly linked together.
Moreover, it is to be seen what the effect of the present tensions with Russia will
be, since the region includes a strongly anti-Russian country, Poland, and a country
maintaining strong economic and political ties with Russia, Hungary.

In spite of their differences, the V4 countries managed the crisis relatively
well, better anyway than other EU countries, particularly in Southern Europe.
Convergence of living standards proceeded and the countries became significant
world players in trade and industrial production. In spite of sacrifices and costs in
terms of unemployment, they were able to regain control over their finances, while
managing to keep enviably low levels of inequality. In spite of periodic turbulence
in the relations with the EU, particularly by Hungary and Poland in the present and
Slovakia in the past, and with role differences due to the countries' varying sizes
and the determination of governments, these countries appear to be well placed
and active participants in the Union. Their future will be played out in this context.

Thus the region seemed to have moved uncomfortably between the respect
for general principles of good economic management and adaptation to local circumstances. The most difficult moments and conflicts were in Slovakia in the
1990s, in Hungary in the 2010s and in Poland in 2016. Uneasy moments could
also be found in the Czech Republic, in particular under Václav Klaus. These
were moments of the pre-eminence of local circumstances in conflict with the
general principles represented by the European Union. The latter tried, sometimes
in a bureaucratic and rigid way, to lead the member countries along the good
general principles considered to be at the basis of the Union's treaties, pacts, rules
and policies.

The Union's approach was debated and sometimes opposed on two grounds:
because those rules and policies were considered to be wrong, being based on the
idea of austerity and discipline equal for every country, largely independent from
the country's particular features and situation. Moreover, the negative effects of
austerity were not compensated for by a nonexistent common government. This
debate was between alternative models and views of sound economic principles.
A different debate, sometimes overlapping with the former, started from local
circumstances and was aimed at giving priority to the latter. The soundness of
economic principles was of little relevance and only the priority of local circumstances—however interpreted—mattered. This approach was particularly strong
in Slovakia in the 1990s, in Hungary mainly in the 2010s and in Poland in 2016.

The real issue at stake, in the European integration and V4 countries more than
anywhere else, is to make the two fundamental principles coexist and complement each other. This will require the ability of the V4 countries, in particular of
Poland, to upgrade their situation in global value chains to compensate growing
costs. It will also require, particularly in Hungary, a stronger integration between
the home sector and the foreign-owned sector. In all the countries, but particularly in the Czech Republic, bolder growth policies are urgently needed to fully
overcome the negative effects of the crisis and austerity policies. In Slovakia,

unemployment is still a serious problem, together with regional disparities, the latter is also an important problem in Hungary and Poland. The ability to solve these problems, while maintaining fundamental financial stability, will determine the economic future of these countries.

Notes

1 According to Rae (2013), the need to win political majorities led a liberal party such as Citizens' Platform (*Platforma Obywatelska*) in Poland to adopt moderate economic policies. Myant et al. (2013) find that there were key policy differences in dealing with the crisis related to public budgets and support for a demand stimulus that descended from the social-democratic or neoliberal nature of the governments.

2 The Hungarian insolvency law was passed in 1991 and included harsh conditions. According to the law, a business was required to declare bankruptcy within eight days of realizing its inability to pay a debt, and within ninety days of the debt becoming due. The law was amended in July 1993, and the harsh conditions removed due to the high number of bankruptcy petitions filed in 1992 (14,000 overall) (Gerlach 1998, Gray et al. 1995, Mitchell 1993).

3 According to the Ameco database, Poland ranks third, the Czech Republic fifth, Slovakia twelfth and Hungary thirteenth among the EU-28 in the number of hours worked on average in the period 2009–14. The number of hours are respectively 2,043, 1,920, 1,783 and 1,782. The EU-15 average in the same period was 1,584. These differences correspond to an "excess" individual working time of 29.0 percent in Poland, 21.2 percent in the Czech Republic, 12.6 percent in Slovakia and 12.5 percent in Hungary over the EU-15 average.

4 The average number of hours actually worked per year per full-time employee in industry, construction and services increased by 14 hours to 1,749 hours in the Czech Republic between 2008 and 2012. The number decreased in each of the three other countries: by 2 in Hungary to 1,780 hours, by 13 in Poland to 1,685 hours and by 10 in Slovakia to 1,705. The corresponding decrease in the EU-28 were 14 hours to 1,736 hours (Eurostat database).

5 In Poland, the growth of nominal unit labor costs was similar to the EU average, with the per hour indicator growing slightly faster than the per person indicator. The growth pace slowed down with the crisis. In the Czech Republic, unit labor costs per person moved as in the EU average, while costs per hour were much slower and stagnated both in 2009 and after 2012. In Slovakia, both costs per person and per hour increased slowly, but both accelerated in 2014. Costs per person increased slightly faster than per hour (as in EU and the Czech Republic). Costs decreased in 2009 after years of fast growth (Eurostat database).

6 Makó and Illéssy (2015) distinguish four clusters of the Hungarian economy: the Hungarian manufacturing sector, personal service providers and business service providers, and the foreign-owned business segment. They use the results of the first nation-wide Employment Relations in the Workplace Survey: 2010, to assess the segmentation of the Hungarian economy. They find that segmentation is reflected in such structural features as ownership, number of employees, market structure and geographical location of the firms, and is the cause of the low level of integration that threatens the country's development perspectives.

7 The Fiscal Compact (Treaty on Stability, Coordination and Governance in the Economic and Monetary Union) is an intergovernmental treaty that rendered the provisions of the Stability and Growth Pact stricter. It was signed by all EU member countries on March 2, 2012, except for the Czech Republic, the United Kingdom and Croatia. The treaty entered into force in the 16 countries which completed ratification on January 1, 2013 and for the remaining 9 in April 2014.

8 Poland was the first to introduce such a provision (public debt/GDP ratio of 60 percent) in its constitution, as early as 2004. The Act of November 26, 1998 on Public Finances had already imposed prudential and remedial procedures when debt exceeded 50 percent of GDP, procedures aimed at preventing the 60 percent limit to be exceeded. In Hungary, a debt ceiling of 50 percent of GDP was introduced in the Constitution in 2011.

9 The Fiscal Responsibility Law of 2012 establishes a debt ceiling of 60 percent of GDP and introduced a set of automatic enforcement mechanisms when the ceiling is close to being breached.

10 The IMF shares the view of the EC and stresses the need to sustain the recovery by means of a "growth-friendly medium-term fiscal strategy," including "structural reforms to encourage investment and enhance productivity; and continued efforts to preserve financial stability and achieve the central bank's inflation target are the top priorities" (IMF 2015b).

11 Behind the controversial policy measures in the Hungarian economy, the real nature of the Orban governments and the dangers that this may cause both domestically and internationally are the subject of a growing domestic and international debate. Ungváry (2014), Sárközy (2012, 2014) and Magyar (2013) represent a good critical spectrum of opinions.

12 According to *Financial Times online* (http://www.ft.com/intl/cms/s/0/0e01c370-06de-11e0-8c29-00144feabdc0.html#axzz3nUf7gvys), the Hungarian government forced the transfer of almost Ft3,000bn (US$14bn) in mandatory private pension savings to the state. A further consequence of the government's decision was a dramatic decrease of the number of members in private pension funds, from more than 3 million in 2010 to a bare 60,000 in September 2011. As a matter of fact the Hungarian case was the harshest, although not the only case of a government seizing pension funds. Other cases include Bulgaria, France, Ireland and Poland.

13 Johnson and Barnes (2015) defines the government stance as Hungary's financial nationalist turn and maintain that the Hungarian government's willingness and ability to use unorthodox, financial nationalist policies to control government deficits and debt both reduced EU and IMF leverage over Hungary and encouraged international bond markets to assume a tolerant behavior.

14 According to the World Bank (World Development Indicators online), exports of goods and services amounted to 90 percent of GDP in Slovakia and Hungary since 2011 and to 80 percent in the Czech Republic. Exports decreased significantly in 2009, particularly in Slovakia, after which they resumed the consistent and significant growth experienced since the start of transformation. In Poland, exports increased at a slower pace as a share of GDP. The corresponding figure for Poland was around 45 percent.

Conclusion
Back to the future?

The Soviet economic system was founded on classical Leninist "socialist" principles (Lenin 1917). Stalin imposed his version of the model on Central-Eastern Europe in the early post-war era. Soviet and Central European Communist Party rulers before 1954 had criminalized private property (nationalization of the means of production), private business (markets) and entrepreneurship. It was illegal for non-state actors to own income-producing assets, engage in for-profit activities, or use nationalized assets on the state's behalf without official authorization, although some marginal private activities were tolerated in various countries. The intention was to substitute the "rule of wise communist men" (socialism at the penultimate stage before the advent of stateless communism) for the "freely competitive rule of men" (capitalist rule).

Communist authorities likewise criminalized rival political parties or obliged them to merge with the Communist Parties because only Communist Parties were deemed loyal and reliable. The Communist Party claimed to rule in accordance with the proletariat's will, asserting that people's democracy was a million times more democratic than bourgeois parliamentary democracy (Lenin 1920). Soviet and Central-Eastern European leaders adhered more or less strictly to these ideological constructs under Stalin's watchful eye, but administrative command planning always coexisted in the Soviet Union and Central-Eastern Europe with managerial incentives, open private/cooperative market activities and a large informal economy. The scope of these parallel self-guided market-stimulating and competitive activities gradually expanded after Stalin's death in March 1953, most visibly in Hungary and Poland. Changes were induced by the evident flaws of the Stalinist political guidance and the negative consequences that an inefficient economic system and deeply unbalanced economic priorities had for the standard of living of those countries' citizens. The ensuing economic, political and social crises offered the opportunity to "national communists," the main political victims of the Stalinist trials that took place at the end of the 1940s in the "popular democracies" of Central-Eastern Europe, to take the lead of the early reforms. The most noticeable cases were Imre Nagy in Hungary in 1953–55, Władisław Gomułka in Poland since 1956 and János Kádár in Hungary from 1957 (Fejtő 1957, 1971).

The hallmark of Soviet and Central European communist economic systems was physical systems management; that is, state planning, command, administration, control, regulation and incentive guided direction carried out on an engineering basis without regard for private demand (consumer sovereignty) and competitive opportunity costs (Rosefielde 2007a). The primary instruments of physical systems management were: state ownership of the means of production; central planning, command production, ministerial enterprise supervision, the state inspectorate, the secret police (in every enterprise), worker committees (state watchdogs), state appointed "red directors" (enterprise managers), one-man-red director rule, stringent labor discipline, material incentives, tight bank control over enterprise plan compliance and expenditures, prohibition of entrepreneurial initiative, planned state investment, state-run science and technology research, state product design, state standards, state price fixing based on the labor theory of value (*sebestoimost'*), state wage setting, state bonus-incentive formation, state wholesaling and retailing, state monopoly of banking and finance, state provision of basic services (child care, elder care, education, medical care, utilities, public transportation, insurance and foreign trade).

There was some room for dancing between the rain drops, but the Communist Party's physical systems management control over production and distribution repressed and stifled most efforts at circumvention. The state authorized or prohibited the production of tens of millions of goods and services, and chose their characteristics. It allocated resources (including labor), and determined the structure of output, distribution and the redistribution of private wealth (personal property). The system was a Procrustean bed without democratic political alternatives. The Communist Party portrayed itself as the guardian of the proletariat. It claimed that its compassionate priorities protected the people from their baser instincts. All this translated into over-centralization and forced economic growth in the USSR and Central-Eastern Europe (Kornai 1959, 1973), based on the priority given to the production of investment goods and military equipment, at the disadvantage of consumption.

The system initially produced remarkable economic and social results, but quickly degenerated. It wasn't long before fresh achievements were merely paper illusions. Goods produced often were defective, with the partial exception of priority branches in the military, and waste was enormous. Most importantly, sacrificing consumption caused growing popular discontent. Inefficiencies and imbalances increased dangerously and undermined the development of a well-functioning socialist welfare state. The Soviet Union and Central-Eastern European countries continuously introduced reforms after Stalin died, but preserved many of the pillars of administrative command planning.

The implementation of reforms in Central Europe was carried out by national communists who around 1956 replaced the Muscovite communists who had taken power in 1948–49.[1] The replacement took place with the support of the liberal component of the Soviet leadership after Stalin's death and later on, the tolerance of succeeding Soviet leaders, from Khrushchev to Brezhnev. Their efforts succeeded, enabling countries with strong national communists, notably Hungary and Poland, to acquire considerable economic freedom. However, Hungary alone was really able to implement consistent and far-reaching systemic reform after a lengthy period of preparation. Later, after Hungary's pioneering efforts, Czechoslovakia devised and gradually tried to achieve far-reaching political and social liberalization.

In economic terms, reforms were an attempt to move towards a hybrid system. Price liberalization was intended to make the system more sensitive to the needs and the preferences of buyers, giving them expanded consumer choice without full consumer sovereignty. The softening of central planning and the replacement of commands in most cases with parameters and benchmarks were intended to increase the potency of material incentives and enhance economic potential. Successful reforms discarded important components of the command economy but failed to replace them with a sustainable market economy. Free markets were mimicked, perhaps implemented in marginal areas with beneficial results in terms of improved product quality. What came out of reforms were softer, budget-constrained and imbalanced economies that generated shortages and growing external indebtedness. Only Czechoslovakia had a sufficiently conservative approach to maintain a balanced economy.

The moment of truth occurred in the late 1980s when a new generation of party and government leaders realized that the administrative command planning was a dead end and that reforms were insufficient to revitalize the economy to a level comparable with that of western countries. They mustered their resolve and tried to liberalize the system, including politics, without destroying it, with the intention to make it more efficient and democratic. At this point, the paths of the Soviet Union and most of its successor countries on one side and Central Europe and the Baltic countries on the other departed radically. Russia and Ukraine scuttled Marxist-Leninism, but refused to commit themselves to any specific systemic alternative. They moved toward democracy and markets without working out the details, hoping to successfully improvise and muddle through.

Central European and the Baltic countries followed a more radical approach, with remarkable internal differences. Their Communist Parties and governments (initially Poland and Hungary, but to a certain degree also Czechoslovakia) discussed the future with the social opposition, which was organizing into a political opposition. They accepted democratic electoral competitions, hoping to foster a social-democratic future. East Germany moved quickly towards unification with West Germany. The Balkan countries, Bulgaria and Romania, entered a period in which the old elites initially successfully maintained power by changing their political stance. Yugoslavia entered a destructive civil war. All these countries sought to become members of the European Union, an aim which required deep changes under the external control of the European Commission, facilitated with substantial financial assistance.

This meant that transformations in the former Soviet Union and Central Europe were managed differently. In the former case, transformation was never engineered to culminate in democratic free enterprise, social democracy, German social market economy, or American liberal economy, rhetoric to the contrary notwithstanding. The decision was made to discard the command economy, but this was merely an invitation to rival adventurers, insiders, factions and social forces to place their stamp on the new normal. The result was a fierce political war against communism and its command institutions, which prioritized plunder and destruction over asset preservation, value creation and efficiency.

The war was bloody. In Russia, it claimed 3.4 million excess fatalities in 1990–98 (Rosefielde 2001). Eventually however, "roving bandits" (in Mancur Olson's terminology) became stationary bandits, establishing new orders that differed substantially from command communism (Olson 1993). By the start of the third millennium, Russia and Ukraine sported rent-granting and market supply mechanisms responsive to consumer demand in varying degrees. Physical systems management was eradicated in the private consumer goods sector, but consumer sovereignty remained broadly subordinated to a variety of state actors.

The evolution and outcomes of Central Europe were definitely more favorable. These countries started with a greater degree of social cohesion and economies in better shape than the post-Soviet ones. Also, their history and cultural roots were an important component of western ones. Their economies were much more integrated with western economies well before 1989. Their membership in international economic organizations (in particular the IMF and the World Bank) and even more so their willingness to enter the EU played an important role during transformation. They had a clear and well-defined external anchor—the EU—and a clear initial reference in the Washington Consensus. Right or wrong, both these factors provided Central European countries with clear transformation blueprints and goals, at least in their main guidelines, in both the economy and polity.

Nonetheless, the particularities of the process of Central European transformation mattered. Large-scale privatization provided ample opportunities for plundering, misappropriation and corruption. Scandals and social discontent abounded. However, the judicial system and EU supervision had some beneficial effect in keeping negative effects within tolerable limits. Social conditions did not deteriorate as they did in the former Soviet Union, and even improved on average, in spite of growing unemployment and destitution. Outlooks and life expectancy improved throughout Central Europe during transformation (Mackenbach et al. 2015). Transformation widened the economic gap and political gulf between Russia and Central Europe.

Transformation was achieved in Russia, Ukraine and Central Europe. It was real and deep, but it wasn't obviously a transition to an optimal system or canonical democratic free enterprise, social democracy, German social market economy, or North American liberal economy. The destruction of command communism and reformed economies instead culminated in the creation of distinct systems (mixed rent-granting/market/state-managed), each dominated by its own power configurations, spanning the spectrum from well-working and dynamic market economies (Poland and Slovakia) and effective democracies (the Czech Republic) to under-performing authoritarian rent-granting regimes (Russia and Ukraine).

The new Russian system was just what the *siloviki* had been hoping for: a liberal authoritarian martial police state capable of providing the Kremlin with military superpower and a workably competitive consumer economy to mollify civil discontent. Putin resurrected the VPK, renationalized the weapons sector and supporting economic activities, and engineered an ambitious arms modernization program. Following the precedent of Russia's tsars, he created legions of servitors, oligarchs and kleptocrats as foundation stones for his authoritarian power. He encouraged direct foreign investment and technology transfer (but not outsourcing and integration into western supply chains), allowing small- and medium-sized enterprises to satisfy consumer demand. Once upon a time, Henry Rowen and Charles Wolf (1990) stigmatized the USSR as an impoverished superpower. The *siloviki* successfully disposed of the paradox by eliminating Soviet Russia's impoverishment with small- and medium-sized competitive businesses, and imported western consumer goods.

Ukraine also had a long history of authoritarianism and rent-granting, but its autocrat was Russian, not Ukrainian. When the Soviet Union dissolved, the Kremlin's authority evaporated and was not re-established in Kyiv. This allowed local clan rivals to battle each other for plunder and state rent-grants without deferring to a higher authority—behavior that largely explains the country's dire straits. Ukraine authorized markets, and privatized and dismantled many command institutions like state price fixing, but clan value destruction continues to take precedence over value creation.

Transformation led both groups of countries to evolve back to their futures with different scripts. The Central Europeans had been captive nations during the Cold War and sought shelter in the West after the Soviet Union's collapse to preclude subsequent recapture and restore their western historical and cultural essence. This prompted Hungary, Poland, the Czech Republic and Slovakia to join NATO and the European Union. All have been integrated into western corporate supply chains, and embraced parliamentary democracy. They have re-established their western cultural identities with "special" national characteristics that could significantly affect their comparative long-run economic performance. Russia and Ukraine remain broadly outside the West's democratic cultural paradigm.

The international crisis hit these countries in different ways and had different consequences. The impact of the 2008 global financial crisis was milder in Central Europe than other western countries. This was beneficial, but also had some negative effects. On the positive side of the ledger, Central European countries managed to maintain lower public debts, reduced production costs, had strong foreign bank and corporate presences in their domestic economies, high inflow and stocks of FDI and stronger integration in global value chains, particularly German ones, and some of them had more dynamic economies. But, on the negative side, they preserved lower financial development, greater specialization in productions making use of cheap and unskilled labor, greater specialization in raw material exports, and greater dependence on foreign investors and markets.

Impacts, however, varied. Poland and Slovakia emerged from the crisis well, in spite of structural and governance weaknesses. Their growth was remarkable also during the crisis, although based excessively on extensive factors that could turn out to be a weakness in the long run. The Czech Republic and even more so Hungary had unexpectedly weak performances, although both countries have aspects of strength that could turn out to be important in the long run. Russia was ravaged, but the crisis and its post-recovery performance has been mediocre. Its excessive reliance on raw materials represents a great economic weakness and an important vulnerability to external economic conditions. Ukraine's situation is desperate, due to political and social tensions and clan rivalries.

The big story at the end of the day is that all of the former command economies investigated in this study have transformed into economies which are different from each other and from what they had been in the communist past. They are no longer ruled by Communist Parties. They have replaced command with markets, but arrived at distinctly different destinations. Was the voyage worth it?

The answer depends on realities which are often concealed by statistical fog. If Soviet and Cold War-era Central European statistics are taken at face value, destroying the command economy and communism was a colossal mistake. Living standards would be far higher than they are today if communism had stayed the course. Russia, Ukraine and Central Europe would have been shielded from the ravages of hyper-depression, inflation, high unemployment and inequality. Millions would have been spared from dying prematurely. Their only consolation would be enhanced consumer sovereignty.

However, neither communist statistics nor the CIA's Soviet-era estimates can be taken at face value. Communist countries exclude most services from their national income statistics. The meaning of their economic data were distorted by planners' sovereignty, hidden inflation and sundry fraud (Rosefielde 2007a). Real national income growth was substantially less than officially reported. Gorbachev even claimed that Soviet GDP stopped growing in the late 1970s. Consumers in Russia, Ukraine and some Central-Eastern European countries received only what the state chose to offer, not what they wanted. Hungarian, Czech, Slovak and Polish consumers fared better, but they progressively lost ground related to comparable democratic market economies, such as Austria. Living standards in the Soviet Union were much lower than purchasing power parity calculations indicated. Soviet leaders fully understood that if they clung to command communism, their economy was destined to languish (*zastoi*). The situation in Central Europe was better but unsustainable because of the massive foreign indebtedness. Their national communist leaders rightly believed that the difference didn't justify preserving their brands of communism.

The quality of life and long-term growth prospects across most of these countries are significantly better today than they would have been without transformation. Ukraine is the sole exception. The decision to transform in the final analysis turned out to be the right one. But the transformation path chosen was unbalanced, ineffective and, in various cases, inhumane. Excessive costs were imposed upon large portions of the populations, although Central European welfare and taxation were somehow effective in moderating the increase of inequalities. Improvement in many cases is undeniable, but it often harbors the seeds of further and future problems.

Finally, it should be noted that China has demonstrated that command communism can be scuttled and society liberalized without generating hyper-depression and catastrophic excess mortality. The misery caused by shock therapy in Russia and Ukraine was avoidable and so were some excesses in Central Europe. Those responsible for *katastroika* absolve themselves from responsibility for their callous actions and destructive advice by tirelessly arguing that the ends justified the means, but the rationalization is disingenuous.

Note

1 In Central Europe, Communist Parties were typically composed of two groups of leaders and cadres. One was that of so-called national communists, the communist leaders and cadres who spent the periods between the two World Wars and during World War II in their own countries. They were often put in jail for their beliefs and activities and took part in liberation wars during the German occupation. They were supporters of strategies of national ways to socialism and politically akin to Yugoslav Titoism. The other group was made of communist leaders and cadres who spent the same period in the Soviet Union, typically working within international organizations such as Cominform and Comintern. They were true Muscovite cadres in the satellite countries when they returned and took power in 1948 and 1949. They were generally orthodox defenders of the unique line to socialism and communism, the Stalinist line in all countries.

Bibliography

Acemoglu, Daron and James A. Robinson (2012), *Why Nations Fail: The Origins of Power, Prosperity, and Poverty*, New York: Crown Business Books.

Adachi, Yuko (2009), 'Subsoil Law Reform in Russia under the Putin Administration', *Europe-Asia Studies*, Vol. 61, No. 8, October, pp. 1393–414.

—— (2010), *Building Big Business in Russia: The Impact of Informal Corporate Governance Practices*, London: Routledge.

Adam, Jan (1987), 'The Hungarian Economic Reform of the 1980s', *Soviet Studies*, Vol. 39, No. 4, pp. 610–27.

—— (1989), *Economic Reforms in the Soviet Union and Eastern Europe since the1960s*, London: Palgrave Macmillan.

—— (1994), 'Mass Privatization in Central and East European Countries', *MOST: Economic Policy in Transitional Economies*, Vol. 4, No. 1, pp. 87–100.

Addo Awadzi, Elsie (2015), 'Designing Legal Frameworks for Public Debt Management', *IMF Working Paper* WP/15/147 (http://www.imf.org/external/pubs/ft/wp/2015/wp15147.pdf).

Aganbegyan, Abel G. (1988), *The Challenge. Economics of Perestroika*, London: Hutchinson.

—— (1989), *Inside Perestroika: The Future of the Soviet Economy*, New York: Harper and Row.

Ahrens, Joachim (1994), 'The Transition to a Market Economy: Are there Useful Lessons from History?', in Alfred Schipke and Alan M. Taylor (eds.), *The Economics of Transformation: Theory and Practice in the New Market Economies*, Berlin: Springer Verlag, pp. 17–46.

Aiyar, Shekhar, Bartek Augustyniak, Christian Ebeke, Ehsan, Ebrahimy, Selim Elekdag, Nir Klein, Subir Lall, Hongyan Zhao and Dirk Muir (2013), 'German-Central European Supply Chain: Cluster Report', International Monetary Fund, *IMF Country Report No. 13/263*, July 1.

Allison, Christine and Dena Ringold (1996), 'Labor Markets in Transition in Central and Eastern Europe 1989–1995', *World Bank Technical Paper No. 352*, Social Challenges of Transition Series, Washington, DC: The World Bank (http://documents. worldbank.org/curated/en/1996/12/695067/labor-markets-transition-central-eastern-europe-1989-1995).

Amsden, Alice H., Jacek Kochanowicz and Lance Taylor (1994), *The Market Meets Its Match: Restructuring the Economies of Eastern Europe*, Cambridge, MA: Harvard University Press.

Andor, László (2010), *Eltévedt éllovas. Siker és kudarc a rendszerváltó gazdaságpolitikában* (Wrong charge. Success and defeat in the economic policy of systemic change), Budapest: Napvilág Kiadó.

Antal, László, Lajos Bokros, István Csillag, László Lengyel and Matolcsy György (1987), 'Fordulat és reform' (Turn and reform), *Közgazdasági Szemle*, Vol. XXXIV, June, pp. 642–63.

Aron, Leon (2000), *Yeltsin: A Revolutionary Life*, New York: St. Martin's Press.

—— (2012), 'A Tormenting in Moscow', *Foreign Policy*, April.

Arthur, Brian W. (1994), *Increasing Returns and Path Dependence in the Economy*, Ann Arbor: University of Michigan Press.

Ash, Ken (2015), 'The Emergence of Global Value Chains: Implications for Trade Policies and Trade Agreements', in Bruno Dallago and John McGowan (eds.), *Crises in Europe in the Transatlantic Context: Economic and Political Appraisals*, Abingdon, Oxfordshire: Routledge, pp. 21–34.

Åslund, Anders (1992), 'Post-Communist Economic Revolutions: How Big a Bang?', *Creating the Post Communist Order*, Vol. XIV, No. 9, p. 106.

—— (1995), *How Russia Became a Market Economy*, Washington, DC: Brookings Institute.

—— (2002), *Building Capitalism: The Transformation of the Former Soviet Bloc*. New York: Cambridge University Press.

—— (2007), *How Capitalism Was Built: The Transformation of Central and Eastern Europe, Russia, the Caucasus, and Central Asia*, Cambridge: Cambridge University Press.

—— (2009), *How Ukraine Became a Market Economy and Democracy*, Washington, DC: Peterson Institute for International Economics.

Atkinson, Tyler, David Luttrell and Harvey Rosenblum (2013), 'How Bad Was It? The Costs and Consequences of the 2007–09 Financial Crisis', *Staff Papers Federal Reserve Bank of Dallas*, No. 20, July.

Baker, Peter and Susan Glasser (2005), *Kremlin Rising: Vladimir Putin's Russia and the End of Revolution*, New York: Scribner's.

Bańbuła, Piotr, Witold Koziński and Michał Rubaszek (2011), 'The Role of the Exchange Rate in Monetary Policy in Poland', *BIS Papers No. 57* (http://www.bis.org/publ/bppdf/bispap57t.pdf).

Barrell, Ray, E. Philip Davis, Tatiana Fic and Ali Orazgani (2009), 'Household Debt and Foreign Currency Borrowing in New Member States of the EU', *Economics and Finance Working Paper Series, Working Paper No. 09-23*, Brunel University, June.

Bauer, Tamás (1981), *Tervgazdaság, beruházás, ciklusok* (Planned Economy, Investment, Cycles), Budapest: Közgazdasági és Jogi Könyvkiadó.

—— (1983), 'The Hungarian Alternative to Soviet-Type Planning', *Journal of Comparative Economics*, Vol. 7, No. 3, September, pp. 304–16.

Baumol, William J. (1993), *Entrepreneurship, Management, and the Structure of Payoffs*, Cambridge, MA: The MIT Press.

Beblavý, Miroslav (2010), 'Slovakia's Transition to a Market Economy and the World Bank's Engagement', *Social Science Research* Network (http://ssrn.com/abstract=1530284).

Bekker, Zsuza (1995), 'On Jánossy's Trendline at the End of Century, or, Can We Get Rid of Our Past?', *Acta Oeconomica*, Vol. 47, No. 1–2, pp. 95–110.

Berend, Iván T. (1990), *The Hungarian Economic Reforms 1953–1988*, Cambridge: Cambridge University Press.

—— (1996), *Central and Eastern Europe 1944–1993: Detour from the Periphery to the Periphery*, Cambridge: Cambridge University Press.

—— (2009), *History in My Life: A Memoir of Three Eras*, Budapest and New York: Central European University Press.

—— and György Ránki (1974), *Economic Development of East-Central Europe in the 19th and 20th Centuries*, New York: Columbia University Press.

Bergson, Abram (1938), 'A Reformulation of Certain Aspects of Welfare Economics', *Quarterly Journal of Economics*, Vol. 52, No. 1, pp. 310–34.

—— (1950), 'Soviet National Income and Product in 1937', parts I and II, *Quarterly Journal of Economics*, Vol. 64, Nos. 2, 3, (May–August), pp. 208–41.

—— (1953), 'Reliability and Usability of Soviet Statistics: A Summary Appraisal', *American Statistician*, Vol. 7, No. 3, (June–July), pp. 13–16.

—— (1964), *The Economics of Soviet Planning*, New Haven, CT: Yale University Press.

Berkowitz, Daniel, Katharina Pistor and Jean-Francois Richard (2003a), 'Economic Development, Legality, and the Transplant Effect', *European Economic Review*, Vol. 47, pp. 165–95.

——, Katharina Pistor and Jean-Francois Richard (2003b), 'The Transplant Effect', *American Journal of Comparative Law*, Vol. 51, No. 1, pp. 163–204.

Birman, Igor (1983), *Ekonomika Nedostach* (The Economy of Shortages), Benson Vermont: Chalidze Publishing.

Bischof, Günter, Stefan Karner and Peter Ruggenthaler (eds.) (2009), *The Prague Spring and the Warsaw Pact Invasion of Czechoslovakia in 1968*, Plymouth: Lexington Books.

Blagojević, Sandra and Jože P. Damijan (2013), 'The Impact of Corruption and Ownership on the Performance of Firms in Central and Eastern Europe', *Post-Communist Economies*, Vol. 25, No. 2, pp. 133–58 (DOI: 10.1080/14631377.2013.787734).

Blanchard, Olivier and Daniel Leigh (2013), 'Growth Forecast Errors and Fiscal Multipliers', *IMF Working Paper WP/13/1*, January.

Błaszczyck, Barbara, Grazyna Gierszewska, Michal Górzynski, Titus Kaminski, Wojciech Maliszewski, Richard Woodward and Aleksander Zolnierski (1999), 'Privatization and Company Restructuring in Poland', in Iván Major (ed.), *Privatization and Economic Performance in Central and Eastern Europe: Lessons To Be Learnt from Western Europe*, Cheltenham: Edward Elgar, pp. 303–73.

Blinder, Alan S. (2013), 'The Macroeconomic Policy Paradox: Failing by Succeeding', *The Annals of the American Academy of Political and Social Science November*, Vol. 650, No. 1, pp. 26–46.

Blokker, Paul (2015), 'The European Crisis as a Crisis of Democratic Capitalism', in Bruno Dallago and John McGowan (eds.), *Crises in Europe in the Transatlantic Context: Economic and Political Appraisals*, Abingdon, Oxfordshire: Routledge, pp. 137–51.

Blyth, Mark (2013), *Austerity. The History of a Dangerous Idea*, Oxford: Oxford University Press.

Bocchiaro, Piero (2009), *Psicologia del male*, Bari: Laterza.

Bofinger, Peter (1993), 'The Output Decline in Central and Eastern Europe: A Classical Explanation', *CEPR Discussion Paper No. 784*, May, London.

Bologna, Pierluigi, Arianna Miglietta and Marianna Caccavaio (2014), 'EU Bank Deleveraging', *VOX CEPR's Policy Portal*, October 14 (http://www.voxeu.org/article/eu-bank-deleveraging).

Bondar, Anatoli and Boo Lilje (2002), *Land Privatization in Ukraine*, Fig. XXII International Congress; Washington, DC, April 19–26 (https://www.fig.net/pub/fig_2002/Ts7-6/TS7_6_bondar_lilje.pdf).

Bonefeld, Werner (2012), 'Freedom and the Strong State: On German Ordoliberalism', *New Political Economy*, Vol. 17, No. 5, pp. 633–56.

Bonini, Nicolao and Costantinos Hadjichristidis (2009), *Il sesto senso. Emozione e ragione nella decisione*, Milan, Il Sole 24 Ore.

Bornstein, Morris (1994), 'Privatization in Central and Eastern Europe: Techniques, Policy Options and Economic Consequences', in László Csaba (ed.), *Privatization, Liberalization and Destruction: Recreating the Market in Central and Eastern Europe*, Aldershot: Dartmouth, pp. 233–58.

Boughton, James M. (2001), *Silent Revolution. The International Monetary Fund 1979–1989*, Washington, DC: International Monetary Fund, October 1 (http://www.imf.org/external/pubs/ft/history/2001/).

Brada, Josef C. and Arthur E. King (1992), 'Is There a J-Curve for the Economic Transition from Socialism to Capitalism?', *Economics of Planning*, Vol. 25, No. 1, pp. 37–53.

Brazova, Vera-Karin, Piotr Matczak and Viktoria Takacs (2013), *Regional Organization Study: Visegrád Group*, Anvil (Analysis of Civil Security Systems in Europe), July.

Briguglio, Lino, Gordon Cordina, Nadia Farrugia and Stephanie Vella (2009), 'Economic Vulnerability and Resilience: Concepts and Measurements', *Oxford Development Studies*, Vol. 37, No. 3, pp. 229–47 (part of a special issue on 'Vulnerability in Development: Advances in Concept and Measurement', pp. 183–309).

Brown, Archie (1996), *The Gorbachev Factor*, Oxford: Oxford University Press.

Burki, Shahid Javed and Guillermo E. Perry (1998), *Beyond the Washington Consensus: Institutions Matter*, Washington, DC: The World Bank.

Buti, Marco and André Sapir (eds.) (1998), *Economic Policy in EMU: A Study by the European Commission Services*, Oxford: Clarendon Press.

Calvo, Guillermo A. and Fabrizio Coricelli (1993), 'Output Collapse in Eastern Europe: The Role of Credit', *IMF Staff Papers*, Vol. 40, No. 1, March pp. 32–52.

Cariolle, Joël (2011), 'The Economic Vulnerability Index. 2010 Update', *Working Paper 9: Development Indicators*, Fondation pour les études et recherches sur le développement international, March (http://www.ferdi.fr/sites/www.ferdi.fr/files/publication/fichiers/I9-Cariolle-Eng_web.pdf).

Carlin, Wendy, John Van Reenen and Toby Wolfe (1995), 'Enterprise Restructuring in Early Transition: The Case Study Evidence from Central and Eastern Europe', *Economics of Transition*, Vol. 3, pp. 427–58.

CEPI (2014), *Central Europe Fit for the Future. Visegrad Group Ten Years after EU Accession*, Report by the High Level Reflection Group, Bratislava and Warsaw: Central European Policy Institute (CEPI), Bratislava, and demosEUROPA (dE)—Centre for European Strategy, Warsaw, January.

Chen, Vivian, Abhay Gupta, Andre Therrien, Gad Levanon and Bart van Ark (2010), 'Recent Productivity Developments in the World Economy: An Overview from The Conference Board Total Economy Database', *International Productivity Monitor*, No. 19, Spring, pp. 3–19.

CIA (1992), *Handbook of International Economic Statistics*, CPAS92-10005, September.

—— (2008), *The World Factbook 2008*, Washington, DC: Central Intelligence Agency.

Cohn, Theodore H. (2012), *Global Political Economy. Theory and Practice*, Boston, MA: Longman, sixth edn.

Comisso, Ellen (1997), 'Legacies of the Past or New Institutions: The Struggle over Restitution in Hungary', in Beverly Crawford and Arend Lijphart (eds.), *Liberalization and Leninist Legacies: Comparative Perspectives on Democratic Transitions*, Research Series, No. 96, Berkeley: University of California, pp. 184–227.

Commander, Simon, Andrei Tolstopiatenko and Ruslan Yemtsov (1999), 'Channels of Redistribution: Inequality and Poverty in the Russian Transition', *Economics of Transition*, Vol. 7, No. 1, pp. 411–65.

Cooper, Julian (2012), *Reviewing Russian Strategic Planning: The Emergence of Strategy 2020*, NDC Research Review, NATO Defense College, www.ndc.nato.int.

Cordina, Gordon (2004), 'Economic Vulnerability and Economic Growth: Some Results from a Neo-Classical Growth Modelling Approach', *Journal of Economic Development*, Vol. 29, No. 2, December, pp. 21–39.

Coricelli, Fabrizio (1996), 'Inter-enterprise Arrears in Economies in Transition: Analytical, Empirical and Policy Issues', in Bruno Dallago and Luigi Mittone (eds.), *Economic Institutions, Markets and Competition: Centralisation and Decentralisation in the Transformation of Economic Systems*, Cheltenham: Edward Elgar, pp. 291–318.

Csaba, László (1995), *The Capitalist Revolution in Eastern Europe: A Contribution to the Economic Theory of Systemic Change*, Aldershot: Edward Elgar.

—— (2003), 'The Role of Financing in the Growth of the SME Sector: The Case of Hungary', in Robert J. McIntyre and Bruno Dallago (eds.), *Small and Medium Enterprises in Transitional Economies*, Houndmills, Basingstoke: Palgrave Macmillan, pp. 185–205.

Curtis, Glenn E. (ed.) (1992), *Poland: A Country Study*, Washington, DC: GPO for the Library of Congress (http://countrystudies.us/poland/60.htm).

Dallago, Bruno (1981), 'Commercio estero e strategia di sviluppo: Polonia e Ungheria negli anni settanta' (Foreign trade and Development Strategy: Poland and Hungary in the Seventies), *Commercio*, No. 10, pp. 123–42.

—— (1982), *Sviluppo e cicli nelle economie est europee* (Development and Cycles in Eastern European Economies), Milan: Franco Angeli.

—— (1987), 'Les interprétation des fluctuations et cycles dans les économies de type soviétique', in Bernard Chavance (ed.), *Régulation, cycles et crises dans les économies socialistes*, Paris: Editions de l'Ecole des Hautes Etudes en Sciences Sociales, pp. 17–44.

—— (1989), 'The Non-Socialized Sector in Hungary: An Attempt at Estimation of Its Importance', *Jahrbuch der Wirtschaft Osteuropas/Yearbook of East-European Economics*, Vol. 13, No. 2, pp. 67–92.

—— (1991), 'Hungary and Poland: The Non-Socialized Sector and Privatization', *Osteuropa-Wirtschaft*, Vol. 36, No. 2, pp. 130–53.

—— (1993), *Sistemi economici comparati* (Comparative Economic Systems), Rome: La Nuova Italia Scientifica.

—— (1996a), 'Investment, Systemic Efficiency and Distribution', *Kyklos*, Vol. 49, No. 4, pp. 615–41.

—— (1996b), 'Between Spontaneity and Economic Engineering: Path Dependence in the Process of Economic Transition', in *Economic Developments and Reforms in Cooperation Partner Countries: The Social and Human Dimension*, Brussels: NATO, pp. 73–86.

—— (1996c), 'The Market and the State: The Paradox of Transition', *Most*, No. 4, pp.1–29.

—— (1997), 'The Economic System, Transition and Opportunities for Entrepreneurship', in *Entrepreneurship and SMEs in Transition Economies*, Paris: LEED/OECD, pp. 103–24.

—— (1999), 'Privatization: The Teaching of Western Experiences', in Iván Major (ed.), *Privatization and Economic Performance in Central and Eastern Europe: Lessons To Be Learnt from Western Europe*, Cheltenham: Edward Elgar, pp. 1–42.

—— (2003), 'SME Development in Hungary: Legacy, Transition and Policy', in Robert J. McIntyre and Bruno Dallago (eds.), *Small and Medium Enterprises in Transitional Economies*, Houndmills, Basingstoke: Palgrave Macmillan, pp. 78–97.

—— (2004), 'Comparative Economic Systems and the New Comparative Economics', *The European Journal of Comparative Economics*, Vol. 1, No. 1, pp. 59–86.

—— (2009), 'The State and the Transformation of Economic Systems', in Shinichi Ichimura, Tsuneaki Sato and William James (eds.), *Transition from Socialist to Market Economies*, Houndmills, Basingstoke: Palgrave Macmillan, pp. 164–87.

—— (2015), *One Currency, Two Europes*, Singapore: World Scientific.

—— and John McGowan (2015), 'Introduction. The European Crisis in the Transatlantic Context', in Bruno Dallago and John McGowan (eds.), *Crises in Europe in the Transatlantic Context: Economic and Political Appraisals*, Abingdon, Oxfordshire: Routledge, pp. 1–18.

Darvas, Zsolt, Pia Hüttl, Silvia Merler, Carlos de Sousa and Thomas Walsh (2014), 'Analysis of Developments in EU Capital Flows in the Global Context Final Report', Bruegel, November, No. MARKT/2013/50/F.

Das, Udaibir S., Michael G. Papaioannou and Christoph Trebesch (2012), 'Sovereign Debt Restructurings 1950–2010: Concepts, Literature Survey, and Stylized Facts', *IMF Working Paper WP/12/203*, August, Washington, DC: International Monetary Fund (https://www.imf.org/external/pubs/ft/wp/2012/wp12203.pdf).

David, Paul (1985), 'Clio and the Economics of QWERTY', *American Economic Review*, Papers and Proceedings, Vol. 75, No. 2, pp. 332–7.

De Backer, Koen and Sébastien Miroudot (2013), 'Mapping Global Value Chains', *OECD Trade Policy Papers*, No. 159, OECD (http://dx.doi.org/10.1787/5k3v1trgnbr4-en).

—— and Sébastien Miroudot (2014), 'Mapping Global Value Chains', European Central Bank, *Working Paper Series No. 1677*, May.

De Grauwe, Paul (2014), *Economics of Monetary Union+*, Oxford: Oxford University Press, tenth edn.

d'Hombres, Beatrice, Lorenzo Rocco, Marc Suhrcke and Martin McKee (2006), 'Does Social Capital Determine Health? Evidence from Eight Transition Countries', *MPRA Paper No. 1862* (http://mpra.ub.uni-muenchen.de/1862/).

——(2010), 'Does Social Capital Determine Health? Evidence from Eight Transition Countries', *Health Economics*, Vol. 19, No. 1, pp. 56–74.

Djankov, Simeon and Gerhard Pohl (1997), 'The Restructuring of Large Firms in Slovakia', The World Bank, *Policy Research Working Paper 1758*, April.

—— and Peter Murrell (2002), 'Enterprise Restructuring in Transition: A Quantitative Survey', *Journal of Economic Literature*, Vol. XL, September, pp. 739–92.

——, Rafael La Porta, Florencio Lopez-de-Silanes and Andrei Shleifer (2008), 'The Law and Economics of Self-Dealing', *Journal of Financial Economics*, Vol. 88, No. 3, pp. 430–65.

——, Edward L. Glaeser, Rafael La Porta, Florencio Lopez-de-Silanes and Andrei Shleifer (2003), 'The New Comparative Economics', *NBER Working Paper Series* 9608, April.

Draghi, Mario (2014), *Unemployment in the Euro Area*, Annual central bank symposium in Jackson Hole, August 22 (https://www.ecb.europa.eu/press/key/date/2014/html/sp1 40822.en.html).

Durand, Mattine and Claude Giorno (1987), 'Indicators of International Competitiveness: Conceptual Aspects and Evaluation', *OECD Journal: Economic Studies*, Paris: OECD, Vol. 9, pp. 147–82 (https://www1.oecd.org/eco/outlook/33841783.pdf).

Eberstadt, Nicholas and Nick Eberstadt (1988), *The Poverty of Communism*, New Brunswick, NJ: Transaction Publishers.

EBRD (2000), *Transition Report 2000*, London: European Bank for Reconstruction and Development.

EC (2014), 'Convergence Report 2014', *European Economy*, No. 4/2014, European Commission.

—— (2015a), *Assessment of the 2015 Convergence Programme for Czech Republic*, Brussels: European Commission, May 27.

—— (2015b), *Country Report Czech Republic 2015*, Commission Staff Working Document [COM(2015) 85 final], Brussels: European Commission, February 26.

—— (2015c), 'Macroeconomic Imbalances. Country Report: Hungary 2015', *European Economy Occasional Papers 220*, Brussels: European Commission.

—— (2015d), *Country Report Hungary 2015. Including an In-Depth Review on the Prevention and Correction of Macroeconomic Imbalances*, Commission Staff Working Document [COM(2015) 85 final], Brussels: European Commission, March 18.

—— (2015e), *Assessment of the 2015 Convergence Programme for Poland*, Brussels: European Commission, May 27.

—— (2015f), *Recommendation for a COUNCIL DECISION Abrogating Decision 2009/589/EC on the Existence of an Excessive Deficit in Poland* [COM(2015) 243 final], Brussels: European Commission, May 13.

—— (2015g), *Country Report Poland 2015*, Commission Staff Working Document [COM(2015) 85 final], Brussels: European Commission, February 26.

—— (2015h), *Country Report Slovakia 2015*, Commission Staff Working Document [COM(2015) 85 final], Brussels: European Commission, March 18.

Ederer, Peer (2006), *The European Human Capital Index*, Lisbon Council Policy Brief, Brussels: The Lisbon Council.

——, Philipp Schuller and Stephan Willms (2007), 'The European Human Capital Index: The Challenge of Central and Eastern Europe', *Lisbon Council Policy Brief*, Vol. 2, No. 3.

EEAG (2012), *The EEAG Report on the European Economy*, 'The Hungarian Crisis', CESifo, Munich 2012, pp. 115–30.

Epstein, Rachel A. (2013), 'Central and East European Bank Responses to the Financial "Crisis": Do Domestic Banks Perform Better in a Crisis than Their Foreign-Owned Counterparts?', *Europe-Asia Studies*, Vol. 65, No. 3, pp. 528–47.

—— (2014), 'Special Issue: Assets or Liabilities? Banks and the Politics of Foreign Ownership versus National Control', *Review of International Political Economy*, Volume 21, Issue 4, pp. 765–89.

Etkind, Alexander (2011), *Internal Colonization: Russia's Imperial Experience,* London: Polity Press.

European Bank for Reconstruction and Development(2014), *Country Assessments: Ukraine*, 2013 (http://tr.ebrd.com/tr13/en/country-assessments/3/ukraine); *World Bank Group—Ukraine Partnership: Country Program Snapshot*, April: (worldbank.org/content/dam/Worldbank/document/Ukraine-Snapshot.pdf).

Faini, Riccardo (2006), 'Europe: A Continent in Decline?', in Paul W. Rhode and Gianni Toniolo (eds.), *The Global Economy in the 1990s: A Long-Run Perspective*, Cambridge: Cambridge University Press, pp. 69–88.

Fallenbuchl, Zbigniew (1985), 'National Income Statistics for Poland, 1970-1980', *Staff Working Paper No. SWP 776*, Washington, DC: The World Bank (http://documents.worldbank.org/curated/en/1985/11/1554693/national-income-statistics-poland-1970-1980).

Fejtő, François (1957), *Ungheria 1945-1957* (Hungary 1945–1957), Turin: Einaudi.

—— (1971), *A History of the People's Democracies: Eastern Europe Since Stalin*, New York: Praeger.

Ferge, Zsuzsa (2010), *Társadalmi áramlatok és egyéni szerepek* (Social Flows and Individual Roles), Budapest: Napvilág Kiadó.

Fischer, Stanley and Alan Gelb (1991), 'The Process of Socialist Economic Transformation', *Journal of Economic Perspectives*, February, Vol. 5, No. 4, pp. 91–105.

——, Ratna Sahay and Carlos A. Végh (1996), 'Stabilization and Growth in Transition Economies: The Early Experience', *Journal of Economic Perspectives*, Vol. 10, No. 2, Spring, pp. 45–66.

Fite, Brando (2012), *U.S. and Iranian Strategic Competition: The Impact of China and Russia*, Washington, DC: CSIS, March.

Fitzsimmons, Michael (2002), 'Investment Privatization Funds, Banks and Corporate Governance in the Czech Republic and Russia', *Chazen Web Journal Of International Business*, Columbia Business School, Fall (www.gsb.columbia.edu/chazenjournal).

Flemming, John and John Micklewright (1999), 'Income Distribution, Economic Systems and Transition', *Innocenti Occasional Papers*, Economic and Social Policy Series No. 70, May.

Focus Economics (2015a), *Ukraine Economic Outlook*, June 9 (http://www.focus-economics.com/countries/ukraine).

—— (2015b), *Ukraine—Consumption*, June 19, 2015 (http://www.focus-economics.com/country-indicator/ukraine/consumption).

Foy, Henry (2015), 'Candidates Put Euro at Centre of Polish Presidential Race', *Financial Times online*, April 1 (http://www.ft.com/intl/cms/s/0/f36f72f2-d6a7-11e4-a99f-00144 feab7de.html#axzz3d444RWr5).

Freeland, Chrystia (1997), 'Tidings of Prosperity', *Financial Times*, January 6.

Friss, István (1971), *Reform of the Economic Mechanism in Hungary*, Budapest: Akadémiai Kiadó.

Fukuyama, Francis (1992), *The End of History and the Last Man Standing*, New York: Free Press.

—— (2014a), 'America in Decay: The Sources of Political Dysfunction', *Foreign Affairs*, Vol. 93, September/October.

—— (2014b), *Political Order and Political Decay: From the Industrial Revolution to the Globalization of Democracy*, New York: Farrar, Straus and Giroux.

Gaddy, Clifford and Barry Ickes (2013), *Bear Traps on Russia's Road to Modernization*, London: Routledge.

Gaidar, Yegor and Karl Otto Pöhl (1995), *Russian Reform/International Money* (Lionel Robbins Lectures), Cambridge, MA: The MIT Press.

GAO (2013), *Financial Regulatory Reform: Financial Crisis Losses and Potential Impacts of the Dodd-Frank Act*, GAO-13-180, US Government Accountability Office, January.

Gates, Robert (2014), *Duty: Memoirs of a Secretary at War*, New York: Alfred A. Knopf.

Garner, Thesia and Katherine Terrell (1998), 'A Gini Decompositon Analysis of Inequality in the Czech and Slovak Republics During the Transition', *The Economics of Transition*, Vol. 6, No. 1, pp. 23–46.

George, Konstantin (1998), 'How IMF Shock Therapy was Imposed on Russia', *EIR*, Vol. 25, No. 32, August 14, pp. 56–62.

Gerlach, Helmut (1998), 'Bankruptcy in the Czech Republic, Hungary, and Poland and Section 304 of the United States Bankruptcy Code, Proceedings Ancillary to Foreign Bankruptcy Proceedings', *Maryland Journal of International Law*, Vol. 22, No. 1, Art. 4, pp. 81–115 (http://digitalcommons.law.umaryland.edu/cgi/viewcontent.cgi?article=1484&context=mjil).

Gerschenkron, Alexander (1962), *Economic Backwardness in Historical Perspective*, Cambridge, MA: Harvard University Press.

Glaeser, Edward L. and Andrei Shleifer (2002), 'Legal Origins', *NBER Working Paper No. 8272* (http://www.nber.org/papers/w8272.pdf).

Goldman, Marshall (2003), *The Piratization of Russia: Russian Reform Goes Awry*, London: Routledge.

—— (2010), *Petrostate: Putin, Power, and the New Russia*, London: Oxford University Press.

Gomułka, Stanisław (1991), 'The Causes of Recession Following Stabilization', *Comparative Economic Studies*, Vol. 33, No. 2, pp. 71–89.

Gorbachev, Mikhail (1987), *Perestroika: New Thinking for Our Country and the World*, New York: HarperCollins.

—— (1988), *Perestroika: New Thinking for Our Country and the World*. New York: Harper & Row.

—— (1996), *Memoirs*, New York: Doubleday.

Gray, Cheryl, Sabine Schlorke and Miklos Szanyi (1995), 'Hungary's Bankruptcy Experience, 1992–93', *Policy Research Working Paper 1510*, Washington, DC: The World Bank, September.

Greenspan, Alan (2013), 'Never Saw it Coming', *Foreign Affairs*, November/December (http://www.foreignaffairs.com/articles/140161/alan-greenspan/never-saw-it-coming).

Gregory, Paul and Robert Stuart (1997), *Comparative Economic Systems*, Boston, MA: Houghton.

Gretschmann, Klaus (forthcoming), 'The EU in Stormy Seas: Beginning of the End or End of the Beginning?', in Bruno Dallago, Gert Guri and John McGowan (eds.), *A Global Perspective on the European Economic Crisis*, Abingdon, Oxfordshire: Routledge (forthcoming).

Grossman, Gregory (1963), 'Notes for a Theory of the Command Economy', *Soviet Studies*, Vol. 15, No. 2, pp. 101–23.

—— (1977), 'The "Second Economy" of the USSR', *Problems of Communism*, September–October, pp. 25–40.

—— (1987), 'The Second Economy: Boon or Bane for the Reform of the First Economy?', *Berkeley-Duke Occasional Papers on the Second Economy in the USSR*, No. 11, December.

—— (1995), *Origins of Russian Organized Crime*, paper presented at the Fifth Trento Workshop on *Privatization and Distribution: The Consequences of Privatization of State Ownership for Distribution and Chances for Development*, Department of Economics, University of Trento and European Association for Comparative Economic Studies, Trento, March 3–4.

Guillaumont, Patrick (1999), 'On the Economic Vulnerability of Low Income Countries', CERDI-CNRS, Université d'Auvergne (http://siteresources.worldbank.org/INTPOVERTY/Resources/WDR/stiglitz/Guillau2.pdf).

—— (2009), 'An Economic Vulnerability Index: Its Design and Use for International Development Policy', *Oxford Development Studies*, Vol. 37, No. 3, pp. 193–228.

—— (2011), 'The Concept of Structural Economic Vulnerability and Its Relevance for the Identification of the Least Developed Countries and other Purposes (Nature, Measurement, and Evolution)', *CDP Background Paper No. 12*, September (http://www.un.org/en/development/desa/policy/cdp/cdp_background_papers/bp2011_12.pdf).

Hall, Peter A. and David W. Soskice (eds.) (2001), *Varieties of Capitalism: The Institutional Foundations of Comparative Advantage*, Oxford: Oxford University Press.

Hare, Paul (1987), 'Economic Reform in Eastern Europe', *Journal of Economic Surveys*, Vol. 1, No. 1–2, pp. 25–58.

—— Mohammed Ishaq and Saul Estrin (1996), 'The Legacies of Central Planning and the Transition to a Market Economy: Ukrainian Contradictions', *CERT*, October 1996, pp. 1–26 (http://www.sml.hw.ac.uk/downloads/cert/wpa/1996/dp9618.pdf).

Harre, Romano and P.F. Secord (1972), *The Explanation of Social Behaviour*, Oxford: Basil Blackwell.

Hart-Landsberg, Martin (2013), 'Lessons from Iceland. Capitalism, Crisis, and Resistance', *Monthly Review*, Vol. 65, No. 5, October.

Hashi, Iraj (2000), 'The Polish National Investment Fund Programme: Mass Privatisation with a Difference?', *Comparative Economic Sudies*, Vol. XLII, No. 1, pp. 87–134.

Hayden, Jacqueline (2006), *The Collapse of Communist Power in Poland: Strategic Misperceptions and Unanticipated Outcomes*, Abingdon and New York: Routledge.

HCB (2015), 'Hungary's Balance of Payments: 2014 Q4', press release, Hungarian Central Bank, March (http://english.mnb.hu/Root/Dokumentumtar/ENMNB/Statisztika/mnben_statkozlemeny/mnben_fizetesi_merleg/BPM6_press_2014_Q4_EN.pdf).

HCSO (2010), *Hungary 1989–2009*, Budapest: Hungarian Central Statistical Office.

Hedström, Peter and Charlotta Stern (2008), 'Rational Choice and Sociology', *The New Palgrave Dictionary of Economics*.

Hellie, Richard (2005), 'The Structure of Russian Imperial History', *History and Theory*, No. 44, pp. 88–112.

Hellman, Joel S. (1998), 'Winners Take All: The Politics of Partial Reform in Post-communist Transitions', *World Politics*, Vol. 50, pp. 203–34.

Hewett, Ed (1990), 'The New Soviet Plan', *Foreign Affairs*, Vol. 69, No. 5, pp. 146–66.

Hirschman, Albert O. (1970), *Exit, Voice, and Loyalty: Responses to Decline in Firms, Organizations, and States*, Cambridge, MA: Harvard University Press.

Hollis, Martin and Edward J. Nell (1975), *Rational Economic Man*, Cambridge: Cambridge University Press.

Huntington, Samuel (1996), 'The West: Unique, Not Universal', *Foreign Affairs*, Vol. 75, No. 6, pp. 28–46.

Hurník, Jaromír , Zdeněk Tůma and David Vávra (2010), 'The Czech Republic on Its Way to the Euro: A Stabilization Role of Monetary Policy Revisited', in Ewald Nowotny, Peter Mooslechner and Doris Ritzberger-Grünwald (eds.), *The Euro and Economic Stability: Focus on Central, Eastern and South-Eastern Europe*, Cheltenham: Edward Elgar, pp. 48–68.

IMF (2001), 'Structural Conditionality in Fund-Supported Programs', Policy Development and Review Department, International Monetary Fund, 16 February (http://www.imf.org/external/np/pdr/cond/2001/eng/struct/cond.pdf).

—— (2011), 'Changing Patterns of Global Trade', International Monetary Fund, Strategy, Policy, and Review Department, June 15 (http://www.imf.org/external/np/pp/eng/2011/061511.pdf).

—— (2014a), Republic of Poland. 2014 Article IV Consultation—Staff Report; Press Release; and Statement by the Executive Director for the Republic of Poland, *IMF Country Report No. 14/173*, June.

—— (2014b), 'Slovak Republic. 2014 Article IV Consultation—Staff Report; and Press Release', *IMF Country Report No. 14/254*, September.

—— (2014c), *Annual Report on Exchange Arrangements and Exchange Restrictions 2014*, Washington, DC: International Monetary Fund.

—— (2015a), Hungary. 2015 Article IV Consultation—Staff Report; Press Release; and Statement by the Executive Director for Hungary, *IMF Country Report No. 15/92*, April.

—— (2015b), 'Czech Republic: Concluding Statement of the 2015 Article IV Mission', May 20 (https://www.imf.org/external/np/ms/2015/052015a.htm).

—— (2015c), 'Republic of Poland: Concluding Statement of the 2015 Article IV Mission', May 18 (http://www.imf.org/external/np/ms/2015/051815.htm).

—— (2015d), 'Slovak Republic: Staff Concluding Statement of the 2015 Article IV Mission', November 3 (http://www.imf.org/external/np/ms/2015/110315.htm).

Ioffe, Julia (2014), 'Booting Russia from the G8 Ends 16 Years of Pretending Moscow Should Sit at the Big-Kids Table', *New Republic*, March 24 (http:newrepublic.com/article/117140/g7-boots-russia-g8-relief).

Jánossy, Ferenc (1966), *A gazdasági fejlödés trendvonala és a helyreállítási periódusok* (The Trend of Economic Development and Reconstruction Periods), Budapest: Közgazdasági és Jogi Kiadó.

—— (1975), *A gazdasági fejlődés trendvonaláról* (On the Trend of Economic Development), Budapest: Magvető Könyvkiadó, second edn.

Jedlička, Jan, Juraj Kotian and Rainer Münz (2014a), 'Visegrad Four—10 years of EU Membership', *CEE Special Report*, Erste Group Research, April 23.

——, Juraj Kotian and Rainer Münz (2014b), '25 years after Communism, Does CEE Still Hold Key to Growth?', *CEE Special Report*, Erste Group Research, 11 November.

Johnson, Juliet and Andrew Barnes (2015), 'Financial Nationalism and Its International Enablers: The Hungarian Experience', *Review of International Political Economy*, Vol. 22, No. 3, pp. 535–69.

Johnson, Simon, Rafael La Porta, Florencio Lopez-de-Silanes and Andrei Shleifer (2000), 'Tunneling', *American Economic Review*, Vol. 90, No. 2, pp. 22–7.

Judt, Tony (2005), *Postwar: A History of Europe Since 1945*, Harmondsworth: The Penguin Press.

Jütting, Johannes, Denis Drechsler, Sebastian Bartsch and Indra de Soysa (eds.) (2007), *Informal Institutions: How Social Norms Help or Hinder Development*, Paris: OECD.

Kahneman, Daniel and Amos Tversky (1984), 'Choices, Values, and Frames', *American Psychologist*, Vol. 39, No. 4, pp. 341–50.

—— and Amos Tversky (eds.) (2000), *Choices, Values and Frames*, Cambridge: Cambridge University Press.

——, Paul Slovic and Amos Tversky (eds.) (1982), *Judgment under Uncertainty: Heuristics and Biases*, Cambridge: Cambridge University Press.

Kakutani, Shizuo (1941), 'A Generalization of Brouwer's Fixed Point Theorem', *Duke Mathematical Journal*, Vol. 8, No. 3, pp. 457–9.

Kaminski, Bartlomiej (1991), *The Collapse of State Socialism: The Case of Poland*, Princeton, NJ: Princeton University Press.

Kaser, Michael (1965), *Comecon: Integration Problems of the Planned Economies*, London: Oxford University Press.

Kattel, Rainer and Ringa Raudla (2013), 'The Baltic Republics and the Crisis of 2008–2011', *Europe-Asia Studies*, Vol. 65, No. 3, May, pp. 426–49.

Keeney, Ralph L. (2004), 'Framing Public Policy Decisions', *International Journal of Technology, Policy and Management*, Vol. 4, No. 2, pp. 95–115.

Keynes, John Maynard (1962), *Essays in Persuasion*, New York: W.W. Norton.

Kingston, Christopher and Gonzalo Caballero (2009), 'Comparing Theories of Institutional Change', *Journal of Institutional Economics*, Vol. 5, No. 2, pp. 151–80.

Kiss, Tibor (1969), *Hol tart a KGST-integráció?* (The Comecon Integration), Budapest: Kossut Kiadó.

Klich, Jacek (1998), 'The Concept of Mass Privatization in Poland: Theoretical and Practical Considerations', in Demetrius S. Iatridis and June G. Hopps (eds.), *Privatization in Central and Eastern Europe: Perspectives and Approaches*, Westport, CT: Praeger, pp. 85–95.

Knight, Jack (1992), *Institutions and Social Conflict*, Cambridge: Cambridge University Press.

Kočenda, Even (2003), 'The Impact of Czech Mass Privatisation on Corporate Governance', *Journal of Economic Studies*, Vol. 30, No. 3/4, pp. 278–93.

Kolodko, Grzegorz W. (1988), 'Crisis, Adjustment and Development in Socialist Economies: The Case of Poland', *Monetary Policy and Banking Research Institute Working Paper*, No. 1, National Bank of Poland, Warsaw, December.

—— (1989), 'Reform, Stabilization Policies and Economic Adjustment in Poland', *WIDER Working Papers*, WP 51, World Institute for Development Economics Research of the United Nations University, Helsinki, January.

—— (1991), 'Polish Hyperinflation and Stabilization 1989–1990', *Moct/Most*, Nomisma Economic Journal on Eastern Europe and The Soviet Union, No. 1, pp. 9–36.

—— (2000), *From Shock to Therapy: The Political Economy of Postsocialist Transformation*, Oxford: Oxford University Press.

—— (2001), 'Post-Communist Transition and Post-Washington Consensus: The Lessons for Policy Reforms', in Mario I. Blejer and Marko Skreb (eds.), *Transition: The First Decade*, Cambridge, MA: The MIT Press, pp. 45–83.

——, Danuta Gotz-Kozierkiewicz and Elzbieta Skrzeszewska-Paczek (1992), *Hyperinflation and Stabilization in Postsocialist Economies*, New York: Kluwer.

Korbonski, Andrei (1989), 'The Politics of Economic Reforms in Eastern Europe: The Last Thirty Years', *Soviet Studies*, Vol. 41, No. 1, January, pp. 1–19.

Kornai, János (1959), *Overcentralization in Economic Administration*, Oxford: Oxford University Press.

—— (1973), *Forced and Harmonic Growth*, Budapest: Akadémiai Kiadó.

—— (1979), 'Resource-Constrained Versus Demand-Constrained Systems', *Econometrica*, July, Vol. 47, No. 4, pp. 801–19.

—— (1980), *Economics of Shortage*, Amsterdam: North-Holland.

—— (1986), 'The Hungarian Reform Process: Visions, Hopes and Reality', *Journal of Economic Literature*, Vol. 24, No. 4, pp. 1687–737.

—— (1990), *The Road to a Free Economy: Shifting from a Socialist System—The Example of Hungary*, New York: W. W. Norton and Budapest: HVG Kiadó.

—— (1992a), *The Socialist System: The Political Economy of Communism*, Princeton, NJ: Princeton University Press and Oxford: Oxford University Press.

—— (1992b), 'The Postsocialist Transition and the State: Reflections in the Light of Hungarian Fiscal Problems', *American Economic Review*, Vol. 82, No. 2, pp. 1–21.

—— (1994), 'Transformational Recession: The Main Causes', *Journal of Comparative Economics*, Vol. 19, No. 1, August, pp. 39–63.

—— (1997a), 'Paying the Bill for Goulash Communism: Hungarian Development and Macro Stabilization in a Political-Economy Perspective', in János Kornai, *Struggle and Hope: Essays on Stabilization and Reform in a Post-Socialist Economy*, Cheltenham: Edward Elgar, pp. 121–79.

—— (1997b), 'The Welfare State in Postsocialist Societies', *World Development*, Vol. 25, No. 8, pp. 1183–6.

Koyama, Yoji (2015), *The EU's Eastward Enlargement: Central and Eastern Europe's Strategies for Development*, Singapore: World Scientific Publishers.

Koyame-Marsh, Rita O. (2011), 'The Complexities of Economic Transition: Lessons from the Czech Republic and Slovakia', *International Journal of Business and Social Science*, Vol. 2, No. 19, Special Issue, October, pp. 71–85.

Krugman, Paul (2009), *The Return of Depression Economics and the Crisis of 2008*, New York: W.W. Norton Company.

Kryshtanovskaya, Olga and Stephen White (1996), 'From Soviet *Nomenklatura* to Russian Élite', *Europe-Asia Studies*, Vol. 48, No. 5, pp. 711–33.

Lane, David, György Lengyel and Jochen Tholen (eds.) (2007), *Restructuring of the Economic Elites after State Socialism: Recruitment, Institutions and Attitudes*, Stuttgard: ibidem Verlag.

Lane, Philip R. (2013), 'Capital Flows in the Euro Area', *European Economy*, Economic Papers 497, April.

La Porta, Rafael, Florencio Lopez-de-Silanes, Andrei Shleifer and Robert W. Vishny (1998), 'Law and Finance', *Journal of Political Economy*, Vol. 106, No. 6, pp. 1113–55.

Lavigne, Marie (1974), *The Socialist Economies of the Soviet Union and Europe*, London: Martin Robertson.

—— (1995), *The Economics of Transition: From Socialist Economy to Market Economy*, Houndmills: Macmillan Press.

—— (1999), *The Economics of Transition: From Socialist Economy to Market Economy*, London: Palgrave Macmillan.

Lee, Barbara and John Nellis (1990), 'Enterprise Reform and Privatization in Socialist Economies', *World Bank Discussion Papers n. 104*, Washington, DC: The World Bank.

Legvold, Robert ed. (2007), *Russian Foreign Policy in the Twenty-First Century and the Shadow of the Past*, New York: Columbia University Press.

Lenin, Vladimir (1917), *State and Revolution*, Moscow.

—— (1920), *The Proletarian Revolution and Kautsky the Renegade*, Moscow.

Lévesque, Jacques (1997), *The Enigma of 1989: The USSR and the Liberation of Eastern Europe*, Berkeley: University of California Press.

Linotte, Daniel (1992), 'The Fall of Industrial Output in Transition Economies: A New Interpretation', Working Paper 3/1992, Leuven: Leuven Institute for Central and East European Studies.

Lipton, David and Jeffrey D. Sachs (1990), 'Creating a Market in Eastern Europe: The Case of Poland', *Brookings Papers on Economic Activity*, Vol. 20, No. 1, pp. 75–147.

LoC (1987), *Czechoslovakia: A Country Study*, Country Studies Series by Federal Research Division of the Library of Congress, September (http://www.country-data.com/cgi-bin/query/r-3711.html).

—— (1989), *Hungary: A Country Study*, Country Studies Series by Federal Research Division of the Library of Congress, September (http://www.country-data.com/cgi-bin/query/r-5870.html).

Lohmann, Susanne (2008), 'Rational Choice and Political Science', in Steven Durdaul and Lawrence Blume (eds.), *The New Palgrave Dictionary of Economics*, London: Palgrave Macmillan, second edn.

Louzek, Marek (2014), 'Structural Problems of the Czech Economy', *Journal Mittelforum and Next Europe*, Vol. 1, No. 1 (http://transitionacademiapress.org/jmne/article/view/15).

Lukowski, Jerzy (2006), *A Concise History of Poland*, Cambridge: Cambridge University Press.

Lukyanov, Fyodor (2009), 'Putin's Russia: The Quest for a New Place', *Social Research: An International Quarterly*, Vol. 765, No. 1, Spring, pp. 117–50 (http://muse.jhu.edu/journals/social_research/summary/v076/76.1.lukyanov.html).

Mackenbach, Johan P., Marina Karanikolos, Jamie Lopez Bernal and Martin Mckee (2015), 'Why Did Life Expectancy in Central and Eastern Europe Suddenly Improve in the 1990s? An Analysis by Cause of Death', *Scandinavian Journal of Public Health*, December, Vol. 43, No. 8, pp. 796–801.

Mačys, Gediminas (2012), 'The Crisis and Economic Recovery in Baltic Countries', *International Journal of Humanities and Social Science*, Vol. 2, No. 19, pp. 202–9.

Maddison, Angus (2003), *The World Economy: Historical Statistics*, Paris: OECD.

Magyar, Bálint (2013) (ed.), *A magyar polip. A posztkommunista maffiaállam* (The Hungarian Polip. The Postcommunist Mafia State), Budapest: Noran Libro.

Makó, Csaba and Miklós Illéssy (2015), 'Segmented Capitalism in Hungary: Diverging or Converging Development Paths? (Lessons from the First Nation-Wide Employment Survey)', Gödöllő and Budapest: Centre for Learning Economy and Innovation, Szent István University and Institute of Sociology, Hungarian Academy of Sciences.

Malle, Silvana (1992), 'Soviet Cooperatives and the Labour Market', in Bruno Dallago, Gianmaria Ajani and Bruno Grancelli (eds.), *Privatization and Entrepreneurship in Post-Socialist Countries: Economy, Law and Society*, Basingstoke and New York: Macmillan and St. Martin's Press, pp. 275–305.

Manyika, James, Jacques Bughin, Susan Lund, Olivia Nottebohm, David Poulter, Sebastian Jauch and Sree Ramaswamy (2014), *Global Flows in a Digital Age: How Trade, Finance, People, and Data Connect the World Economy*, McKinsey Global Institute.

Marcus, Jonathan (2014), 'Ukraine Crisis: Transcript of Leaked Nuland-Pyatt Call', *BBC*, February 7 (www.bbc.com/news/world-europe-26079957).

Marelli, Enrico and Marcello Signorelli (2010), 'Transition, Regional Features, Growth and Labour Market Dynamics', in Floro Ernesto Caroleo and Francesco Pastore (eds.), *The Labour Market Impact of the EU Enlargement: A New Regional Geography of Europe?*, AIEL Series in Labour Economics, AIEL—Associazione Italiana Economisti del Lavoro, Vol. 1, No. 4, December, pp. 99–147.

Marer, Paul (2015), 'The Euro and Eastern Europe', in Bruno Dallago, Gert Guri and John McGowan (eds.), *A Global Perspective on the European Economic Crisis*, Abingdon, Oxfordshire: Routledge.

—— and Salvatore Zecchini (eds.) (1991), *The Transition to a Market Economy*, Vol. 2, Paris: OECD.

McDaniel, Tim (1996), *The Agony of the Russian Idea*, Princeton, NJ: Princeton University Press.

McFaul, Michael and Kathryn Stoner-Weiss (2008), 'Mission to Moscow: Why Authoritarian Stability is a Myth', Foreign Affairs, January/February.

Mckinnon, Ronald (1992), *The Order of Economic Liberalization: Financial Control in the Transition to a Market Economy*, Baltimore, MD: Johns Hopkins University Press.

Mend, Sarah (2002), 'The View From Above: An Insider's Take on Clinton's Russia Policy', *Foreign Affairs*, July/August.

Mertlik, Pavel (2000), 'Transparency: The Importance for the Economic Growth', at the *Joint Annual Discussion Boards of Governors*, 2000 Annual Meetings, Prague, September 26–28, International Monetary Fund and World Bank Group, Press Release No. 7 (https://www.imf.org/external/am/2000/speeches/pr07cze.pdf).

Meyer, Bruce D. and James X. Sullivan (2013), 'Consumption and Income Inequality and the Great Recession', *American Economic Review: Papers & Proceedings*, Vol. 103, No. 3, pp. 178–83.

Mihályi, Péter (2010), *A Magyar privatizáció enciklopédiája* (The Encyclopedia of Hungarian Privatization), Vol. 2, Veszprém and Budapest: Pannon Egyetemi Könyvkiadó and MTA Közgazdaságtodományi Intézet.

—— (2012), 'The Causes of Slow Growth in Hungary during the Post-Communist Transformation Period', *Discussion Papers MT-DP-2012/16*, Institute of Economics, Research Centre for Economic and Regional Studies, Hungarian Academy of Sciences, March.

—— (2013), *A Magyar gazdaság útja az adósságválságba 1945–2013* (The Road to Indebtedness of the Hungarian economy), Budapest: Corvina.

Milanovic, Branko (1998), *Income, Inequality, and Poverty during the Transition from Planned to Market Economy*, Washington, DC: World Bank.

Mitchell, Janet (1993), 'Creditor Passivity and Bankruptcy: Implications for Economic Reform', in Colin Mayer and Xavier Vives (eds.), *Capital Markets and Financial Intermediation*, Cambridge: Cambridge University Press, pp. 197–229.

Mizsei, Kálmán (1990), *Lengyelország. Válságok, reformpótlékok és reformok* (Poland. Crises, Reform Surrogates and Reforms), Budapest, Közgazdasági és Jogi Könyvkiadó.

Molnár, Miklós (2001), *A Concise History of Hungary*, Cambridge: Cambridge University Press.

Monaghan, Andrew (2012), 'The Vertikal: Power and Authority in Russia', *International Affairs*, Vol. 88, No. 1, January.

Murrell, Peter (1992), 'Evolutionary and Radical Approaches to Economic Reform', *Economics of Planning*, Vol. 25, pp. 79–95.

—— (1993), 'What Is Shock Therapy? What Did It Do in Poland and Russia', *Post-Soviet Affairs*, Vol. 9, No. 2, 1993, pp. 111–40 (http://econ-server.umd.edu/~murrell/articles/What%20is%20Shock%20Therapy.pdf).

Myant, Martin (1989), *The Czechoslovak Economy 1948–1988: The Battle for Economic Reform*, Cambridge: Cambridge University Press.

—— (2003), *The Rise and Fall of Czech Capitalism: Economic Development in the Czech Republic since 1989*, Cheltenham: Edward Elgar.

——, Jan Drahokoupil and Ivan Lesay (2013), 'The Political Economy of Crisis Management in East–Central European Countries', *Europe-Asia Studies*, Vol. 65, No. 3, pp. 383–410.

Nawojczyk, Maria (1993), 'Rise and Fall of Self-Management Movement in Poland', *Polish Sociological Review*, No. 104, pp. 343–54.

Nee, Victor (1995), 'Norms and Networks in Economic and Organizational Performance', *American Economic Review*, Vol. 88, No. 2, Papers and Proceedings, May, pp. 85–9.

Neményi, Judit and Gábor Oblath (2012), 'Az euró hazai bevezetésének újragondolása' (Revisiting Hungary's euro-adoption)', *Kozgazdasagi Szemle*, Vol LIX, June, pp. 569–684.

Neumann, Iver B. (2001), 'Regionalization and Democratic Consolidation', in Jan Zielonka and Alex Pravda (eds.), *Democratic Consolidation in Eastern Europe. Volume Two: International and Transnational Factors*, Oxford: Oxford University Press, pp. 58–75.

Norris, Floyd (2014), 'Borrowers in Hungary Learn Tough Lessons', *The New York Times*, November 13.

North, Douglas C. (1990), *Institutions, Institutional Change and Economic Performance*, Cambridge: Cambridge University Press.

——, John Joseph Wallis and Barry R. Weingast (2009), *Violence and Social Orders: A Conceptual Framework for Interpreting Recorded Human History*, Cambridge: Cambridge University Press.

Nuti, Domenico Mario (1981), 'The Polish Crisis: Economic Factors and Constraints', *The Socialist Register 1981*, pp. 104–43 (https://www.google.it/?gfe_rd=cr&ei=xjCuVZfU BKSO8Qfpg4HQAw&gws_rd=ssl#q=foreign+debt+of+poland+1980s).

—— (1992), 'The Role of New Cooperatives in the Soviet Economy', in Bruno Dallago, Gianmaria Ajani and Bruno Grancelli (eds.), *Privatization and Entrepreneurship in Post-Socialist Countries: Economy, Law and Society*, Basingstoke and New York: Macmillan and St. Martin's Press, pp. 247–73.

—— (2015), 'The Euro Area: Premature, Diminished, Divergent', in Bruno Dallago and John McGowan (eds.), *Crises in Europe in the Transatlantic Context: Economic and Political Appraisal*, London and New York: Routledge, pp. 171–9.

OECD (1994), *Unemployment in Transition Countries: Transient or Persistent?*, Paris: OECD.

—— (1999), *OECD Economic Surveys: Slovak Republic 1999*, Paris: Organization for Economic Cooperation and Development.

—— (2006), *Economics Surveys: Russian Federation 2006*, Paris.

—— (2008), *Reforms for Stability and Sustainable Growth: An OECD Perspective on Hungary*, Paris: OECD.

—— (2009) *FDI in Ukraine: New Approach*: oecd.org/globalrelations/psd/43361570.pdf.

—— (2012), 'Economic Policy Reforms 2012: Going for Growth'.

—— (2012), 'Mapping Global Value Chains', Paris: OECD, Working Party of the Trade Committee, December 3, TAD/TC/WP/RD (2012)9 (http://www.oecd.org/dac/aft/ MappingGlobalValueChains_web_usb.pdf).

Olson, Mancur (1982), *The Rise and Decline of Nations: Economic Growth, Stagflation, and Social Rigidities*, New Haven, CT: Yale University Press.

—— (1993), 'Dictatorship, Democracy, and Development', *American Political Science Review*, Vol. 87, No. 3, 1993, pp. 567–76.

Orlowski, Lucjan T. and Anna Tsibulina (2014), 'Integration of Central and Eastern European and the Euro-Area Financial Markets: Repercussions from the Global Financial Crisis', *Comparative Economic Studies*, Vol. 56, Issue 3, pp. 376–95.

Orszag, Peter (2007), 'Estimated Costs of U.S. Operations in Iraq and Afghanistan and of Other Activities Related to the War on Terrorism', *CBO Testimony before the Committee on the Budget*, US House of Representatives, October 24.

Pasimeni, Paolo (2015), 'Assessing the Europe 2020 Strategy', in Bruno Dallago, Gert Guri and John McGowan (eds.) (2015), *A Global Perspective on the European Economic Crisis*, Abingdon, Oxfordshire: Routledge.

Pejovich, Svetozar (1996), 'The Market for Institutions v. the-Strong-Hand-of-the-State: The Case of Eastern Europe', in Bruno Dallago and Luigi Mittone (eds.), *Economic Institutions, Markets and Competition. Centralisation and Decentralisation in the Transformation of Economic Systems*, Cheltenham: Edward Elgar, pp. 111–26.

Pejovich, Svetozar (2006), 'The Effects of the Interaction of Formal and Informal Institutions on Social Stability and Economic Development', in Kartik Roy and Jörn Sideras (eds.), *Institutions, Globalisation and Empowerment*, pp. 56–74.

Pfeffer, Fabian T., Sheldon Danziger and Robert F. Schoeni (2013), 'Wealth Disparities before and after the Great Recession', *The Annals of the American Academy of Political and Social Science November*, Vol. 650, No. 1, pp. 98–123.

Piattoni, Simona (2015), 'Institutional Innovations and EU Legitimacy after the Crisis', in Bruno Dallago and John McGowan (eds.), *Crises in Europe in the Transatlantic Context: Economic and Political Appraisals*, Abingdon, Oxfordshire: Routledge, pp. 119–36.

―― (forthcoming), 'The European Crisis: Testing the Trust Foundations of an Economic and Monetary Union', in Bruno Dallago, Gert Guri and John McGowan (eds.), *A Global Perspective on the European Economic Crisis*, Abingdon, Oxfordshire: Routledge.

Pistor, Katharina and Andrew Spicer (1998), 'Investment Funds in Mass Privatization and Beyond: Evidence from the Czech Republic and Russia', Harvard Institute for International Development (http://www.cid.harvard.edu/hiid/565.pdf).

Pipes, Richard (1997), *The Formation of the Soviet Union, Communism and Nationalism, 1917–1923*, Cambridge, MA: Harvard University Press.

Polisensky, Josef V. (1991), *History of Czechoslovakia in Outline*, Prague: Bohemia International.

Popov, Vladimir (2000), 'Shock Therapy versus Gradualism: The End of the Debate (Explaining the Magnitude of Transformational Recession)', *Comparative Economic Studies*, XLII, No. 1, pp. 1–57.

Prečan, Vilem (2013), 'The Czech Twentieth Century?', *Czech Journal of Contemporary History*, Vol. I, Prague: Institute for Contemporary History, Academy of Sciences of the Czech Republic, pp. 7–19.

Ptak, Ralf (2009), 'Neoliberalism in Germany: Revisiting the Ordoliberal Foundations of the Social Market Economy', in Philip Mirowski and Dieter Plehwe, *The Road from Mont Pèlerin: The Making of the Neoliberal Thought Collective*, Cambridge, MA: Harvard University Press, pp. 124–5.

Rae, Gavin (2013), 'Avoiding the Economic Crisis: Pragmatic Liberalism and Divisions over Economic Policy in Poland', *Europe-Asia Studies*, Vol. 65, No. 3, pp. 411–25.

Rahman, Jesmin and Tianli Zhao (2013), 'Export Performance in Europe: What Do We Know from Supply Links?', *IMF working Paper 13/62*, March, Washington, DC: International Monetary Fund.

Razin, Assaf and Steven Rosefielde (2011) 'Currency and Financial Crises of the 1990s and 2000s', *NBER Working Paper Series*, Working Paper 16754, February (http://www.nber.org/papers/w16754).

Reddaway, Peter and Dmitri Glinski (2001), *The Tragedy of Russia's Reforms: Market Bolshevism against Democracy*, US Institute of Peace Press, Washington, DC: USIP Press Books.

Reich, Robert (2007), *Supercapitalism: The Battle for Democracy in an Age of Big Business*, New York: Alfred A. Knopf.

Rider, Christine and Edward K. Zajicek (1995), 'Mass Privatization in Poland: Processes, Problems and Prospects, *International Journal of Politics, Culture and Society*, Vol. 9, No. 1, pp. 133–48.

Rodrik, Dani (1994), 'Foreign Trade in Eastern Europe's Transition: Early Results', in Olivier Blanchard, Kenneth Froot and Jeffrey Sachs (eds.), *Transition in Eastern Europe*, Vol. 2, Chicago, IL: University of Chicago Press, pp. 319–56.

―― (2007), *One Economics, Many Recipes: Globalization, Institutions, and Economic Growth*, Princeton, NJ: Princeton University Press.

Rogoff, K. (2011), 'The Second Great Contraction', *Project Syndicate*, Online (http://www.project-syndicate.org/commentary/rogoff83/English).

Roland, Gérard (2000), *Transition and Economics: Politics, Markets, and Firms*, Cambridge, MA: MIT Press.

―― (2004), 'Understanding Institutional Change: Fast-Moving and Slow-Moving Institutions', *Studies in Comparative International Development*, Vol. 38, No. 4, pp. 109–31.

Rosefielde, Steven (1998), *Efficiency and the Economic Recovery Potential of Russia*, Aldershot: Ashgate.

—— (2000), 'The Civilian Labor Force and Unemployment in the Russian Federation', *Europe-Asia Studies*, Vol. 52, no. 8, December, pp. 1433–47.

—— (2001), 'Premature Deaths: Russia's Radical Transition', *Europe-Asia Studies*, Vol. 53, No. 8, December 2001, pp. 1159–76.

—— (2003), 'Russia's Productive Potential: Limitations of Muscovite Authoritarianism', *Comparative Economic Studies*, No. 10, July, pp. 83–4.

—— (2005a), 'An Abnormal Country', *The European Journal of Comparative Economics*, Vol. 2, No. 1 (2005), pp. 3–16.

—— (2005b), 'Illusion of Transition: Russia's Muscovite Future', *Eastern Economic Journal*, Vol. 31, No. 2, Spring, pp. 283–96.

—— (2005c), *Russia in the 21st Century: Prodigal Superpower*, Cambridge: Cambridge University Press.

—— (2005d), 'Tea Leaves and Productivity: Bergsonian Norms for Gauging the Soviet Future', *Comparative Economic Studies*, Vol. 47, No. 2, pp. 259–73.

—— (2007a), *Russian Economy from Lenin to Putin*, New York: Wiley.

—— (2007b), 'The Illusion of Westernization in Russia and China', *Comparative Economic Studies*, Vol. 49, pp. 495–513.

—— (2010), *Red Holocaust*, London: Routledge.

—— (2011a), 'Postcrisis Russia: Counting on Miracles in Uncertain Times', in Carolina Vendil Pallin and Bertil Nygren, eds., *Russian Defense Prospects*, New York: Macmillan.

—— (2011b), 'Review of Andrey Vavilov, The Russian Public Debt and Financial Meltdowns, New York: Palgrave Macmillan, 2010', Slavic Review.

—— (2012a), 'Economics of the Military-Industrial Complex', in Michael Alexeev and Shlomo Weber (eds.), *The Oxford Handbook of Russian Economy*, Oxford: Oxford University Press.

—— (2012b) 'The Impossibility of Russian Economic Reform: Waiting for Godot', US Army War College, Carlisle Barracks.

—— (2013a), *Asian Economic Systems*, Singapore: World Scientific Publishers.

—— (2013b), 'Soviet Economy: An Ideocratic Reassessment', *Ekonomicheskaya Nauka Sovremennoy Rossii*, No. 3, November.

—— (2014), 'Cold Peace: 'Reset' and Coexistence', *The Northeast Asian Review*, Vol. 1, No. 3, March, pp. 39–50.

—— (2016), *The Kremlin Strikes Back: Russia and the West after Crimea's Annexation*, London: Cambridge University Press.

—— and Stefan Hedlund (2008), Russia Since 1980: Wrestling with Westernization, Cambridge: Cambridge University Press.

—— and Quinn Mills (2013), *Democracy and its Elected Enemies*, Cambridge: Cambridge University Press.

—— (2015), *Global Economic Turmoil and the Public Good*, Singapore: World Scientific Publishers.

—— (forthcoming), *Realpolitik in an Age of Ignorance: Exiting the Global Morass*, Oxford: Oxford University Press.

—— and Ralph W. Pfouts (2014), *Inclusive Economic Theory,* Singapore: World Scientific Publishers.

Rowen, Henry and Charles Wolf (1990), *Impoverished Superpower: Perestroika and the Soviet Military Burden*, Palo Alto: ICS Publishers.

Roxburgh, Angus (2014), 'Russia's Revenge: Why the West will Never Understand the Kremlin', *New Statesman*, March 27: www.newstatesman.com.

Sachs, Jeffrey (2000), 'Russia's Tumultuous Decade', *The Washington Monthly*, March (http://www.washingtonmonthly.com/books/2000/0003.sachs.html).

Sakwa, Richard (1998), *Soviet Politics in Perspective*, London: Routledge, second edn.

—— (2009), *Quality of Freedom: Putin, Khodorkovsky and the Yukos Affair*, Oxford: Oxford University Press.

—— (2014), *Putin and the Oligarchs: The Khodorkovsky-Yukos Affair*, Washington, DC: I.B. Tauris.

Sárközy, Tamás (2012), *Magyarország kormányzása 1978–2012* (Governing Hungary 1978–2012), Budapest: Park Kiadó.

—— (2014), *Kétharmados túlzáskormányzás, avagy gólerős csatár a mély talajú pályán* (Excessive Government with Two Thirds, or a Strong Forward in a Muddy Field), Budapest: Park Kiadó.

Schnyder, Gerhard and Mathias Siems (2013), 'The Ordoliberal Variety of Neoliberalism', in Suzanne J. Konzelmann and Marc Fovargue-Davies (eds.), *Banking Systems in the Crisis: The Faces of Liberal Capitalism*, Abingdon: Routledge, pp. 250–68 (http://papers.ssrn.com/sol3/papers.cfm?abstract_id=2142529).

Schroeder, Gertrude (1979), 'The Soviet Economy on a Treadmill of "Reforms"', in *Soviet Economy in a Time of Change*, Joint Economic Committee of Congress, Washington, DC, October 10, pp. 312–66.

—— (1982), 'Soviet Economic "Reform" Decrees: More Steps on the Treadmill', in *The Soviet Economy in the 1980s: Problems and Prospects*, Vol. 1, Washington, DC: Joint Economic Committee of the Congress of the United States, pp. 79–84.

Schütte, Clemens (2000), *Privatization and Corporate Control in the Czech Republic*, Cheltenham: Edward Elgar.

Shatalin, Stanislav (1990), *Transition to the Market: 500 Days*, Moscow: Arkhangelskoe.

Shleifer, Andrei (2002), 'The New Comparative Economics', *NBER Reporter*, Fall, pp. 12–15.

—— (2005), *A Normal Country: Russia after Communism*, Cambridge, MA: Harvard University Press.

—— and Daniel Treisman (2001), *Without a Map: Political Tactics and Economic Reform in Russia*, Cambridge, MA: MIT Press.

—— (2004), 'Russia: A Normal Country', *Foreign Affairs*, Vol. 83, March/April, pp. 20–38.

—— and Robert W. Vishny (1998), *The Grabbing Hand: Government Pathologies and Their Cures*, Cambridge, MA: Harvard University Press.

Shlykov, Vitaly V. (2006), 'Back into the Future, or Cold War Lessons for Russia', *Russia in Global Affairs*, No. 2, April–June (http://eng.globalaffairs.ru/number/n_6571).

Simatupang, Batara (1994), *The Polish Economic Crisis: Background, Circumstances and Causes*, Abingdon, Oxfordshire: Routledge.

Šimečka, Milan (1984), *The Restoration of Order: The Normalization of Czechoslovakia, 1969–1976*, London: Verso.

Simon, Herbert (1957), 'A Behavioral Model of Rational Choice', in Simon, *Models of Man: Social and Rational—Mathematical Essays on Rational Human Behavior in a Social Setting*, New York: Wiley.

—— (1990), 'A Mechanism for Social Selection and Successful Altruism', *Science*, Vol. 250, No. 4988, pp. 1665–8.

—— (1991), 'Bounded Rationality and Organizational Learning', *Organization Science*, Vol. 2, No, 1, pp. 125–34.

Smallbone, David and Friederike Welter (2001), 'The Distinctiveness of Entrepreneurship in Transition Economies', *Small Business Economics*, Vol. 16, No. 4, pp. 249–62.

—— and Friederike Welter (2012), 'Entrepreneurship and Institutional Change in Transition Economies: The Commonwealth of Independent States, Central and Eastern Europe and China Compared', *Entrepreneurship & Regional Development: An International Journal*, Vol. 24, No. 3–4, pp. 215–33.

Smith, Hedrick (1990), *The New Russians*, New York: Random House.

Sobják, Anita (2013), 'From the Periphery to the Core? Central Europe and the Economic Crisis', *Policy Paper*, Warszaw: PISM, No. 7 (55), April (https://www.pism.pl/files/?id_plik=13326).

Soós, Károly Attila (1986), *Terv, kampány, pénz. Szabályozás és ciklusok Magyarországon és Jugoszláviában*, (Plan, Campaign, Money. Regulation and Cycles in Hungary and Yugoslavia), Budapest: Közgazdasági és Jogi Kiadó.

Stalin, Joseph (1952), *Economic Problems of Socialism in the U.S.S.R.*, Moscow: Foreign Languages Publishing House.

Stanovaya, Tatiana (2014),'In Search of Lost Ideology', *Institute of Modern Russia*, April 25 (http://www.imrussia.org/en/society/725-in-search-of-lost-ideology).

Stark, Antal (2009), *Rögös úton. Nemzetgazdaságunk rendszerváltás előtti és utáni két évtizede* (On a Rugged Road. Two Decades of Our National Economy before and after Systemic Change), Budapest: Akadémiai Kiadó.

Stark, David (1996), 'Recombinant Property in East European Capitalism', *American Journal of Sociology*, Vol. 101, No. 4, pp. 993–1027.

Stiglitz, Joseph E. (1998), 'More Instruments and Broader Goals: Moving Toward the Post-Washington Consensus', The 1998 WIDER Annual Lecture, Helsinki, January, reprinted as Chapter 1 in Ha-Joon Chang (ed.), *The Rebel Within*, London: Wimbledon Publishing Company, 2001, pp. 17–56.

Stiglitz Joseph E. (2010), *Freefall: America, Free Markets, and the Sinking of the World Economy*, New York, W.W. Norton & Company.

—— and Linda J. Bilmes (2008), *The Three Trillion Dollar War: The True Cost of the Iraq Conflict*, New York: W.W. Norton & Company.

Sutela, Pekka (1991), *Economic Thought and Economic Reform in the Soviet Union*, Cambridge: Cambridge University Press.

—— (1996), 'Economics under Socialism: The Russian Case', paper presented to the conference on *Economics and Systemic Change*, Berlin, June 27–30.

—— (2012), 'The Underachiever: Ukraine's Economy Since 1991', *Carnegie Endowment for International Peace*, March 9 (http://carnegieendowment.org/2012/03/09/underachiever-ukraine-s-economy-since-1991/a1nf#).

Svejnar, Jan (1999), 'Labor Markets in the Transitional Central and East European Economies', in Orley Ashenfelter and Richard Layard (eds.), *Handbook of Labor Economics*, Vol. 3, Part B, pp. 2809–57, Amsterdam: North-Holland.

—— (2002), 'Transition Economies: Performance and Challenges', *Journal of Economic Perspectives*, Vol. 16, No. 1, Winter, pp. 3–28.

Szomolányi, Soňa (2004), 'Slovakia: From a Difficult Case of Transition to a Consolidated Central European Democracy', in Tadayuki Hayashi (ed.), *Democracy and Market Economics in Central and Eastern Europe: Are New Institutions Being Consolidated?*, pp. 149–88, Sapporo: Slavic Research Center, Hokkaido University (http://src-home.slav.hokudai.ac.jp/sympo/03september/pdf/S_Szomolanyi.pdf).

Teichova, Alice (1988), *The Czechoslovak Economy 1918–1980*, London and New York: Routledge.

Tversky, Amos and Daniel Kahneman (1981), 'The Framing of Decisions and the Psychology of Choice', *Science*, Vol. 211, No. 4481, pp. 453–58.

UNECE (2003), 'The Single Window Concept', Geneva: United Nations Economic Commission for Europe, ECE/TRADE/324, April (http://www.unece.org/fileadmin/DAM/trade/ctied/ctied7/ece_trade_324e.pdf).

Ungváry, Rudolf (2014), *A láthatatlan valóság* (The Invisible Reality), Bratislava: Kalligram.

United States Congress (1992), *The December 1, 1991 Referendum/Presidential Election in Ukraine* (A Report Prepared by the Staff of the Commission on Security and Cooperation in Europe) (http://www.google.com/url?sa=t&rct=j&q=&esrc=s&source=web&cd=13&ved=0CG8QFjAM&url=http%3A%2F%2Fcsce.gov%2Findex.cfm%3FFuseAction%3DFiles.Download%26FileStore_id%3D297&ei=jxlRU6LYMMmnsQS-sIHgBw&usg=AFQjCNHx62W05zpwiYDWmrDK9DDDBLiYzQ&bvm=bv.65058239,d.cWcOn).

Van Herpen, Marcel (2014), *Putinism: The Slow Rise of a Radical Right Regime in Russia*, New York: Rowman & Littlefield Publishers.

—— (1993), 'Development and the "Washington Consensus"', *World Development*, Vol. 21, pp. 1239–336.

Valentinyi, Akos (2012), 'The Hungarian Crisis', VOX CEPR's Policy Portal, March 19 (http://www.voxeu.org/article/hungarian-crisis).

van Brabant, Jozef M. (1992), *Privatizing Eastern Europe: The Role of Markets and Ownership in the Transition*, Dordrecht: Kluwer.

Voszka, Éva (1996), 'The Revival of Redistribution in Hungary', in Bruno Dallago and Luigi Mittone (eds.), *Economic Institutions, Markets and Competition: Centralisation and Decentralisation in the Transformation of Economic Systems*, Cheltenham: Edward Elgar, pp. 273–90.

Wädekin, Karl-Eugen (1973), *The Private Sector in Soviet Agriculture*, ed. by George Karcz, Berkeley: University of California Press.

—— (1982), *Agrarian Policies in Communist Europe: A Critical Introduction*, Totowa, NJ: Allanheld, Osmun & Co.

—— (1990), 'Il ruolo dei produttori individuali in un'agricoltura socializzata' (The Role of Private Producers in a Socialized Agriculture), in Bruno Dallago, Gianmaria Ajani and Bruno Grancelli (eds.), *Quaderni di economia e banca*, No. 10, pp. 113–38.

Wasilewski, Jacek (1998), 'Hungary, Poland and Russia: The Fate of Nomenklatura Elites', in Mattei Dogan and John Higley (eds.), *Elites, Crises, and the Origins of Regimes*, Lanham, MA: Rowman and Littlefield, pp. 147–67.

WEF (2014), *The Global Competitiveness Report 2014–2015*, ed. by Klaus Schwab, Geneva: World Economic Forum (http://www3.weforum.org/docs/WEF_Global CompetitivenessReport_2014-15.pdf).

Wemer, David A. (2013), 'Europe's Little Tiger? Reassessing Economic Transition in Slovakia under the Mečiar Government 1993–1998', *The Gettysburg Historical Journal*, Vol. 12, No. 7 (http://cupola.gettysburg.edu/ghj/vol12/iss1/7).

Williams, Kieran (1997), *The Prague Spring and its Aftermath: Czechoslovak Politics, 1968–1970*, Cambridge: Cambridge University Press.

Williamson, John (1989), 'What Washington Means by Policy Reform', in John Williamson (ed.), *Latin American Readjustment: How Much Has Happened*, Washington, DC: Institute for International Economics.

—— (1990), 'What Washington Means by Policy Reform', Chapter 2 in John Williamson (ed.), *Latin American Adjustment: How Much Has Happened?*, Washington, DC: Institute for International Economics.

—— (1999), 'What Should the Bank Think about the Washington Consensus', background paper to the World Bank's World Development Report 2000, July.

—— (2004), 'A Short History of the Washington Consensus', paper presented at Foundation CIDOB conference 'From the Washington Consensus Towards a New Global Governance', Barcelona, September 2004.

Williamson, Oliver E. (2000), 'The New Institutional Economics: Taking Stock, Looking Ahead', *Journal of Economic Literature*, Vol. XXXVIII, September, pp. 595–613.

Wilson, Andrew (2000), *The Ukrainians: Unexpected Nation*, New Haven, CT: Yale University Press.

Winiecki, Jan (2012), *The Distorted World of Soviet-Type Economies*, London: Routledge.

Wolff, Edward N. (2014), 'Household Wealth Trends in the United States, 1983–2010', *Oxford Review of Economic Policy*, Vol. 30, No. 1, pp. 21–43.

World Bank (1998), *Slovak Republic: A Strategy for Growth and European Integration*, Washington, DC: The World Bank.

—— (1999), *Czech Republic: Toward European Union Ascension. Main Report*, Volume 2, Washington, DC: The World Bank.

—— (2002), *Transition. The First Ten Years: Analysis and Lesson or Eastern Europe and the Former Soviet Union*, Washington, DC: The World Bank.

—— (2005), 'Review of World Bank Conditionality: Content of Conditionality in World Bank Policy-Based Operations: Public Sector Governance, Privatization, User Fees, and Trade', PREM GROUP and World Bank, June 30 (www:http://siteresources. worldbank.org/PROJECTS/Resources/ContentofConditionality7-21.pdf).

World Bank (2011a), *Country Partnership Strategy (CPS) for the Russian Federation*, Report No. 65115-RU, November.

—— (2011b), *Ukraine System of Financial Oversight and Governance of State-Owned Enterprises*, Report No. 59950-UA, February 22, 2011: http://www wds.worldbank. org/external/default/WDSContentServer/WDSP/IB/2012/05/21/000425970_20120521 113855/Rendered/PDF/599500ESW0P1120mance0budgeting0MTEF.pdf.

—— (2014a),'Russian Economic Report 31: Confidence Crisis Exposes Economic Weakness', March 26 (http://www.worldbank.org/en/news/press-release/2014/03/26/ russian-economic-report-31).

—— (2014b), *Ukraine Partnership: Country Program Snapshot*, April.

Young Choi, Jae (2011), 'A Survey of Single Window Implementation', *WCO Research Paper No. 17*, World Customs Organization, August.

Zaslavskaya, Tatiana I. (1984), 'The Novosibirsk Report', *Survey,* Vol. 28, No. 1, pp. 88–108.

Zenger, Todd R., Sergio G. Lazzarini and Laura Poppo (2000), 'Informal and Formal Organization in New Institutional Economics', in Paul Ingram and Brian S. Silverman (eds.) *The New Institutionalism in Strategic Management*, Bingley: Emerald Group Publishing Limited, pp. 277–305.

Index